D1745346

Die Einheit der Schrift und die Vielfalt des Kanons
The Unity of Scripture and the Diversity of the Canon

Beihefte zur Zeitschrift für die neutestamentliche Wissenschaft

und die Kunde der älteren Kirche

In Verbindung mit
James D. G. Dunn · Richard B. Hays
Hermann Lichtenberger

herausgegeben von
Michael Wolter

Band 118

Walter de Gruyter · Berlin · New York
2003

Die Einheit der Schrift und die Vielfalt des Kanons

The Unity of Scripture and the Diversity of the Canon

Herausgegeben von / edited by
John Barton und/and Michael Wolter

Walter de Gruyter · Berlin · New York
2003

⊗ Gedruckt auf säurefreiem Papier,
das die US-ANSI-Norm über Haltbarkeit erfüllt.

ISBN 3-11-017638-6

Bibliografische Information Der Deutschen Bibliothek

Die Deutsche Bibliothek verzeichnet diese Publikation in der Deutschen
Nationalbibliografie; detaillierte bibliografische Daten sind im Internet
über <http://dnb.ddb.de> abrufbar.

Printed in Germany
Einbandgestaltung: Christopher Schneider, Berlin
Druck und buchbinderische Verarbeitung: Hubert & Co., Göttingen

Inhaltsverzeichnis

Einleitung

Seit mehr als einem Vierteljahrhundert gibt es zwischen der Theologischen Fakultät der University of Oxford und der Evangelisch-Theologischen Fakultät der Rheinischen Friedrich-Wilhelms-Universität Bonn eine Partnerschaft, die sich in einer Vielzahl gemeinsamer Seminare von Studierenden, Doktoranden und Dozenten konkretisiert hat und auch einen regelmäßigen Austausch von Studierenden und Gastvorlesungen einschließt. Seit Mitte der 90er Jahre des vergangenen Jahrhunderts hat sich die Kooperation zudem in konkreten Forschungsprojekten verdichtet, die Wissenschaftler aus den beiden Theologischen Fakultäten über mehrere Jahre hinweg zu einer intensiven Arbeit an einem bestimmten theologischen Sachthema zusammengeführt haben. Die Ergebnisse eines ersten Projekts zum Thema „Revelation and Story" wurden unlängst publiziert.[1] Die dabei gewonnenen Erfahrungen ermutigten uns, die Zusammenarbeit in einem weiteren Projekt fortzusetzen, das erneut vom Deutschen Akademischen Austauschdienst und vom British Council gefördert wurde und dessen Ertrag wir in diesem Band vorlegen. Die einzelnen Beiträge wurden auf mehreren Tagungen, zu denen wir uns in den Jahren 1999 bis 2002 abwechselnd in Oxford und Bonn zusammenfanden, vorgestellt und intensiv diskutiert.

Maßgeblich geprägt wurde die gemeinsame Arbeit durch die in mehrfacher Hinsicht „pluralistische" Zusammensetzung unserer Gruppe, die ihr nicht nur ein internationales, sondern auch ein interkonfessionelles und interdisziplinäres Profil gab: Unser Projekt führte britische und deutsche Wissenschaftler, Anglikaner, Lutheraner und Baptisten sowie Alttestamentler, Neutestamentler, Kirchenhistoriker und Systematiker zusammen. Es wurde dadurch möglich, eine mehrdimensionale Vielfalt unterschiedlicher theologischer Traditionen und wissenschaftlicher Ansätze miteinander ins Gespräch zu bringen. Auf diese Weise wurden wir in die Lage versetzt, die im wissenschaftlichen Alltag bestehenden Grenzen in überaus fruchtbarer Weise zu überwinden.

---

[1] Gerhard Sauter/John Barton (Ed.), Revelation and Story. Narrative Theology and the Centrality of Story, Aldershot 2000; dt.: John Barton/Gerhard Sauter (Hrsg.), Offenbarung und Geschichten. Ein deutsch-englisches Forschungsprojekt, Frankfurt a.M. u.a. 2000.

Das Thema, das wir zum Gegenstand unserer Arbeit gemacht haben, besteht aus zwei Begriffspaaren, die einander zugeordnet werden: „Einheit und Vielfalt" sowie „Schrift und Kanon". Von maßgeblicher Bedeutung ist dabei zunächst, dass wir mit dem Gegenüber von *„Einheit"* und *„Vielfalt"* eine *ekklesiologische Kategorie* aufnehmen. Bereits Paulus greift mehrfach auf sie zurück, um die besondere Eigenart der christlichen Ekklesia zu beschreiben (vgl. Röm 12,4–5; 1.Kor 10,17; 12,12–13.20; s. auch Gal 3,28), und für seinen Umgang mit diesem Begriffspaar ist charakteristisch, dass er die ihm innewohnende semantische Spannung nicht als ein sich ausschließendes Konkurrenzverhältnis versteht, sondern eine dynamische Integration entstehen lässt: Die Einheit der an Jesus Christus Glaubenden und auf ihn Getauften hebt deren Unterschiedlichkeit nicht auf, sondern umschließt sie.

Der ekklesiologische Bezug dieses Begriffspaares findet dann im 20. Jahrhundert seinen Ausdruck darin, dass es zur Leitkategorie der ökumenischen Bewegung wurde. Es waren hier gerade die Arbeiten der Kommission für Faith and Order – und nicht die Einheitsbemühungen der Kommission für Life and Work –, in denen die Frage nach der Einheit im Blick auf die Bibel im Mittelpunkt stand und die damit zu erkennen geben, dass sie von einer spezifischen Auffassung von Einheit, Konsens und Kirche geleitet waren.

Sie nahm ihren Ausgangspunkt von der Wahrnehmung der konfessionellen Ausdifferenzierung der christlichen Kirchen als „Spaltung", „Zertrennung" und „Uneinigkeit", die unbedingt zu überwinden sei, weil das eine Christusbekenntnis auch die „sichtbare Einheit" der Christenheit verlange. Erst nach mehreren Jahrzehnten ökumenischer Verständigungsbemühungen, bei denen vor allem strittig blieb, welche Konzeption von „sichtbarer Einheit" verwirklicht werden könnten, traten Entwürfe in den Vordergrund, die „Einheit" und „Vielfalt" nicht mehr als einander ausschließende Gegensätze, sondern als komplementäre ekklesiologische Kategorien begriffen und sich zu Formeln wie „Einheit in der Vielfalt", „Vielfalt in der Einheit", „Einheit in versöhnter Verschiedenheit", „Konziliare Gemeinschaft der Verschiedenen" oder „Ökumene in Gegensätzen" verdichteten.

Aus demselben kirchen- und theologiegeschichtlichen Kontext stammt auch die Übertragung dieser beiden Kategorien auf das Begriffspaar *„Schrift und Kanon"*. Auch über das Wie der jeweiligen Zuordnung bestand ein grundsätzlicher Konsens, denn zu den unumstrittenen Überzeugungen, von denen sich die ökumenische Bewegung von ihren Anfängen an getragen wusste, gehörte der *Zusammenhang von „Einheit" und „Schrift"*, und zwar in einer doppelten Hinsicht:[2] Zum einen wurde die Schrift bzw. die Bibel,

---

2   Vgl. dazu M. Haudel, Die Bibel und die Einheit der Kirchen. Eine Untersuchung der Studien von „Glauben und Kirchenverfassung" (KiKonf 34), Göttingen 1993.

weil sie von der gesamten Christenheit als gemeinsame Grundlage und Quelle ihres Glaubens und Lebens anerkannt war, als Fundament einer auch ekklesiologisch qualifizierbaren „Einheit" wahrgenommen. „The Bible, the Holy Scripture, is the biggest thing we have in common" – diese von Willem A. Visser 't Hooft 1963 formulierte Einsicht in Bezug auf das einheitstiftende Potential der Schrift[3] artikuliert eine Gewissheit, die sich wie ein roter Faden durch die gesamte Geschichte der ökumenischen Bewegung hindurchzieht.[4] Zum anderen galt umgekehrt „Einheit" aber auch stets als ein theologisches Prädikat, das die Größe „Schrift" auszeichnet, ja mehr noch: Es war allererst diese Eigenschaft, die es möglich machte, dass der Schrift auch eine ekklesiologische Relevanz zugeschrieben und sie zur Grundlage für die Suche nach der angestrebten Sichtbarmachung der Einheit aller Christen werden konnte.

Aus der Korrelation dieser beiden Zuordnungen der Größen „Einheit" und „Schrift" folgte dann mit einiger Konsequenz, dass sich vor allem in der zweiten Hälfte des 20. Jahrhunderts die ökumenischen Verständigungsbemühungen verstärkt auf die Suche nach gemeinsamen Prinzipien der biblischen Hermeneutik richteten. Beide Grundannahmen – das Postulat der *Einheit der Schrift* und die ihr zugeschriebene konstitutive Bedeutung für die *Einheit der Kirchen* – wurden dabei so zusammengeführt, dass gewissermaßen eine dritte Einheitsebene an ökumenischer Aufmerksamkeit gewann: die *Einheit der Schriftauslegung*.[5] Über viele Jahre hinweg standen dementsprechend vor allem diejenigen Fragen und Problemzusammenhänge im Zentrum der Diskussion, an denen die konfessionellen Differenzen am deutlichsten sichtbar wurden: die Autorität und Normativität der Schrift, das Verhältnis von Schrift und Tradition sowie das Verhältnis von Altem und Neuem Testament.

Zu einem nicht geringen Problem musste unter dieser Voraussetzung natürlich das Bewusstwerden der *inneren theologischen Vielfalt des Kanons* werden. Wie groß das Problem tatsächlich war, wird vor allem an den heftigen Reaktionen erkennbar, die Ernst Käsemanns Vortrag aus dem Jahre 1951 evozierte, aus dem vor allem immer wieder dieselben beiden Spitzensätze herausgegriffen wurden: „Der neutestamentliche Kanon begründet als solcher

---

3   W.A. Visser 't Hooft, The Bible and the Ecumenical Movement, in: Bulletin of the United Bible Societies 56 (1963) 165–172, S. 168.
4   Vgl. auch S. de Diétrich, The Bible, a Force fo Unity, Ecumenical Review 1 (1948/49) 410–416, S. 412: „Here is truly the one possible meeting-place for Catholics, Orthodox and Protestants. That such a meeting-place exists, is acknowledged as really existing, is perhaps the greatest gift of God to His Church in this generation."
5   Aus naheliegenden Gründen sei an dieser Stelle vor allem an die Konferenz erinnert, die im Jahre 1949 im Wadham College in Oxford stattfand und zu einer von allen Teilnehmern getragenen Verständigung über „Guiding Principles for the Interpretation of the Bible" führte (veröffentlicht in: ER 2 [1949/50] 81–86).

nicht die Einheit der Kirche. Er begründet als solcher, d.h. in seiner dem Historiker zugänglichen Vorfindlichkeit dagegen die Vielzahl der Konfessionen."[6] Dadurch fielen „Kanon" und „Schrift" auseinander – womit in einem
etwas veränderten Gewand Johann Salomo Semlers Thesen[7] in der ökumenischen Bewegung wirksam wurden –, und die Behandlung des Kanons als
eine historische und literarische Größe, die ein Produkt der Alten Kirche war,
schien die theologische Dignität der „Schrift" zu depotenzieren und damit
überhaupt deren ekklesiologisches Potential in Frage zu stellen, das eben auf
der Korrelation von „Einheit der Kirche" und „Einheit der Schrift" basierte.
In dem Maße jedoch, wie in ekklesiologischer Hinsicht „Einheit" und „Vielfalt" nicht mehr als einander ausschließende Gegensätze galten, sondern als
miteinander vereinbar angesehen wurden (s.o.), konnte auch die Vielfalt des
Kanons in ein Konzept von Einheit integriert werden, das den Kanon geradezu zu einem ökumenischen Dokument par excellence macht.[8] Denn ebensowenig wie der Glaube eine empirisch wahrnehmbare Größe ist, ebensowenig
kann natürlich auch die *Gemeinschaft* des Glaubens, in der alle Christen miteinander verbunden sind, empirisch aufweisbar sein. Angesichts dessen ist es
darum an ganz prominenter Stelle gerade der Kanon, der die prinzipiell unobjektivierbare Einheit der Kirche zeichenhaft zur Anschauung bringt.

Unser Projekt setzt diese Vorgeschichte als Kontext voraus. In den einzelnen Beiträgen sollen darum vor allem solche Fragen aufgegriffen werden,
die sich aus der vorstehend skizzierten Spannung zwischen dem kirchlichen
Schriftgebrauch und der Tatsache ergeben, dass es allererst die Alte Kirche
war, die uns den Kanon als Erbe hinterlassen hat. Sie bricht z.B. immer dann

---

6   E. Käsemann, Begründet der neutestamentliche Kanon die Einheit der Kirche?, EvTh 11
    (1951/52) 13–21 = ders. (Hg.), Das Neue Testament als Kanon. Dokumentation und kritische Analyse zur gegenwärtigen Diskussion, Göttingen 1970, 124–133, S. 131. In dieselbe Richtung ging auch Käsemanns Vortrag auf der 4. Weltkonferenz für Glauben und
    Kirchenverfassung in Montréal im Jahr 1963 über „Einheit und Vielfalt der neutestamentalichen Lehre von der Kirche" (ÖR 13 [1964] 58–63 = ders., Exegetische Versuche
    und Besinnungen II, Göttingen ³1968, 262–267.
7   Vgl. J. S. Semler, Abhandlung von freier Untersuchung des Canon, Halle 1771–75; hg.
    v. H. Scheible, Göttingen ²1980.
8   Vgl. z.B. H.-R.Weber, The Bible: Critical Guide for the Ecumenical Movement, JTSA 1
    (1972) 23–36, S. 31: „What in biblical studies is discovered about the diversity and the
    unity of the Bible can safeguard the churches in the ecumenical movement from both the
    danger of uniformity and a cheap pluralism"; R. Stahl, Grunddimensionen einer ökumenischen Ekklesiologie, ThLZ 111 (1986) 81–90, Sp. 85: „Der Kanon des Neuen Testaments oder der gesamten Bibel begründet eben doch die Einheit der Kirche, qualifiziert
    diese Einheit aber nun als Verbindung verschiedener Positionen und ‚Konfessionen'";
    H.-G. Link, Der Kanon in ökumenischer Sicht, JBTh 3 (1988) 83–96, S. 96: „Der biblische Kanon kann auch im Blick auf die ökumenische Einheit der Christenheit ... seine
    wegweisende Kraft erweisen. Denn er ist und bleibt das beste Modell sichtbarer Einheit
    der Verschiedenen, das die Christenheit besitzt."

auf, wenn historisch-kritische Exegese mit der dogmatischen Überlieferung vermittelt werden soll und umgekehrt. Es soll dementsprechend danach gefragt werden, ob und wie wir heute an einer Überwindung dieser Diastase mit einigen Erfolgsaussichten arbeiten können.

Wir wollen aber auch noch darüber hinausgehen und diejenigen Fragen behandeln, bei denen die Differenz zwischen britischen und deutschen theologischen Traditionen in der Vergangenheit besonders deutlich zutage getreten ist und die innerhalb des vorstehend skizzierten Diskussionszusammenhangs unterbestimmt geblieben sind bzw. über ihn hinausweisen. Im einzelnen lassen sich nennen:

– Welchen Stellenwert hat die Frage nach der theologischen Beziehung von Altem und Neuem Testament in Bezug auf das Verhältnis des ökumenischen Dialogs zum christlich-jüdischen Dialog? Wie ist in dieser Hinsicht mit den Unterschieden (z.B. zwischen dem hebräischen, dem griechischen, dem lateinischen und dem äthiopischen Kanon des Alten Testaments) umzugehen?

– Ist das Alte Testament für Christen nur durch das Neue Testament hindurch präsent oder spricht es zu ihnen mit einer eigenen Stimme?

– Erweist sich das ökumenische Modell „Vielfalt in der Einheit" u.ä. nicht lediglich als ein billiger Formelkompromiss, wenn er auf den Kanon übertragen wird? Hat er nicht eine hermeneutische Beliebigkeit zur Folge, weil jeder der Schrift das entnehmen kann, was ihm passt? Kann man der Schrift unter dieser Voraussetzung überhaupt noch Autorität oder Normativität zubilligen, die auch theologische Sachkritik möglich und erforderlich macht? Oder nötigt die Einsicht in das historische Gewordensein des Kanons gar zu der Feststellung, dass die Schrift von der Tradition verschlungen wurde?

– Ist es, umgekehrt gefragt, theologisch legitim, dem Problem der inneren Vielfalt des Kanons durch die Suche nach einem „Kanon im Kanon" oder einer „Mitte der Schrift" zu begegnen oder ist nicht vielmehr die innerbiblische Vielfalt vom Kanon umgriffen und in ihm aufgehoben?

– Kann dem Kanon der neutestamentlichen Schriften angesichts seines historischen Gewordenseins überhaupt noch eine theologische Qualität zukommen oder muss er nicht vielmehr gerade aus theologischen Gründen zur Disposition gestellt werden?

– Kann es überhaupt noch so etwas wie eine ‚Theologie des Alten Testaments' und eine ‚Theologie des Neuen Testaments' und gar eine ‚Biblische Theologie' geben?

– Inwiefern kann die theologische Vielfalt der biblischen Schriften wirklich helfen, die Einheit des Glaubens und die Einheit der geglaubten Kirche zu entdecken? Handelt es sich womöglich um unterschiedliche Konzepte von „Einheit" bzw. „Vielfalt"?

– Wie verhalten sich „Kanon" und „Schrift" zueinander? Ist es möglicherweise so, dass die im Kanon enthaltenen „Texte" allererst durch den Kanon
und seinen Gebrauch in der Christenheit zur „Schrift" geworden sind und
damit die die „Schrift" allererst eine rezeptionshermeneutisch sich konstituie-
rende Größe ist, die von Christen mit der Erwartung in ihre Lebensgeschich-
ten eingelesen wird, in ihr der Offenbarung Gottes zu begegnen.

In diesem Sinne macht *John Barton* in seinem Beitrag darauf aufmerksam, dass man in der Vielfalt des biblischen Kanons nicht nur ein Problem,
sondern auch einen Vorteil sehen kann. Wurde sie als Problem angesehen,
zog dies ganz unterschiedliche Lösungsversuche nach sich: Die Texte wurden geändert oder man bemühte sich um den Nachweis, dass die bestehenden
Spannungen und Widersprüche nur an der Oberfläche existierten und von
einer übergeordneten Einheit umgriffen und in ihr aufgehoben seien. Umgekehrt ist es aber wohl eher ein Geschenk für die Christenheit, dass sie die
Bibel nicht als einen monolithischen Block vorfindet, sondern als eine ausgesprochen pluralistische Vielfalt ganz unterschiedlicher Schriften, die eben
genau dadurch christliche Freiheit ermöglicht.

Horst Seebass fragt nach der hermeneutischen Bedeutung, die dem ge-
wöhnlicherweise „Altes Testament" genannten Teil des *einen* biblischen Kanons für eine christliche Theologie zukommt, die ihn als integralen Bestandteil einer Juden und Christen *gemeinsamen* Tradition ernstnehmen will.

In dem Beitrag von *Michael Wolter* geht es um den sachgerechten hermeneutischen Umgang mit dem Kanon als Schrift angesichts seines historischen
Gewordenseins und seiner inneren Vielfalt. Er versucht zu zeigen, dass die
theologische Verbindlichkeit des Kanons nicht *a priori*, sondern nur *a posteriori*, d.h. von seiner Rezeption und seinem Gebrauch in den christlichen Kirchen her, begründet werden kann. Ihm kann damit im Sinne Umberto Ecos
eine *intentio operis* zugeschrieben werden, die im Kanon als literarischer
Größe den Willen zur Einheit und in seiner Rezeption als „Schrift" das
Merkmal der Vielfalt wahrnimmt.

Morwenna Ludlow untersucht in ihrem Beitrag die altkirchlichen An-
schauungen von Verfasserschaft, Gebrauch und Rechtgläubigkeit kanonischer Texte. Sie hält es für irreführend, in ihnen *Kriterien* für die Feststellung
von Kanonizität zu sehen, weil eine solche Annahme impliziert, dass die Kirche – noch *bevor es den biblischen Kanon gab* – eine Vorstellung davon hatte, welche Eigenschaften ein ‚kanonischer' Text haben musste, und sie diese
Vorstellung dann benutzt, um bestimmte Bücher in den Kanon aufzunehmen
und andere auszuschließen. Das Nachdenken über Kanonizität beginnt vielmehr *in media res*: Es liefert die Begründung dafür, warum bestimmte Schriften als bedeutsam galten und andere nicht, denn es setzt eine bereits existie-

rende Beziehung zwischen der Kirche und den Texten voraus. Damit ist nicht gesagt, dass die Kirche die kanonischen Schriften rein passiv empfing und an ihrer Hervorbringung weitgehend unbeteiligt war. Die Texte bestimmten und gestalteten die Kirche ebenso wie die Kirche die Texte den Kanon gestaltete und bestimmte. Innerhalb dieser komplexen Wechselseitigkeit lässt sich darum ein Kanonisierungsprozess identifizieren, der sowohl historisch als auch theologisch erklärbar ist.

John Webster fragt in seinem Beitrag nach dem präzisen dogmatischen Ort des Kanons angesichts der verbreiteten Enttheologisierung des Kanon-Konzepts innerhalb der neuzeitlichen Theologie. Er gibt einen Überblick über unterschiedliche Aspekte dieser Enttheologisierung (historische Kritik, religionsgeschichtlicher Vergleich, sozio-politische Theorie, postmoderne Zurückweisung von kanonischer Bestimmtheit) und setzt sich mit unterschiedlichen theologischen Strategien zur Restitution des Kanonischen auseinander, vor allem mit den Versuchen, den Kanon an die Gemeinschaft zu binden. Im Anschluss daran liefert er eine konstruktive dogmatische Beschreibung des Kanonischen. Er verortet es innerhalb des Mitteilungsgeschehens von Gottes Heilshandeln, verweist auf die Vorstellung von der Heiligkeit eines Textes, bestimmt die Hervorbringung des Kanons durch die Kirche als einen Vorgang der Entgegennahme und nimmt das Wirken des Geistes im Leser des Kanons in den Blick.

Paul S. Fiddes erblickt im Kanon ein zwar durch Grenzen beschlossenes Gebiet, dies aber so, dass es nach wie vor eine Spannung zwischen Offenheit (‚space') und Bestimmtheit (‚place') von Bedeutung zu bedenken gibt, welch letztere in der Begegnung mit Gottes selbstoffenbarendem Wort zutage tritt. Solche Orte der Bestimmtheit sind es, die uns an die Stelle Anderer treten lassen. Dies können die Autoren der Texte sein, unsere Mitmenschen hier und jetzt – und letztlich auch der dreieinige Gott. Zwar kommt es auch bei der Lektüre *aller* Texte zur Begegnung mit derartigen Orten, doch lenkt das Bild vom Kanon als einem begrenzten Raum unsere Aufmerksamkeit auf diejenigen Texte, die sich *sowohl* innerhalb wie außerhalb dieses Raumes befinden. Für die Christenheit bleibt der biblische Kanon gleichwohl normativ, und zwar sowohl aus christologischen als auch aus sozio-kulturellen Gründen. Der Vorteil einer solchen Grenzziehung besteht darin, dass sie von uns verlangt, die Binnentexte zu erkunden, und uns einlädt, mit Hilfe der außerhalb gelegenen Texte das Geschäft der Kritik zu beginnen, um dadurch das Urteil Gottes über den Leser und den Text als solchen vernehmen zu können.

Robert Morgan thematisiert das Problem, das christlicher Glaube und christliche Theologie mit der theologischen Vielfalt der Schrift haben, wenn sie sie als normative Instanz ernstnehmen wollen. Er nimmt Ernst Käsemanns Prinzip des „Kanon im Kanon" als ein christologisches Kriterium, von dem die Schriftauslegung geleitet wird. Die christliche Identität wird demnach mit hinreichender Deutlichkeit im ständigen Gespräch der unterschiedlichen christlichen Schriftauslegungen greifbar. Die neutestamentlichen Schriften setzen ein Wissen von Gott und der Welt voraus, das die Kirche von Anfang an mit der Synagoge geteilt hat und das in ihr auch weiterhin als Lebensgrund von Glaube und Theologie in Geltung steht. Mit Ernst Käsemann und Brevard S. Childs teilt er das Anliegen einer sauberen theologischen Schriftauslegung, und wie Käsemann hält auch er es für erforderlich, dass es ein christologisches Kriterium ist, das als hermeneutischer Maßstab fungiert. Gleichwohl möchte er als anglikanischer Theologe diesen Maßstab gerne inklusiver formuliert sehen, als dies in der Rechtfertigungslehre zum Ausdruck kommt.

Caroline Schröder-Field geht in ihrem Beitrag der Beobachtung nach, dass zwar viele vom Kanon sprechen, dies aber in unterschiedlicher Weise und mit den verschiedensten Erwartungen tun. Eine Annäherung zwischen den theologischen Disziplinen im Blick auf den biblischen Kanon ist zu erhoffen, wo derartige Erwartungen aufgedeckt und mitbedacht werden. Das gilt besonders da, wo der Kanonbegriff vom protestantischen Schriftbegriff her bestimmt wird – eine durchaus frag-würdige, zumeist unreflektierte Verbindung, die vor allem, aber nicht nur für die Dogmatik evangelischer Provenienz bezeichnend ist.

Gerhard Sauter fragt nach dem Verhältnis von Kanon und Kirche: *Dass* die christliche Kirche bei der Entstehung des Kanons beteiligt war, ist historisch unbestritten. Doch *wie* sich die Kanonbildung für die Kirche auswirkte und mit welchen Gründen, ist eine – zumindest theologisch – offene Frage geblieben. Antworten auf diese Frage spiegeln unterschiedliche Vorstellungen von kirchlicher Einheit wider. Sie werfen auch ein Licht auf verschiedene Leseweisen, die wiederum von der Auffassung der Einheit der „Schrift" abhängen, wie sie durch den Kanon umrissen worden ist. Dieser komplexe Befund macht darauf aufmerksam, dass der Kanon einen Raum bildet, der Grenzen setzt, die zugleich verschiedene Wahrnehmungen des Handelns Gottes freisetzen und deshalb eine spannungsvolle Offenheit ermöglichen. Solche Offenheit wird von dem Vertrauen auf einen gemeinsamen Weg geleitet, der verspricht, alle zusammenzuführen, die mit der Bibel leben, so verschiedenartig sich die Schritte auf diesem Wege auch ausnehmen mögen.

Auch für den Beitrag von *Günter Bader* ist die durch Johann Salomo Semler 1771 eröffnete freie Untersuchung des Kanons die unhintergehbare Voraussetzung der Argumentation. Demnach sieht es so aus, dass die von

Semler reflekierte innerkirchliche Relativierung des Kanons erst dann in vollem Umfang als neuzeitliches Phänomen verstanden, wenn sie zugleich als ausserkirchliche Relativierung erkannt wird. Indem sie erstmals erlaubt, den Kanonbegriff auf Texte ausserhalb der hl. Schrift zu übertragen, macht die Schwäche des kirchlichen Kanonbegriffs den ausserkirchlichen Kanonbegriff stark. Damit ist die aktuelle Situation eingetreten, in der der einzig verfügbare Kanonbegriff die Kanonmetapher ist. Um in dieser Situation von einem Kanon hl. Schrift überhaupt sprechen zu können, sieht Bader sich zur Durchführung der umständlicheren These veranlasst: Die Einheit des Kanons liegt im Schnittpunkt einer Zweiheit von Kanonbegriffen.

Bei der Herstellung der Druckvorlage haben uns Dipl. Theol. Jochen Flebbe und stud. theol. Leonie Panenka unterstützt. Beiden sei an dieser Stelle herzlich gedankt!

Oxford und Bonn   John Barton
im November 2002   Michael Wolter

Unity and Diversity in the Biblical Canon

by John Barton

That the biblical canon contains diversity is obvious to most readers; that it is nevertheless a unity is the conviction of those for whom it functions as Holy Scripture. In the history of Christian thought there have been many ways of trying to hold together an awareness of both diversity and unity. I shall highlight some salient moments in the debate by examining, first, approaches to the Bible in which diversity is seen as a problem – a problem with a number of possible solutions; and secondly, some which perceive it as a virtue, as one of the positive advantages that Christians gain from having as their holy book this complex, interrelated set of diverse documents, rather than some simple and uncomplicated text with strong internal unity.

1. Diversity as a Problem

'Rab Judah said in Rab's name: In truth, that man, Hananiah son of Hezekiah by name, is to be remembered for blessing: but for him, the book of Ezekiel would have been hidden, for its words contradicted the Torah. What did he do? Three hundred barrels of oil were taken up to him and he sat in an upper chamber and reconciled them.'[1]

This anecdote reminds us that in post-biblical, rabbinic Judaism it is essential for the teaching of Scripture to be consistent in matters of *halakhah*. It is not possible to tolerate diversity, because clear rulings are needed on matters of conduct if one is to lead an observant Jewish life. It is perhaps difficult to imagine a religion which ascribed 'scriptural' status to a collection of books and yet was indifferent to their mutual consistency – a problem that Christian ethicists who wish to use the Bible still grapple with today. It may be worth noting, however, that it is consistency on matters of torah that seems to be of concern in Judaism. There are no rabbinic debates about how to reconcile Kings and Chronicles, for example, probably because in that case no issues of *halakhah* arise: consistency in telling the history of the kingdoms of Israel

---

1   b. Shabbat 13b.

and Judah is not an essential part of Judaism. What is essential is that Scripture shall speak with a single voice on those matters that are central to the actual operation of the religious system.

Josephus, it is true, did defend the historical consistency of the Jewish Scriptures:

> 'We do not possess myriads of inconsistent books, conflicting with each other. Our books, those which are justly accredited, are but two and twenty, and contain the record of all time.'[2]

But his context is polemical. He is contrasting the consistency of Jewish books with the chaotic muddle, as he sees it, of Greek histories. The argument is unfair, since the contrast is not between similar things – the whole of Greek literature is being compared with the narrow compass of the biblical books in Judaism, not with all books written by Jews. Nevertheless the argument that the scriptural books are consistent historically is clearly a powerful debating point. Christians, later, were to find Scripture (both Testaments) attacked by pagans as riddled with inconsistencies, and in patristic writings some space is devoted to attempts to confute this objection.

It seems to me likely that the earliest Christians were interested principally in one particular kind of consistency in Scripture. Whereas for Jews the Bible needed to be read as presenting a coherent picture of how Jewish life was to be led, so that inconsistency was a problem where matters of *halakhah* were concerned, for Christians the crucial question was the consistency of the prophecies that pointed forward to Jesus Christ. If God had 'spoken through the prophets', he must have announced through them a consistent scheme of salvation. Collections of testimonia, whether as free-standing texts or in the form of lists of prophecies embedded in other works, aimed to show that God had predicted the coming of Christ in a self-consistent way. Christianity could not live with alternative schemes of salvation-history, but needed to show that the prophetic message was coherent and pointed in a single direction.

It is thus clear that, in both early Judaism and early Christianity, there were at any rate certain kinds of inconsistency or diversity that could not be tolerated in Scripture. The possession of holy texts that could be read as fully self-consistent was a feature that might be used to commend either religion, and significant inconsistency was a problem.[3] I think this continues to be the case for most people who turn to the Bible as an inspired or authoritative or

---

2   *C. Ap.* 1:37–143.
3   Cf. H. Merkel, *Die Pluralität der Evangelien als theologisches und exegetisches Problem in der Alten Kirche* (TCh 3), Bern/Frankfurt a.M.: Peter Lang, 1978.

sacred text. They expect it to be consistent, and are worried if they find within it a level of diversity that makes it difficult to hold all its material in the mind at the same time. This may be called a common-sense reaction, found among ordinary Christians and Jews alike.

At the same time careful readers of the Bible have always noticed that there are in fact problems about its internal consistency, and that its contents are extremely diverse. There are inconsistencies in the historical information the text imparts, in its moral teaching, and in its theological understanding. It is felt, rightly, that the so-called historical-critical method has been particularly alive to such problems, and has forced them to the forefront of attention. It was not until the rise of historical criticism that inconsistencies within the text of the Bible became a tool with which it was possible to reconstruct an account of the political or intellectual history sharply at variance with what emerges from a naïve reading of the text. It is not true to say, however, that biblical criticism *imported* inconsistencies into Scripture or *deliberately* read the text as inconsistent – though this is sometimes said nowadays by scholars who regard historical criticism as having been a mistaken avenue in biblical studies. The presence of (at least apparent) diversity and inconsistency is a matter of empirical observation, and in many cases 'pre-critical' interpreters were well aware of the difficulties. What was new in historical criticism was a refusal to deal with such inconsistencies through the kinds of traditional means I outline below.

Thus it is difficult to read either the Old or the New Testament carefully without becoming aware of the presence of diversity and inconsistency, and both in the early church and in modern times Christians have devised ways of dealing with it in such a way as to retain a belief in the authority and integrity of Scripture. Three such approaches may be outlined.

1.1. Deletion and Alteration

One way of dealing with observed inconsistency in Scripture is – to put it crudely – to decide which of the various positions adopted in the text is correct, and then to excise all others by deleting verses, chapters, or even books. What is given is the apparent meaning of particular books or sections, and this cannot be changed so as to conform to what the Christian reader believes to be the truth (historical truth, theological truth, ethical truth, etc.). If the meaning of books or sections is at variance with this truth, then so much the worse for these books or sections: the Christian reader is entitled to demand that they be omitted or, at least, sidelined – shunted into an 'apocrypha' or supplement to the Bible, or read only under special terms and conditions.

This radical solution to the perceived problem of diversity in the canon has had few proponents, even in modern times, but those it has had have been of considerable historical importance. We might list Marcion, Tatian, Luther, Bultmann, and Käsemann! Indeed, the list should perhaps begin even before Marcion, with Luke, who believed that other Gospel writers had presented an account of the life of Jesus which was historically inaccurate and ought to be improved upon. (Maybe even he had a precursor in the Chronicler, who was dissatisfied with the mistelling of the history of Israel in Samuel-Kings and wanted to present a 'corrected' version of it. In this case, as in that of Luke, the replacement and what it replaced were in the end both canonized.) Marcion (and perhaps Luke) had a theory about the Gospel tradition which was not unlike the theory about the Old Testament in the Pseudo-Clementines, according to which false teachers had interfered with the accuracy of the text, and their errors should be corrected by changing or omitting material in the commonly received version.[4] Celsus was aware of such theories, which he saw as devices to enable Christians to make their Scriptures less open to criticism than they really were: 'some of the faithful, as though coming from a drinking bout, fight one another and alter the Gospel after it had first been written down three or four times, indeed many times, and falsify it, so that they can reject arguments against it (better).'[5]

It is unlikely that Marcion had genuinely independent information about the life of Jesus. Rather, he had a theological conviction that certain things were true (above all, the distinction between the saving God of Jesus and the Creator-God of the Jews) and that Jesus – being himself the truth incarnate – *can* only have taught such true things. But whereas the 'orthodox' might have treated this as a hermeneutical obligation to read whatever the Gospels delivered as Jesus' teaching *as though* it taught these things, Marcion refused to 'falsify' the plain sense of the Gospel tradition in its Lukan version, and preferred simply to delete it. He recognized material that contradicted his own position when he saw it, and drew the entirely logical conclusion that, since it must be untrue, it ought not to be read as though it had authority. Out it went.[6]

---

4   On this theory see H. v. Campenhausen, *The Formation of the Christian Bible*, London: Adam and Charles Black, 1972, p. 79.

5   Origen, *C. Cels.* 2:27.

6   Cf. H. Merkel, *Die Widersprüche zwischen den Evangelien* (WUNT 13), Tübingen: Mohr, 1971, and see my discussion in J. Barton, *The Spirit and the Letter: Studies in the Biblical Canon*, London: SPCK, 1997 (= idem, *Holy Writings, Sacred Text: The Canon in Early Christianity*. Louisville, KY: Westminster John Knox Press, 1997), pp. 35–62.

Tatian's *Diatessaron*, though far more reverent in its approach to received tradition and widely accepted in the East for some centuries, belongs logically to the same type as Marcion. Whereas 'reconcilers' argued that the four Gospels *already* made coherent sense despite their *apparent* conflicts, Tatian like Marcion (and like modern biblical critics) thought that they could not all be correct because their conflicts were real.[7] He therefore eliminated the discrepancies to produce a single consistent narrative. He does not seem — in this he was unlike Marcion — to have censored the Gospel material theologically; what he rectified were the historical inconsistencies.[8] No doubt this is one reason why his version endured for so much longer than Marcion's expurgated Luke, being untainted by heretical teaching and attractive in offering a coherent picture of the life of Jesus. Indeed, it could be said that it represents the only really successful attempt to deal with inconsistency through deletion, for even after it was officially replaced in the Syrian churches by the four-Gospel canon (thanks to Theodore of Mopsuestia), it went on being read and translated into many languages. Tatian's spirit lives on in Lives of Jesus, and even, one could say, in the various Quests of the Historical Jesus, which are interested in the facts about Jesus as these can be historically established, rather than in the 'canonical' version of his life — though the tools they use to get at the facts are of course quite different from those available to Tatian, who had only his eye for inconsistency to guide him.

Martin Luther's treatment of Esther, James, Hebrews, and Revelation seems to me to inhabit the same mental universe as these early thinkers, in that it results from refusing to harmonize them with the rest of the Bible or to read them 'in the light of' other Scripture, as 'canonical critics' would put it. He insisted on attending to the 'plain sense' of such texts, and judged that sense to be more or less incompatible with the truth of the Gospel as he had heard it from other biblical books and especially, of course, from Romans and Galatians. Like Marcion, he would not 'allegorize' in order to force texts to witness to Christ when they did not, in his judgement, really do so. He preferred to remove them from the canon, even if he bowed so far to tradition as to translate them and keep them available, like the Apocrypha, for Christian readers. They have continued to be read in all the churches of the Reformation despite Luther's structures: their 'deletion' is more theoretical than actual. Nevertheless Luther established the *possibility* of criticising biblical

---

7   Tatian may have been following his teacher Justin, who is thought to have used a gospel harmony: cf. M. Hengel, *The Four Gospels and the One Gospel of Jesus Christ*, London: SCM Press, 2000, p. 26.

8   Logically harmonizations between the Gospels in the textual tradition belong to this same movement of thought.

books on the basis of a theological principle. But it is remarkable how comparatively seldom even biblical 'critics' follow him and actually 'criticise' the Bible in this sense. Julius Wellhausen was one great exception – he used to call a spade a spade, and expressed himself freely about portions of the Old Testament of which he disapproved. But such has never become the standard practice in biblical studies.

There has been, however, a certain willingness among Lutheran scholars – albeit in a more polite way – to question the value of parts of the canon. One thinks above all of Rudolf Bultmann's negative judgements on the Old Testament as a whole, which more conservatives Christians are apt to dub 'neo-Marcionite', though in fact they are surely far less hostile than Marcion's or even, for that matter, Adolf v. Harnack's. Käsemann's famous strictures on the Lukan corpus belong in the same camp: they too, rest on a judgement about where Christian truth lies, and a willingness to use that judgement as a criterion by which to assess the adequacy of Scripture. None of these scholars, to the best of my knowledge, has actually gone so far as to propose a revision of the canon. But they are not to be persuaded that the canon contains a 'higher unity' (see below) which turns their critical comments into matters of mere detail: Käsemann's famous argument that the New Testament canon is the basis not for the unity but for the *dis*unity of the Church is proof enough of his unwillingness to think of the theological discords in the Bible as ultimately expressive of some grand symphonic design. In short, the ability to engage in theological criticism of the contents of the canon has a sharp cutting edge – one which the Church ought perhaps to beware of deliberately blunting for the sake of peace.

The theory that there is a 'canon within the canon' represents the 'deletion' approach in a more nuanced form. The less important parts of the canon are not rejected, but a hierarchy is established whereby Scripture has a core surrounded by a penumbra of decreasing value. Judaism may be said to operate in practice with such a theory, in that the Torah is of vastly greater importance for the religion than the rest of the Bible: indeed, Mishnah and Talmud matter considerably more than (say) Kings or Chronicles. While as a conscious theory the 'canon within the canon' has been prominent in particular types of German-language theology, it may reasonably be said that almost all Christians informally espouse such an approach. Most people who read the Bible have an 'effective' canon which is smaller than the theoretical one.

This can be illustrated from lectionaries, which (even when they attempt to be as even-handed as the *Revised Common Lectionary* now used widely by all kinds of churches) inevitably tend to foreground some books and soft-pedal others. Liturgically, indeed, the Gospels have had for Christianity something like the kind of centrality that the Pentateuch has for Jews – the parallel extends even to the existence of specially written or printed texts (evangeliars) containing liturgical Gospel readings, and produced to a higher standard than volumes containing the rest of Scripture. Although Luke and Acts appear to be volumes 1 and 2 of a single work, we have no evidence that they have ever been treated equally: Acts, in fact, is particularly little-cited in early Christian literature[9], and liturgical readings from it have always had the status of an 'Epistle' rather than a 'Gospel'. And of course the two Testaments have traditionally had a different status in many varieties of Christianity; except in parts of the Reformed tradition, the Old Testament normally plays second fiddle to the New. This is not Marcionism, but a nearly universal Christian belief that ultimate authority in Christianity lies with the new revelation in Christ, even though, because this revelation was 'in accordance with the Scriptures', the Old Testament can never be abandoned. The 'second rank' character of the Old Testament as Scripture is perhaps more marked in Lutheran than in other Christian thinking; there is a slight paradox here, in that the New Testament book one might most plausibly appeal to in support of such an idea is probably the Epistle to the Hebrews, whose own status was in doubt for Luther himself! In fact even Hebrews does not challenge the authority of the Old Testament, but it does interpret it as making sense only in the context of the new covenant in Christ.

Incidentally, there are anticipations in early Judaism of all the tendencies I have included under the umbrella category 'deletion and alteration', even apart from the general and continuing Jewish tendency to privilege the Pentateuch. The Qumran community similarly corrected the Pentateuch when it felt the need:

'There are five versions of the reworked Pentateuch (4Q158; 4Q364-367), which is not dissimilar to the Samaritan Pentateuch in purpose and even in the form of its text. This composition adjusts the text of the books of the Law in various minor ways so that its consistency is enhanced and its style and grammar improved … The many copies of the Book of *Jubilees* and of compositions somewhat similar to it (e.g. 4Q225-227) reflect a similar interest in rewriting the biblical accounts of Genesis and Exodus so as to have particular halakhic views incorporated within an authoritative text.'[10]

---

9 Cf. F. Stuhlhofer, *Der Gebrauch der Bibel von Jesus bis Euseb. Eine statistische Untersuchung zur Kanonsgeschichte*, Wuppertal: R. Brockhaus, 1988, and my comments in *The Spirit and the Letter* (see n. 6), pp. 14–24.

10 G. Brooke, 'The Dead Sea Scrolls', in: J. Barton (ed.), *The Biblical World I*, London: Routledge, 2002, pp. 257–258.

1.2. Reconciliation

The word 'harmonization' often appears in discussion of traditional ways of
reading the Bible and coping with its inconsistencies, but it is a slippery term
which I shall avoid here. The problem is that it can describe one of two
things which it is important to keep separate, since they are in many respects
actually opposites. One is the attempt to show that a number of documents
(for example, the four Gospels) are in fact fully consistent with each other as
they stand in spite of apparent or *prima facie* inconsistencies. (This is the
kind of 'harmonization' practised by Hananiah b. Hezekiah in the anecdote
quoted above.) The other consists in changing one or more of the texts concerned to make them all convey the same message, often by omitting passages in which there is conflict, in other words the method described above
as 'deletion and alteration'. Scholars sometimes fail to draw this distinction:
thus, for example, S.J. Patterson in his article 'Harmony of the Gospels'[11]
writes 'a gospel harmony rests on the proposition that the four canonical gospels are in fundamental or substantive agreement (*consensus evangelistarum*)
in their presentation of the life of Jesus'.[12] But a gospel 'harmony', in the
sense of a single account produced by weaving together incidents and sayings
from the four separate Gospels, is more likely to *change* the individual accounts: indeed, it is impossible to produce a consistent account without doing
so, and we have already looked at some efforts in this direction. This procedure is very different from (indeed, diametrically opposed to) trying to show
that there is no difference that would require a change anyway.

What I am concerned with in this section is 'harmonization' in the first
sense: the attempt to demonstrate that inconsistencies between biblical texts
are only apparent. For this 'reconciliation' is a less ambiguous term. In the
English-speaking world at least, reconciliation of biblical texts is nowadays
associated with fundamentalism. At the level of historical fact, it may take
the form of trying to reconcile dates and figures between Kings and Chronicles, or of seeking to show that the four Gospels present a single and consistent account of the events leading up to the crucifixion, or of the resurrection
appearances. At a more theological level, it may consist of demonstrations
that there is really no tension between Paul and James, or that the Pentateuch
has a single theological message rather than representing a compromise between the theology of the various sources discovered by historical critics.

---

11 S.J. Patterson, Art. 'Harmony of the Gospels', *AncBD* 3 (1992) 61.
12 Cf. The much fuller discussion in D. Wünsch, Art. 'Evangelienharmonie', *TRE* 10
(1982) 626–636, pp. 631–635.

But reconciliation was certainly not invented by fundamentalists. It has an ancient pedigree. Its best patristic representative is perhaps Augustine's *De consensu evangelistarum*, and it can be seen clearly at work in Andreas Osiander's great harmony of the Gospels, which does not correct one Gospel by another but simply adds together all the data in all the Gospels, so that Jesus cleanses the Temple three times, and heals four blind men.[13] An early example of reconciliation is the attempt to make John consistent with the Synoptic Gospels by proposing that the events recorded in John took place before John the Baptist was imprisoned, part of the life of Jesus which the Synoptics largely pass over in silence:

'The three Gospels already written were in general circulation and copies had come into John's hands. He welcomed them, we are told, and confirmed their accuracy, but remarked that the narrative only lacked the story of what Christ had done first of all at the beginning of his mission.'[14]

1.3. The Search for a Higher Unity

An alternative approach – or perhaps in a way a more sophisticated form of 'reconciliation' – is to argue that the admitted diversity, even inconsistency, in Scripture is subordinate to a higher unity. The texts do not all speak with a single voice, yet taken together they witness to a unified truth. In this way of understanding the Bible there is no attempt to deny the empirical evidence that shows we are dealing with many writers and points of view, and that all do not say the same thing. The intuition of ordinary readers that there are inconsistencies in Scripture is acknowledged to be correct, and in modern versions of this approach even the observation of historical critics to the effect that the biblical text is highly variegated and uneven is not necessarily denied. But it is held that, properly read, the scriptural texts have a unity of purpose and message which is more important than their mutual tensions and disagreements in detail. I think there are two versions of such a 'search for a higher unity'.

(a) One takes the form of arguing that the overarching unity of the Bible is just as empirically observable as the internal inconsistencies, provided one reads it with an open mind. That is to say, the Scriptural writers really were communicating an essentially unified vision of the truth, even though they differed on points of detail. In ancient times such is the view, for example, of Origen, writing on the four Gospels:

---

13 Cf. Hengel, *The Four Gospels* (see n. 7), p. 23.
14 Eusebius, *Hist. Eccl.* III:34.

'I do not condemn them if they even sometimes dealt freely with things which to the eye of history happened differently, and changed them so as to subserve the mystical aims they had in view … Jesus is many things, according to the conceptions of him, of which it is quite likely that the Evangelists took up different notions; while yet they were in agreement with each other in the different things they wrote.'[15]

'Just as the Gospel which several people preach is one, so (too) that which has been written by many is in its spirit-gifted significance one, and therefore in truth the Gospel, which consists of four texts, is one.'[16]

In modern biblical study, such an approach seems to me to characterize most of what describes itself as 'biblical theology', at least where this discipline has set itself the task of producing a complete 'Theology of the Old/New Testament', or even the whole Bible.[17] None of the great biblical theologies of the twentieth century assumes that the texts are to be harmonised; they are perfectly aware of diversity and inconsistency, and make a point of trying to hear the separate witnesses to theological thought of different strands in the Bible. But they affirm, in various ways, that there is some underlying unity within the texts, and that to read them as having a centre or fundamental theme is not a matter of the interpreter's choice, but corresponds to something that is and *always was* true to their content.

Walther Eichrodt,[18] for example, was not saying that the idea of covenant was one we might *choose* as a key to the Old Testament, but rather that it was (though often not overtly expressed) the concept that held all this disparate material together. Equally, for Gerhard von Rad[19] the *Heilsgeschichte* was the thread on which all the scriptural beads had been strung by their authors and tradents and compilers. By articulating it he was not imposing a unity on the Old Testament, but rather was elucidating the unity it really had. The American 'Bible Theology Movement' of the 1950s and 1960s often expressed a measure of disenchantment with what it portrayed as the 'fragmentation' of the text common in historical criticism. In doing so it was claiming that the text was more truly unified than the historical critics believed. They were not wrong to identify detailed points of diversity and inconsistency, but they were in danger of not seeing the wood for the trees, ignoring the equal or greater volume of evidence that pointed to unity and singleness of purpose.

Thus most kinds of biblical theology were interested in unity as a historical fact about the text, just as important as (or more important than) the ele-

---

15 Origen, *Comm. on John* X:4.
16 Origen, *Comm. on John* V:5; cited in Hengel, *The Four Gospels* (see n. 7), p.12.
17 Cf. M. Oeming, *Gesamtbiblische Theologien der Gegenwart*, Stuttgart u.a.: Kohlhammer, 1985; H. Gese, *Vom Sinai zum Zion*, Munich: Chr. Kaiser, 1974; J. Barr, *The Concept of Biblical Theology: An Old Testament Perspective*, London: SCM Press, 1999.
18 W. Eichrodt, *Theology of the Old Testament*, 2 vols., London: SCM Press, 1960/67.
19 G. von Rad, *Old Testament Theology*, 2 vols., Edinburgh: Oliver and Boyd, 1962/65.

ment of variety and disparity which was admittedly not to be denied. There was a clear sense that the true unity of the biblical witness was being *discovered*, not *imposed*.

So far as I can see this remains true of the biblical theologies still being produced today. Otto Kaiser, for example, in taking the Torah as the 'centre' of the biblical canon is making a historical claim about the text: that the Pentateuch emerged as central in Judaism precisely because it really was the focal point around which other biblical material had gathered.[20] In treating Torah as the fundamental unifying principle of the Old Testament we are doing justice to something inherent in the texts themselves, recognizing what is really there. To put it in terms developed by Umberto Eco: there is a real diversity in the texts, because the *intentio auctoris* is in each case different; but there is a unity at the level of the *intentio operis*, the 'intention' (using the term metaphorically) of the work taken as a whole.[21]

(b) There is, however, another way of seeking a higher unity in the Bible, and this lies in proposing that the text should be *read as* unified – whatever the historical facts about its origins may be – in accordance with a hermeneutical imperative which flows from the Church's recognition of it as Holy Scripture. This, it seems to me, is essentially what is proposed in the 'canonical approach' of Brevard S. Childs.[22] Here the unity of the Bible is not a matter of empirical observation, on a par with the equally empirical observation of its diversity, but a theologoumenon deriving from a doctrine of Scripture. What Childs suggests is that Christians *ought* to read the Bible as a unified text because of what they believe about its status as Scripture for the community. There is here no harmonizing tendency: it is entirely open to a 'canonical' reader to think that, as a matter of empirical fact, there is a great deal of variety and even contradiction within the biblical text. In so far as it is read *as Scripture*, however, this variety is to be subsumed in a higher unity. The unity that is to be looked for in the canon may quite well be a complex unity: the Bible is multi-faceted, not simple. But Christian readers *qua* Christian are

---

20 See O. Kaiser, *Der Gott des Alten Testaments. Theologie des Alten Testaments. I. Grundlegung*, Göttingen: Vandenhoeck & Ruprecht, 1993.

21 See U. Eco, *Zwischen Autor und Text*, Munich: dtv, 1996, pp. 71ff. I am grateful to Michael Wolter for this suggestion. It may go some way, incidentally, to meet James Barr's objection to Brevard Childs's phrase 'canonical intentionality', which he dismisses as 'a mystic phrase' (see B.S. Childs, *Introduction to the Old Testament as Scripture*, London: SCM Press, 1979, p. 78; J. Barr, 'Childs' Introduction to the Old Testament as Scripture', *JSOT* 16 (1980) 12-23, esp. p. 13). Cf. my comments in: J. Barton, *Reading the Old Testament: Method in Biblical Study*, London: Darton, Longman and Todd, 1984, p. 224.

22 See B.S. Childs, *Introduction* (see n. 21); idem, *Old Testament Theology in a Canonical Context*, London: SCM Press, 1985; idem, *Biblical Theology of the Old and New Testaments: Theological Reflections on the Christian Bible*, London: SCM Press, 1992.

not at liberty to expound this multi-faceted character as evidence of a basic disunity or inconsistency. They are to read Scripture as an integrated work, in which all the diverse parts witness to the one God revealed in Christ and believed in the Church. Historical-critical observations of disunity are perfectly acceptable *in the context of historical study*, but they do not have the power to overrule the Church's perception of the unity of Scripture once we move on to the level of a *theological* appropriation of the text.[23]

I have suggested elsewhere that Childs's proposal, though novel in the context of modern academic study of the Bible, is (as indeed he himself claims) quite close to how many 'ordinary' Christian readers instinctively approach the Bible.[24] People expect the Bible to be consonant with their Christian faith, and though they are open (unless they are hard-line fundamentalists) to variety and inconsistency on detailed points, they do not regard reading the Bible as a collection of wholly disparate and unrelated items as a serious option for the Christian. What Childs offers is a theologically-informed and academically underpinned argument to support Christians in approaching the Bible as they are in any case likely to do, unless biblical critics tell them otherwise. The important point here is that the 'canonical' approach is a hermeneutic of the text – and one that chimes in with the perceptions of most Christians – rather than a critical observation about it. It is issued in the imperative, not the indicative mood.

2. Diversity as a Virtue

> 'Turn it, turn it, for everything is in it'
> (mAboth V:22)

Despite the freedom of earlier forms of Judaism, (such as the Qumran community, as discussed above) later rabbinic Judaism did not easily tolerate discrepancies between different parts of the Bible on matters of *halakhah*. But in all other areas Jews have tended to be far more relaxed than Christians about the diversity within the canon. Because the real and effective authority for the practice of Judaism is the oral law, not the text of Scripture, it does not matter very much if there are different points of view and even factual disagree-

---

23 For a strongly argued statement of this case see R.W.L. Moberly, *The Bible, Theology, and Faith: A Study of Abraham and Jesus*, Cambridge: Cambridge University Press, 2000.

24 See J. Barton, 'Canon and Old Testament Interpretation', in: E. Ball (ed.), *In Search of True Wisdom: Essays in Old Testament Interpretation in Honour of Ronald E. Clements* (JSOT.S 300), Sheffield: Sheffield Academic Press, 1999, pp. 37–52.

ments between different parts of the biblical text. Catholicism, though in theory committed to the infallibility of Scripture and so unable to take the matter in such a relaxed way, has similarly in practice not been very concerned about inconsistencies within the text, because it is the church's magisterium, not the contents of the Bible, that directs what shall be believed. It is Protestant Christians for whom the shoe pinches most, because for them Scripture is the ultimate court of appeal and has to act as its own interpreter, there being no higher court which can adjudicate when it seems to give an uncertain judgement. It is perhaps this Protestant attribution of *all* authority to the Bible that leads to the need to find a 'canon within the canon', to take over the role that traditional authoritative teaching plays in both Judaism and Catholicism.

Nevertheless, at least in modern Protestant thinking the diversity in Scripture has sometimes been given a favourable spin. Diversity, after all, though it can be a source of confusion or a sign of muddle, can also be a mark of richness and subtlety, and can point to a mystery that lies beyond precise formulation:

'As the second century superscriptions remind us, none of the Gospels is *the* Gospel. They are all fallible human witnesses. Their theological subject-matter lies beyond the text and beyond anything the historian can draw from these sources. The biggest danger of the so-called quest of the historical Jesus is the suggestion that the historian's conclusions might provide not simply one critical norm amongst others but the foundation and substance of Christian faith. This critical reduction to a single norm, like Tatian's solution to the plurality of the Gospels, would be in danger of making *the* Gospel into a new law. The variety of witnesses (which include the other New Testament writers) to the one Lord is one way of ensuring that this Lord transcends not only these witnesses but also all subsequent Christian theological and ethical positions and decisions ...

A normative portrait of Jesus would perhaps facilitate theological criticism of unsatisfactory faith images and judgements. But any simple measuring of these against that would rapidly extinguish the freedom of the spirit. It would also imply that the Christian gospel could be identified with any one formulation of it. Perhaps Matthew, and certainly later harmonizers, wanted this. One can understand why. The Christian church has always had to exercise some control over the enthusiasms of faith. Perhaps that is why the Gospels were composed. But it seems to have been a higher wisdom which resulted in a plurality of Gospels in the canon.'[25]

In precisely this form such an idea is perhaps a modern perception. But the four-Gospel canon is, after all, not in itself a modern product, but something on which Christians agreed from quite early times. Despite the influence of Tatian in the Syrian churches, in both East and West there was the early authority of Irenaeus to support the importance of there being four Gospels, no more and no less, by the end of the second century. Irenaeus does not exactly see the four Gospels as four different *portraits* of Jesus, each with its own

---

25 R. Morgan, 'The Hermeneutical Significance of Four Gospels', *Interp.* 33 (1979) 376-388; the quotations are from pp. 387 and 388.

character: it has taken redaction criticism to develop this idea in detail. He thinks more in terms of each supplementing the others by providing additional (rather than alternative) information. Nevertheless, he never produced a harmony of the Gospels, and he was clearly aware, for example, of the divergent character of John as against the Synoptics, to be summed up in Clement of Alexandria's description of it as a 'spiritual' Gospel designed to teach truths of a different *kind* from Matthew, Mark, and Luke.

It is possible to argue that Irenaeus's defence of the four separate Gospels rests on an earlier idea already implied in the titles 'According to X' which seem to derive from a time before the tendency developed of referring to them as 'The Gospel of X'. Even though Justin seems to know of the use of 'Gospel' as a genre-description, he himself refers to them as the 'memoirs' (ἀπομνημονεύματα) of the apostles, and it is not until Origen that they are called simply 'the Gospels'. The earlier perception is that they are four *versions* of the (single) 'gospel', that is, of the message about Jesus.[26] Even if each was originally intended by its author or compiler to be the one authoritative account of the life of Jesus – only Luke makes this explicit – and were so used in the community that produced them, that very early period is now wholly hidden from our view. As soon as we have evidence of their use, it is as multiple accounts of equal standing, although, as is well known, Matthew tends to be cited more than the others by most writers from the second century onwards, and is often thought of as the earliest. The diversity of the Gospels seems not to have been thought of as a problem, even if it was not actively promoted as a benefit.

One reason for this may have been, as I have argued elsewhere,[27] that they were felt to be codified extracts from a larger corpus, the traditions about the acts and sayings of Jesus, which existed primarily in oral tradition and on which Christian teachers were free to some extent to extemporize.[28] 'Clement does not yet quote the text of a Gospel literally, because he feels bound up with the teaching of Jesus through the living oral tradition … The fact that it was there in different versions gave him freedom to shape his own.'[29] The looseness of patristic citation from the Gospels, which is such a headache to textual critics, may not indicate sloppiness or carelessness but more an attitude of freedom towards written sources which died out only

---

26 Cf. Hengel, *The Four Gospels* (see n. 7), p. 3.

27 Barton, *The Spirit and the Letter* (see n. 6), pp. 79–91.

28 Cf. also Hengel, *The Four Gospels* (see n. 7), pp. 61–65: "Euangelion" or "the Kyrios".

29 Ibid., pp. 128–190. Cf. p. 134: 'Appeal to the "word of the Lord" always made a better impression, referring directly to a pre-existent, incarnate and exalted Kyrios rather than to a mere writing … It was in the nature of things for his words still to be quoted freely from memory.'

slowly in the Church and may, indeed, still be seen today in the way preachers and others commonly conflate and combine sayings from several Gospels.

In a similar vein David C. Parker has argued that the early textual tradition of the sayings of Jesus is often flexible not merely in practice but in principle. The sayings were not treated in the Church of the first two of three centuries as holy Writ in the same way as the Old Testament, but were seen as enshrining basic ideas which could be developed flexibly in different situations. The flexibility was not infinite, but its bounds were not exactly defined, and they certainly were not so tight that we can confidently reconstruct, from the words a given writer cites as Jesus', precisely what he found in the manuscript of the Gospels he habitually used. Against this background the existence of four varying versions of the life and teachings of Jesus, and perhaps even of other texts such as the putative Q and the Gospel of Thomas, was not the problem it has been for later, more 'literalistic' readers. The existence of variant versions of what Jesus said or did on any particular occasion may have helped to authorize the preacher's freedom to tell the story in a new way, not corresponding exactly to any of the written accounts.

Along these lines one might argue that diversity, even inconsistency, was seen at least by some in the early Church as having a distinctive value, rather than being simply a problem. This cannot have been a universal perception, or there would be no Diatessaron nor any patristic treatises on the 'consensus of the evangelists', but it may have been a common one.

'... the church came into being through the Spirit, as the community of the Spirit. The oral and written traditions together were and remain a principal element in the church's finding its calling. But the tradition is manifold. There are four quite different Gospels, none with a claim to authority over the other three; there is no authoritative text beyond the manuscripts which we may follow without further thought ... Rather than looking for right or wrong readings, and with them for right or wrong beliefs and practices, the way is open for the possibility that the church is the community of the Spirit even in its multiplicities of texts, one might say in its corruptions and restorations. Indeed, we may suggest that it is not in spite of the variety but because of them that the church is that community.'[30]

Where the Old Testament was concerned, there was of course no corresponding sense of a freely adaptable text. These books had been written Scripture from time immemorial, and inconsistencies within them could hardly be handled in the same way. When Origen encounters pagan objections to the Old Testament based on its diversity, he does not argue that this diversity is beneficial, but meets the argument head-on by trying to rebut the accusation of inconsistency. Sometimes, as Philo had done before him, he will try to show

---

30 D.C. Parker, *The Living Text of the Gospels*, Cambridge: Cambridge University Press, 1997, p. 212.

that the surface inconsistency points to some deeper truth, which does in a sense amount to making a virtue of what had been raised as an objection.[31] But it would be hard, I think, to find a patristic author who takes the kind of delight in the sheer diversity of the Old Testament evinced in the rabbinic saying with which this section began.

For a modern Christian, diversity and inconsistency in the biblical canon is likely to be seen as a fact of life. Given what we know of how haphazard and unplanned was the growth of the canon, it would be surprising if this were not so. Despite the best efforts of biblical theologians and canonical critics to show that the Bible exhibits, or can or should be read as if it exhibited, an impressive unity, anyone who has engaged in the detail of modern biblical study is likely to have a stronger sense of its variegated and untidy character. To commend such a book honestly as a vehicle for the Word of God must somehow involve seeing this diversity not merely as no worse than neutral, but rather as in some respects a positive advantage. One may say, for example, that scriptural diversity is a check on authoritarianism, part of an insistence on there being legitimately different Christian perceptions of the truth: the freedom within the canon permits Christians also to explore freely. The Church thus acquires the benefits of a fixed corpus of texts but without the straitjacket it would impose if all those texts spoke with a single voice. Protestant Christians are convinced that the Bible 'contains all things necessary for salvation', as Anglican formularies put it: but it is its unity of witness to central Christian truth that matters, not a total inner accord on all matters however small. Martin Hengel sums this up very well:

'The early church could therefore endure and make fruitful the offence which was caused by its four very different Gospels and which continually threatened to be a stumbling block, because it knew that despite all the differences, indeed manifest contradictions, these four reports were grounded in the Lord and his work of salvation for God's lost creatures and because beyond all the contradictions, this 'plurality' pointed to a wealth of theological thought and narrative which first fully developed this work of salvation in its various perspectives. The work of Christ and the message which goes out from it cannot adequately be summarized in the theological outline of a single Christian teacher. From the beginning the difference between the Gospels was necessary and was not only tolerated by the church but willed in this form.'[32]

---

31 For examples see J. Barton, *Oracles of God: Perceptions of Ancient Prophecy in Israel after the Exile*, London: Darton, Longman and Todd, 1986, New York/Oxford: Oxford University Press, 1988, pp. 250–251.
32 Hengel, *The Four Gospels* (see n. 7), pp. 166–167.

Erstes oder Altes Testament?[1]

von Horst Seebass

Die Themenstellung fragt nach einer Ortsbestimmung in einem neuen Streit um die Hermeneutik der Schriftensammlung, für die der Titel „Altes Testament" in Wissenschaft und kirchlichem Gebrauch der geläufigste ist. Der Streit erwächst aus dem erfreulicherweise seit einiger Zeit in Gang gekommenen christlich-jüdischen Gespräch. Angesichts der Begegnung von Christen und Juden als Vertreter einer je lebendigen Glaubensweise war und ist es sowohl unvermeidlich als auch wünschenswert, auf die gemeinsame biblische Tradition zurückzugreifen, für die beide Seiten je ihre eigene Sichtweise mitbringen, die aber für beide – und das erscheint als große Chance – nicht als gesicherter Besitz gelten kann, sondern als etwas Einzuholendes, Wiederzugewinnendes.[2] Dies gilt jedenfalls dann, wenn man sich beiderseits um jene Tradition in historisch-kritisch und metakritisch geschulter Weise bemüht, wie das wissenschaftlich kaum anders möglich ist. Zwar fehlt der exegetischen Bemühung um die alten Texte derzeit ein tragender Konsens der Meinungen, wie er für die vorige Forschergeneration weithin gegeben war. Aber

---

1 Eine erste Fassung dieses Beitrags ging aus einer Vorlesung zur Hermeneutik des Alten Testaments im WS 1999/2000 hervor. Eine korrigierte Fassung hatte ich meinem Bonner Kollegen Gerhard Sauter zum 65. Geburtstag gewidmet. Der Anlass ist vorbei, die Verbundenheit geblieben.

2 Um keine Missverständnisse aufkommen zu lassen: Ich meine etwas je neu Einzuholendes nach der zunächst verfremdenden Bearbeitung durch die historisch-kritische Methode, die von den namhaften jüdischen und christlichen Wissenschaftlern und Wissenschaftlerinnen für unabweislich gehalten wird. Ich gehe grundsätzlich davon aus, dass das Wort der heiligen Schriften zumindest christlich zum *verbum externum* zu werden vermag und so die Möglichkeit in sich birgt, Überraschendes in je neue Situationen zu sagen wie etwa in die gegenwärtige. Zwar gibt es eine erhebliche Differenz zwischen dem exegetischen Bemühen um die alten Texte und dem systematisch-gegenwärtigen Bemühen zum Vernehmen des *verbum externum* (s. jüngst M. Grohmann, Aneignung der Schrift. Wege einer christlichen Rezeption jüdischer Hermeneutik, Neukirchen-Vluyn 2000, 1–17, die sich m.E. zuviel vorgenommen hat; s. meine Rezension in ThLZ 126 [2001] 1183f.). Aber man darf an eine Analogie zwischen beiden Bemühungen denken, sofern sie beide theologisch sind, als eine mögliche Notwendigkeit oder notwendige Möglichkeit gemeinsamen Bemühens über die Disziplingrenzen hinaus. Hat nicht z.B. erst der Rückgriff auf die „fremde", neu gehörte heilige Schrift den bescheidenen Konsens zwischen Lutheranern und Katholiken in der *Gemeinsamen Erklärung zur Rechtfertigungslehre* vom 31. Oktober 1999 zur Akzeptanz geführt?

dies dürfte bei einer spezifisch theologischen, kanonischen Fragestellung nicht so gravierend sein wie bei religionsgeschichtlichen, literarhistorischen und historischen. So ist der historische Abstand zu den Quellen, d.h. den alten Schriften, der umso konkreter, fassbarer und andringender wird, je weiter die Arbeit fortschreitet, einerseits für beide, Judentum und Christentum, ein Problem, andererseits aber eine Chance, den gemeinsamen Ursprüngen näher zu kommen, als es Jahrhunderte lang geschah.[3]

Den an diesem Gespräch Beteiligten ist zu einem Teil die Bezeichnung „Altes Testament" suspekt geworden, weil an ihr eine unheilvolle Geschichte der Abwertung sowohl dieser Schriftensammlung als des Judentums als einer lebendigen Religion verbunden zu sein scheint. Inzwischen ist zwar genug an Klarstellung erfolgt, dass ein solcher Automatismus nicht zwangsläufig ist und dass bisher alle Versuche, einen neuen Titel zu finden, nicht überzeugend ausgefallen sind. Zunächst kam der Terminus „Hebräische Bibel" auf; aber seine Schwächen sind bekannt, und er wird z.T. auch nur beiläufig verwendet:[4] Dan 2–7 und Teile aus Esr 4–6; 7 sind aramäisch verfasst, daher trifft der Terminus nicht zu. Der Partnerbegriff könnte auch nicht „Neues Testament" sein, sondern etwa „Griechische Bibel". Die aber würde neben dem Neuen das Alte Testament in seiner Septuaginta-Übersetzung umfassen. Ähnlich steht es mit dem Terminus „Erstes Testament".[5] Das Zahlwort erlaubt eine unbegrenzte Zahl weiterer Testamente[6] und würde damit dem

---

3   Eine ausgezeichnete Ausarbeitung zu dem hier verhandelten Thema, mit anderen Akzenten im Detail, lieferte B. Janowski, Der eine Gott der beiden Testamente. Grundfragen einer biblischen Theologie, ZThK 95 (1998) 1–36 = ders., Beiträge zur Theologie des Alten Testaments. II. Die rettende Gerechtigkeit, Neukirchen-Vluyn 1999, 249–298. Ob jüdische Orthodoxie und christlicher Fundamentalismus darauf ansprechbar sind, kann hier offen bleiben.

4   Dies gilt eher für die Diskussion im deutschen Sprachraum als für die im angelsächsischen. Denn es scheint so, als dominiere in den USA die Bezeichnung „Hebrew Bible", weil „Old Testament" antijüdisch verstanden werden kann und dort schon dieser Verdacht genügt, um die m.E. zweckmäßige Bezeichnung „Altes/Old Testament" unmöglich zu machen (Weiteres s.u.). Wie lange wird es dauern, bis im englischen Sprachraum das Gefühl aufkommt, „Hebrew Bible" solle Christen einen Teil ihrer Bibel wegnehmen? Zur Sache vgl. den wichtigen, leider entlegenen Beitrag von J. Barton, Biblical Studies 2: Old Testament or Hebrew Bible?, in: M. Rogers (Hg.), Farmington Papers BS 2 (Sept. 1996) sowie Janowski, Gott (s. Anm. 3), 249f., der den Begriff „Altes Testament" nur für den christlichen Kanonteil reklamiert.

5   Er scheint eher im deutschen Sprachraum propagiert zu werden. Gewichtig im angelsächsischen Bereich ist jedoch J.A. Sanders, First Testament and Second, BTB 17 (1987) 47–49.

6   Bei Testamenten ist nun mal das spätere, d.h. das mit der höheren Zahl, das jeweils verbindliche, das letzte das einzig verbindliche. Im Gespräch der Weltreligionen denke man nur an den Islam, der den Kor'an als letztgültige Offenbarung nach Altem und Neuem Testament versteht. Der Titel „Erstes Testament" beabsichtigt dagegen eine Aufwertung der gemeinten Schriftensammlung als (fast einzig) fundamental. Das ergibt sich aus dem Titel aber nicht und bedarf auch sachlich der Prüfung. Weiteres s.u.

spannenden Moment der Kanonizität des Alten Testaments im Christentum und noch stärker der Tanach-Grenze als Vorgabe im Judentum sicher nicht gerecht.

Vielleicht darf man nicht ausschließen, dass im Zuge weitergehender Diskussionen ein befriedigenderer Ausdruck für die hier zu behandelnde Schriftensammlung auftaucht als der des Alten Testaments.[7] Mir scheint aber die dahinter stehende historische und theologische Problematik jeder nur möglichen Bezeichnung weitaus wichtiger. Es muss also primär darum gehen, wie die Christenheit mit dem Kanonteil „Altes Testament" ihres Gesamtkanons lebt und wissenschaftlich mit ihm verfahren sollte. Hat er Normativität neben und mit dem Neuen Testament? Hat er eine nur eingeschränkte? Oder begibt man sich aus dem normativ Christlichen heraus, wenn man dem Alten Testament Normativität, und sei es nur eine eingeschränkte, zuschreibt?

So verweist die Themenstellung auf das oben angesprochene Grundproblem des Verstehens einer zwischen Judentum und Christentum gemeinsamen Tradition. Es ist dem (in einer ersten Diskussionsrunde) von Robert Morgan[8] verhandelten Problem einer Biblischen Theologie nicht unähnlich, hat also mit ihm ein gemeinsames Feld.[9] Jedoch kann die Themenstellung das Problem vielleicht distanzierter angehen als das Programm einer Biblischen Theologie, indem sie ein nicht nur innerchristliches Problemfeld anzeigt.[10] Und im Rahmen einer Betrachtung zum Kanon als der Sammlung klassisch-verbindlicher Schriften im Christentum ergibt sich eine weitere Entlastung insofern, als in diesem Rahmen die christliche Identifikation mit einzelnen Büchern auch des Neuen Testaments Unterschiede zulässt, ohne das Insgesamt des Neuen Testaments in Frage zu stellen.

Ich möchte also erst am Schluss zur Frage der Bezeichnungen zurückkommen. Im Zentrum wird stehen müssen, wie man als christlicher Theologe

---

7 Grohmann, Aneignung (s. Anm. 2), 17ff. schlug nach dem neutestamentlichen Sprachgebrauch „Schrift(en)" vor, was wohl nur im wissenschaftlichen Diskurs sinnvoll sein kann und Näherbestimmungen benötigt.

8 What is Biblical Theology – and what should it be? Or: Another bite at an overchewed cherry. R. Morgan hat inzwischen den für ihn entscheidenden Gesichtspunkt der Normativität des Christuszeugnisses präzisiert (s. dazu seinen Beitrag in diesem Band).

9 S. dazu Janowski, Gott (s. Anm. 3), passim (mit viel Literatur).

10 Bekanntlich hat J.D. Levenson, Warum Juden sich nicht für biblische Theologie interessieren, EvTh 51 (1991) 402–430; ders., The Hebrew Bible. The Old Testament and Historical Criticism, Louisville, KY 1993, dazu manches Treffende gesagt. Unsachlich provozierend ist seine Bemerkung, die hebräische Bibel sei das einzige nichtchristliche Buch, das immer noch christlich interpretiert werde (Hebrew Bible 10), weil auch Judenchristen Juden sind und das Alte Testament seit den Anfängen ein christliches Buch war und ist. Veraltet ist die Behauptung, historische Kritik sei antijudaistisch (Warum 42).

bzw. als christliche Theologin hermeneutisch mit dem Kanon umgeht, soweit es die Schriftensammlung angeht, die man einstweilen „Altes Testament" nennen kann.

1950 publizierte Rudolf Bultmann in dem Sammelband „Welt ohne Hass" den bekannten Aufsatz „Die Bedeutung der alttestamentlich-jüdischen Tradition für das christliche Abendland".[11] Dem Motiv „Welt ohne Hass" sind wir nach breiterer Reflexion zur Schoah einerseits und neuen Erfahrungen im christlich-jüdischen Gespräch andererseits wohl noch gründlicher verpflichtet als Bultmann, obwohl solche Komparative bei Würdigung der unterschiedlichen historischen Situation immer ihre Schwächen haben. Ich erwähne das aber, weil man nur zu gut die Gefahren kennt, die bei der anstehenden Kanonbetrachtung lauern:[12]

Wie wird das Judentum nicht enteignet, wenn man christlich das Alte Testament als ersten Teil der zweigeteilten Bibel liest? Kann man sich einer wie auch immer gearteten Abwertung des Alten Testaments gegenüber dem Neuen entziehen, wenn man sich strikt an die Offenbarung des Christus Jesus gebunden weiß? Wenn man das Alte Testament im Kanon nicht abwertet, sondern als vom Neuen Testament unterschieden in gleicher Weise gelten lässt, kann man dann noch zureichend die Einzigartigkeit des Christus Jesus geltend machen[13], oder wird das Neue Testament mit seinem Christus zu einem Anhängsel des einzig fundamentalen „Ersten Testaments"?[14]

---

11 Wiederabgedruckt in: ders., Glauben und Verstehen II, Tübingen [4]1965, 236–245.

12 In der theologischen Debatte ist manches durch einen Übereifer und im Gegenschlag durch besondere Zurückhaltung schwierig, so dass es wohl tut, bei einem Physiker und Philosophen – nämlich C.F.v. Weizsäcker, Gerschom Scholem und die Kabbala, in: ders., Wahrnehmung der Neuzeit, München [2]1986, 180–184 – sehr Hilfreiches zum Verhältnis von Judentum und Christentum zu finden.

13 Ich denke hier an gewichtige Fragen neutestamentlicher Forschung, die sich in der Tradition von R. Bultmann weiß. Eine entsprechende Rücksichtnahme findet man in dem ausgezeichneten Buch von A.H.J. Gunneweg, Vom Verstehen des Alten Testaments. Eine Hermeneutik (ATD.E 5), Göttingen 1977, Kap. VII: „Das Alte Testament als Teil des christlichen Kanons".

14 So E. Zenger, Das Erste Testament. Die jüdische Bibel und die Christen, Düsseldorf 1991, 130f. – Janowski, Gott (s. Anm. 3), passim, bemühte sich sinnvoll, solche Spitzensätze Zengers nicht zu zitieren, sondern ihn in eine Diskussion einzubinden, um die Bedeutung des Christus Jesus für Christen im Verbund mit dem um das Jüdische im Christentum besorgten Zenger angemessen zu profilieren. Ich zitiere also nur historisch; s. jetzt E. Zenger, Einleitung in das Alte Testament, Stuttgart [3]1998, 12–36. Eine exzellente Entfaltung des alttestamentlich zu Christus zu Sagenden findet man inzwischen bei H.J. Hermisson, Jesus Christus als externe Mitte des Alten Testaments, in: Ch. Landmesser u.a. (Hg.), Jesus Christus als die Mitte der Schrift (BZNW 86), Berlin/New York 1997, 199–233.

Ältere Problemfragen habe ich so noch nicht einmal genannt. Sie waren ja nicht weniger wichtig als die jetzigen.[15] Für die Themenstellung beschränke ich mich auf die genannten Fragen. Es wird sich zeigen, wie weit sie beantwortbar sind. Vorweg aber möchte man wiederholen, dass fundierte Antworten eine größere Einigkeit der alttestamentlichen Wissenschaft in Grundfragen verlangten, als sie zur Zeit existiert. Ihr fehlt zur Zeit die ganz große Synthese oder wenigstens eine große Synthese.[16] Daran haben die folgenden Ausführungen ihre Grenze. Wie aber bereits erwähnt, dürfte dies bei der hier verfolgten Fragestellung nicht so durchschlagen wie etwa bei religionsgeschichtlichen oder literarhistorischen.[17]

Im Folgenden soll thesenhaft geklärt werden, wie die in der Themenstellung enthaltene Problematik eine Lösung finden könnte.

1. Als Basis sehe ich an, dass die Offenbarung, an die Christen und Christinnen sich halten, nicht die Bibel ist wie der Kor'an für den Islam, sondern Gott in Jesus Christus.[18] Im Neuen Testament ist sie bezeugt, ohne das Alte Tes-

---

15 S. etwa Gunneweg, Verstehen (s. Anm. 13); H. Graf Reventlow, Hauptprobleme der alttestamentlichen Theologie im 20. Jahrhundert (EdF 173), Darmstadt 1982; ders., Hauptprobleme der Biblischen Theologie im 20. Jahrhundert (EdF 302), Darmstadt 1983; H.D. Preuß, Das Alte Testament in christlicher Predigt, Stuttgart u.a. 1984, 10–164; O. Kaiser, Der Gott des Alten Testaments. Theologie des Alten Testaments. I. Grundlegung (UTB 1747), Göttingen 1993, 13–89. – Aus der gegenwärtig noch andauernden Debatte habe ich die Frage gemieden, ob im Neuen Testament nicht nach der Schoah Textpartien wegen ihres in der Diskussion behaupteten Antijudaismus abgewiesen werden müssen. M.E. gehört diese Frage in das weiterreichende Problem theologischer Sachkritik, das man kaum auf das Neue Testament beschränken kann. Das mit jener Frage angesprochene Gelände dürfte besonders vermint und die Diskussion dazu sicher nicht abgeschlossen sein.

16 Für mich selbst verleugne ich nicht, dass die großen Synthesen zu den Pentateuchquellen und zur großen Prophetie der vorigen Forschergeneration immer noch tragfähig sind, selbstverständlich mit manchen Modifikationen. Aber das ist z.Z. nur eine Position unter vielen. Anders als C. Dohmen, Wenn die Argumente ausgehen, BiKi 53 (1998) 113–117, S. 114 meint, ist nicht diese Position, sondern die diesbezügliche Forschung in der Krise, weil Konsensfähiges kaum in Sicht ist.

17 Es dürfte nicht mehr rückgängig zu machen sein, dass nach dem 2. Weltkrieg die theologische Dimension des Alten Testaments mit Macht wiederentdeckt worden ist. Auch wenn die Forschung im einzelnen differiert, dürfte jene Dimension selbst nicht mehr strittig sein. Religionsgeschichtliche Forschung ist damit ebenso wenig überflüssig wie zum Neuen Testament. S. dazu die Diskussion in: Religionsgeschichte Israels oder Theologie des Alten Testaments?, JBTh 10 (1995), in der die dort von R. Albertz (Religionsgeschichte Israels statt Theologie des Alten Testaments! Plädoyer für eine forschungsgeschichtliche Umorientierung [S. 3–24]; Hat die Theologie des Alten Testaments doch noch eine Chance? Abschließende Stellungnahme in Leuven [S. 177–188]) promulgierte These, die alttestamentliche Theologie sei durch Religionsgeschichte zu ersetzen, von N. Lohfink (Fächerpoker und Theologie [S. 207–230]) als nicht möglich erwiesen wurde.

18 Dieser Satz verdankt sich letzten Endes K.H. Miskotte, Wenn die Götter schweigen, München 1963. In dem schönen Buch von G. Sauter, Zugänge zur Dogmatik (UTB

tament ist sie nicht verständlich.[19] Neutestamentliche Belege, die dies verdeutlichen wie etwa 1.Kor 15,3ff.; Lk 24,25–27 sind nicht etwa wegen ihrer
damaligen Methodik zu destruieren, sondern mit unseren Methoden ist das
Äquivalent zu erbringen. Insbesondere ist die Idee der Menschwerdung des
Logos Gottes zwar im Neuen Testament formuliert, aber im Alten Testament
geboren, indem der einzigartige und darum einzige Gott sich ein begrenztes
historisches Volk zum menschlichen Partner nahm, unter Umständen durch
eine Einzelperson vertreten wie durch Mose in Ex 32,10–14; Num 14,11–22,
um sein Wesen grundlegend zur Kenntnis zu geben.[20]

2. Da das Wort „Testament" über griech. $\delta\iota\alpha\theta\acute{\eta}\kappa\eta$ auf hebräisch *berît* zurückgeht, ist es signifikant, dass der Bund Gottes mit seinem Volk Israel weder
im Alten noch im Neuen Testament als von Gott gekündigt gilt.[21] Vor allem

---

2064), Göttingen 1998 habe ich, weil ich seiner Zustimmung gewiss war, nach einem
solchen Satz gesucht. Wohl wegen seiner Zurückhaltung gegenüber dem Begriff „Offenbarung" findet man ihn nicht genau so, wohl aber durchgehend die Grundlegung in
Jesus Christus. Neutestamentlich wird der Satz in dem Beitrag von M. Wolter präzisiert
(s.u. S. 63ff.).

19 So z.B. expliziert in einer auch jüdische Diskussionen berücksichtigenden Weise von Janowski, Gott (s. Anm. 3), 260–265; Hermisson, Jesus Christus (s. Anm. 14), passim. Die
   in dem obenstehenden Satz vorgenommene vorsichtige Unterscheidung in der Art der
   Bezeugung versucht, die Überlegungen von R. Morgan in diesem Band aufzunehmen.

20 Dieser Gedanke wird unten näher erläutert. Ausgangspunkt ist der existential-
   theologische Ansatz von R. Bultmann, wonach man von Gott nicht reden könne, ohne
   von *dem* Menschen bzw. präziser von sich selbst zu reden. M.E. müsste es biblisch heißen: Man kann nicht vom Gott der Bibel reden, ohne von seinen Menschen zu reden.
   Hierzu freue ich mich über die grundlegende Übereinstimmung mit Janowski, Gott (s.
   Anm. 3), 265ff., der das Inkarnatorische an einer Schekina-Theologie zu verdeutlichen
   suchte, die in Judentum und Christentum je unterschiedliche Weiterführungen erfahren
   hat. Als jüdischer Gesprächspartner ist bemerkenswert vor allem M. Wyschogrod, Inkarnation aus jüdischer Sicht, EvTh 55 (1995) 13–28. Eine gewichtige Aufarbeitung zu
   dem Thema leisten W. Dietrich/Ch. Link, Die dunklen Seiten Gottes. I. Willkür und
   Gewalt, Neukirchen-Vluyn [2]1997; II. Allmacht und Ohnmacht, ebd. 2000: Es sei nicht
   zu vergessen, dass alttestamentlich das menschliche Gegenüber Gottes eben Israel heißt
   und ist.

21 Dass nach dtn-dtr Konzept das Bundbrechen des Volkes das Exil verständlich mache,
   damit aber zugleich dem Volk eine Berufung auf den Bund verwehrt war, hat vor allem
   N. Lohfink, Art. Bund, NBL 1 (1992) 344–348, Sp. 346 nachgewiesen. Für Dtr gab es
   eine Lösung dann nur entweder, wenn Jahwe die Umkehr herbeiführte, oder jeremia-
   nisch, indem Gott einen neuen Bund kreiert. – Zur eng begrenzten Aussagekraft des
   Wortes „Bund" für das Verhältnis von Altem und Neuem Testament s. besonders einerseits E. Gräßer, Der alte Bund im Neuen. Exegetische Studien zur Israelfrage nach dem
   Neuen Testament (WUNT 35), Tübingen 1985, 1–134, andererseits N. Lohfink, Der
   niemals gekündigte Bund. Exegetische Gedanken zum christlich-jüdischen Dialog, Freiburg u.a. 1989, 25–47 sowie Christen und Juden III. Schritte der Erneuerung im Verhältnis zum Judentum. Eine Studie der Evangelischen Kirche in Deutschland, Gütersloh
   2000, 19–46; Kirche und Israel. Ein Beitrag der reformatorischen Kirchen Europas zum
   Verhältnis von Christen und Juden (Leuenberger Texte 6), im Auftrag des Exekutivaus-
   schusses für die Leuenberger Kirchengemeinschaft hg. v. H. Schwier, Frankfurt a.M.

die einzige Bezugsstelle vom neuen Bund, Jer 31,31–34[22] (für die Herren-
mahlsworte nach Lk 22,20 und 1.Kor 11,25 sowie für 2.Kor 3 und Hebr 8–
10), spricht nicht von einer Aufhebung des Bundes durch Gott, sondern vom
Bundbrechen des Volkes, und kündigt eine radikale anthropologische Erneuerung des Gottesvolkes Israel durch Gott an.[23] Wenn Jer 31,31–34 dabei speziell auf die Tora abhebt, wird das noch zu bedenken sein. Einstweilen bleibt
die Hauptsache festzuhalten: keine Kündigung des Bundes von Gottes Seite.
2.Kor 3 und Hebr 8–10 sprechen jedoch von einem Defizit des dort erst als
alten Bund verstandenen Mosebundes (2.Kor 3,14).[24] Das führt zu einem
weiteren, m.E. ausschlaggebenden Punkt.

2001, 46f.; Das jüdische Volk und seine Heilige Schrift in der christlichen Bibel (Ver-
lautbarungen des Apostolischen Stuhls 152), Bonn 2001.

22 Verfehlt sind Versuche, Bundesschlüsse, die im Alten Testament selbst nicht als neue
deklariert werden, trotzdem als neu zu bezeichnen wie z.B. Zenger, Das Erste Testament
(s. Anm. 14), 108ff.; ders., Bundestheologie – ein derzeit vernachlässigtes Thema der
Bibelwissenschaft und ein wichtiges Thema für das Verhältnis Israel – Kirche, in: ders.
(Hg.), Der neue Bund im Alten. Die Bundestheologie der beiden Testamente (QD 146),
Freiburg u.a. 1993, 13–50; C. Dohmen, Der Sinaibund als neuer Bund in Ex 19–34, in:
ebd., 51–84; dagegen m.R.: A. Schenker, Der nie aufgehobene Bund. Exegetische Beobachtungen zu Jer 31,31–34, in: ebd., 85–112. Der theologische Gebrauch des Wortes
berît im Alten Testament ist solcher Art, dass Gott einen bestehenden Bund ergänzen
kann, ohne ihn zu ändern. Dahin gehören u.a. die so wichtigen Ankündigungen eines
ewigen Bundes in Dtn 32,36–41; Ez 16,59–63; 36,24–28. Leider hat bereits Lohfink, Der
niemals gekündigte Bund (s. Anm. 21), 63ff. den Befund verwischt, indem er die bis
heute bei Juden und Christen nicht erfüllte Verheißung eines neuen Herzens, das von
niemanden einer Belehrung bedarf (Jer 31,34) auf die Selbigkeit der Tora im Rahmen
dieser Verheißung sowie auf die nach Jer 31 gewiss nach dem Exil anhebende Vergebung Gottes reduziert. Ebd., 73f. hat er die Bitte um ein reines Herz (Ps 51,12) umge-
münzt zur Bitte um ein neues Herz. Der Text lautet aber: „Schaffe in mir, Gott, ein reines Herz und mache neu für mich einen beständigen Geist"; von *berît* ist da nicht die
Rede. Weiteres s.u.

23 Hebr 8,13 nennt den alten Bund einen zum Schwinden gekommenen, weil er dessen
Gottesvolk nicht untadelig vor Gott gemacht habe. Dazu hat E. Gräßer, An die Hebräer
II (EKK XVII/2), Zürich/Neukirchen-Vluyn 1993, 98f. herausgearbeitet, dass der Autor
das im Neuen Testament ohnehin selten zitierte Jer 31,31–34 (96 Anm. 3) nicht in vollem Umfang auswertet (und zudem als Anklage versteht; 97), sondern auf die Zusage der
Sündenvergebung reduziert, die er für seine Interpretation des Hohepriestertums Christi
benötigt. Die drei übrigen Elemente – Toraverheißung, Bundesverheißung, Erkenntnis-
verheißung – lässt er unberücksichtigt. „Im Zentrum des Hebr steht eben nicht die *Stiftung* der Sinai-Diatheke per Toraübermittlung, sondern ihr In-Kraft-Treten durch das
Besprengungsblut (Ex 24,8), dem in der Zion-Diatheke das Blut des Kreuzesopfers Jesu
entspricht (9,12.14). ... Bund und Opferblut sind das eigentliche Leitthema im folgenden
9,1 – 10,18, zu dem unser Text überleitet" (99). Gräßer kann zudem erweisen, dass Hebr
den alten Bund durch den neuen überboten und nicht einen absolut anderen sieht (vgl. 94
Anm. 161). Er erklärt ferner pointiert, dass der Text nicht antijüdisch zu lesen ist, da a)
der alte Bund regelmäßig als Stiftung Gottes gilt, und b) dessen Volk der Titel ‚Gottesvolk' nicht abgesprochen wird (106f.).

24 Zwar führte Lohfink, Der niemals gekündigte Bund (s. Anm. 21), 52–54 an, dass Paulus
in 2.Kor 3 nicht ein Defizit des alten Bundes, der ja (als „Mose") ausdrücklich auch von
Christen zu lesen ist, darstellen wollte, sondern das Defizit lediglich in der Hülle beste-

3. Wenn Paulus in 2.Kor 1,20 sagt: „Soviele Verheißungen Gottes es nämlich gibt, ist in ihm (Christus, dem Sohn Gottes) das Ja; deswegen ist durch ihn auch das Amen, Gott zum Lob (durch uns, die Verkündiger)", so sind damit jedenfalls alttestamentliche Verheißungen erfasst. Bekanntlich gibt es eine Fülle von Zusagen und bzw. Verheißungen Gottes, deren Erfüllung oder Nichterfüllung sich darunter nicht einfach subsumieren lässt.[25] Zweifellos aber sieht Paulus die von ihm apostrophierten Verheißungen als nicht vom Ganzen des Alten Testaments zu trennen an. Im Kern betrifft das von ihm zugesprochene Ja in Christus u.a. auch eine so grundlegend verankerte Vergebung für das Gottesvolk Israel,[26] dass Gottes durch die große Prophetie einst verkündete Vernichtung Israels wegen seiner Gottesverfremdung keinen Raum mehr hat. Wie also Paulus in Röm 4 und 9–11 des Näheren ausführt, wird die Erwählung Israels durch Christus um eine Basis tiefer gelegt. Abraham erscheint ihm im Licht des neutestamentlichen Glaubens an den Gott, der von den Toten erweckt (nach Röm 4 ist dies die Verheißung eines Erben nach dem Ende der generativen Phase Abrahams und Saras). Demgemäß wird in Röm 9–11 einerseits die Wurzel Abraham im Sinne jenes Glaubens zum Maßstab für die Erlösung der Juden, und andererseits kann eben wegen dieser neuen Basis die Fülle der Völker in die Wurzel Abraham, d.h. in den Glauben an den die Toten erweckenden Gott, neu eingepfropft werden.[27] Die

---

he, die wie einst auf Moses Angesicht jetzt auf dem Bund (= Mose) liege, aber vergehe (sic!; V.14b), wenn der Hörer sich Christus als dem Herrn zuwende. „Der ‚neue Bund' ist nichts anderes als der enthüllte ‚alte Bund', der Gottes in ihm stets schon enthaltene Herrlichkeit ausstrahlt." Der Kontext von 2.Kor 3,6ff. an spricht m.E. in der Tat von einer Herrlichkeit des alten Bundes. Aber diesem ist der Dienst des Todes zugeordnet (weil den Tod als der Sünde Sold nicht überwindend), so dass erst die Herrlichkeit des Herrn (sc. Christi) in ‚Mose' hineinkommen muss, um zum Leuchten der Apostel und der Christusglaubenden zu werden. M.E. muss es daher heißen: der ‚neue Bund' erfasst den alten durch Christus mit einer neuen, unerahnten Herrlichkeit. Das macht den Mosebund zwar alt, aber eben nicht veraltet, sondern ganz grundlegend für das Wort vom Kreuz. – In der Interpretation der paulinischen Theologie folge ich M. Limbeck, Das Gesetz im Alten und Neuen Testament, Darmstadt 1997, 115–124, der die von E.P. Sanders, Paulus und das palästinische Judentum. Ein Vergleich zweier Religionsstrukturen (StUNT 17), Göttingen 1985 eingeleitete Wende in der Paulusforschung zu dessen Judentumsinterpretation selbständig nachvollzogen hat.

25 Ich erinnere hier gern an F. Hesse, Das Alte Testament als Buch der Kirche, Gütersloh 1966.

26 Entscheidend ist für diese Argumentation, dass die Vergebung nicht nur einzelnen aus Israel, sondern dem Gottesvolk insgesamt gelten soll, dass also der Satan wie ein Blitz vom Himmel gestürzt werden muss (Lk 10,18) und die Taufe des Weltenrichters allen gilt.

27 Allerdings mit der Folge, dass nicht alle Nachfahren Abrahams auch Erben Abrahams sind, sondern es eine Unterscheidung zwischen Nachfahren und Nachfahren gibt (vgl. schon Gen 17,15–20; 28,1–9). Desungeachtet sagt Paulus weiterhin, dass „der Retter" einst ganz Israel in die Erbschaft Abrahams einholen werde, und zwar mit der so wichtigen Begründung (Röm 11,29), dass Gott die einmal gegebene Zusage, für immer Israels

Erwählung Israels wird damit bestätigt, indem sie ein Ja und Amen erhält, welches das Alte Testament zwar als Tat Gottes ankündigte, aber nicht substantiierte. Das Alte Testament muss daher als Teil der christlichen Bibel nicht nur nicht den neutestamentlichen Topoi angepasst werden, es darf es auch nicht. Wie ein Edelstein sich dadurch nicht ändert, dass Licht in ihn einfällt, der ihn allerdings zum Leuchten bringt, so fällt das Licht des Ja und Amen Gottes in das Alte Testament.[28]

Wenn das richtig ist, so scheint mir zweierlei klar: a) Dieser Gedankengang ist sicher nicht antijüdisch, sondern für sein Verständnis u.a. auch innerjüdisch bzw. israelitisch. Er macht möglich, die ältere Sammlung heiliger Schriften als Altes Testament zu benennen, aber gerade nicht im Sinne von Veraltetem, sondern von Vorgegebenem, als Gottes bleibende Gabe. b) Es besteht nicht die geringste Gefahr, die Einzigartigkeit der Offenbarung des Christus Jesus, die vom ersten Gebot für Christen nicht zu trennen ist, verwischt zu sehen.[29] Inner(jüdisch-)christlich ist das erste Gebot nicht ohne den Christus Jesus zu haben. Vielmehr kann man hier den Prolog des Johannesevangeliums (Joh 1,1–18) beiziehen, nach dem es Gott nicht erst zur Zeit des Imperium Romanum einfiel, seinen Logos, der (prädikativ) Gott ist (V. 1c), in die Welt zu senden, oder den Christus-Hymnus in Phil 2,6–11.[30] In diesem Sinne ist m.E. die im Alten Testament enthüllte Zeit der Erwählung (um das Wort „Geschichte" zu vermeiden)[31] nicht einfach vorlaufend mit der Tendenz „vorläufig" zu nennen, sondern paradigmatisch.[32]

Gott zu sein, nicht zurücknimmt, da er sie nicht kündigt (anders als z.B. die Zusage an König Saul in geschichtlicher Konkretion). S. dazu die hilfreichen Ausführungen von Lohfink, Der niemals gekündigte Bund (s. Anm. 21), 75ff. zur geschichtlichen Dimension der Zweiheit von Judentum und Christentum, auch meinen Versuch in: Der Gott der ganzen Bibel, Freiburg u.a. 1982, 67–75.

28 Dies im Anschluss an die schönen Ausführungen von C. Dohmen, in: ders./G. Stemberger, Hermeneutik der Jüdischen Bibel und des Alten Testaments, Stuttgart u.a. 1996, 206 und 190f. über das Dictum Augustins zu Ex 20,20: „Sowohl im Alten ist das Neue verborgen, wie das Alte im Neuen offenliegt."

29 Dies dezidiert im Einholen von Bedenken aus der Tradition R. Bultmanns und seiner Nachfolger.

30 In einer ersten Fassung zitierte ich auch Joh 8,48: „Ehe Abraham war, *bin* ich." Da hier Abrahams Name anders als bei Paulus gebraucht wird, empfiehlt sich eher der Prolog des Johannesevangeliums. Der Gedanke einer tieferen Basis für die Abraham- bzw. Israel-Erwählung herrscht jedoch auch bei Joh, da nach 4,22 das Heil von den Juden kommt.

31 Dies versuchsweise in Anlehnung an K. Barth, Kirchliche Dogmatik II/2, Zürich [4]1959, § 32–35: „Gottes Gnadenwahl". Das Wort „Geschichte" zu vermeiden, empfiehlt sich im Nachgang zu der Diskussion um den für die theologische Dimension des Alten Testaments so wichtigen Entwurf von G.v. Rad, s. dazu besonders M. Oeming, Gesamtbiblische Theologien der Gegenwart, Stuttgart u.a. [2]1987, 20–80. Mit G.v. Rad scheint mir allerdings die geschichtliche Schwere des Alten Testaments für die Entfaltung seiner Theologie unaufgebbar. Das Wie kann hier nicht ausgeführt werden.

32 Vgl.hierzu trotz einiger anderer Akzentuierungen den Vorschlag von Preuß, Das Alte Testament (s. Anm. 15), 120–139, der von einer „Strukturanalogie" spricht.

4. Im Zuge dessen kann man erst voll ermessen, was es heißt, dass das Neue Testament das Wort „Gott" nicht mehr erklären muss, weil es ihm vom Alten geklärt ist. Grundlegend dafür ist, dass die Einzigkeit Gottes wegen seines alttestamentlichen Eigennamens nicht einer Reflexion auf den Gottesbegriff zu verdanken ist, sondern in einem Raum polytheistischer Konzeptionen einzig und allein einem Gottesverstehen, nach dem das Profil seiner Einzigkeit aus dem Gegenüber zu seinen Menschen (und der zugehörigen Schöpfung) bis hin zur Möglichkeit eines Leidens Gottes an seiner Liebe zu seinen Menschen in Zorn und Erduldung erwächst[33] und demgegenüber – so Deuterojesaja – die anderen Götter samt und sonders nicht gotteswürdig sind.[34] Wie oben gesagt, ist damit die Idee der Menschwerdung Gottes vorbereitet, wenn auch nicht unmittelbar substantiiert.[35]

Von da ausgehend scheint es mir wichtig, nicht nur die allgemein anerkannten, theologisch über das Neue Testament überschießenden Topoi wie die Schöpfung in ihrer alttestamentlichen Fassung, das Hohelied, die Hiobtheodizee usw. ins Gespräch zu bringen, sondern viel weitergehend zu sagen: Man wird das Alte Testament als ganzes, z.B. auch in seinen bisher schlecht oder wenig theologisch erfassten Partien – wie z.B. den Kultordnungen in Leviticus[36] und Numeri[37] oder den Völkersprüchen[38] – benötigen, um

---

33 S. dazu besonders Dietrich/Link, Die dunklen Seiten Gottes (s. Anm. 20).

34 Andernorts wird über den Vorschlag von O. Loretz, Des Gottes Einzigkeit. Ein altorientalisches Argumentationsmodell zum „Schma Jisrael", Darmstadt 1997 zu reden sein, die Einzigkeit Gottes im Alten Testament sei nur eine Radikalisierung der Einzigkeit eines Königsgottes wie z.B. des Baal in Ugarit in Dtn 6,4. Loretz hat schwerlich den Sinn von Dtn 6,4 getroffen, von dem man V.5 nicht trennen darf, s. dazu im Einzelnen H. Seebass, Gott der einzige. Bemerkungen zur Religionsgeschichte und Theologie des Alten Testaments. FS Peter Weimar, 2002 (im Druck). Als Verdienst von O. Loretz sehe ich an, dass er Dtn 6,4f. für jede Theologie des Alten Testaments angemahnt hat.

35 S. im einzelnen Seebass, Gott (s. Anm. 27), 35ff., dort auch zu Joh 1,14 als einem spezifisch christlichen Verstehen der im Alten Testament bezeugten Inkarnation (50); sorgfältig gegen Antijudaismus absichernd Janowski, Gott (s. Anm. 3), 281ff., da das Judentum das Theologoumenon der Inkarnation überwiegend verwirft. Wie o. Anm. 13 bereits erwähnt, beziehe ich den Gedanken darauf, dass die Eigenart Jahwes nicht durch den Unterschied zum Charakter anderer Götter bestimmt wird, sondern sein Charakter (der „Name") durch Geschichten von seinen Menschen als einzigartig herauskommt. Dies erlaubt natürlich, auch hellenistische Geschichten seines Volkes einzubeziehen (z.T. werden ja die beiden Chronikbücher ins 3. Jh. v. Chr. datiert, einiges sogar in die Makkabäerzeit). Zur in der Gegenwart vertretbaren Gotteslehre bestehen m.E. unausgeschöpfte Gesprächsmöglichkeiten zwischen Exegese und systematischer Theologie. Oder sind es sogar Notwendigkeiten, wenn man die Bedeutung der heiligen Schrift für die meisten christlichen Denominationen bedenkt?

36 Einen anthropologischen Zugang zu diesen bietet M. Douglas, Leviticus as Literature, Oxford 1999. Schade, dass R. Rendtorff, Leviticus (BK.AT III/1–3), Neukirchen-Vluyn 1985–92, nicht weiter produziert.

37 Das Buch rückt inzwischen ganz neu in das Interesse der Forschung, nicht zuletzt wegen seiner Rolle für ein Gesamtverständnis des Pentateuch. Einem neuen, auch theologischen Verstehen sind D.T. Olson, Numbers, Interpretation, Louisville, KY 1996; T. Staubli,

das Gottesverstehen und damit ineins das Menschenverstehen der Bibel Alten Testaments zu erfassen. Mit Robert Morgan (s.o.) ist dann die religionsgeschichtlich-historische Erforschung von Altem und Neuem Testament nicht nur nötig, sondern auch erleichternd. Es sollte manche Urteile mancher Forscher über das Alte Testament entspannen, wenn man berücksichtigt, dass es eine ähnliche, wenn auch nicht gleichartige religionsgeschichtliche Distanz zu manchen Theologoumena im Neuen Testament gibt wie zu manchen im Alten. Jon D. Levenson[39] hat zum christlich-jüdischen Gespräch treffend angemerkt, dass Juden nicht jedem Text ihres Tanach eine theologische Bedeutung abgewinnen müssten wie Christen, weil sie wegen ihrer geschichtlichen Kontinuität ganz gut auch manches als Teil der Vergangenheit einfach stehen lassen können. M.E. gilt dies ganz analog für jede christlich-theologische Bemühung in Wahrnehmung einer Kontinuität zur Bibel Alten Testaments zu den frühesten christlichen Anfängen, da man oft über eine plausible geschichtliche Einordnung nicht hinauskommen kann, auch nicht sollte, sie aber trotzdem nicht unwichtig ist. Zum Neuen Testament darf man nicht etwa nur an 1.Kor 14,34f. und 1.Tim 2,14 erinnern, sondern auch daran, dass Joh 8,44 „Euer (sc. der Juden) Vater ist der Teufel" ein Wort aktueller Auseinandersetzung gewesen ist und nicht die nichtchristliche Judenheit der Jahrtausende beurteilt.[40] Umgekehrt steht die christlich-theologische Forschung vor der großen Aufgabe, bisher Unerschlossenes nicht älteren Urteilen zu überlassen, sondern vom christlich-jüdischen bzw. christlich-interreligiös-atheis-

---

Die Bücher Levitikus und Numeri (NSK.AT 3), Stuttgart 1996 und mein Numeri-Kommentar (BK.AT IV/2, Neukirchen-Vluyn 2002) gewidmet (Num 10,11 – 22,1). Ausgezeichnet sind die jüdischen Kommentare von J. Milgrom, Numbers (JPS), Philadelphia 1990, und B.A. Levine, Numbers 1–20 (AncB 4A), New York 1993; Numbers 21–36 (AncB 4B), New York 2000, die ebenfalls auf eine zeitgemäße Erklärung ausgehen.

38 In einem persönlichen Gespräch stellte R. Albertz in Aussicht, einen neuen Zugang zu ihnen durch Vergleich mit babylonischen Texten zu eröffnen. Bekanntlich gibt es hier besonders große Probleme, man denke etwa an Obadja u.ä.

39 Warum (s. Anm. 10); ein Beispiel: Zur Zeit wird mit großem Recht Altisraels Kultsystem aus einer theologischen Nebenkammer herausgeholt und höchst respektabel religionsgeschichtlich-theologisch interpretiert, ohne dass man sogleich oder regelmäßig einen Gegenwartsbezug herstellen müsste. Aber über den Geist solcher Texte gab und gibt es nicht wenige Vorurteile, die sinnvoll zu bereinigen sind.

40 Maßstab ist bei Joh die Verfallenheit an „den Kosmos", die Welt, so dass in gegenwärtiger Auslegung gerade auch Christen und Christinnen betroffen wären, soweit solche Verfallenheit auch für sie gilt (mit Rudolf Bultmann). Dietrich/Link, Die dunklen Seiten Gottes I (s. Anm. 20), 44f. distanzieren sich von Mt 27,25, wo Mt das ganze jüdische Volk sagen lässt: „Sein Blut komme über unser Haupt." Nach Mt 27,20 ist diese Aussage jedoch von der hohepriesterlichen Partei und den Ältesten veranlasst, und diese sind es darum auch, die nach Mt 21,33–43 zusammen mit den Pharisäern den Weinberg Gottes zugunsten anderer verlieren, nicht das Volk.

tischen Gespräch beflügelt, an die Arbeit zu gehen. Mit Jan Assmann[41] darf man es als ein Zeichen der Überlebensfähigkeit ansehen, dass Israeliten-, Juden- und Christentum stets interpretierende Kulturen waren und sind, weil Vergangenheiten als Potentiale für die Zukunft tradiert werden und so die Gegenwart je sowohl herausfordern als auch sich von ihr herausfodern lassen.

Wegen des Gewichts von Jer 31,31–34 für das neutestamentliche Zeugnis soll hier noch speziell das in ihm wichtige Stichwort „Tora" aufgegriffen werden. Im christlich-jüdischen Gespräch ebenso wie im wissenschaftlichen ist dazu viel gesagt worden, was hier im einzelnen nicht anzuführen nötig ist. Wichtig aber scheint mir der Gesichtspunkt, dass in alttestamentlicher Zeit mindestens die dtn Tora inzwischen ganz deutlich als *programmatischer Entwurf* erkannt wird, dessen Umsetzung in die tatsächliche Rechtsprechung höchstens ausnahmsweise vorkommt. Ihre Programmatik bezog sich sehr wahrscheinlich auf eine Abwehr der Forderung unbedingter Loyalität durch neuassyrische Könige des 7. Jahrhunderts v. Chr. derart, dass eine solche Loyalität Jahwe allein zukommen konnte und von da aus das dtn, später das dtr Programm entworfen wurde.[42] Dabei geht es nicht nur um die allenthalben erkennbare Zeitbedingtheit dieses Programms, sondern vor allem um die Tatsache, dass dieses Programm sozusagen eine historisch-politische Umsetzung des spezifisch israelitischen Gottesverstehens in die damalige Völkerwelt sein sollte (der Terminus „Erwählung" ist nicht zufällig erst deuteronomistisch, dann deuterojesajanisch: 6. Jh.).[43] Fand Lothar Perlitt das Dtn auf dem Wege zum Judaismus[44] und Georg Braulik als Evangelium im Alten Testament,[45] so darf man jedenfalls sagen, dass es auf das *Gottes*verstehen perspektivisch angelegt ist (vgl. besonders Dtn 6,4f. durch das Liebesgebot) und deswegen so geeignet war, mit dem ersten Gebot den Maßstab für das dtr Geschichtswerk herzugeben.[46] Für das sog. Heiligkeitsgesetz (Lev 17–26)

---

41 J. Assmann, Das kulturelle Gedächtnis. Schrift, Erinnerung und politische Identität in frühen Hochkulturen, München 1997, 196ff.

42 Spätestens seit M. Weinfeld, Deuteronomy and the Deuteronomic School, Oxford 1972 = 1992, 81ff. (der selbst Anreger nennt) hat sich diese Überzeugung durchgesetzt. Selbstverständlich bedeutet dies nicht, dass im ältesten Bestand des Deuteronomiums alles auf Antiassyrisches zurückzuführen wäre (auf Einzelheiten kann ich hier nicht eingehen; ich habe nur ein Hauptmotiv benannt).

43 Vgl. H. Seebass, Art. Erwählung I, TRE 10 (1982) 182–189.

44 L. Perlitt, Hebraismus – Deuteronomismus – Judaismus, in: Biblische Theologie und gesellschaftlicher Wandel. FS Norbert Lohfink, Freiburg u.a. 1993, 279–295.

45 Vgl. z.B. G. Braulik, Gesetz als Evangelium. Rechtfertigung und Begnadigung nach der deuteronomischen Tora, in: ders., Studien zur Theologie des Deuteronomiums (SBAB 2), Stuttgart 1988, 123–160.

46 Instruktiv dazu z.B. E. Otto, Treueid und Gesetz. Die Ursprünge des Deuteronomiums im Horizont neuassyrischen Vertragsrechts, ZAR 2 (1996) 1–52.

gilt offenbar dasselbe nach dem Motto von Lev 19,2: „Ihr seid/sollt heilig/sein, denn ich, euer Gott, bin heilig."[47] Tatsächlich findet man im Alten Testament noch keine eigentliche Umsetzung in nachweisbare Rechtspraxis, die wohl erst in hellenistischer Zeit vorangetrieben wurde.[48] Demgemäß haben wir es nicht mit der Geltung, sondern mit einer theologischen Wertung von Tora zu tun. Das erlaubt es insgesamt, Jer 31,31–34 angemessen zu verstehen und nicht etwa auf das Deuteronomium oder die berühmten 613 Torot des späteren Judentums festzulegen.[49] Denn die dtr Tora ist bekanntlich auf das erste Gebot reduzierbar[50], und diese Programmatik ist selbstverständlich auch für Christen nicht vergangen.

5. Zur Themenstellung zurückkehrend, dürfte ein hermeneutischer Vorschlag von Christoph Dohmen[51] eine gute Basis für die weitere Forschung bieten. Demnach hat man einerseits zwischen Erst- und Zweitadressaten zu unter-

---

47 Zum Heiligkeitsgesetz und seiner Theologie vgl. vor allem K. Grünwaldt, Das Heiligkeitsgesetz Leviticus 17–26 (BZAW 271), Berlin/New York 1999; theologisch ganz ähnlich, nur spätdatierend E. Otto, Innerbiblische Exegese im Heiligkeitsgesetz Levitikus 17–26, in: H.J. Fabry u.a. (Hg.), Levitikus als Buch (BBB 119), Berlin 1999, 125–196; anders A. Ruwe, „Heiligkeitsgesetz" und „Priesterschrift". Literaturgeschichtliche und rechtssystematische Untersuchungen zu Leviticus 17,1 – 26,2 (FAT 26), Tübingen 1999.

48 M. Hengel, Judentum und Hellenismus (WUNT 10), Tübingen ³1988, 92–105 verwies auf die Übernahme der Zehntabgabe durch die Priester gegen Num 18 (95 Anm. 374), auf die Ausnutzung ritueller Vorschriften für die Handelseinschränkungen (101) sowie auf Hekataios v. Abdera (Anfang 3. Jh. v. Chr.), nach dem die Juden während der persischen und makedonischen Herrschaft wegen der Vermischung mit Fremden viele väterliche Gesetze geändert hätten. Zusätzlich darf man pauschal an die Halacha-Verschärfung der Qumran-Gemeinschaft erinnern.

49 Die Pointe von Jer 31,31–34 in Bezug auf die Tora findet sich in V. 34: Die Tora soll ins Herz geschrieben werden, so dass Groß und Klein Jahwe erkennen: Um Gotteserkenntnis also muss es gehen. Dieser Akzent scheint Gräßer, Hebr II (s. Anm. 23), 102 entgangen zu sein, wenn er seinem Gewährsmann C. Levin, Die Verheißung des neuen Bundes in ihrem theologiegeschichtlichen Zusammenhang ausgelegt (FRLANT 137), Göttingen 1985, 134f. u.ö. folgt, der die zweite Hälfte von V. 34 als nicht-alttestamentlich unverbraucht deklarierte: „Denn ich will ihre Schuld vergeben, und ihrer Sünde will ich nicht mehr gedenken." – Angesichts solch außergewöhnlicher Texte wie Num 11,*11–24 und Ex 32,10–14 ist Jer 31,34b jedoch nicht so singulär wie V. 34a, in dem eine anthropologische Wende verheißen wird. Erst zu *dieser* Wende gehört, dass dann niemand es mehr nötig haben wird, von anderen im Gottesvolk belehrt zu werden – eine Zusage, deren Einlösung bis heute offensichtlich noch aussteht.

50 Wie oben dargelegt, waren für die Deuteronomisten *berît* und Tora auswechselbar und Israel nach ihrer Gewissheit seiner Bundesverpflichtung nicht nachgekommen (s. L. Perlitt, Bundestheologie im Alten Testament (WMANT 36), Neukirchen-Vluyn 1969, 7–53), also für diesen Traditionsstrom auch Gott an seinen Bund nicht mehr gebunden. Neues konnte nur von Gott ausgehen, und dies erfasste jener Traditionsstrom spät-dtr vor allem durch das Motiv der konditionslosen Vätererwählung (z.B. Dtn 7,7), allenfalls in der Ankündigung eines ewigen Bundes (Dtn 32; Ez 11; 36 [s.o.]). Vgl. dazu Lohfink, Art. Bund (s. Anm. 21). Der neue Bund in Jer 31 ist demgegenüber also eigenständig.

scheiden, andererseits zwischen der Bibel des vorchristlichen Altisrael und dem Alten Testament für Christen bzw. dem Tanach für nichtchristliche Juden.[52] Die Unterscheidung von Erst- und Zweitadressaten leitet Dohmen aus einer Auseinandersetzung mit der Rezeptionstheorie als Pragmatik ab: Auch wenn jedes Verstehen von Texten nicht ohne vorgegebene, bereitstehende Verstehensmöglichkeiten des Interpreten bzw. der Interpretin zustande kommen kann, sei pragmatisch zwischen den Erstadressaten und späteren Lesern/Hörern durchweg zu unterscheiden. Beim Kanon gilt dies nach Dohmen in besonderem Maße, da er eben um der Erwartung willen Kanon ist, vor allem verbum externum zu vermitteln und nicht einfach im Verstehen der Rezipienten aufzugehen.[53] Wissenschaftliche Untersuchungen der Bibel Israels haben demnach – so Dohmen – die Aufgabe, den den Erstadressaten gewidmeten Sinn zu ermitteln und diesen dann auch für die Interpretation als Altes Testament bzw. als Tanach fruchtbar zu machen, ihn also zugrunde zu legen. Allerdings identifiziert Dohmen die Erstadressaten ohne Einschränkung mit Israeliten und nicht, wie man das semiotisch müsste, mit der Zeitgenossenschaft etwa des 3.–1. Jahrhunderts v. Chr. So einleuchtend also seine Korrelation von Erstadressaten und Bibel Israels (Genetivus subjectivus!) ist, die eine griffige Formel für die weitere Untersuchung schafft, so wenig berücksichtigt Dohmen die seit der Existenz der LXX belegte viel breitere Leser- und Hörerschaft.

Dohmen trägt mit seinem Modell zwar dem Umstand Rechnung, dass die Tradition der Bibel Israels sich im Umkreis der Zeitenwende gabelt in die christliche Tradition von Juden oder Nichtjuden und in die nichtchristliche jüdische Tradition. Wie viele Forscher vor ihm meint Dohmen, dass die nichtchristlich-jüdische Tradition der Bibel Israels unmittelbarer folge als die christliche, was m.E. das hervorragende hellenistisch-jüdische Schrifttum und die Breite der zeitgleichen Diskussion, die im frühen Christentum vielfältig rezipiert wurde, zu leicht übergeht. Wenn er dann schreibt, der erste und größte Teil der christlichen Bibel, der dem Christentum vorausliegt, sei zuvor und weiterhin „Glaubensurkunde einer anderen Religion", nämlich des Judentums[54], dann verspielt er den Gewinn seiner Hermeneutik.[55] Denn zumin-

---

51 Vgl. Dohmen/Stemberger, Hermeneutik (s. Anm. 28), 192ff.
52 Es ist ungerechtfertigt, in wissenschaftlicher Literatur die Existenz christlicher Juden und Jüdinnen zu übergehen, und so zu tun, als gäbe es sie nicht (so z.B. Dohmen, ebd.).
53 S. dazu den Literaturbericht von J. Barton, The Significance of a Fixed Canon of the Hebrew Bible, in: M. Sæbø (Hg.), Hebrew Bible/Old Testament. The History of Its Interpretation I, Göttingen 1996, 67–83.
54 Dohmen/Stemberger, Hermeneutik (s. Anm. 28), 211.
55 Es ist nicht überflüssig, daran zu erinnern, dass etwa die rabbinische Auslegungspraxis an Religionsentscheidungen für ihre jeweilige Gegenwart interessiert war, die hermeneutisch gegenüber dem Wortlaut des Tanach leitend waren, ihn also nicht auszulegen beab-

dest Paulus und Matthäus unterscheiden, soweit ich das verstehe[56], ganz zeit-
und situationsgemäß zwischen Judentum und Judentum, nämlich einem, das
sich der Offenbarung des Christus Jesus verpflichtet wusste und deswegen zu
den Nichtjuden keinen „Zaun" (Metapher nach Eph 2,14) hat (auch sie erfasst
der Begriff Israel bei Paulus), und Juden, die sich dem Christus Jesus nicht
verpflichtet wussten.

Nachdem wir wissenschaftlich und d.h. auch wissenschaftlich-theologisch
die Bibel Altisraels in vielen (sehr notwendigen) Mühen wiederentdeckt und
damit sowohl profan-wissenschaftlich als auch glaubensmäßig als Gewinn
gefunden haben, in der Auslegung des ersten Teils unseres Kanons auf jede
nur denkbare Stimme zu hören, gewiss aber auch auf die äußerst verwandten
nichtchristlich-jüdischen zu hören – und zwar nicht nur aus schlechtem Gewissen, sondern nach überdimensionalen Menschheitserfahrungen überzeugt
–, kann Zukunft m.E. nur haben, dass Judentum und Christentum die gemeinsamen Ursprünge besser, eben auch gesprächsweise besser verstehen, um
Differenzierungen nicht für trennend zu halten, die längst vorher und dann
intern jeweils möglich waren und sind. Das Gemeinsame würde sich gewiss
ebenso in das Neue Testament und in die christliche Traditionsbildung hinein
verfolgen lassen wie in die große jüdische Traditionsbildung, ohne dass eine
Vereinnahmung oder eine Schwächung des jeweils Spezifischen erfolgen
müsste. Aber das ist natürlich Zukunftsmusik.

6. Damit mag die Themafrage wenigstens beleuchtet sein. Dem Titel „Erstes
Testament" für den ersten Kanonteil der christlichen Bibel kommt eine Deu-
tekraft nur zu, wenn man, wie das nicht wenige tun, in Röm 11,16ff. den
Wurzelstock Abraham mit dem geburtlichen, faktisch fassbaren Judentum
identifiziert,[57] was aber Paulus in Röm 9,6ff. ausgeschlossen hatte. Man kann
sehr wohl den Gedanken fassen, dass es ein Segen war, als innerjüdische
Kräfte auf die physische und religiöse Erhaltung des Ethnos der Juden in den
Diasporai sich konzentrierten, und man darf nicht übersehen, dass solche Be-

---

sichtigten, sondern von ihm ausgehend zu eigenen Entscheidungen zu kommen (s. die
Rolle der mündlichen Tora Moses). Grohmann, Aneignung (s. Anm. 2), 73–130.167–
230 hat dies treffend wiedergegeben, dies aber ausgerechnet einem entsprechenden
christlichen Gebrauch empfohlen.
56 So aber auch Janowski, Gott (s. Anm. 3), 255f. Zum Mt-Ev s. etwa W. Schmithals, Art.
Evangelien, Synoptische, TRE 10 (1982) 570–626, S. 616–620. Dietrich/Link, Die
dunklen Seiten Gottes I (s. Anm. 20), 36–76 gehen allerdings davon aus, dass Mt eine
schroffe Abgrenzung vom Judentum beabsichtigte. Nach Schmithals ging es dagegen um
eine Differenzierung im Judentum und unter wohl ernsthafter Bedrohung, s. auch Limbeck, Gesetz (s. Anm. 24), 129–145.
57 So früher Zenger, Das Erste Testament (s. Anm. 14), passim.

strebungen bereits in nachexilischer Zeit ihren Anfang hatten.[58] Wenn man
das tut – völlig legitim –, dann dürfte man umso mehr nicht daran vorüberge-
hen, dass, soweit es um religiöse Verwurzelung und Identität geht, diese auch
im Ethnos Judentum nicht monolithisch sein können und mit den genannten
neutestamentlichen Zeugen eine innere Gliederung erfordern. Würde dies
durch den Titel „Erstes Testament" hinreichend bezeichnet? Vielleicht; aber
selbst dann blieben die eingangs genannten Vorbehalte gegen eine numeri-
sche Titelei. Der Titel „Altes Testament" kann zwar die eingangs genannten
Befürchtungen auslösen; aber das ist eben wenig zwangsläufig. Ein gewalti-
ger Impuls für jene ist gewiss die im Zuge der Aufklärung entdeckte, völlig
eigenständige religiöse Welt des Alten Testaments gegenüber der in Europa
geläufigen.[59] Weil aber zum Alten Testament seither solche Fehlurteile in die
oberflächliche Diskussion eingedrungen sind wie „Gott der Rache", „Gott
des wilden Zorns", „Gott der Rückgratverkrümmung" usw., nützt eine Na-
mensänderung wenig. Es müsste besser gelingen, Inhalte zu transportieren,
und dieser Weg wird längst eingeschlagen.

Der Titel „Altes Testament" erweckt ja kaum die Assoziationen von
2.Kor 3 oder Hebr 8–10, sondern hat eher den Sinn einer Buchbezeichnung
angenommen. Und in dieser Hinsicht ist er deswegen nicht schlecht, weil er
ein ganz entscheidendes Moment frühchristlicher Selbstfindung bewahrt und
wiedergibt: Das Christentum hat das Alte Testament nicht umgeschrieben,
sondern im wesentlichen unverändert tradiert als eine ihm eigene, vorgegebene, „alte" Tradition.[60] Dies macht das Alte Testament nicht alt, sondern

---

58 Dabei ist vor allem an Neh 1–6; *12,27 – 13,31 zu denken. Zum kanonischen Esr-Neh-
    Buch vgl. S. Grätz, Der königliche Erlaß über den Jerusalemer Tempel und den Auftrag
    Esras. Eine Untersuchung zum religionspolitischen und historischen Umfeld von Esr
    7,12–26, Theol. Hab.schr. Bonn o.J. [2002].
59 Verdienstlich knapp entfaltet von Kaiser, Gott (s. Anm. 15), 47–59.
60 Dies hat m.R. C. Dohmen hervorgehoben (vgl. Dohmen/Stemberger, Hermeneutik [s.
    Anm. 28]). – In der Diskussion wandte M. Wolter ein, dass die vom Christentum de fac-
    to kanonisierte LXX das Alte Testament jedenfalls nicht unverändert übernommen habe.
    Jedoch ist die LXX-Tradition nach den neuesten Ausgaben ein Ort für Ort zu bändigen-
    des Chaos an Lesarten, das, wenn man von Einzelheiten absieht, nach Aussage eines Ex-
    perten wie R. Hanhart im wesentlichen auf alexandrinisch-jüdische Lesarten zurückgeht.
    Davon abgesehen ist die LXX, seitdem die Auswertung der Qumranfunde mit großen
    Schritten vorankommt, ein wichtiger Zeuge dafür, dass die endgültige Festlegung ver-
    schiedener kanonischer Texte bis in neutestamentliche Zeit Unterschiede aufweist, s. E.
    Tov, Der Text der Hebräischen Bibel. Handbuch der Textkritik, Stuttgart u.a. 1997.
    Wenn also zur Zeit nach einer französischen auch noch eine deutsche Bemühung im
    Gange ist, die LXX durch eine Übersetzung für weitere Kreise wieder zugänglich zu
    machen, und wenn etwa die römisch-katholische Kirche die Vulgata zugrundelegt, ver-
    lassen sie alle nicht den Bereich jüdischer Tradition. Man hat keinen Grund, dies bloß
    apologetisch zu sagen. Denn in der Tat ist es kaum zu überschätzen, dass die Christen-
    heit das Alte Testament nicht von sich aus und für sich redigiert hat; eben darauf kommt
    es an.

verleiht dem Christentum eine Tiefendimension, die die Eigentümlichkeit von Zeit in der Formulierung „Als aber die Zeit erfüllt war" und die Eigenart von Erwählung bei uneingeschränktem Universalismus Gottes wach hält.

Die Vielfalt der Schrift und die Einheit des Kanons

von Michael Wolter

1. Der Stand der Dinge

1.1. Vor knapp 30 Jahren leitete Ernst Käsemann seine Einführung zu dem von ihm herausgegebenen Sammelband *Das Neue Testament als Kanon* mit den Sätzen ein: „Über die Entstehung und Geschichte des neutestamentlichen Kanons sind wir vortrefflich informiert. Seine theologische Relevanz ist dagegen heftiger denn zuvor umstritten."[1] – Während das zuversichtliche Urteil des ersten Satzes sich inzwischen als Illusion erwiesen hat[2], gilt die Feststellung des zweiten Satzes nach wie vor uneingeschränkt. Sie basiert im wesentlichen auf zwei Sachverhalten:

Ihr liegt zum einen die Einsicht zugrunde, dass der Kanon der neutestamentlichen Schriften das Produkt eines historischen Entwicklungsprozesses ist und die endgültige Entscheidung über seinen Umfang nicht nur relativ spät erfolgte[3], sondern auch von Zufälligkeiten und aktuellen kirchenpoliti-

---

1 E. Käsemann, Einführung, in: ders. (Hg.), Das Neue Testament als Kanon. Dokumentation und kritische Analyse zur gegenwärtigen Diskussion, Göttingen 1970, 9–12, S. 9.

2 Umstritten sind hier vor allem die Rolle Marcions (war sein Kanon Anstoß für die Ausbildung des kirchlichen Kanons oder Teil des allgemeinen Kanonisierungsprozesses?), die zur Kanonbildung führenden Motive und die Frage, ob die Entstehung des neutestamentlichen Kanons als „Selbstdurchsetzung" oder als „autoritative Entscheidung" zu begreifen sei (bzw. ob das überhaupt eine Alternative ist; vgl. dazu A.M. Ritter, Die Entstehung des neutestamentlichen Kanons: Selbstdurchsetzung oder autoritative Entscheidung?, in: A. Assmann/J. Assmann [Hg.], Kanon und Zensur, München 1987, 93–99). Vgl. auch J. Barton, Holy Writings, Sacred Texts. The Canon in Early Christianity, Louisville, KY 1997, 1ff.

3 So ist z.B. der Hirt des Hermas wie auch der Barnabasbrief Bestandteil des Codex Sinaiticus und wird noch im Kanonverzeichnis des Codex Claromontanus aufgeführt (wie auch Barn, ActPaul und ApkPetr). Dass auch noch Didymus v. Alexandrien ihn zur heiligen Schrift zählte, hat B.D. Ehrman, The New Testament Canon of Didymus the Blind, VigChr 37 (1983) 1–21, gezeigt (11–13). Die Canones Apostolicae führen unter den „heiligen Büchern" auch die beiden Clemensbriefe und die Apostolischen Konstitutionen auf (Can. 85). – Umgekehrt fehlen z.B. Jak, 1./2.Petr und ein Johannesbrief im Canon Muratori, die Apk u.a. im Kanonverzeichnis Cyrills v. Jerusalem (Catech. VI,36)

schen Faktoren beeinflusst war.[4] Dabei wurde nicht nur der Kompro-
misscharakter des Kanons erkannt, sondern man wurde sich auch bewusst,
dass der Kanonisierungsprozess, der regional unterschiedlich verlief, durchaus auch mit einem anderen Ergebnis hätte enden können.[5] – Die durch diese
Einsicht ausgelöste Ernüchterung dokumentiert sich am deutlichsten in William Wredes bekanntem Diktum:

> „Keine Schrift des Neuen Testaments ist mit dem Prädikat ‚kanonisch' geboren. Der Satz:
> ‚eine Schrift ist kanonisch' bedeutet zunächst nur: sie ist nachträglich von den maßgebenden
> Faktoren der Kirche des 2. bis 4. Jahrhunderts – vielleicht erst nach allerlei Schwankungen
> im Urteil – für kanonisch erklärt worden. ... Wer also den Begriff des Kanons als feststehend
> betrachtet, unterwirft sich damit der Autorität der Bischöfe und Theologen jener Jahrhunder-
> te. Wer diese Autorität in anderen Dingen nicht anerkennt – und kein evangelischer Theolo-
> ge erkennt sie an –, handelt folgerichtig, wenn er sie auch hier in Frage stellt."[6]

Zum anderen speist sich das Urteil Ernst Käsemanns aus der inneren Disparatheit des neutestamentlichen Kanons, die dazu nötige, „nicht nur erhebliche
Spannungen, sondern nicht selten auch unvereinbare theologische Gegensätze zu konstatieren"[7]. Dieser Sachverhalt kollidiert geradezu zwangsläufig mit
dem vom Kanon als Kanon ausgehenden Anspruch der theologischen Gleich-
rangigkeit der in ihm enthaltenen Schriften, der z.B. dem Römerbrief denselben – sc. ‚kanonischen' – Status verleiht wie dem Judasbrief.

1.2. Auch der Umgang mit dieser Problemlage lässt sich in zweifacher Weise
beschreiben:

a) Zum einen erklärte man den Kanon und die durch ihn gezogenen Grenzen gegenüber den außerkanonischen Schriften des frühen Christentums für
bedeutungslos.[8] Dies hatte zur Folge, dass die literarische Größe ‚Neues Tes-

---

und im Kanon der Synode von Laodicea (Can. 60). Eusebius v. Caesarea führt Jak, Jud,
2.Petr und 2.–3.Joh unter den ἀντιλεγόμενα auf, nicht ohne jedoch zu vermerken, dass
sie „bei den meisten in Ansehen stehen" (Hist. Eccl. III,25,3). Unter den νόθα, d.h. den
„unechten" Schriften, nennt er neben Hermas, ApkPetr, Barn und Did auch, „wenn man
will", die Apk, die „von den einen verworfen, von anderen aber zu den echten Schriften
gerechnet wird" (ebd., III,25,4).
4 Vgl. W. Schneemelcher, Art. Bibel III, TRE 6 (1980) 22–48, S. 47; s. auch den
   Überblick über die neuere Literatur bei C. Markschies, Neue Forschungen zur Kanonisierung des Neuen Testaments, Apocrypha 12 (2001) 237–262.
5 Vgl. z.B. die Überblicke bei Schneemelcher, ebd., 22–48; H.Y. Gamble, The New Testament Canon. Its Making and Meaning, Philadelphia 1985, 23ff.; B.M. Metzger, Der
   Kanon des Neuen Testaments, Düsseldorf 1993.
6 W. Wrede, Über Aufgabe und Methode der sogenannten neutestamentlichen Theologie
   (1897); zitiert nach dem Wiederabdruck in: G. Strecker (Hg.), Das Problem der Theologie des Neuen Testaments (WdF 367), Darmstadt 1975, 81–154, S. 85.
7 E. Käsemann, Begründet der neutestamentliche Kanon die Einheit der Kirche?, in: ders.
   (Hg.), Das Neue Testament als Kanon (s. Anm. 1), 124–133, S. 128.
8 Vgl. dazu exemplarisch das oben zitierte Dictum W. Wredes.

tament' ihren Charakter als Schrift mit einem produktionsorientiert beschreibbaren distinkten theologischen Profil verliert und zu einer Anthologie von Texten wird. Sie umfasst lediglich einen Ausschnitt aus der literarischen Produktion des frühen Christentums, und dessen Zustandekommen lässt sich dementsprechend ausschließlich unter Rückgriff auf rezeptionshermeneutische Kategorien beschreiben. Die Folge dieser Destruktion des neutestamentlichen Kanons wird zur Zeit vor allem darin greifbar, dass an die Stelle der wissenschaftlichen Literaturgattungen der ‚Theologie des Neuen Testaments' bzw. ‚Einleitung in das Neue Testament' in programmatischer Umsetzung der von W. Wrede eingeforderten „geschichtliche(n) Methode"[9] die Darstellungen einer ‚Theologiegeschichte des Urchristentums'[10], einer ‚urchristlichen Religionsgeschichte'[11] bzw. einer ‚Literaturgeschichte des Urchristentums'[12] treten können, in die dann auch die außerkanonischen Schriften einbezogen werden.

b) In einer umgekehrten Bewegung suchte man den theologischen Spannungen und Widersprüchen innerhalb des neutestamentlichen Kanons dadurch zu begegnen, dass man einen doppelten Kanonbegriff einführte.[13] Vom „formale(n) Kanon"[14] der 27 Schriften des Neuen Testaments wird ein „Kanon im Kanon" unterschieden. – Große Bedeutung gewann in diesem Zusammenhang vor allem die Frage nach der sog. „Mitte der Schrift". Dieser Größe wird gewissermaßen die Funktion eines Gravitationszentrums zugeschrieben, von dem man in doppelter Weise Gebrauch machen kann: zum einen als Differenzkriterium, mit dessen Hilfe sich Nähe und Ferne zur Mitte feststellen lassen, und zum anderen als einheitsstiftende Sachaussage, die allen Schriften des neutestamentlichen Kanons in ihrer spannungsreichen Vielfalt gemeinsam ist.

Als Beispiel für den kritischen Gebrauch dieses Kriteriums ist natürlich an erster Stelle Martin Luthers „Was Christum prediget und treibet" zu nennen, die ihn zu einer Dreiteilung des neutestamentlichen Kanons geführt hat: In der Mitte stehen „die rechten und edelsten Bücher des Neuen Testaments",

---

9   Vgl. Wrede, Aufgabe (s. Anm. 6), 124.
10 Dies ist der gleichlautende Titel der Bücher von K. Berger (Tübingen/Basel [2]1995) und W. Schmithals (Stuttgart 1994).
11 Vgl. dazu jetzt vor allem die Arbeiten von H. Räisänen, Beyond New Testament Theology, London 1990; ders., Neutestamentliche Theologie? Eine religionswissenschaftliche Alternative (SBS 186), Stuttgart 2000 sowie G. Theißen, Die Religion der ersten Christen, Gütersloh 2000; zum Problem vgl. J. Schröter, Religionsgeschichte des Urchristentums statt Theologie des Neuen Testaments?, BThZ 16 (1999) 3–20, bes. S. 5ff.
12 Vgl. G. Strecker, Literaturgeschichte des Neuen Testaments, Göttingen 1992, Abschn. 1.1.3 (S. 20ff.): „Literaturgeschichte als Kritik der Kanongrenzen".
13 Vgl. I. Lönning, „Kanon im Kanon", Oslo/München 1972.
14 W. Künneth, Art. Kanon, TRE 17 (1988) 562–570, S. 565,10.

nämlich „Sankt Johannis Evangelium und seine erste Epistel, Sankt Paulus Epistel, sonderlich die zu den Römern, Galatern, Ephesern, und Sankt Peters erste Epistel", denn „das sind die Bücher, die dir Christus zeigen und alles lehren, was dir zu wissen not und selig ist, obschon du kein ander Buch noch Lehre nimmer sehest noch hörest".[15] An den Rand[16] stellt er Hebräer-, Jakobus- und Judasbrief sowie die Johannesoffenbarung, welche Schriften er expressis verbis von den „rechten gewissen Hauptbücher(n) des Neuen Testaments" unterscheidet[17]. Die übrigen Schriften stehen dazwischen: Luther rechnet sie zu den „gewissen", nicht aber zu den „edelsten" Büchern des Neuen Testaments. – Für die Rezeption dieses Kriteriums in der 2. Hälfte des 20. Jahrhunderts sei vor allem auf W.G. Kümmel verwiesen, der die „innere Grenze des Kanons" durch „die zentrale Christusverkündigung" markiert sieht[18], auf E. Käsemann („die Rechtfertigung des Gottlosen ... als Kanon im Kanon")[19] und auf W. Schrage (als „Sachmitte des Neuen Testaments" sei „der Christus iustificans oder ... der Christus pro nobis" anzusehen).[20]

Dieses Konzept trägt jedoch einen schweren Geburtsfehler mit sich herum, und das ist die historische Bedingtheit der Auswahlkriterien und ihre Abhängigkeit von individuellen theologischen Positionen. Illustrieren lässt sich das am Beispiel von Marcion, Luther und Käsemann, auf die bereits John Barton in seinem Beitrag hingewiesen hat[21]: Allen dreien ist gemeinsam, dass sie bestimmte theologische Positionen vertraten und der Meinung waren, dass der neutestamentliche Kanon sich an diesen Positionen auszurichten habe: Bei *Marcion* war der Kanonisierungsprozess noch nicht abgeschlossen, und darum konnte er einen eigenen Kanon zusammenstellen, der zu seiner Theologie passte. – Für *Martin Luther* war dies so nicht mehr möglich, weil es inzwischen ja einen Kanon gab. Er konnte ihn darum nur dadurch seiner Theologie anpassen, dass er die genannten Umstellungen vornahm. – Beide Wege waren *Ernst Käsemann* natürlich verschlossen, denn

---

15 WA.DB 6,10. – Sprachliche Modernisierung nach H. Bornkamm (Hg.), Luthers Vorreden zur Bibel, Göttingen ³1989, 173.174.

16 Und zwar im eigentlichen Sinne des Wortes: Die genannten Schriften werden in seiner Übersetzung des Neuen Testaments aus der Zählung herausgenommen und ans Ende gestellt; vgl. WA.DB 6,12f.

17 Vorrede auf die Epistel an die Hebräer: Bornkamm (Hg.), Luthers Vorreden (s. Anm. 15), 214.

18 W.G. Kümmel, Notwendigkeit und Grenze des neutestamentlichen Kanons, in: E. Käsemann (Hg.), Das Neue Testament als Kanon (s. Anm. 1), 62–97, S. 96 u.ö.

19 E. Käsemann, Zusammenfassung: ders. (Hg.), Das Neue Testament als Kanon (s. Anm. 1), 405.

20 W. Schrage, Die Frage nach der Mitte und dem Kanon im Kanon des Neuen Testaments in der neueren Diskussion, in: Rechtfertigung. FS Ernst Käsemann, Tübingen/Göttingen 1976, 415–442, S. 439.

21 S. o. S. 14.

dank des Buchdrucks und der durch ihn möglich gewordenen Bibelverbrei-
tung wurde in der Neuzeit eine unüberwindliche Barriere gegen solche Ein-
griffe aufgerichtet.

Dasselbe kann man im übrigen auch von der Festlegung des äthiopischen Kanons im 15.
Jahrhundert sagen, auch wenn sie in die entgegengesetzte Richtung führt: Bekanntlich enthält der äthiopische Kanon sehr viel mehr Bücher als der in den anderen christlichen Kirchen
in Gebrauch stehende (nämlich insgesamt 81). Und diejenigen Schriften, die im 15. Jahrhundert dazukamen, taten dies, weil der damals regierende Kaiser das so wollte, und zwar aufgrund ganz aktueller religionspolitischer Interessen[22]: „Das Henochbuch wurde vom Kaiser
als Ergänzung zur Danielapokalypse in den Kanon eingereiht, um mit den äthiopischen Juden (Falasha) über den messianischen Charakter Christi diskutieren zu können", das Testamentum Domini nostri wurde aufgenommen, „weil es die vom König geforderte Sabbat-
Observanz stützte" und die Didaskalia schließlich „wegen ihrer ... Distanzierung vom jüdischen Ostertermin"[23].

Wenn demgegenüber nach der theologischen Kohärenz der neutestamentlichen Schriften gefragt wird, so ist es – ohne dass ich dies durch Beispiele
belegen müsste – stets die Selbstoffenbarung Gottes in Jesus Christus, die als
einheitsstiftendes Kriterium benannt wird.

c) Beide Konzepte können jedoch das Kanonproblem nicht einmal im
Ansatz lösen, denn sie geben zwar vor, sie würden die bestehenden Kanongrenzen respektieren, de facto stellen jedoch auch sie den Kanon zur Disposition. Dies gilt sowohl für den kritischen als auch für den einheitsstiftenden
Gebrauch des Kriteriums ‚Mitte der Schrift':

Beim Konzept „Kanon im Kanon" „(läuft) die eigentliche Grenze des Kanons ... durch den Kanon mitten hindurch"[24], womit natürlich der Anspruch
des Kanons als Kanon, der allen in ihm enthaltenen Schriften ein und denselben Status verleiht, suspendiert ist. Die katholischen Kritiker dieses Programms haben seine Schwäche in diesem Punkt dann auch mit aller Schärfe
herausgestellt.[25]

Umgekehrt werden beim Konzept „Mitte der Schrift" die Kanongrenzen
nach außen hin geöffnet, weil kein theologisches Kriterium denkbar ist, das
in eine sachlich begründete Korrelation mit den Kanongrenzen gebracht werden könnte. Jede theologische Aussage, der in dieser Weise einheitsstiftende
Funktion innerhalb der Pluralität des neutestamentlichen Kanons zugeschrieben wird, ermöglicht immer auch die theologische Integration der außerkanonischen Schriften, und es gibt dann keinen inhaltlichen Grund, der eine

---

22 Vgl. zum Folgenden F. Heyer, Art. Äthiopien, TRE 1 (1977) 572–596, S. 576ff.
23 Ebd., 577.
24 Kümmel, Notwendigkeit (s. Anm. 18), 96.
25 Vgl. die knappe Darstellung bei Schrage, Frage (s. Anm. 20), 417f.; s. auch Gamble,
    New Testament Canon (s. Anm. 5), 88.

Unterscheidung zwischen kanonischen und nichtkanonischen Schriften recht-
fertigte.

Im Blick auf die eingangs zitierte Feststellung Ernst Käsemanns sieht es
darum so aus, als sei der Streit um die theologische Relevanz des Kanons
inzwischen entschieden: Es scheint überaus fraglich geworden zu sein, ob sie
sich überhaupt noch verteidigen lässt.

2. Neues Licht auf das Problem

2.1. Zur Formulierung einer Fragestellung, die möglicherweise neues Licht
auf das Kanonproblem werfen kann, möchte ich zwei unterschiedliche Ansatzpunkte miteinander ins Gespräch bringen:

a) Jon D. Levenson hat in seinem Aufsatz „Warum Juden sich nicht für
biblische Theologie interessieren"[26] die These formuliert, dass es sich bei der
„Bemühung, eine systematische, einheitliche theologische Aussage aus den
unsystematischen und polydoxen Materialien in der Hebräischen Bibel zu
konstruieren", um ein spezifisch christliches Interesse handele, das es vom
Judentum unterscheide[27]. Er bezeichnet in diesem Zusammenhang die
Grundannahme, „dass die zu interpretierende Einheit das Testament ist", als
eine „moderne christliche Vorstellung".[28] Sie sei dem Judentum fremd, weil
in ihm „die Tendenz (besteht), den Text als Problem mit vielen Facetten zu
sehen, von denen jede Beachtung verdient"[29]. – Levenson's Beobachtungen
beziehen sich zwar auf den Umgang der christlichen Exegeten mit dem Alten
Testament, doch denke ich, dass wir sie mutatis mutandis auch auf die Dis-

---

26 EvTh 51 (1991) 402–430; amerik. Original: Why Jews Are Not Interested in Biblical
    Theology, in: Judaic Perspectives on Ancient Israel, ed. J. Neusner/B.A. Levine/E.S.
    Frerichs, Philadelphia 1987, 281–307.
27 Ebd., 421; s. auch 423: „... ist es unwahrscheinlich, dass die Suche nach der einen großen
    Idee, die die Hebräische Bibel durchdringt und zusammenhält, Juden interessiert". 425f.
    – Vgl. auch M. Tsevat, Theologie des Alten Testaments – eine jüdische Sicht, in: M.
    Klopfenstein u.a. (Hg.), Mitte der Schrift? Ein christlich-jüdisches Gespräch, Bern u.a.
    1987, 329–341, der die Darstellung einer Theologie des Alten Testaments aus jüdischer
    Sicht mit einer „Zoologie des Einhorns" vergleicht (329).
28 Ebd., 425.
29 Ebd., 426. – Vgl. auch die Kritik am Programm der ‚Biblischen Theologie' bei G.T.
    Sheppard, Canonization. Hearing the Voice of the Same God through Historically Dis-
    similar Traditions, Interp. 36 (1982) 21–33, S. 32f.: „The hermeneutic of the biblical
    theology movement, usually a modern intentionality theory of meaning, was as alien to
    Judaism as the use of the term *unity* which took on an almost mathematical quality as the
    objective historian sought to find a single constant factor in the tradition-historical proc-
    ess (...) or a 'center' in the writers' original intents (...)."

kussion um Einheit und Vielfalt des Neuen Testaments übertragen können. Gefragt werden soll dabei, ob nicht die Frage nach einer Sachmitte des Kanons und die Unmöglichkeit, sie so oder so – d.h. als kritisches („Kanon im Kanon") oder als einheitsstiftendes („Mitte der Schrift") – mit dem vorliegenden Kanon des Neuen Testaments in eine theologisch begründete Korrelation bringen zu können, als integraler Bestandteil der Konstitutionsbedingungen des Christentums zu gelten hat.[30]

b) Den zweiten Ansatzpunkt markiert der Primat der Mündlichkeit vor der Schriftlichkeit, der in der Diskussion um den Kanon in der Regel nicht ausreichend beachtet wird.[31] Gemeint ist damit nicht die an das Medium der Mündlichkeit gebundene ursprüngliche Überlieferungsgeschichte der Jesustradition[32], sondern dass das frühe Christentum über mehrere Jahrzehnte hindurch als eine Überzeugungsgemeinschaft existieren konnte, ohne über einen Kanon eigener Schriften als identitätsstiftenden und identitätssichernden Symbolbestand zu verfügen. Etwas plakativ formuliert: Christentum gab es auch schon vor der Entstehung des Kanons, und insofern kann man nicht sagen, dass der Kanon unabdingbar zum *Wesen* des Christentums gehört[33]. Diese Leerstelle kann nicht durch das Alte Testament in Gestalt der Hebräischen Bibel oder der Septuaginta aufgefüllt werden, auch wenn es als autoritatives Zeugnis für das Evangelium von Jesus Christus gelesen wurde, denn (a) war und ist es als solches natürlich nicht in der Lage, eine distinkte *christliche* Identität zu begründen, (b) wurde es nicht als Ganzes, sondern immer nur selektiv rezipiert und (c) ist für den Umgang mit ihm kennzeichnend, dass es immer nur von der Vorgabe einer christologischen Hermeneutik her sachgerecht verstanden wurde (vgl. exemplarisch 2.Kor 3,7–18).

---

30 Eine ähnliche Vermutung in Bezug auf die Frage nach einer – im christlichen Sinne – gesamtbiblischen Theologie äußert bereits E. Brocke, Von den ‚Schriften' zum ‚Alten Testament' – und zurück?, in: Die Hebräische Bibel und ihre zweifache Nachgeschichte. FS Rolf Rendtorff, Neukirchen-Vluyn 1990, 581–594, S. 585: „Kann es sein, daß sich hinter der christlichen Suche nach einer ‚Einheit der Schrift' oder nach ihrer ‚Mitte' verbergende Problem kein exegetisches und auch kein methodisches, sondern ein christlich-existentielles ist?"

31 Dies gilt z.B. auch für die Darstellung von U.H.J. Körtner, Literalität und Oralität im Christentum, in: Text und Geschichte. FS Dieter Lührmann (MThSt 50), Marburg 1999, 76–88, S. 76ff.

32 Vgl. dazu im Zusammenhang der Frage Mündlichkeit/Schriftlichkeit: W.H. Kelber, The Oral and the Written Gospel, Philadelphia 1983; G. Sellin, „Gattung" und „Sitz im Leben" auf dem Hintergrund der Problematik von Mündlichkeit und Schriftlichkeit synoptischer Erzählungen, EvTh 50 (1990) 311–331; ders./F. Vouga (Hg.), Logos und Buchstabe. Mündlichkeit und Schriftlichkeit im Judentum und Christentum der Antike, Tübingen/Basel 1997; J. Schröter, Erinnerung an Jesu Worte (WMANT 76), Neukirchen-Vluyn 1997.

33 Vgl. auch Gamble, New Testament Canon (s. Anm. 5), 57ff.

Wir haben darum in Rechnung zu stellen, dass die für das Christentum
entscheidenden anfänglichen Konstituierungs- und Differenzierungsprozesse
im Wege einer unliteralen, d.h. *mündlichen* Interaktion und Kommunikation
abliefen. Und war es in diesem Zusammenhang doch erforderlich, auf das
Medium der Schrift zurückzugreifen, so lassen die Briefe, die Paulus an die
von ihm gegründeten Gemeinden schrieb, deutlich erkennen, dass sie die
persönliche Anwesenheit ihres Verfassers bei den Adressaten vertreten und
insofern Ersatz für mündliche Interaktion sein wollen, die aufgrund der räum-
lichen Distanz nicht realisierbar war.

2.2. Wenn wir beide Ansatzpunkte miteinander verknüpfen, so ergibt sich für
unsere Fragestellung zunächst eine nicht unerhebliche Erhöhung der Komplexität:

Für eine Aufnahme in den Kanon standen von vornherein nur diejenigen
Äußerungen zur Verfügung, die innerhalb der Kommunikationsprozesse des
Urchristentums im Medium der Schriftlichkeit ausformuliert worden waren.
Es ist mithin ein rein formales Kriterium, das am Anfang des frühchristlichen
Kanonisierungsprozesses steht. Stimmen und Positionen, die sich lediglich
mündlich artikuliert hatten, mussten zwangsläufig unter den Tisch fallen,
ohne dass dabei die von ihnen vertretenen Inhalte irgendeine Rolle spielten.
„Die Zensur, die" nach A. und J. Assmann „im Schatten eines Kanons auftaucht" und „ein nicht zu eliminierender Störfaktor" bleibt[34], ist darum zunächst in einer ganz elementaren Hinsicht ein mediales Phänomen: Sie unter-
drückt theologische Positionen einzig und allein aus dem Grund, weil ihre
Vertreter – als Beispiele genannt seien Petrus und Jakobus – keine schriftlichen Texte produziert haben.

Hinter der Pluralität des Kanons wird damit eine sehr viel weitergehende
Pluralität erkennbar, die durch den Kanon lediglich aus formalen Gründen
reduziert wurde. Dieser Sachverhalt verlangt nun aber, auch die aufgrund
ihres medialen Aggregatszustandes ausgeschlossenen Positionen in unsere
Fragestellung einzubeziehen. Hierbei zeigt sich nun ziemlich schnell, dass
wir auf dasselbe Phänomen stoßen, das Jon D. Levenson als typisch christlichen Umgang mit der Vielfalt des Kanons identifizieren zu können meinte[35]:
dass nämlich die intensive Suche nach einer sprachlich wie existentiell aus-
differenzierbaren und einheitsstiftenden ‚Mitte' der christlichen Identität und
die Unmöglichkeit, sie eindeutig und verbindlich zu bestimmen, bereits von
Anfang an integraler Bestandteil der geschichtlichen Existenz der christlichen

---

34 A. und J. Assmann, Kanon und Zensur, in: dies. (Hg.), Kanon und Zensur (s. Anm. 2),
    7–27, S. 20.
35 S. o. bei Anm. 27.

Gemeinden war. Die Spannung zwischen Einheit und Vielfalt wäre demnach nicht ein erst mit dem Kanon gegebenes Problem, sondern eine fundamentale und damit unaufhebbare Gegebenheit der geschichtlichen Existenz des Christentums überhaupt.[36]

3. Exemplarische Illustration

3.1. Drei Beispiele können die vorstehende These illustrieren:

a) Apg 15,1.5 und der Galaterbrief lassen eine Kontroverse erkennen, in der es darum ging, ob das Bekenntnis zu Jesus Christus den Unterschied zwischen Juden und Heiden aufhebt oder nicht. Während Paulus diese Frage rückhaltlos bejaht, wurde sie von einer starken judenchristlichen Gruppe, der auch die von Paulus im Galaterbrief bekämpften Gegner zuzuordnen sind, entschieden verneint. Sie vertrat die Überzeugung, dass um der in Abraham erfolgten Erwählung Israels willen die Zueignung des durch Jesus Christus vermittelten Heils an die Heiden deren Übertritt zum Judentum, und d.h. konkret: deren Beschneidung, erforderlich macht. Obwohl die Mehrheit der Jerusalemer Urgemeinde und ihre Leiter auf dem Apostelkonvent Paulus und Barnabas das theologische Recht zur beschneidungsfreien Heidenmission und damit auch dem Bekenntnis zu Jesus Christus einen gemeinschaftsbildenden Stellenwert zuerkannten, war das Problem nicht grundsätzlich gelöst. Dies zeigt der in Gal 2,11–14 geschilderte Konflikt in Antiochien, bei dem es darum ging, ob das gemeinsame Christusbekenntnis von Juden und Heiden auch die bedingungslose Tischgemeinschaft jener mit diesen möglich machen kann. Es kam hierbei zu dem Kompromissvorschlag des sog. Aposteldekrets (Apg 15,11–21.28f.), der in Anknüpfung an Lev 17–18 den Heidenchristen von Antiochien und Umgebung auferlegte, sich des Genusses von Götzenopferfleisch, von Blut und des Fleisches nichtgeschächteter Tiere sowie der Unzucht zu enthalten. Nur unter dieser Bedingung sei den Juden(christen) eine Tischgemeinschaft mit den Heiden(christen) möglich. Während Petrus und Barnabas und wohl auch die Gemeinde in Antiochien diesen Kompromiss akzeptierten, lehnte Paulus ihn rigoros ab.

---

36 E. Brocke beschreibt den Grund für das christliche Interesse an einer ‚Mitte‘ eher auf der kognitiven Ebene: „... weil nur mit Hilfe eines in sich geschlossenen Systems die Diskrepanz zwischen den beiden Teilen der christlichen Bibel kaschiert werden kann" (‚Schriften‘ [s. Anm. 30], 584f.). Sie vereinfacht damit die Problematik, weil es die von ihr geltend gemachte Diskrepanz natürlich nicht nur im Verhältnis der beiden Testamente gibt, sondern auch innerhalb der beiden Bibelteile selbst.

b) In den Gemeinden von Korinth und Rom gab es Kontroversen zwischen zwei verschiedenen Gruppen um die Notwendigkeit der Beachtung von Speisetabus: In Korinth (vgl. 1.Kor 8; 10,23–33) ging es um die Frage, ob Christen Götzenopferfleisch essen dürfen oder nicht, und in Rom lehnten die „Schwachen im Glauben" das Essen von Fleisch überhaupt ab (vgl. Röm 14,1f.). – Während Paulus die eine wie die andere Position für vertretbar hält, solange die jeweils andere toleriert wird (vgl. Röm 14,5b–6), ging es den beiden miteinander streitenden Gruppen auch hier um ein zentrales Problem ihrer christlichen Identität. Zwischen ihnen stand zur Debatte, was die durch das christliche Bekenntnis konstituierte Zugehörigkeit zur eschatologischen Heilsgemeinschaft für den lebensweltlichen Umgang mit den überkommenen kulturellen Normen und Gewohnheiten bedeutete: Verlangt bzw. ermöglicht sie Kontinuität, oder tut sie dies nicht? – In beiden Fällen stellt sich Paulus theologisch auf die Seite der „Starken" (1.Kor 8,1a.4f.8; 10,25; Röm 14,14.17), empfiehlt diesen aber, aus Rücksicht auf die „Schwachen" (1.Kor 8,9.13; 10,24.28f.; Röm 14,21; 15,1f.) auf eine öffentliche Vertretung ihrer von ihm für richtig gehaltenen Einsicht zu verzichten.

c) Beim letzten Beispiel geht es um die Frage, wie ein christliches Sexualethos auszusehen hat: In der korinthischen Gemeinde gibt es auf der einen Seite eine Gruppe, die die Position vertritt, dass Christen überhaupt auf jeglichen Sexualverkehr verzichten sollten (1.Kor 7,1)[37]. Auf der anderen Seite wird in 5,1–5 der Fall eines jungen Mannes bekannt, der mit der „Frau seines Vaters" zusammenlebt (so beschreibt jedenfalls Paulus den Sachverhalt, und zwar unter Rückgriff auf die Begrifflichkeit von Lev 18,8)[38]. Die korinthische Gemeinde nahm daran keinen Anstoß, weil man es offenbar als Privatsache ansah und sich für die Beurteilung des Alltagslebens ihrer Mitglieder unzuständig fühlte. Demgegenüber fordert Paulus die Gemeinde dazu auf, den jungen Mann aus ihrer Mitte zu entfernen, und er begründet dies damit, dass ein einzelner Unzuchtsünder den Heilsstatus der gesamten Gemeinde gefährdet, wenn diese ihn in ihrem Kreise duldet (5,6–8).

3.2. Wenn wir zunächst einmal davon absehen, welche dieser Positionen wirkungs- und rezeptionsgeschichtlich sanktioniert wurden, müssen wir ihnen

---

37 Es spricht alles dafür, dass es sich in der Formulierung καλὸν ἀνθρώπῳ γυναικὸς μὴ ἅπτεσθαι um ein Zitat handelt, das die Position dieser Gruppe wiedergibt (s. auch V. 28.36). – Wahrscheinlich ist diese Gruppe mit derjenigen identisch, die auch den Verzehr von Götzenopferfleisch ablehnte.

38 Aller Wahrscheinlichkeit nach handelte es sich bei ihr um die ehemalige Konkubine seines verstorbenen Vaters, die nicht zur christlichen Gemeinde gehörte; vgl. dazu C.S. de Vos, Stepmothers, Concubines and the Case of πορνεία in 1 Corinthians 5, NTS 44 (1998) 104–114.

allen zunächst das gleiche Recht zubilligen, denn sie alle galten ihren Vertretern als identitätsstiftende und darum unaufgebbare Konstituenten ihrer christlichen Existenz. Hierin wird erkennbar, dass die Ausdifferenzierung des einen Bekenntnisses in unterschiedliche und miteinander konkurrierende Heilskonzepte einschließlich ihrer lebensweltlichen Implikationen nicht als Verlust einer ursprünglichen Einheit verstanden werden darf[39], sondern ein integraler Bestandteil der Plausibilität des Bekenntnisses selbst gewesen ist, ohne die die Rezeption der christlichen Heilsbotschaft nicht möglich gewesen wäre.

Bei den vorstehend beschriebenen Vorgängen handelt es sich nun um notwendige Inkulturations- oder Kontextualisierungsprozesse, auf die christliche Identität zwingend angewiesen ist, wenn sie denn auch als soziale Identität zur Anschauung gebracht werden will. Diese Prozesse gehen dabei stets so vor sich, dass die christliche Heilsbotschaft in einen vorgegebenen kulturellen Kontext eintritt und in einer Weise Gestalt gewinnt, die zum einen von den jeweils in Geltung stehenden kulturellen Paradigmen geprägt ist und zum anderen eine Reinterpretation dieser Paradigmen zur Folge hat.

3.3. Von entscheidender Bedeutung ist nun aber, dass dem christlichen Bekenntnis innerhalb des kulturellen Pluralismus der hellenistisch-römischen Welt des 1. Jh. n. Chr. zu keinem Zeitpunkt eine gewissermaßen chemisch reine Urgestalt eignete, die sich aus seiner kontextuellen Einbettung herausdestillieren ließe. In diesem Sinne setzt bereits das als christliches Urbekenntnis anzusehende Osterbekenntnis ("Gott hat Jesus von den Toten auferweckt"; vgl. Röm 4,24b; 8,11; 10,9; 2.Kor 4,14; Gal 1,1; Eph 1,20; Kol 2,12; 1.Petr 1,21) das jüdische Wirklichkeitsverständnis voraus. Damit einher ging innerhalb dieses Rahmens dann eine Ausdifferenzierung des Bekenntnisses durch unterschiedliche Trägerkreise, die unmittelbar mit deren spezifischem Ort innerhalb des kulturellen Gesamtkontextes zusammenhängt. Nachweisen lässt sich dies z.B. für die Differenzen zwischen der Jerusalemer Urgemeinde (den aus Palästina stammenden, aramäisch sprechenden "Hebräern"; Apg 6,1) und den aus der Diaspora zugewanderten, griechisch sprechenden "Hellenisten" (ebd.) des Stephanuskreises in bezug auf die Konsequenzen des Bekenntnisses für die eigene Bindung an die identitätsstiftenden Elemente des Judentums (vgl. Apg 2,46 mit 6,11–15). Schon in den Anfangsjahren des Christentums implizierte das Bekenntnis zu Jesus Christus somit einen Inkulturationsvorgang, der notwendig mit erheblichen Normen- und

---

39 Vgl. auch G. Ebeling, Zur Geschichte des konfessionellen Problems, in: ders., Wort Gottes und Tradition, Göttingen 1964, 41–55, S. 41.

Loyalitätskonflikten einherging, die sich ihrerseits wiederum in Identitäts-
und Orientierungskrisen niederschlugen. Diese waren um so gravierender, je
größer die Unterschiede zwischen den kulturellen Kontexten waren, die hierbei aufeinandertrafen. An Hand der oben genannten Beispiele lässt sich dies
illustrieren:

a) Beim Konflikt in Antiochien (Gal 2,11–14) ging es darum, ob eine
christliche Gemeinde, zu der Juden und Heiden gehören, sich an den Normen
der jüdischen Halacha zu orientieren hat oder ob die Integration des christlichen Bekenntnisses in einen nichtjüdischen Kontext auch eine kulturelle
Neuorientierung der Judenchristen erforderlich macht: Petrus hatte zunächst
mit den antiochenischen Heidenchristen Tischgemeinschaft praktiziert (2,12)
und sich damit im Sinne des letztgenannten Modells verhalten. Aufgrund der
Vorhaltungen von Judenchristen, die aus Jerusalem („von Jakobus") gekommen waren, geriet er aber in einen Loyalitätskonflikt und fürchtete um den
Verlust seiner jüdischen Identität, so dass er die Tischgemeinschaft zusammen mit Barnabas und anderen antiochenischen Judenchristen wieder auf-
kündigte (ebd.). Aufschlussreich ist, dass der zur Lösung des Konflikts ein-
gebrachte Kompromiss des Aposteldekrets gerade auf die Tora-Vorschriften
von Lev 17–18 zurückgreift: Hier werden rituelle Forderungen für diejenigen
formuliert, die als Beisassen in Israel leben wollen. Auch hinter diesem
Kompromiss steht damit die Überzeugung, dass als Plausibilitätsbasis für das
christliche Bekenntnis allein ein solcher Kontext gelten kann, der durch kulturelle Orientierungsnormen definiert ist, die die jüdische Identität konstituie-
ren. Das Aposteldekret ordnet die Heidenchristen nicht dem Christusbekenntnis, sondern Israel zu.

b) Während es sich bei den Differenzen zwischen den „Schwachen" und
„Starken" innerhalb der römischen Gemeinde wiederum um einen Konflikt
zwischen jüdischen und nichtjüdischen kulturellen Gewohnheiten handelt,
lässt sich die Auseinandersetzung um den Verzehr von Götzenopferfleisch in
der Gemeinde von Korinth als eine Kontroverse verständlich machen, die aus
der Inkulturation des Evangeliums in einen paganen Kontext erwachsen ist:
Wenn die ablehnende Haltung der „Schwachen" auf deren „bis jetzt (andau-
ernde) Gewöhnung an den Götzen" zurückgeführt wird (1.Kor 8,7), so heißt
dies: Die religiösen Paradigmen des kulturellen Kontextes, innerhalb dessen
die Hinwendung zum christlichen Bekenntnis erfolgte, bleiben auch im Rahmen der neuen Existenzorientierung der „Schwachen" in einer Weise präsent,
der die fortdauernde Abgrenzung von ihnen erforderlich machte. Für sie üben
die alten Götter weiterhin Macht aus. Im Verzehr von Fleisch, das ursprünglich den Göttern geweiht war, sahen sie sich wieder in Verbindung mit den
früher von ihnen verehrten Göttern gebracht und dementsprechend ihre neu-

gewonnene Identität verloren gehen. Demgegenüber ging bei der anderen
Gruppe die Übernahme des Christusbekenntnisses mit einer Bewahrung ihrer
bisherigen Gewohnheiten einher. Möglich wurde dies dadurch, dass die
christliche Heilsbotschaft einen Prozess anstieß, der bei ihnen zu einer Entta-
buisierung ihres religiösen Kontextes führte (vgl. den wiederholten Hinweis
auf ihre „Erkenntnis" und ihr „Wissen": 8,1f.4.7.10f.). Wir haben hier also
einen Inkulturationsvorgang, der auf der einen Seite eher affektiv und auf der
anderen eher kognitiv abläuft, und G. Theißen hat darum wohl Recht mit
seiner Annahme, dass hinter dieser Differenz eine unterschiedliche soziale
Schichtenzugehörigkeit der beiden Gruppen steht.[40]

c) Als Hintergrund von 1.Kor 5,1–13 schließlich steht die Spannung zwischen jüdischem und nichtjüdischem Sexualethos. In diesem Zusammenhang
ist wichtig, dass – anders als dies in der älteren Forschung durchweg angenommen wird – die von Paulus kritisierte Praxis durchaus nicht in einem li-
bertinistischen Enthusiasmus gründet, der aus der paulinischen Freiheitspre-
digt abgeleitet wurde. Es ist vielmehr davon auszugehen, dass das von Paulus
kritisierte Verhalten nichts weiter ist als ein im kulturellen Kontext einer hel-
lenistischen Stadt sozial akzeptiertes Ethos, das für die betroffenen Angehö-
rigen der Gemeinde bereits vor ihrer Christwerdung selbstverständlich war
und von ihnen dann nach der Taufe einfach fortgesetzt wurde. Wenn Paulus
demgegenüber diesen Sachverhalt unter Rückgriff auf Lev 18,8 beschreibt,
wird daran erkennbar, dass er ihn durch die jüdische Brille betrachtet und
sich in seinem Urteil von den Kategorien und Normen der jüdischen Sexualethik leiten lässt.[41]

3.4. Die von Jon D. Levenson und anderen[42] als spezifisch christlich bezeichnete Suche nach einer „Mitte" bzw. einem einheitsstiftenden Kriterium des
Kanons weist damit auf eine Problemlage hin, die sich nicht erst aufgrund der
Existenz des Kanons eingestellt hat, sondern bereits ein integraler Bestandteil
der urchristlichen (und d.h. der präkanonischen) Inkulturationsprozesse war.
Insofern es bei diesen Auseinandersetzungen darum ging, welchem kulturellen Kontext die christliche Heilsorientierung anzuverwandeln ist[43], lässt sich

---

40 G. Theißen, Die Starken und die Schwachen in Korinth, in: ders., Studien zur Soziologie
   des Urchristentums, Tübingen ²1983, 272–289.
41 Vgl. dazu jetzt M. Wolter, Der Brief des sogenannten Unzuchtsünders, in: Liebe –
   Macht – Religion. Gedenkschrift für Helmut Merklein, Stuttgart 2003 (im Druck).
42 S. Anm. 27.
43 Aus diesem Grunde geht auch E. Käsemanns Urteil an der Sache vorbei: Er hatte seinerzeit die theologische Disparatheit des neutestamentlichen Kanons historisch darauf zurückgeführt, „dass bereits in der Urchristenheit eine Fülle verschiedener Konfessionen
   nebeneinander vorhanden war, aufeinander folgte, sich miteinander verband und gegeneinander abgrenzte" (Begründet [s. Anm. 7], 221). Er stellt sie als „Lehrgegensätze" dar

als Hintergrund für diese Unsicherheit, die dann eben zu den skizzierten Kontroversen führte, ziemlich leicht eine für das Christentum – und zwar m.E. nicht nur für das Urchristentum, sondern für das Christentum überhaupt – konstitutive Gegebenheit anführen, die man vielleicht am besten – da Glaube als solcher empirisch nicht aufweisbar ist – als ‚lebensweltliche Unanschaulichkeit‘ des Glaubens bezeichnen kann:[44]

Der für alle christlichen Gemeinden entscheidende identity marker war in den ersten Jahrzehnten zweifelsohne die πίστις[45]. Hierin kommt zum Ausdruck, dass die Gemeinden in dieser Zeit aus Menschen bestanden, die auf die Christusverkündigung mit Zustimmung reagiert hatten (vgl. z.B. Röm 10,14f.; 1.Thess 1,8–10), ohne dass damit allerdings die Festlegung auf einen bestimmten kulturellen Kontext, der sich in einem bestimmten lebensweltlichen Ethos zur Anschauung bringen konnte, verbunden war. So konnten z.B. judenchristliche Gemeinden weiterhin more judaico leben, und heidenchristliche nicht. Oder – im Blick auf die korinthische Gemeinde gesagt: Die eine Gruppe konnte aus ihrer Bekehrung die Forderung ableiten, dass nunmehr Speise- und Sexualtabus zu beachten sind, die andere konnte ihren bisherigen Lebensstil unverändert fortsetzen. Analog war für die paulinischen Gegner in Galatien Christentum nur als kultureller Bestandteil des Judentums denkbar. Kurz gesagt: die allen gemeinsame πίστις Χριστοῦ blieb ohne eine korrespondierende einheitsstiftende Objektivation in der lebensweltlichen Existenz der Glaubenden. Die Bedeutung dieses Sachverhalts für unsere Fragestellung liegt auf der Hand: Während die Urchristenheit sich der Gemeinsamkeit ihrer *kognitiven* Identität gewiss war, blieb dabei aufgrund ihrer disparaten kulturellen Herkunft die Frage nach ihrer *sozialen* Identität, d.h. nach der kontextuellen Anverwandlung des Glaubens offen. Die von mir angeführten Beispiele lassen erkennen, wie intensiv um ihre Beantwortung gerungen wurde.

---

und erklärt sie „aus der verschiedenen theologisch-dogmatischen Haltung" der Autoren (ebd., 220.216).

44 Vgl. dazu ausführlicher M. Wolter, Ethos und Identität in paulinischen Gemeinden, NTS 43 (1997) 430–444; ders., Die ethische Identität christlicher Gemeinden in neutestamentlicher Zeit, in: Marburger Jahrbuch Theologie. XIII. Woran orientiert sich Ethik? (MThSt 67), hg. v. W. Härle/R. Preul, Marburg 2001, 61–90, S. 65ff.

45 Dies findet seinen Ausdruck darin, dass quer durch das gesamte Neue Testament die Christen mit Hilfe eines absoluten Partizips als οἱ πιστεύοντες identifiziert werden, ohne dass dabei der Gegenstand ihres Glaubens durch ein Attribut näher bestimmt wird; vgl. Apg 2,44; Röm 3,22; 4,11; 1.Kor 1,21; 14,22; Gal 3,22; 1.Thess 1,7; 2,10.13; Eph 1,19; 1.Petr 2,7; s. auch Mk 16,17; Apg 4,32; 2.Thess 1,10; Hebr 4,3 (jeweils Aorist) und Apg 18,27; 19,18 (jeweils Perfekt). In der außerchristlichen Literatur ist diese Verwendung von οἱ πιστεύοντες als Gruppenbezeichnung demgegenüber völlig unbekannt.

4. Konsequenzen für das Kanonproblem

Für unsere Fragestellung ergeben sich daraus die folgenden Konsequenzen:

4.1. Die oben genannten Beispiele haben erkennen lassen, dass die Spannung von Einheit und Vielfalt als theologisches Problem nicht erst in der Eigenart des neutestamentlichen Kanons als eines schriftlichen Symbolbestandes begründet ist, sondern bereits als integraler Bestandteil der vorkanonischen (d.h. der mündlich ablaufenden) Kontextualisierungsprozesse des frühen Christentums anzusehen ist. Dasselbe gilt auch für die Frage nach der Grenze des Kanons, d.h. für die Frage nach seiner Offenheit und Unverbindlichkeit resp. Geschlossenheit und Verbindlichkeit.

Obwohl natürlich die Bedeutung des Lexems ‚Kanon' für das theologische Sachproblem nicht entscheidend ist, sei zur Illustration dieses Sachverhalts noch auf seine Verwendung in Gal 6,16 hingewiesen: Mit Hilfe der anaphorischen Deixis τοῦτο kennzeichnet Paulus den Grundsatz οὔτε γὰρ περιτομή τί ἐστιν οὔτε ἀκροβυστία ἀλλὰ καινὴ κτίσις (6,15) als unbedingt verbindlichen κανών, der das Identitätszentrum der christlichen Existenzorientierung markiert. Das Demonstrativpronomen τοῦτο ist spezifizierend zu verstehen, und darum ist dieser Text für unsere Fragestellung wichtig: In der Auseinandersetzung zwischen Paulus und seinen (christlichen!) Gegnern in Galatien ging es wie zuvor schon beim antiochenischen Konflikt um die einheitsstiftende Verbindlichkeit eben dieses paulinischen ‚Kanons': ob der Unterschied zwischen Juden und Heiden ἐν Χριστῷ irrelevant geworden ist, weil Glaube und Taufe aus ihnen neue Geschöpfe machen (vgl. auch 1.Kor 12,13; 2.Kor 5,17; Gal 3,26–28; 5,6), oder ob ihm nach wie vor eine unheilsgeschichtliche Qualität zukommt und ein christlicher κανών darum inhaltlich ganz anders zu formulieren wäre. Wenn man so will, kann man sagen, dass hier wie auch anderswo eine Auseinandersetzung um ‚das Kanonische' geführt wird.

Der uns überlieferte schriftliche Kanon des Neuen Testaments als historisch gewordene Größe verhält sich in ambivalenter Weise zu seiner Vorgeschichte: Im Blick auf die Vielfalt der in ihn aufgenommenen Texte will der Kanon gerade in seiner Intentionalität und in seiner „dem Historiker zugänglichen Vorfindlichkeit"[46] ohne Zweifel nichts anderes als die Einheit der identitätsstiftenden Grundlagen der Kirche zum Ausdruck bringen. Wir können dies vor allem an zwei Beispielen erkennen:

Zum einen können wir auf das Nebeneinander der vier Evangelien mit ihren Abweichungen und Widersprüchen verweisen: Dass die Verschiedenheit der Evangelien als von einer übergeordneten theologischen Einheit umgriffen

---

46 Käsemann, Begründet (s. Anm. 7), 131.

angesehen wurde, zeigen ihre Überschriften[47]. Obwohl deren handschriftliche Überlieferung divergiert, wird doch jede einzelne Evangelienschrift immer nur als εὐαγγέλιον κατὰ Μαθθαῖον, εὐαγγέλιον κατὰ Μᾶρκον usw. bezeichnet. Diese Formulierungen bringen zum Ausdruck, dass *das* Evangelium nicht mit einer einzelnen Evangelien*schrift* zu identifizieren ist; zu übersetzen ist dementsprechend „das Evangelium *in der Fassung* des Matthäus/Markus/Lukas/Johannes". Die Diversität der einzelnen Schriften wird damit zusammengehalten durch die Größe des einen Evangeliums, das in ihnen lediglich individuelle unterschiedliche literarische Gestalt angenommen hat.

Ein anderes Beispiel ist die Ergänzung des Corpus Paulinum um die Katholischen Briefe: Sie ist, wie Dieter Lührmann gezeigt hat[48], in Orientierung an Gal 2,9 vorgenommen worden und soll das theologische Zeugnis der Jerusalemer „Säulen" dem des Paulus komplementär an die Seite stellen. Hierbei handelt es sich zweifellos um ein recht eindrucksvolles Zeugnis kanonischer Ökumenizität.

Beiden Beispielen entspricht, dass in den altkirchlichen Texten, die den Kanonisierungsprozess begleiten und kommentieren, der Gesichtspunkt der theologischen Kohärenz der neutestamentlichen Schriften an keiner einzigen Stelle auch nur die geringste Rolle spielt. Im Vordergrund steht vielmehr in vielen Texten das Konsensargument: Als wichtiges Kriterium wird immer wieder angeführt, dass eine bestimmte Schrift in vielen Kirchen „gelesen", „benutzt" oder „anerkannt" wird: Und je verbreiteter eine Schrift war, desto größer war die Chance, dass sie in den Kanon Eingang fand.

Es lohnt sich, an dieser Stelle in einem kleinen *Exkurs* einen kurzen Blick auf die außerbiblischen Kanonisierungsprozesse in hellenistisch-römischer Zeit zu werfen.[49] Sie unterscheiden sich natürlich in vielfacher Hinsicht von den neutestamentlichen Kanonisierungsprozessen, doch können wir auch interessante Analogien feststellen: Demnach fanden sich nach den Eroberungen Alexanders d. Gr. in allen von ihm eroberten Territorien und in zumeist neugegründeten Städten Griechen wieder. Sie lebten dort zwar in leitender Position in Verwaltung, Wirtschaft und Militär, doch blieben sie ethnische und kulturelle Minderheiten innerhalb

---

47 Vgl. dazu vor allem M. Hengel, Die Evangelienüberschriften (SHAW.PH 1984/3), Heidelberg 1984.

48 D. Lührmann, Gal 2,9 und die katholischen Briefe, ZNW 72 (1981) 65–87, S. 70ff. – Besonders eindrücklich wird dieser Zusammenhang auch durch die Entsprechungen in der Reihenfolge: In den meisten griechischen Handschriften werden die Jerusalemer Säulen in Gal 2,9 in der Reihenfolge Jakobus, Kephas (Petrus), Johannes genannt, und dem entspricht auch die Reihenfolge der Katholischen Briefe in den jeweiligen Handschriften. Anders der Codex Claromontanus (D 06): Er hat in Gal 2,9 die Reihenfolge Petrus, Jakobus, Johannes und ordnet auch die Katholischen Briefe in der Abfolge 1./2.Petr, Jak, 1.–3.Joh, Jud an.

49 Vgl. zum Folgenden T. Morgan, Literate Education in the Hellenistic and Roman Worlds, Cambridge 1998; A. Dihle, Literaturkanon und Schriftsprache, in: J. Dummer/M. Vielberg (Hg.), Leitbilder der Spätantike – Eliten und Leitbilder, Stuttgart 1999, 9–30.

eines fremden Umfeldes. Sie waren aus diesem Grunde darauf angewiesen, Strategien zur Bewahrung und Vergewisserung ihrer griechischen Identität zu entwickeln, und sie taten dies – das lassen die erhaltenen Schultexte deutlich erkennen –, indem sie sich auf eine begrenzte Zahl von ‚klassischen' Autoren verständigten, deren Texte gelesen und für die Erziehung und Ausbildung herangezogen wurden.

Natürlich sind die Differenzen nicht zu übersehen, doch treten auch die Gemeinsamkeiten deutlich zutage: Hier wie dort haben wir eine Minderheitensituation und ein ihr entsprechendes Elitebewusstsein. Hier wie dort haben wir das Bewusstsein einer gemeinsamen Identität, die in der Lektüre derselben Texte ihren Ausdruck findet. Hier wie dort haben wir das Phänomen der Überlokalität: Der Gebrauch derselben Texte kompensiert dies und stellt Gemeinsamkeit her. Und hier wie dort geht es schließlich um Schriften einer als normativ angesehenen Vergangenheit.

Man kann also vielleicht sagen, dass die Ausbildung des Kanons im Kontext einer Krise des frühen Christentums erfolgte, die sich nach zwei Seiten hin beschreiben lässt: Zum einen, und zwar in diachronischer Hinsicht, lässt sie sich als eine *Kontinuitätskrise* verstehen, die ihren Grund in dem zunehmenden Abstand von den identitätsstiftenden Anfängen der Christentumsgeschichte hatte. Dem Kanon kommt in diesem Zusammenhang die Funktion zu, diese Anfänge bleibend vergegenwärtigen zu können bzw. die Verbindung mit diesen Anfängen bleibend zu bewahren. – Zum anderen, und zwar in synchronischer Hinsicht, war diese Krise auch eine *Kohärenzkrise*, insofern nämlich die Fixierung des Kanons mit der zunehmenden Ausdifferenzierung des Christentums in eine Vielzahl von miteinander konkurrierenden Christentümern entgegentreten wollte. Auf diese Gefahr reagiert der Kanon, indem einerseits diejenigen Schriften aufgenommen wurden, die konsens- oder auch mehrheitsfähig waren, während andererseits Schriften, die lediglich von Randgruppen ‚benutzt' wurden, ausgegrenzt wurden.[50]

Umgekehrt reduziert der Kanon aber auch die Vielfalt der frühchristlichen Inkulturations- und Kontextualisierungsprozesse, und verantwortlich für diese Reduktion sind ausschließlich mediale Gesichtspunkte: Theologische Positionen, die nur mündlich vertreten worden waren, wurden damit – anders als dies bei den Positionen der Textproduzenten der Fall war – der Möglichkeit beraubt, in die ökumenische Vielfalt des Kanons aufgenommen zu werden. Diesem Vorgang liegt keine inhaltliche Entscheidung zugrunde, und darum ist es auch nicht legitim, einer theologischen Position nur deshalb theologische Verbindlichkeit zuzuerkennen, weil sie schriftlich formuliert wurde.

4.2. Daraus folgt nun aber, dass es eine sachlich problematische Verkürzung wäre, wenn das Problem der Spannung zwischen Einheit und Vielfalt als ein für den neutestamentlichen Kanon spezifisches Problem behandelt würde:

---

50 Vgl. auch die Beschreibung der bei der Entstehung des Kanons wirksamen Faktoren bei Theißen, Religion (s. Anm. 11), 339ff.

Die genannte Spannung war von Anfang an integraler Bestandteil derjenigen Inkulturations- und Differenzierungsprozesse, die den frühchristlichen Gemeinden in der Pluralität ihrer kulturellen Kontexte soziale Identität vermittelten. Die Spannung von Einheit und Vielfalt ist darum kein Problem des *Kanons*. Gleichzeitig ist sie aber auch kein *Problem* des Kanons, denn er spiegelt – trotz der oben skizzierten Reduktion – die Vielfalt der genannten Kontextualisierungsprozesse wider, und es entspricht auch der Intentionalität seines Kompromisscharakters, die Disparatheit der unterschiedlichen Fassungen des einen Evangeliums sowie der unterschiedlichen theologischen Entwürfe ungewichtet nebeneinander zu stellen. Und ebensowenig wie ,das Christentum' über eine kontextuell objektivierbare ,Mitte' verfügt, widerspricht es auch der Eigenart des neutestamentlichen Kanons, in ihm so etwas wie einen „Kanon im Kanon" auszudifferenzieren oder eine „Mitte" zu bestimmen, zu der die einzelnen Schriften in unterschiedlicher Nähe oder Ferne stehen.[51] Die Pluralität des Kanons hält vielmehr bleibend fest, dass christliche Identität sich in unterschiedlichen Plausibilitätsstrukturen kontextuell ausdifferenzieren kann und muss, um soziale Identität gewinnen zu können, ohne sich dabei an einen individuellen Kontext auszuliefern oder in ihm aufzugehen.

4.3. Die zuletzt formulierte Einschränkung ist von zentraler Bedeutung, denn sie wirft nun doch die Frage nach dem Kriterium auf, das ein Auseinanderfallen der sozialen Identität(en) des Christentums in eine beliebige Vielfalt von Kontextualisierungen verhindert und eine theologische Sachkritik an denjenigen Glaubens- und Lebensformen erforderlich macht, die die kontextuellen Objektivationen zum Gegenstand der Heilsorientierung erheben.

Greifbar ist dieses Kriterium in nichts anderem als im Christusbekenntnis als einer außerhalb des Kanons existierenden Größe, insofern es seine Unverwechselbarkeit darin findet, dass es das Bekenntnis zum gekreuzigten Gottessohn ist: Sein unaufgebbares Zentrum ist die Paradoxie, dass Gott gerade im abgründigen Geschehen des Kreuzes zum Heil aller Menschen gehandelt hat. Gemeint ist damit: Weil Gott am Kreuz „die Weisheit der Welt zur Torheit gemacht hat" (1.Kor 1,20), hat er auch jeden Versuch einer Heilsorientierung, die das Skandalon des Kreuzes (1.Kor 1,23; Gal 5,11)

---

51 S. auch I.U. Dalferth, Die Mitte ist außen. Anmerkungen zum Wirklichkeitsbezug evangelischer Schriftauslegung, in: Ch. Landmesser u.a. (Hg.), Jesus Christus als die Mitte der Schrift (BZNW 86), Berlin/New York 1997, 173–198, S. 178: „... *die Mitte* gibt es nicht – allenfalls einen Streit um literarische, religiöse, theologische, poetische, rechtsgeschichtliche oder sonstige Schwerpunkte, Hauptthemen oder Höhepunkte, einen Streit, der hermeneutisch nie letztgültig entschieden werden kann" (Hervorhebung im Original).

durch kontextuelle Paradigmen substituiert und es dadurch zu umgehen sucht, zum Scheitern verurteilt. Mit Paulus gesagt: „Mir soll es nicht geschehen, dass ich mich rühme, außer des Kreuzes unseres Herrn Jesus Christus, durch das mir die Welt gekreuzigt ist und ich der Welt" (Gal 6,14). Paulus führt dann in V. 15 zur Begründung dieser Aussage den bereits oben zitierten Satz von der Aufhebung der theologischen Qualität von περιτομή und ἀκροβυστία an. Dieselbe Argumentationsfigur verwendet Paulus auch in 1.Kor 1,23: Weil die Verkündigung eines gekreuzigten Heilsbringers „den Juden ein σκάνδαλον" und „den Heiden eine μωρία" ist, zerbricht die Verkündigung der *mors turpissima crucis* als eines Heilsgeschehens alle Wirklichkeitskonstruktionen und Wertesysteme, die auf kontextuellen Gegebenheiten aufruhen, und vermittelt die Gewissheit einer aus ihnen unableitbaren übergeordneten Einheit. Paulus lässt hier nicht weniger als ein völlig neues Universum entstehen. Er konzipiert die Matrix einer Sinnwelt, deren master paradigm das „Wort vom Kreuz" ist. In dieser Funktion sorgt die Verkündigung eines Kreuzestodes als Heilsgeschehen dafür, dass der Unterschied zwischen Juden und Nichtjuden theologisch depotenziert und einer Gemeinsamkeit nachgeordnet wird, die sich durch nichts anderes als durch Zustimmung oder Ablehnung dieser Verkündigung gegenüber konstituiert.

Auf die interne Ausdifferenzierung der korinthischen Gemeinde und die Gefährdung der innergemeindlichen Einheit bezogen, liefert die paulinische Kreuzestheologie darüber hinaus insofern einen theologischen Gegenentwurf, als sie die verschiedenen Parteien mit dem „Wort vom Kreuz" auf ein einheitsstiftendes Kriterium hin anzusprechen vermag, das sogar den Unterschied zwischen Juden und Nichtjuden bedeutungslos werden lässt und eine distinkte *christliche* Identität zu begründen vermag.[52] Hinter dieser Größe treten alle kontextuellen (und dementsprechend auch alle konfessionellen) Differenzen zurück.

Diese alle kontextuellen Ausdifferenzierungen umgreifende Einheit artikuliert sich nirgendwo anders als in der πίστις Χριστοῦ, die eben dadurch gekennzeichnet ist, dass sie das Kreuz als Heilsereignis wahrzunehmen vermag. Erkennbar wird dies vor allen Dingen in der Einbettung von Gal 6,12–16 in den gesamten Argumentationszusammenhang des Galaterbriefs, denn die Rede vom Kreuz in diesem Text steht in sachlicher Entsprechung zu den Aussagen über den Glauben in den anderen Briefteilen: Wie zufolge 6,14f. ein Rühmen, dass sich auf einen Kreuzestod richtet, und dessen Wahrnehmung als Etablierung einer neuen Schöpfung nur möglich sind, weil es nicht

---

52 Vgl. dazu M. Wolter, „Dumm und skandalös". Die paulinische Kreuzestheologie und das Wirklichkeitsverständnis des christlichen Glaubens, in: Das Kreuz Jesu. Gewalt – Opfer – Sühne, hg. v. R. Weth, Neukirchen-Vluyn 2001, 44–63.

ein beliebiger, sondern der Kreuzestod Jesu Christi ist, so gilt Entsprechendes auch vom Glauben: Der Glaube, der Abrahamskindschaft herstellt (3,7.9), durch den Gott die Menschen für gerecht erklärt (2,16; 3,8.11.24), der die Verheißung des Geistes vermittelt (3,2.5.14.22) und der den Unterschied zwischen Juden und Heiden aufhebt (5,6), tut all dies immer nur als πίστις Χριστοῦ (2,16.20; 3,22), d.h. als sich exklusiv auf Jesus Christus richtender Glaube (s. auch 2,16; 3,26). Diese Konvergenz hat zur Folge, dass der christliche Glaube als ein Wirklichkeitsverständnis identifizierbar wird, das seine Unverwechselbarkeit darin findet, dass es in einem Kreuzestod das heilsstiftende Handeln Gottes zu erkennen vermag.

4.4. Daraus ergibt sich für die Kanonfrage: Obwohl der neutestamentliche Kanon in seiner Vielfalt nur einen Ausschnitt aus der Vielfalt der frühchristlichen Kontextualisierungsprozesse repräsentiert und obwohl bei seiner Entstehung auch „die confusio hominum mitgewirkt (hat)", wie Kurt Aland es formuliert hat[53], hat er in rezeptionshermeneutischer Hinsicht als unantastbar zu gelten. Dies gilt nicht, weil den einzelnen Schriften des Kanons eine besondere Qualität zukäme, die den außerkanonischen Schriften fehlte, sondern aus einem ganz positivistischen Grund: Der Kanon ist seit seiner Fixierung zu einem Teil der kulturellen Identität der Kirchen geworden, und er ist dies durch nichts anderes als durch seinen Gebrauch geworden, der ihn zu einem integralen Bestandteil ihrer kollektiven Erinnerung hat werden lassen. In diesem Sinne gibt es – wenn wir von den Einzelschriften ausgehen – keinen Grund, dem Matthäusevangelium einen anderen theologischen Status zuzubilligen als z.B. dem Thomasevangelium, außer dass jenes im Kanon steht und dieses nicht. Die Verbindlichkeit des Kanons lässt sich eben nicht *a priori* begründen, sondern einzig und allein *a posteriori*, d.h. von seiner Rezeption und seinem Gebrauch in den christlichen Kirchen her. Der neutestamentliche Kanon hat damit eine Qualität gewonnen, die Jan Assmann als „Kennzeichen einer textual community", d.h. als „identitäts-definierende Bedeutung eines ... Grundtextes" beschrieben hat.[54] Die theologische Verbindlichkeit des Kanons hat ihren Grund darin, dass der neutestamentliche Kanon in der gesamten Christenheit in ihren unterschiedlichen kontextuellen Ausdifferenzie-

---

53 K. Aland, Das Problem des neutestamentlichen Kanons, in: E. Käsemann (Hg.), Das Neue Testament als Kanon (s. Anm. 1), 134–158, S. 158.
54 J. Assmann, Fünf Stufen auf dem Wege zum Kanon. Tradition und Schriftkultur im frühen Judentum und in seiner Umwelt, Münster u.a. 1999, 26; vgl. auch Th.L. Hettema, The Canon: Authority and Fascination, in: A. van der Kooij/K. van der Toorn (Hg.), Canonization and Decanonization (SHR 82), Leiden u.a. 1998, 391–398, S. 391: „A canonical text is a text that is recognized as being a genuine part of a certain tradition, literary or religious."

rungen als kontinuitäts- und einheitsstiftender Symbolbestand über alle Konfessionsgrenzen hinweg in Geltung steht. Sein einheitstiftender Aussagewille besteht darin, dass die Gemeinsamkeit der christlichen Identität alle theologischen Differenzen umgreift – seien sie auch noch so groß. Das Prädikat „kanonisch" verleiht darum nicht den einzelnen Schriften des Kanons eine besondere Dignität und unterscheidet sie auch nicht von den außerkanonischen Schriften, sondern es zeichnet allein den Kanon in seiner übersummativen Gesamtheit aus. Das Prädikat ‚kanonisch' kommt einer Schrift allein dadurch zu, dass sie gemeinsam mit anderen, theologisch gegebenenfalls völlig unterschiedlichen Schriften im Kanon steht. Keine Schrift ist für sich allein ‚kanonisch', sondern immer nur zusammen mit anderen. Dementsprechend bedeutet ‚kanonisch' auch, dass keine Schrift für sich allein gelesen werden kann, sondern immer nur im Blick auch auf die anderen kanonischen Schriften und im Blick auf den Kanon in seiner Gesamtheit.[55]

Und ebenso wie der Kanon nach außen hin geschlossen ist[56], so ist er auch nach innen hin unteilbar. Jede gewichtende und wertende Differenzierung innerhalb des Kanons führt dazu, dass innerhalb der Vielfalt der kontextuellen Ausdifferenzierungen des Christentums das Trennende auf Kosten des Gemeinsamen in den Vordergrund gestellt wird. Martin Luthers Aufteilung des neutestamentlichen Kanons[57] ist das beste Beispiel dafür: Seine Verschiebung des Hebräer- und des Jakobusbriefes nach hinten wird bis in die Gegenwart hinein von allen Ausgaben der Lutherbibel fortgeschrieben, und so ist allein schon die formale Reihenfolge der Bücher des Neuen Testaments nicht nur zu einem festen Bestandteil des identitätstiftenden Symbolinventars der Tradition nunmehr der *lutherischen* Kirchen geworden, sondern sie macht auch die konfessionelle Trennung zur maßgeblichen Lektüreanweisung für die Rezeption des neutestamentlichen Kanons insgesamt. Konsequenterweise wurde dieser Schritt in der ökumenischen Einheitsübersetzung dann auch wieder rückgängig gemacht.

---

55 S. auch Gamble, New Testament Canon (s. Anm. 5), 75.
56 Das bedeutet natürlich, dass, „wenn morgen ein geistbewährter urchristlicher Brief bzw. Evangelium gefunden würde", er *auf gar keinen Fall* „dem Kanon hinzugezählt werden (würde)" (gegen C.H. Ratschow, Art. Schrift, Heilige. V. Systematisch-theologisch, TRE 30 [1999] 423–432, Zitat S. 426,16ff.). Es gibt keinerlei Kriterium, das eine solche Entscheidung begründen könnte, und vor allen Dingen gilt dies natürlich auch für das von Ratschow selbst genannte: Was heißt überhaupt „geistbewährt"? Und wer stellt das fest, bzw. können Menschen das feststellen? Dies gilt auch für jedes andere Kriterium: Wenn wir einen mit Sicherheit authentischen Paulusbrief finden sollten und ihn dann aufgrund seiner Authentizität in den Kanon aufnähmen, würden wir mit dieser Entscheidung und ihrer Begründung sofort die Kanonizität der neutestamentlichen Pseudepigraphen zur Disposition stellen.
57 S. o. S. 47f.

Wir stehen mithin vor der Situation, dass dem neutestamentlichen Kanon in seiner gewordenen literarischen Gestalt eine *hermeneutische* Qualität zukommt, insofern er nämlich geeignet ist, christliche Identität in authentischer Weise zur Anschauung zu bringen:

Bezogen auf die seit jeher bestehende Spannung zwischen Einheit und Vielfalt des Christentums verfügt der Kanon einerseits zweifellos über das Potential, die Einheit zur Anschauung zu bringen und damit als Realsymbol jener Gewissheit zu fungieren, dass die Gemeinsamkeit seiner (des Christentums) kognitiven Identität, die sich im Glauben an Jesus Christus als den gekreuzigten und auferstandenen Gottessohn artikuliert, über alle Unterschiede dominiert.[58]

Andererseits ist aber auch nicht zu übersehen, dass die einzelnen Kanonexemplare mit ihren Abweichungen voneinander immer noch Teil jener kulturellen Ausdifferenzierung sind, ohne die es das Christentum als geschichtlich existierende Größe nicht geben kann. – Hieraus ergibt sich dann aber auch die theologisch begründete Notwendigkeit, eine Vertauschung der Prädikationen vorzunehmen, die für gewöhnlich den Größen „Schrift" und „Kanon" zugeordnet werden[59], indem als Merkmal der „Schrift" die „Einheit" und als Kennzeichen des „Kanons" die „Vielfalt" herausgestellt wird: Es ist demgegenüber gerade der Wille zur Einheit, der den *Kanon* auszeichnet, und umgekehrt die Vielfalt, die die Rezeption des Kanons als *Schrift* bestimmt. – Daraus können wir nun aber auch Folgen für den exegetischen Umgang mit dem Kanon als Kanon ableiten. Sie lassen sich skizzieren, wenn wir das Kanonthema noch einmal aus einer anderen Perspektive in den Blick nehmen:

5. Von Gebrauch und Interpretation des Kanons

Die Unterscheidung von Gebrauch und Interpretation eines Textes stammt von Umberto Eco.[60] Sie ist so einsichtig, dass ich sie nicht erklären muss. Sie lässt sich für unsere Fragestellung fruchtbar machen, wenn wir sie auf eine

---

58 Vgl. in diesem Sinne gegenüber dem eingangs zitierten Urteil Ernst Käsemanns W. Härle, Dogmatik, Berlin/New York 1995, 134: „Die komplexe Bedeutung des biblischen Kanons wird angemessener beschrieben, wenn man sagt, daß er als solcher in der Vielzahl der Konfessionen bzw. kirchlichen Richtungen die Einheit der *Kirche* (sing.!) bewahrt" (Hervorhebung im Original).

59 Zur semantischen Grundlage der Unterscheidung zwischen Schrift und Kanon vgl. die Ausführungen bei Barton, Holy Writings (s. Anm. 2), 8ff.

60 Vgl. U. Eco, Lector in fabula. Die Mitarbeit der Interpretation in erzählenden Texten, München ³1998, 72ff.

andere Kategorie beziehen, die ebenfalls von U. Eco ins Spiel gebracht wurde: die Kategorie der *intentio operis*, bei der es sich um eine Größe handele, die gewissermaßen zwischen der Intention des Autors und der Intention des Lesers stehe[61]:

Die *intentio operis* ist demzufolge einerseits von der *intentio auctoris* unabhängig, denn sie hat mit der *intentio lectoris* gemeinsam, dass es sich bei ihr wie bei dieser um ein rezeptionshermeneutisches *Zuschreibungsphänomen* handelt. Eco spricht in diesem Zusammenhang von einer „Unterstellung seitens des Lesers"[62]. Text und Autor werden voneinander getrennt, und für die Frage nach dem Sinn eines Textes ist die ursprüngliche Absicht seines Autors völlig unerheblich. Andererseits geht die *intentio operis* eines Textes aber auch nicht in seiner Rezeption auf. Sie besteht nämlich gerade darin, dass der Leser dem Text unterstellt, einen Sinn zu haben, der von seiner eigenen Absicht *verschieden* ist. – Eco will mit dem Begriff der *intentio operis* demnach einen hermeneutischen Schwebezustand abbilden, den ich versuchsweise ,die doppelte Autonomie der Texte' nennen möchte: dass nämlich jeder Text sowohl gegenüber seinem empirischen Autor als auch gegenüber jedem potentiellen empirischen Leser autonom ist.

Wenn wir diese Überlegungen auf den neutestamentlichen Kanon übertragen, müssen wir zunächst das eingangs zitierte Dictum William Wredes[63] in einem wesentlichen Punkt korrigieren: Die Akzeptanz des neutestamentlichen Kanons als geschlossen und unantastbar bedeutet keineswegs, dass wir uns „damit der Autorität der Bischöfe und Theologen" des 2. bis 4. Jahrhunderts" unterwerfen. Sie sind zwar – wenn man so will – die ,Autoren' des Kanons, doch sind die produktionshermeneutischen Faktoren und Intentionen für die Rezeption des Kanons als geschlossen und unantastbar völlig irrelevant. Es ist vielmehr so, dass die mit dem Kanon existierenden Christen diesen immer mit der Unterstellung *gebrauchen*, dass er ihnen als identitätsstiftende Objektivation ihres kulturellen Gedächtnisses vorgegeben ist und dass eben dies dem Kanon einen Eigensinn gibt, der seine Autonomie gegenüber seinen ,Autoren' *und* gegenüber seinen Lesern konstituiert.

Und genau an dieser Stelle kommen dann die Exegese und die Unterscheidung zwischen Gebrauch und Interpretation eines Textes ins Spiel. Meistens ist es ja so, dass beim *Gebrauch* eines Textes die *intentio lectoris* leitend ist, während bei seiner *Interpretation* die Frage nach der *intentio auc-*

---

61 U. Eco, Überzogene Textinterpretation, in: ders., Zwischen Autor und Text. Interpretation und Überinterpretation, München 1996, 52–74, S. 71ff.; ders., Zwischen Autor und Text, in: ebd., 75–98, S. 76ff.
62 Ebd., 72.
63 S. o. S. 46.

toris im Vordergrund steht. Im Blick auf diese Unterscheidung möchte ich nun die naheliegende These aufstellen, dass Exegese allererst dann zu einer *theologischen* Exegese wird, wenn sie dem Kanon eine von den Absichten seiner Autoren und Leser unabhängige Intention, nämlich die beschriebene *intentio operis* unterstellt: wenn sie nämlich diese doppelte Unterscheidung für sich außer Kraft setzt und die *Interpretation* des Kanons als eine Weise seines *Gebrauchs* versteht. Und eben dies ermöglicht es der Exegese, im neutestamentlichen Kanon nicht lediglich eine historisch gewordene und darum unverbindliche Größe zu sehen, sondern ihm einen *theologischen* Status zuzuerkennen, und es verpflichtet sie auch dazu.

'Criteria of canonicity' and the Early Church

by Morwenna Ludlow

The question of how the Christian canon of Scripture was formed consists of several overlapping questions. First, are the historical questions: Which books became part of the canon? When did this happen? Was it as a result of pressures internal to or external to the Church? Secondly, come questions about the nature and significance of its formation: Was it mainly a process of inclusion or exclusion? Did the Church passively receive or actively create the canon? What criteria were involved in the selection of the books?

Theological as well as historical issues are raised by the second type of question – especially the last two, on which this paper will focus. In particular, I want to suggest that the very idea of asking about canonical *criteria* is misleading because it begs some of the other questions which I have listed above.[1] It seems to downplay the idea that much of the canon was the result of the Church's reception of traditional collections of books and it highlights the notion that the Church played a very active role in the creation of the canon. If this were the case, there might be two ways of finding out what criteria were involved in the creation of the canon. One could attempt to derive a common distinguishing factor from the collection of the books which we now know as the Bible. However, besides this being a very speculative approach, it seems extremely difficult to unite the many books of the Bible under one such criterion. Alternatively, one could look for evidence of early Church members' own reflections on the formation of the canon. Here, however, one encounters two problems. The first is that we have insufficient evidence of systematic reflection on the criteria of canonicity from an early enough period.[2] Of course we do have later reflection on whether such doubtful books as Hebrews should be included and whether the Gospel of Peter should be excluded. But, by the time of Irenaeus, a central core of New Tes-

---

1 Perhaps because of this some historical accounts are hesitant about using the term 'criteria': R.P.C. Hanson writes of 'norms of canonicity' (*Tradition in the Early Church*, London: SCM Press, 1962, p. 213); Gamble sometimes uses 'criteria', at others uses 'principles' (H. Gamble, *The New Testament Canon: its making and meaning*, Philadelphia: Fortress, 1985, pp. 67–72, esp. p. 71.

2 See Hanson, *Tradition in the Early Church* (see n. 1), p. 213

tament documents was already generally accepted by the Catholic church. Marcion may to some degree have hastened the formation of a more formal and explicit canon, but the reason why he caused such offence to writers such as Irenaeus and Tertullian was surely that the acceptance of, for example, the four Gospels, was very widespread in the Church at least by the time they were writing, even if it had not been when Marcion himself created his single gospel. Moreover, by Marcion's day the Church was *already* using allegorical exegesis in order to read the Old Testament through the perspective of the New – it was not a new technique designed in opposition to his ultra-literalism.[3] One can thus see Tertullian's logical point: if Marcion edited objectionable passages out of Scriptural texts and 'separated' Old from New Testaments, then he must have known some kind of collection of texts, albeit a very loose and informal one.[4] It was only when the Church's growing habit of treating its texts as some sort of corpus was challenged that it began to reflect on what it had. The Church thus did not react to Marcion by *creating* the first canon of the New Testament; it did, perhaps, react to Marcion by *reflecting* for the first time on the nature of the Scriptures it was already using.

This points to a second problem, which derives from the very nature of the process of canonisation itself. is not just that we lack documentary evidence about the early stages of the formation of the canon. In fact, the Church's self-conscious reflection on the canon of Scripture *always* began *in media res*: with regard to most books it was a question of explaining why it had what it had, rather than deciding on what it should have. Even with doubtful books, there was always some tradition of their use, however minor and short-lived – or the question of canonicity would not have arisen. No council sat down to choose the texts according to some pre-established set of criteria, just as a selection committee might decide on the sort of person they want to fill a post, before interviewing the candidates. Rather, there is some sense in which the canon chose (or formed) the Church, rather than the

---

3   For the view that Marcion was reacting against and trying to halt the Church's progression towards a relatively inclusive biblical canon see: J. Barton, *The Spirit and the Letter*, London: SPCK, 1997, ch. 2 *passim*. My assumptions in this paper about the history of the formation of the canon are greatly indebted to Barton's account.

4   *De praescr.* XXX 'For since Marcion separated the New Testament from the Old, he is (necessarily) subsequent to that which he separated, inasmuch as it was only in his power to separate what was (previously) united' (tr. P. Holmes, *The Ante-Nicene Fathers III: Tertullian*, Edinburgh: T&T Clark, 1997); *Adv. Marc.* IV:4 'if that gospel which among us is ascribed to Luke ... is the same that Marcion by his *Antitheses* accuses of having been falsified by the upholders of Judaism with a view to its being so combined in one body with the law and the prophets that they might also pretend that Christ had that origin, evidently he could only have brought accusation against something he had found there already' (tr. E. Evans, Tertullian *Adversus Marcionem*, Oxford: Clarendon Press, 1972).

Church chose (or formed) the canon. For this reason, then, the whole practice of talking about *criteria* of canonicity is called into question, for what seems to be happening – at least in part – is that the Church is formulating *reasons* or *explanations* for why it has what it has, not *criteria* for choosing what it should have in the future.

In this respect, the process of canonisation could be said to be more like a romance rather than a job interview. There is of course usually a degree to which one chooses one's romantic partner (and even on the verge of marriage one can always say 'no', in true Hollywood fashion). However, through being asked for one's reasons for the choice, one should be brought up against the fact that one was as much the chosen one as the chooser (this very fact, indeed, explains why in real life it is actually very difficult to say 'no' at the last minute). Furthermore, although each party can give retrospective *reasons* for their choice (he has a nice sense of humour, she's intelligent and sympathetic), these reasons seem neither to explain the mutual choice adequately, nor to be very important in comparison with the actual reality created by the choice. (It is a very common experience that one's relationships rarely match up to the criteria that one thought one had for them – and this is not always a disappointment!)

This analogy is, I hope, not entirely trivial. I will return to it in the course of discussing the important interplay between the Church's active and passive role in the formation of the canon. In particular, I want to argue that a study of the early Church's reflection on the canonical books shows that one needs to keep in balance *both* the Church's passive reception *and* its active creation of the canon of Scripture – however paradoxical that may sound. I am not, in other words, denying that at times the Church did *choose* which books should stay in and which should stay out. What I am suggesting, however, is that applying talk of *criteria* to this choice masks the more complex and mutually conditioning relationship between the early Church and its texts. For this reason, I will write mainly of *reasons why* canonicity was attributed, as opposed to 'criteria of canonicity'. The latter phrase fails to match up to the early Church writers' own perception of what they were doing and there is historical as well as theological value in attending to that issue. Whereas it may be impossible to reconstruct the precise history of how the canon came to be, it is possible – and perhaps equally instructive – to give an account of early Church views on the nature of what was going on.

Consequently, in the course of this paper I will focus on early Church writers' own reflections on whether certain books are acceptable or not. I will argue that these reveal the complex relationship between the Church's passive reception and active decisions about the texts, precisely through the way

in which the different reasons justifying canonicity are interrelated, overlap
and blend into each other. Thus, the very thing which seems to be a source of
frustration to some historians of the formation of the canon – that one cannot
draw up a neat list of 'canonical criteria' – becomes key to an understanding
of the canon's formation.

Clearly, this task is complicated by the fact that there is no Latin or Greek
word which is used in the early stages of the debate which exactly corresponds to the English 'canonical'. (The word κανών did not mean a list of
Scriptural texts until Athanasius' day.) However, it can be argued that from
the time of Irenaeus there was a *notion of canonicity*, by comparing how the
fathers write about core texts such as the Pauline epistles and how they describe doubtful and excluded books.[5] Consequently, by a 'canonical' text I
mean one considered in the early Church to be of key importance and to be
part of a collection of such key texts. This meaning clearly will carry with the
connotations that the text is inspired, authoritative, normative and of Scrip-
ture-like character, but it cannot be reduced to these (because there were inspired and authoritative texts which were not considered canonical, for example, and because in the earliest Christian period 'Scripture' referred only
to the Old Testament). The meaning of 'canonical' is thus of necessity rather
vague: precisely the issue here is that it was *not* the case that the early Church
had a concept of canonicity, and was in the process of working out what the
criteria for this should be and which books fitted the criteria. (The Church
was not like a group of children who decide to form a club, know they want
members, but are undecided both as to whom the members should be and
also as to what the criteria for membership might be.) There was no point at
which the notion of a 'club' of texts existed without a notion of which books
and what sort of books were 'clubbable'. Rather, the concept of canonicity
was being worked out at the same time as the canon was being formed. In
other words, in the third and fourth centuries, the early Church was not merely working out an answer to the question 'which books are canonical?'; they
were also only just beginning to formulate the question 'what is canonicity?'.

1. The Early Church's reflection on canonicity: a synthesis

Most commentators on the so-called 'canonical criteria' remark that they
were discussed and applied by the Fathers very unsystematically. Harry
Gamble's remark is typical:

---

5   See Hanson, *Tradition in the Early Church* (see n. 1), p. 130, 143.

'It should be clear that the principles of canonicity in the early church were numerous, diverse, and broadly defined, that their application was not systematic or thoroughly consistent, and that they were used in a variety of combinations.'[6]

Instead of simply making my own list of the factors which are usually cited as criteria of canonicity and commenting on which seem the most important, I would to like to suggest a synthesis which emphasises the logical relations between one factor and another, and between Scripture on the one hand and the canon of faith, the Church and Christian practices on the other. I shall try to deal with the Old and the New Testaments, although clearly some considerations will not apply equally to both. From the evidence of writers such as Irenaeus, Tertullian, Origen, Eusebius of Caesarea and Augustine, it will be shown that the early Church recognised three reasons for holding that a book was canonical: authentic and ancient authorship; appropriate Christian use (by which I mean catholic or universal use; traditional use and use in appropriate contexts), and orthodoxy. As Gamble suggests, these were complementary, not exclusive. I will explain below what I mean by these concepts and give an account of their interrelationships which I hope will reveal why the term 'criteria' is inappropriate. My suggestions are set out diagrammatically at the following figure:

Reasons for attributing canonicity to a text

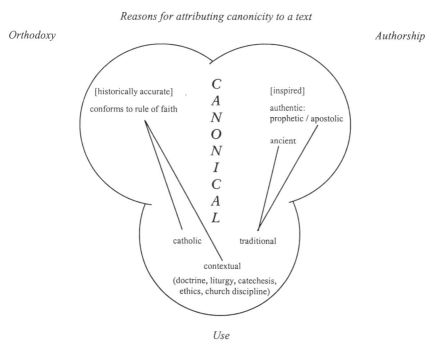

Orthodoxy   *Authorship*

[historically accurate]

conforms to rule of faith

C
A
N
O
N
I
C
A
L

[inspired]

authentic:
prophetic / apostolic

ancient

catholic   traditional

contextual

(doctrine, liturgy, catechesis,
ethics, church discipline)

Use

---

6   Gamble, *The New Testament Canon* (see n. 1), p. 71.

1.1. Authorship: ancient and authentic

Like many people in the ancient world, early Christians respected normative texts partly because they were ancient: antiquity was taken to denote reliability, either in the sense of historical accuracy, or in the sense that they had proved themselves as reliable guides to life. This applies more straightforwardly to the Old Testament which was obviously old and whose continued use was authorised by the practice of Paul and of Christ as reported in the Gospels. The reason applies less simply to the texts of the New Testament. As John Barton points out, clearly these were not originally used because they were old, because some were accepted as normative very quickly.[7] In time, however, it is true to say that antiquity became an important reason for canonicity, despite the difficulties of actually proving that a text was genuinely old.[8] For example, one of Tertullian's main arguments against Marcion rested on the assumption that a new version must necessarily be worse than an old:

'If it is agreed that that has the greater claim to truth which has the earlier priority, and that has the priority which has been so since the beginning, and that has been since the beginning which was from the apostles, there will be no less agreement that that was handed down by the apostles which is held sacred and inviolate in the churches the apostles founded.'[9]

This reason has its problems: on other occasions Tertullian is forced to explain why old heresies are still bad and why the New Testament, though an innovation, is nevertheless good![10] However, both these difficult cases – and the quotation above – underline what is fundamentally important about the antiquity reason with regard to the New Testament: older texts are more reliable because of their apostolic origin (i.e. their more reliable witness to Christ) *and* their safekeeping in the Churches established by the apostles.[11] We will return to this theme again when discussing traditional use.

By 'authenticity' I mean firstly that where a book is attributed to a particular author, the attribution is assumed to be correct. Although the nature and status of pseudonymous literature in the late antique world is hotly de-

---

7   Barton, *The Spirit and the Letter* (see n. 3), p. 67
8   F.F. Bruce, *The Canon of Scripture*, Glasgow: Chapter House, 1988, p. 260.
9   Tertullian *Adv. Marc.* IV:5; see also *Adv. Marc.* IV:4, *De praescr.* XXX, XXXVII.
10 Tertullian *De praescr.* XXXIV; *Adv. Marc.* IV:1.
11 H.v. Campenhausen uses this overlap between the antiquity and the apostolicity criteria to claim that what was important about the apostles' role was their eye-witness to Christ and not their apostolic commission by Christ (*The Formation of the Christian Bible*, London: Adam & Charles Black, 1972, p. 254). This is an exaggeration, being undermined, for example, by Tertullian's emphasis on the role of the apostles 'sent out' to transmit the rule of faith (*De praescr.* XX).

bated it seems unlikely that a New Testament book would have been accepted as Scripture if it had been openly acknowledged to be pseudonymous. Of course, many Scriptural books have no attribution: anonymity was not in itself seen as a problem, although in fact traditions about the authorship of unattributed books quickly grew up. Tertullian's reaction to the anonymity of Marcion's single Gospel suggests a certain amount of discomfort about the idea of a canonical text with no apparent author.[12]

On top of this, I also use 'authentic' to mean that the author of a particular book is taken to be either prophetic or apostolic.[13] Prophetic writers include Moses (presumed by all early Church writers to be the author of the Pentateuch), David (presumed author of the Psalms) and Solomon (supposed by all to have written Proverbs, Song of Songs and Ecclesiastes, and by some to have written Wisdom and Ecclesiasticus). Sometimes, however, 'prophetic' is not so much a reason for a book's canonicity as a characteristic attributed to canonical books. For example, even though Augustine seems to realise that some people reject Wisdom and Ecclesiasticus because they were not written by Solomon, he accepts them as canonical because of a tradition of Church use. His description of Ecclesiasticus' author as 'the prophet' seems to be a consequence of, not an argument for the book's canonicity.[14] Similarly, Origen, in his discussion of the concept of 'gospel' in his *Commentary on John*, seems to imply that apostles are apostles because of what they wrote (i.e. the Gospel, in the sense of 'exhortations intended to produce faith in the things Jesus accomplished'), *not* that a gospel is defined as something written by an apostle.[15]

Apostolicity is a notoriously loose reason for a text's canonicity: it includes not only authorship by an apostle, but also a reliable transmission

---

12 *Adv. Marc.* IV:2.
13 For the division of biblical writers into prophets and apostles see the Muratorian fragment §73 (e.g. in B.M. Metzger, *The Canon of the New Testament,* Oxford: Clarendon Press, 1987, p. 307) and Augustine, *De civitate Dei* 11.3: 'This Mediator [the Son] spoke in former times through the prophets and later through his own mouth, and after that through the apostles ...' (tr. H. Bettenson, *Augustine Concerning the City of God Against the Pagans*, Harmondsworth: Penguin books, 1972).
14 See A.-M. La Bonnardière, 'The Canon of Sacred Scripture', in: P. Bright (ed. and tr.), *Augustine and the Bible*, Notre Dame: University of Notre Dame Press, 1999, p. 33. La Bonnardière implies that the references to 'the prophet' indicate that Ecclesiasticus 'belonged to the prophetic literary genre'. Although Augustine does make a *historia – prophetia* distinction amongst Old Testament books, he also distinguishes between the Old and New Testaments as those written by the prophets and the apostles (see above n. 13) and I think that it is that distinction which is relevant here. Authorship by a prophet or apostle seems to connote inspiration and both appear to be a corollary of canonicity, not vice versa. Hence, the claim that Ecclesiasticus contains 'prophetic words' emphasises for the reader that Augustine accepts its canonical status.
15 Origen, *Comm. on John* I:18 (tr. J.W. Trigg, *Origen*, London: Routledge, 1998, p. 108).

from an apostle – preferably a traceable connection from a specific apostle.
Hence Irenaeus writes that Mark was 'the interpreter and follower of Peter'
and that Luke 'was inseparable from Paul and his fellow-labourer in the Gospel'.[16] Tertullian distinguishes between the twelve 'apostles' (*apostoli*) who
were given the commission to preach the Gospel to all nations by Christ and
'apostolic men' (*apostolici*) who were companions of those original apostles.
Thus:

> 'From among the apostles the faith is introduced to us by John and by Matthew, while from
> among apostolic men Luke and Mark give it renewal, <all of them> beginning with the same
> rules <of belief> (*regulis*), as far as relates to the one only God, the Creator, and to his
> Christ, born of a virgin, the fulfilment of the law and the prophets. It matters not that the ar-
> rangement of their narrative varies, so long as there is agreement on the essentials of the faith
> – and on these they show no agreement with Marcion.'[17]

Irenaeus and Tertullian both argue for the apostolicity of Paul, locating in it
two things.[18] First they stress his commission from Christ, both citing the beginning of Galatians 'Paul an apostle – not from men nor through man, but
from Jesus Christ ...' which they presumably connect with Paul's Damascus
road experience.[19] Secondly, they locate Paul's apostolicity in the fact that
his authority derives from the Gospel itself and the truthfulness with which
he reported it.

> 'For [Paul's] intention in going up to Jerusalem to know and to consult the apostles, was lest
> perchance he had run in vain – that is lest perchance he had not believed as they did, or were
> not preaching the gospel in their manner. At length, when he had conferred with the original
> <apostles> (*cum auctoribus*), and there was agreement concerning the rule of faith, they
> joined the right hands <of fellowship>, and thenceforth divided spheres of preaching the
> gospel ...'[20]

These examples reveal three things. First, they very clearly show that many
people thought that there was something very special about the original apostles' witness to Christ and/or their commission by Christ.[21] Apostolicity thus

---

16 *Adv. Haer.* III:10:5; III:14:1; see also III:1:1 (tr. A. Roberts/J. Donaldson, *The Ante-
    Nicene Fathers. I: The Apostolic Fathers with Justin and Irenaeus*, Edinburgh: T&T
    Clark, 1975).

17 *Adv. Marc.* IV:2.

18 Their Marcionite opponents thought that Paul was the only true apostle (see e.g.
    Irenaeus, *Adv. Haer.* III:1:1; Tertullian, *Adv. Marc.* V:1); consequently, Irenaeus and
    Tertullian are not so much arguing that Paul was an apostle, but that he was an apostle
    in substantially the same sense as the other apostles.

19 Irenaeus, *Adv. Haer.* III:13:2; Tertullian, *Adv. Marc.* V:1. Tertullian follows this up with
    typological evidence from the Old Testament which he claims points to Paul, lest
    Marcionites should doubt the authority of self-attribution.

20 *Adv. Marc.* IV:3; the same story from Gal. 2:1–2 is used by Irenaeus, *Adv. Haer.*
    III:13:3.

21 This is sometimes illustrated with the account of Papias going to great lengths to inter-

became an important reason for canonicity. Second, the Gospel writers and Paul were from very early on accepted as special witnesses and, as it were, granted apostolicity *de facto*, even if they were not believed to be apostles *de jure*. Third, another type of reason has crept in: orthodoxy as judged by the rule of faith. Although Gamble is right to say that 'it would have been non-sensical for the early church to have *inquired* ... *into* the orthodoxy of Paul', it is nevertheless the case that writers felt the need to *defend* the orthodoxy of Paul and the Gospel authors in their unexpurgated form against Marcion, and the way they did this was to insist (as in the above passage) that all these writers shared the original – and apostolic – rule of faith.[22] After all, what was important about apostolicity was what the apostles witnessed, not the men themselves.[23] Furthermore, as we shall see later, the apostolicity of certain gnostic texts was denied not by using the reasons of apostolic authorship or divine inspiration (which the gnostics could themselves easily claim), but on the grounds that they were not consonant with the rule of faith and they were not transmitted by the open and universal Christian tradition.

The looseness of the principle of apostolicity can, I think be attributed to its importance: precisely because it was felt that all, or most, New Testament writers should be apostolic, the principle was stretched to fit. The problem with this is that it ceased to become a very useful reason for attributing canonicity to a text and discussions of the antiquity, use or orthodoxy of a text overtook it. One might even suggest that apostolicity became a *corollary* of canonicity with regard to New Testament texts in the same way that prophetic authorship became a corollary of canonicity with regard to Old Testament texts.[24] Both imply divine inspiration, which several commentators have noted is a corollary of canonicity.[25] And, like inspiration, apostolicity was never a sufficient reason for canonicity. Both seem to lead to an assumption of historical accuracy (apostles are true eye-witnesses; the divinely-inspired writer speaks the truth). Finally, inspiration played for the Eastern church a similar role in discussions of the New Testament to that which Ap-

---

view people who remembered the apostles (e.g. H. Chadwick, 'The Bible and the Greek Fathers', in: D.E. Nineham [ed.], *The Church's Use of the Bible,* London: SPCK, 1963, p. 35–36).

22 Gamble, *The New Testament Canon* (see n. 1), p. 70 (my emphasis). See also Chadwick, 'The Bible and the Greek Fathers' (see n. 21), p. 33.

23 See L. McDonald, *The Formation of the Christian Biblical Canon,* Peabody, Mass.: Hendrickson, [2]1995, p. 233; v. Campenhausen, *The Formation of the Christian Bible* (see n. 11), p. 254.

24 Bruce seems to suggest this when he points out that where the canonicity of 2 John and Revelation was doubted, then their apostolicity was too (*The Canon of Scripture* [see n. 8], p. 258).

25 See e.g. Bruce, *The Canon of Scripture* (see n. 8), p. 264–268; Gamble, *The New Testament Canon* (see n. 1), p. 71–72.

ostolicity did in the West – although the latter was a rather narrower principle.[26]

In sum, the patristic notions of prophetic authorship and of apostolicity seem to rely (albeit in slightly different ways) more on the ancient origin of a text, its harmony with the apostolic rule of faith and its transmission and use by the apostolic succession of the Church than on genuine prophetic or apostolic authorship.

1.2. Use

Within this category I have distinguished traditional, catholic and contextual use, although patristic writers themselves do not always make these distinctions. Notably, however, Eusebius distinguishes the contemporary use of a text from its ancient use, rejecting the former as a good reason for canonicity.[27] Significantly, most of the books he dismisses on these grounds are those – like James, 2 Peter, and the *Acts*, *Gospel*, *Preaching* and *Apocalypse of Peter* – which claimed apostolic authorship: in other words, as we suggested above, a claim to apostolic authorship needed, in the eyes of the more acute church Fathers, to be backed up by a text's ancient provenance.[28] Hence, Richard P.C. Hanson claims that 'what matters above all to Eusebius for establishing canonicity is early attestation or antiquity; recognition by the Church contemporary with Eusebius hardly matters at all.'[29]

However, this statement needs to be qualified slightly. First, although use by the contemporary Church is not given the prominence that it is given by Augustine, for example, it presumably *did* matter to some extent: it would be very strange for someone in Eusebius' day to claim as canonical a book which hardly anyone still used. It is simply the case that he thought that common current use was not a *sufficient* reason for canonicity. Secondly, as is implicit in Hanson's account, it is knowledge of a book's ancient *use* which is important, not just the knowledge that a book is ancient. Thus we read that the elders of old made 'frequent use' of 1 Peter, that 1 John was used by ancient writers and that Hebrews and Hermas' *Shepherd* was used by

---

26 Bruce, *The Canon of Scripture* (see n. 8), p. 264; J.N.D. Kelly, 'The Bible and the Latin Fathers', in: Nineham (ed.), *The Church's Use of the Bible* (see n. 21), p. 33–34. Historical accuracy seems also to be a corollary of a text being called prophetic or apostolic: hence historical accuracy and inspiration are indicated on my diagram only parenthetically.
27 Hanson, *Tradition in the Early Church* (see n. 1), p. 215–216.
28 Hanson, *Tradition in the Early Church* (see n. 1), p. 215.
29 Hanson, *Tradition in the Early Church* (see n. 1), p. 216.

some ancient writers.[30] Connected to the concept of ancient use is the claim that a text has (or has not) been handed down by tradition, because this carries the implication that the book was handed down for some purpose. Slightly different from this are the notions that a book was accepted as canonical in ancient times and that there has been a tradition of regarding certain books as canonical: these indicate a consensus of opinion on the status of a book more than a common use of it. Just as Augustine thinks that contemporary consensus is important, so for Eusebius a diachronic consensus is key.[31] In fact, the idea of consensus and common use do overlap and Eusebius seems to drift between the two: his common phrase 'is/are accepted' appears to cover both.

The fact that Eusebius is not just concerned with the ancient attestation of a text is clear from the way he is also interested in the *different sorts of use* which he thinks are appropriate or in appropriate for canonical texts: an archetype of good use, for example, is the citation of a text by approved ancient Christian writers in their own theological works. Other authors, recognising the fact that Christians continued to use texts which they did not regard in precisely the same way as the unquestionably central books (like the gospels), attempted to distinguish between different sorts of use (or contexts of use) according to whether they were appropriate for canonical books or not. A good example is Jerome: 'while admitting that the Church reads books like Wisdom and Ecclesiasticus which are strictly non-canonical, he insists on their being used solely "for edifying the people, not for the corroboration of ecclesiastical doctrines".'[32] This could be more a nominal than an actual distinction: John Norman Davidson Kelly admits that Jerome 'continued to cite [non-canonical books] as if they were Scripture'![33] Nevertheless, there is at least a *conceptual* distinction evident here. With regard to more recent writings, Rufinus, states that the *Shepherd* of Hermas and the *Didache* are 'ecclesiastical' but not canonical: by this he means that they can be read in Church, but 'appeal should not be made to them on points of faith'[34].

Another type of use considered particularly appropriate for canonical texts was their reading in the course of Church liturgy. In particular, the Muratorian fragment emphasises this, stating that, for example, some do not

---

30   Eusebius, *Hist. Eccl.* III:3:1; III:24:17; III:38:1–3; III:3:6, cited in Hanson, *Tradition in the Early Church* (see n. 1), p. 215–216.

31   See Augustine, *De doctrina Christiana* II:25.

32   J.N.D. Kelly, *Jerome,* London: Duckworth 1975, p. 160–161, quoting Jerome's *Preface to Solomon's Books* (Vulgate); PL 28,1242f. See also Bruce, *The Canon of Scripture* (see n. 8), p. 269.

33   Kelly, *Jerome* (see n. 32), p. 161.

34   Rufinus, *Exposition of the Apostles' Creed* (Metzger, *Canon* [see n. 13], p. 234).

wish the *Apocalypse of Peter* to be read in Church.[35] There is a similar problem with Hermas' *Shepherd*:

'It ought indeed to be read; but it cannot be read publicly to the people in Church either among the prophets, whose number is complete, or among the apostles, for it is after their time.'[36]

The writer of the fragment also suggests that another sort of use had become a *de facto* reason for canonicity: although the informal style of the letters to Philemon, Titus and Timothy might make them borderline candidates for canonicity, nevertheless he concludes that they are canonical because they 'are held sacred in the esteem of the Church for the regulation of Ecclesiastical discipline'.[37]

Catechesis is another important Church activity which seems to have an effect on the way in which certain texts were regarded. John Barton notes, for example, that some books such as Wisdom which did not belong to the Jewish canon were read to Christian catechumens: this practice might explain their later inclusion in some, but not all, Christian canons.[38]

It would be obvious to any early Christian writer that 'all Scripture, being inspired by God, is useful and profitable for teaching, for reproof, for correction, and for training in righteousness' (2 Tim 3:16). The problem is that 'usefulness' could never be a *sufficient* reason for canonicity, because it could easily include too much. Nevertheless, the examples we have studied seem to show attempts – albeit unsystematic – to establish some sort of hierarchy of use. Thus, just as ancient use was more important than contemporary use, the quotation of books by authoritative Christian writers to settle points of doctrine and the Church's use of a text in liturgy were more significant than a text's use for catechesis, moral advice or Church discipline.

Interestingly, while the use of a text in an appropriate context was taken as a reason for (or, perhaps, an indication of) its canonicity, the utter uselessness of a text was sometimes appealed to, at least rhetorically, to exclude some texts. Most strikingly, Irenaeus' and Tertullian's sarcastic attacks on the gnostics' systems (and by implication their texts) take this line.

'Who would not spend his whole fortune to learn that from the tears of Desire ... originated seas and springs and everything wet?'[39]
'If in any instance mirth be excited, this will be quite as much as the subject deserves ... Vain and silly topics are met with especial fitness by laughter.'[40]

---

35 Muratorian frg. § 72.
36 Muratorian frg. §§ 77–80.
37 Muratorian frg. § 62–63.
38 Barton, *Spirit* (see n. 3), Ch. 2.
39 Irenaeus, *Adv. Haer.* I:4:3.
40 Tertullian, *Adv. Val.* 7 (tr. A. Roberts, *The Ante-Nicene Fathers III* [see n. 4]).

Christian authors could also argue that the gnostics' texts were worse than useless – that they led people astray both in doctrine and morals.[41]

The problem with these approaches, however, was that opponents could easily turn round and point to apparently useless or immoral passages in the Scriptures accepted by Christians – especially in the Old Testament. This was particularly Marcion's argument, of course.[42] Irenaeus and Tertullian were well aware of this difficulty and in reply they insisted that their opponents were not reading Scripture properly. Thus the whole issue of what was the proper 'use' or reading of Scripture was in dispute, and Irenaeus and Tertullian had to appeal to a different reason: consequently, they tended to defend their 'canon' of Scripture according to the measure of orthodoxy, or agreement with the rule of faith, and they developed a hermeneutical method based on that which would govern the correct reading or use of the text. Similarly, Origen openly admits that heretics reject various parts of Scripture precisely because they cannot find them useful.[43] He therefore explicitly bases his hermeneutics on the assumption that *all* canonical Scripture is useful and that all apparent 'impossibilities' have a spiritual meaning. Origen too needs a measure for the proper reading of the biblical texts and, therefore, for keeping them in the canon. This measure is again the rule of faith. For Origen, the concept of usefulness is a corollary of canonicity and can no longer be seen as a reason for it.

Hans von Campenhausen famously concluded of patristic views of canonicity that 'in practice the crucial factor is clearly the usage and judgment of the one true Church, spread throughout the world'.[44] However, there are problems with this conclusion. Although we have good reason to think that certain 'doubtful' books were eventually accepted precisely because of their widespread use, we have seen the caution of people like Tertullian, Irenaeus and Origen. Even later Church fathers themselves realised that the idea of catholic use could not be applied with ease as a reason for canonicity. In the following passage, for example, Augustine, struggles between his typical desire for neatness and the difficult facts of the case:

'In the matter of the canonical Scriptures [the most expert investigator of the divine Scriptures] should follow the authority of the great majority of catholic churches, including of course those that were found worthy to have apostolic seats and receive apostolic letters. He

---

41 See, for example, Irenaeus, *Adv. Haer.* I:25:4–5.
42 Irenaeus, *Adv. Haer.* I:27:7: 'Marcion ... developed his teaching by impudently blaspheming the God announced by the law and the prophets, calling him the creator of evils, desirous of wars, inconstant in his thoughts and contradicting himself.'
43 See *Philokalia* 11:1:4.
44 v. Campenhausen, *The Formation of the Christian Bible* (see n. 11), p. 260–261. He thought that antiquity was an important, but ultimately less decisive factor.

will apply this principle to the canonical scriptures: to prefer those accepted by all catholic churches to those which some do not accept. As for those not universally accepted, he should prefer those accepted by a majority of churches, and by the more authoritative ones, to those supported by fewer churches, or by churches of lesser authority. Should he find that some scriptures are accepted by the majority of churches and others by the more authoritative ones (though in fact he could not possibly find this situation) I think that they should be considered to have equal authority.'[45]

What is extraordinary about this passage is that Augustine reverts to no other reason to resolve problem books, but is happy to leave the question slightly open. It also suggests a willingness to accept that some books are more central than others, whilst accepting that all might be canonical.

It is notable here that it is the earlier writers such as Tertullian, Irenaeus and Origen who are most cautious about seeing the usage of a text as a reason for attributing canonicity to a text. Precisely their problem was that some texts which they regarded as central to the catholic faith were used by people they did not regard as catholic. Consequently, they turned to orthodoxy as a means both of affirming the canonicity of certain texts and of excluding believers they thought were heretical. Irenaeus in particular frequently claims that the tradition of the apostles is universal in the Church.[46] What he rarely does, however, is claim the same sort of universality specifically for the use of Scripture. Although he may think that the one Church possesses one collection of canonical texts, it is fairly clear that in his eyes that is not what *makes* them canonical. This seems to be in contrast with the rule of faith, the universality of which does appear to be an indication of its truth: 'Therefore the proclamation of the church is true and solid, since in it one and the same way of salvation is shown forth in the whole world'.[47] When Tertullian argues that 'it ought clearly to be seen to whom belongs the possession of the Scriptures, that none may be admitted to the use thereof who has no title at all to the privilege' he implies that the 'correct title' is orthodoxy, that is the possession of the rule of faith, inherited, like the Scriptures, from the apostles.[48] By the time of Augustine, both the structures of the Church (now a state institution) and the formalised decrees of Councils made it (relatively) clear who was a catholic or not. He, therefore, could more confidently turn to

---

45 Augustine, *De doctrina Christiana* II:25 (tr. R.P.H. Green, Saint Augustine, *On Christian Teaching* [Oxford World's Classics], Oxford: Oxford University Press, 1997).

46 E.g. *Adv. Haer.* I:10:1: 'The Church, dispersed throughout the world to the ends of the earth, received from the apostles and their disciples the faith in one God the Father Almighty' (i.e. the rule of faith); III:3:2: 'Thus the tradition of the apostles [= the rule of faith], manifest in the whole world, is present in every church to be perceived by all who wish to see the truth'; IV:33:8: 'This is true gnosis: the teaching of the apostles and the ancient institution of the church, spread throughout the whole world'.

47 *Adv. Haer.* V:20:1.

48 Tertullian, *De praescr.* XV.

the notion of 'catholic use' as a reason for attributing canonicity. Eusebius, who accepts the notion of ancient catholic use, but is uncertain about the helpfulness of contemporary catholic use perhaps marks a transition between these two points.

1.3. Orthodoxy

As we have seen, there is good evidence that orthodoxy was an important reason for canonicity. This is particularly clear when the apostolicity of a text was doubtful. Thus Origen famously argued for the canonical use of Hebrews because its thoughts were 'admirable', despite thinking that Paul was not the author.[49] Eusebius dismissed the supposedly apostolic gospels of Peter, Thomas, Matthias, and the Acts of Andrew and of John because (amongst other reasons) 'the thought and purport of their contents are completely out of harmony with true orthodoxy and clearly show they themselves that they are the forgeries of heretics'.[50] Even where most people in fact believed that an apostle had written a text, this was not necessarily the most important reason for it being regarded as canonical.[51]

But to say that orthodoxy is a reason for the canonicity of a particular text is to say that that a canonical text is harmonious with some standard of orthodoxy which is external to it.[52] What was that standard for the early Church?

One candidate is historical reliability: a text is canonical if it truly tells the history of the Christ-event (including the pre-history of that event as told in the Old Testament). But the Church had little access to any such standard for historical verisimilitude, for the texts themselves were for the most part their only historical evidence. Some forms of the rule of faith, as we shall see, contained the broad brush-strokes of the history of Christ and this would rule out some of the more extravagant gnostic fantasy-scriptures; but it would otherwise not be very useful as a purely *historical* principle. Given the limited resources that early Church writers had to verify historical events, it would be almost useless applied to the Old Testament and of only limited use with regard to Epistles. Furthermore, to use a historical reason for attributing canonicity would be to miss part of the point of scriptural texts: although a reliable

---

49 Origen quoted by Eusebius, *Hist. Eccl.* VI:25:12 (Metzger, *Canon* [see n. 13], p. 308).
50 Eusebius, *Hist Eccl.* III:25:7 (Metzger, *Canon* [see n. 13], p. 310).
51 J.N. Sanders has argued that Irenaeus enthusiastic defence of John's Gospel was more on doctrinal grounds than because of its alleged apostolicity (*The Fourth Gospel in the Early Church*, Cambridge: Cambridge University Press, 1943, pp. 66–84; cited by Hanson, *Tradition in the Early Church* (see n. 1), p. 217.
52 Gamble. *The New Testament Canon* (see n. 1), p. 69.

witness to Christ was important (hence the importance of apostolicity), that witness cannot be reduced to a mere historical account. The earliest Gospels were already interpretations of the event and exhortations to respond to it, and patristic theologians treated them as such.[53] In fact, the Church tended to assume that whatever was canonical was, for the most part, historical. But patristic exegesis – both allegorical and typological – shows both that historical meaning was not the only or the primary meaning, and that those events which were frankly impossible, historically speaking, were explained in other terms. In other words, historical impossibilities seem not to have been used as a reason for rejecting a text, provided that there were other good reasons for accepting it.

So, it is fairly clear that the reasons for rejecting a text as unorthodox and therefore non-canonical were not so much historical as, broadly speaking, dogmatic. What then was the criterion of dogmatic orthodoxy? In a period of the Church before conciliar pronouncements on doctrine the only possible standard was the rule, or canon, of faith. We have seen above how Tertullian and Irenaeus defend the apostolicity of Paul by reference to the rule of faith shared between him and the other apostles; we also noted that the usefulness of the Scriptures was defended by Irenaeus by means of the concept of the rule of faith. In addition, the rule of faith lay behind the idea of the catholic Church which possessed and used the canonical Scriptures. But how did the rule of faith function more specifically as a reason for attributing canonicity?

On first inspection it is very easy to apply: texts which conform to the rule of faith are included, texts which do not are excluded. Tertullian seems to be implying this when he boldly asserts:

'For wherever it shall be manifest that the true Christian rule and faith shall be, *there* will likewise be the true Scriptures and expositions thereof, and all the Christian traditions.'[54]

Conversely, 'where diversity of doctrine is found, *there*, then, must the corruption both of the Scriptures and the expositions thereof be regarded as existing'.[55] Similarly, Irenaeus argues that the Scriptures 'can be clearly, unambiguously, and understood by all' to teach that 'one only God, to the exclusion of all others, formed all things by his Word' – the idea of one God, Father of Jesus Christ being the basis of his version of the rule of faith.[56] The rule of faith is understood by Irenaeus not just in terms of a (fairly loose)

---

53 See e.g. Origen, *Comm. on John* I:18, I:21 (tr. Trigg, *Origen* [see n. 15], pp. 108,109). Origen's description of John as the 'first-fruits of the gospels' suggests that it is the summit of four different interpretations of the Gospel of Christ.

54 Tertullian, *De praescr.* XIX.

55 Tertullian, *De praescr.* XXXVII.

56 Irenaeus, *Adv. Haer.* II:27:2.

doctrinal proposition, but also as a deposit of salvific teaching from Christ via the apostles:

> 'For indeed the Lord of all gave to his apostles the power of the gospel; and by them we have known the truth, i.e. the teaching of the Son of God ... [This Gospel] was both in the first place preached by them, and afterwards by the will of God handed down to us in the Scriptures, to be the ground and pillar of our faith.'[57]

This idea of the rule of faith seems to be the reason why Bishop Serapion made his judgment against the *Gospel of Peter*. According to Eusebius he commented that 'most of it is in accordance with the true teaching of the Saviour, but some things are additions to that teaching'; it seems that he subsequently banned the use of that book.[58]

However there are several problems with the use of the rule of faith as a reason for attributing canonicity. First, it clearly includes books which were not regarded as canonical. The examples of Jerome and Rufinus, mentioned above show this nicely: Wisdom and Ecclesiasticus are edifying, but not canonical; Hermas' *Shepherd* and the *Didache* can be read in church but cannot be used to ground doctrine. Presumably, then, if books were regarded as fit to read in Church or as moral guides they were not diametrically opposed to orthodoxy – even if they were not clear enough to be used for grounding doctrine. Hence, despite the fact that, as we noted above, the notion of orthodoxy can be seen to lie behind some appeals to catholicity and use in an appropriate context as criteria for canonicity and that orthodoxy was used as a criterion to prove the apostolicity of a text (in the broad sense), one must resist the temptation to think that orthodoxy is the 'root' of all the other reasons for attributing canonicity to a text. For the examples of Jerome and Rufinus show that although orthodoxy may be a necessary reason for asserting a text's canonicity, it cannot be a sufficient reason, because it includes too much.

Secondly, as I have already suggested, although the principle of orthodoxy might seem to *include* too much, it might also, on a strict interpretation, *exclude* too much. Even though it is probably obvious that one should read the Old and New Testaments as referring to the same God, it is not clear that the Old Testament refers to God specifically as the Father of Jesus Christ, as even the minimal interpretations of the rule of faith would seem to require. Even if one ignores Marcion's point about the supposed immorality of God in the Old Testament, his main criticism has some force: why should Christians retain it in their canon? In fact, we can see from the work of Irenaeus and

---

57 Irenaeus, *Adv. Haer.* III:1:1.
58 Eusebius, *Hist. Eccl.* VI:12:3 (tr. Metzger *Canon* [see n. 13], p. 119). This episode is interesting because of its earliness (c. 200) and because it shows a Bishop who clearly thinks that he has Episcopal authority in matters such as the use of Scripture.

Origen in particular that with regard to the Old Testament the rule of faith was not a reason for attributing canonicity to texts, but was a criterion for reading books which were *already* assumed to be canonical.[59] This was especially the case with books such as the Song of Songs and Job which were difficult to fit into a model of the Old Testament as a depiction of the salvation-history leading up to Christ.

This problem with the Old Testament points to a third and broader difficulty: it might be thought that the canon of what we now call the Bible is so diverse that it would be surprising if any one notion of orthodoxy could apply to it all. There are two replies to this, however. First, as I have already mentioned, Gamble stresses that the notion of orthodoxy according to the canon of faith was never applied to the central core of accepted books: rather it was applied mainly to doubtful books and usually then with the aim of excluding unorthodox texts rather than including further orthodox books.[60] Second, it can be argued that the rule of faith is in fact a more general and loose concept than is sometimes assumed. Perhaps then it is flexible enough to apply to the whole Bible, or at least the whole New Testament. This line of argument is supported by the fact that although some passages in writers like Tertullian give an extended and quasi-creedal account of the rule of faith[61], others suggest a more general approach:

'Jesus Christ our Lord ... did, whilst he lived on earth, himself declare what he was, what he had been, what the Father's will was which he was administering, what the duty of man was which he was prescribing ...'[62]

---

59 On Origen see R.P.C. Hanson, *Origen's Doctrine of Tradition*, London: SPCK, 1984, p. 91–113.

60 Gamble, *The New Testament Canon* (see n. 1), p. 70.

61 Tertullian, *De praescr.* XIII: 'Now with regard to this rule of faith – that we may from this point acknowledge that it is which we defend – it is, you must know, that which prescribes the belief that there is one only God and that he is none other than the creator of the world, who produced all things out of nothing through his own Word, first of all sent forth; that this Word is called his Son, *and*, under the name of God, was seen "in diverse manners" by the patriarchs, heard at all times in the prophets, at last brought down by the Spirit and Power of the Father into the Virgin Mary, was made flesh in her womb, and, being born of her, went forth as Jesus Christ; thenceforth he preached the new law and the new promise of the kingdom of heaven, worked miracles; having been crucified, he rose again the third day; (then) having ascended into the heavens, he sat at the right hand of the Father; sent instead of Himself the Power of the Holy Ghost to lead such as believe; will come again with glory to take the saints to the enjoyment of everlasting life and of the heavenly promises, and to condemn the wicked to everlasting fire, after the resurrection of both these classes shall have happened, together with the resurrection of their flesh. This rule, as it will be proved, was taught by Christ, and raises amongst ourselves no other questions than those which heresies introduce, and which make men heretics.'

62 Tertullian, *De praescr.* XX; see also *Adv. Marc.* IV:2, quoted above (see n. 17).

This general approach to the rule of faith is even more evident in Irenaeus, for whom the rule can be briefly summarised as the confession of the unity of God the Creator with God the Saviour, Jesus Christ. This for him is the equivalent of 'the truth', 'the Gospel' (as opposed to the four gospels), 'tradition' and the content of the sayings of Jesus.[63] Furthermore, it is particularly clear that Irenaeus used the rule of faith at least as much to convict his opponents for their interpretation of the Scriptures, as for their doctrinal propositions.[64] In other words it had become a hermeneutical principle for the reading of Scripture, which required the canonical texts to be read together and in the right order. It must therefore by necessity be a flexible enough principle to be applied to the whole Bible. To the extent that this principle forbade additions or mutilations to the text it functioned as a reason for attributing canonicity, but to the extent that it was a principle of interpretation it clearly applied to that which was *already* assumed to be canonical. Similarly, it has been convincingly argued that Origen's concept of the rule of faith was not a 'list of articles of belief or creed' but a more general hermeneutical proposition.[65] Hence, the claim that the Bible is too diverse to be judged, or rather read, according to the rule of faith is not, I think, so serious as one might at first expect. However, it does raise the problem that once the rule of faith is used as a hermeneutical rule it ceases to be a reason for attributing canonicity to a text, because it necessarily applies to all books which are *already* regarded as canonical: its function is, in effect, to enable Christians to keep within the canon those texts which might be treated by the less sympathetic as non-canonical.

Irenaeus' account of the rule of faith also raises a fourth problem; for in his *Adversus Haereses* it becomes clear that Scripture and the rule of faith are mutually related. Although he sometimes suggests that Scripture is record of the rule of faith, at other times he asserts that the rule of faith is derived from, or at least founded on, Scripture. However, this is not as paradoxical as it first seems. Rather, it seems to point to a situation in which Christianity first ex-

---

63 See e.g. J.N.D. Kelly, *Early Christian Creeds*, London: Longmans, Green and Co., 1950, p. 76: '[Irenaeus] favourite word for designating [the substance of tradition] was 'the canon of the truth', by which he did not mean a single universally accepted creed, or indeed any kind of formula as such, but rather the doctrinal content of the Christian faith as handed down in the Catholic Church.'

64 See, for example, A.Y. Reed, 'ΕΥΑΓΓΕΛΙΟΝ: Orality, Textuality, and the Christian Truth in Irenaeus' *Adversus Haereses*', *VigChr* 56 (2002) 11–46, pp. 13–14: 'For Irenaeus, the κανών functions as an extratextual criterion for distinguishing true doctrine from heretical speculations, authentic texts from spurious compositions, and proper Scriptural interpretation from "evil exegesis". ... He never equates κανών directly with any texts at all. Rather, his articulation of this concept within *Adversus haereses* privileges the issue of proper interpretation over the issue of text selection.'

65 Hanson, *Origen's Doctrine of Tradition* (see n. 59), p. 91–113, esp. p. 95.

isted as an oral tradition of faith, then became recorded in authoritative texts which later were regarded as canonical, alongside which continued to exist the original oral tradition – the rule of faith – which gradually became reinforced by reference to Scripture. To quote Gamble, 'by a fruitful synergy, scripture helped to mold the tradition of faith, and the tradition of faith helped to shape the canon of scripture'.[66] In particular, the rule was said to be closely related to core of the New Testament: the gospels and the supposedly Pauline epistles. It was particularly associated with the evangelists' accounts: this can be seen in the frequent ambiguity of Irenaeus' and Tertullian's use of the word 'gospel', which sometimes refers to the rule of faith, sometimes to a text.[67] When Origen says that the ideas of Hebrews 'are not inferior to the acknowledged writings of the Apostle' and therefore should be accepted as canonical, he is in effect judging the periphery of the canon by its core, and, by implication, according to the rule of faith contained in that core.[68]

It is because of this close interaction between Scripture and canon that we do not need to worry too much about the subordination of Scripture to tradition. Scripture and the rule of faith are *both* tradition; but because of the interrelation between them in the earliest days of the Church, Scripture became gradually more settled and formalised and the role of the rule of faith became gradually less prominent. The latter was particularly the case when conciliar decrees and creeds addressing specific issues overtook the more general rule of faith. This is not to say, however that at this point the rule of faith became otiose: rather its role as a specifically hermeneutical criterion, which we saw operating already in Irenaeus and Origen, became ascendant. It is, for example, particularly evident in Augustine.[69]

2. Conclusions

This discussion of the interrelation between the 'canon' of Scripture and the 'canon' of faith sums up the complexity of the whole phenomenon which I have been trying to describe. From the views of the theologians I have reviewed, it seems that no single reason for attributing canonicity is regarded as sufficient in itself; this is because each reason is intimately related to the other reasons and to the life and practice of the Church. One of the reasons I

---

66 Gamble, *The New Testament Canon* (see n. 1), p. 69.
67 On Irenaeus, see Reed, 'ΕΥΑΓΓΕΛΙΟΝ' (see n. 64), esp. pp. 18–24 and pp. 42–46.
68 Origen quoted by Eusebius, *Hist. Eccl.* VI:25:12 (tr. Metzger, *Canon* [see n. 13], p. 308).

have discussed – use – suggests that the Church recognised that it was receiving a canon which had already been created. Another – orthodoxy – suggests a more active role for the Church, in which it saw itself as creating a canon which conformed to its rule of faith. Yet we have seen that this is too sharp a distinction: for the notion of catholic and appropriate use was used by the Church as a means of excluding various books in an active process of canon formation, and the rule of faith became as much a key to reading books which were already assumed to be orthodox, as a reason for deciding that they were orthodox. Finally, although some aspects of authorship affected active decisions about whether to include certain books in the canon, the notion of apostolicity has been seen to be very difficult to call a criterion of canonicity, for it is more usually a quality applied to a book already considered canonical – a corollary rather than a criterion.

Each of the so-called criteria of canonicity which I have assessed thus has a double aspect which reveals the complex interaction between the Church's passive reception of the canon and its ongoing active process of creating it. This is further illustrated by the interrelation of the various 'criteria'. It is for this reason that I have suggested that we should be cautious about talking about *criteria* of canonicity at all. Firstly, the basic meaning of 'criterion' – a principle or standard by which something is judged – suggests that there is a always a self-conscious process of judgment going on, which is somewhat undermined by the very idea of 'use' being a used as a reason for attributing canonicity (for it assumes that the decisions have already been made by the previous generation).

Secondly, the term 'criterion' tends to suggest a principle external to the subject in question, as if the Church had a pre-existent standard of what was canonical and then applied it to all the books in the canon. On the contrary, this paper has emphasised not only that the Church had no *clear* principle or set of principles of judgment, but also that any standards it had were not external to the phenomenon of the canon itself: there never was an abstract concept of what a canonical book should be. Rather, arguments tended to proceed by asking whether a 'doubtful' book was sufficiently like a 'certain' book: is the *Gospel of Truth* sufficiently like the Gospel according to John? Is *Hebrews* similar in important respects to the letters of the (supposedly) Pauline canon? Alternatively, it was asked why a doubtful book was already in use by some people *as if it were* canonical: was it considered to have derived from an Apostle? did it express the rule of faith? was it useful in catechesis or did it witness to an important doctrinal point? Thus the standards

---

69 Augustine, *De doctrina Christiana* III:3,5–6,9,10.

for canonicity which the Church used were always internal to the canon it-self, that is, to those books it already possessed.

If the 'certain' books had been a very uniform collection right from the start, it might have been the case that the Church would have been able to draw from it a simple 'criterion' for canonicity. However, from a very early period the Church accepted a diverse collection of books – both 'passively', in the sense that the four gospels, for example, were its inheritance, and 'actively' in the sense that the Church opted for the four gospels over Marcion's model or Tatian's *Diatessaron*. Consequently, the very diversity of the books of Scripture which is the focus of our project was intimately tied up with the problem of which books should be included or not, just as the same diversity is also tied up with the problem of to what degree individual books are normative. The notion of use is particularly interesting in this respect, for in drawing up what I have suggested is in effect a hierarchy of church-sanctioned uses of Scripture, as a means for attributing canonicity to various books, the Church was also tacitly acknowledging that some books were 'more canonical than others' (and that some books outside the canon were more nearly canonical than others).

It is important to stress that in rejecting language of canonical 'criteria' I am not suggesting that the Church had *no* active role in the formation of the canon. I am suggesting neither that it was the entirely passive recipient of a diverse collection of books which came together as the result of various random social forces, nor that it has these texts imposed on it by a God who knew more clearly that the church did why these texts were canonical. I am merely re-emphasising what others have stated – that the process involved both passive reception and active decision-making. However, I am also claiming that is not just a mere historical fact, but an insight which is important for a theological understanding of the history of Scripture and the Church.

Returning to analogy of a human relationship, I am suggesting that it is very odd to ask 'how did I know that you were "the one for me"?' – unless you are a hopeless romantic with the idea that there is only one person suited to you, with all the fatalistic assumptions that implies. The emphasis on 'how did I *know*' suggests there is some epistemic test, some list of right qualities which identifies the 'right' person. Instead, the better question is 'why did I choose you?' or rather, 'why did we choose each other?'. This recognises both that there *are* reasons for the choice, but also that *some* of these reasons spring neither from the qualities already possessed by the individuals, nor from any state of affairs prior to the relationship, but from the process and existence of the mutual choice itself. By this I mean not just that the reasons *are expressed in terms of* the current relationship, but also that some of the reasons for the (continued) choice actually *arise* from the relationship itself. 'I chose you, because you chose me' (– or 'each of us chose the other because each of us was chosen by the other') might seem weak as the *only* reason for a relationship, but it is usually a central reason, which is bound up with all the other more specific reasons for making the choice. These specific reasons are always important – they help explain why Jack chose Jill and not Edna – but the cause of the relationship can never be *reduced* to a list of such reasons and such reasons can only exist in the context of the subsequent history of the relationship. Thus any reasons one has for explaining the relationship are necessarily internal to the relationship itself.

This is not, I think, fatalistic: to say that the reasons for the relationship spring partly from the fact of the relationship itself is not to say that the relationship is permanent nor to say that it could not have been any other way. Nor is it to be totally relativistic and claim that all relationships are alike in value: when giving reasons for relationships one must allow for the possibilities of relationships which are mistakes, or relationships which never happened, because of missed opportunities. Nor is this reasoning a resort to a romantic, non-rational level of explanation which is totally immune to historical investigation. The origins of a relationship may be difficult to pin down, difficult to explain in terms of cause and effect; but the fact of being able to *give reasons* for it, to explain it in terms of mutual choice is at least to make a start of analysing it, even if a complete and detailed explanation is never possible.

So it is, I would suggest, with the history of the formation of the canon. The questions 'how did the Church know which books were canonical? what *criteria* did it use?' suggest that the process of canonisation was *merely* a question of the Church identifying which books contained those particular key qualities which made them canonical (whether those qualities are natural or supernatural). Much more interesting and constructive is the question: 'why did the Church end up with the canon it now possesses? what *reasons* did it give?' All the specific reasons – particular aspects of authorship, usage and orthodoxy – are very important, but all are inevitably seen from within the context of the already-existing relationship between the Church and these texts. Again, this is not to assert fatalistically that the Church could only ever have ended up with the canon it now has (as if 'canonical' means *only* 'chosen by the Church'): it could have chosen not to include Hebrews,and this could have been a mistake. Nor is it to resort lazily to the sort of 'mystical' explanation which only solves theological problems insofar as it puts them on hold. Rather, the very fact of being able to give *some* reasons for the

Church's choice is evidence of the fact that one can investigate the origins of the canon historically. The mistake is in claiming to be able to reduce the formation of the canon to those reasons alone, to isolate those reasons from the fact of the already-existing relationship.[70]

It might be claimed that my analogy breaks down with regard to the element of mutuality: surely, the Church and the texts did not choose each other in the same way that a couple do? However, while there are clearly differences between the two situations, I would suggest two points. First, the strong sense that the New Testament texts contained a deposit of truth – the Gospel – exerted a force on the early Church fathers which is roughly equivalent to the sense of 'being chosen' in a human relationship. Similarly, there was a 'given' quality to the Old Testament collection them which meant that the Church was faced with the urgent issue of how to deal with them. The texts thus imposed themselves on the Church in a way that was initially beyond the Church's conscious control, yet not in a deterministic manner which guaranteed acceptance by Church: it had to choose over time to (continue to) receive them. To put this another way: the texts posed the Church a question which was unavoidable, but a question which it was not bound to answer one way or the other. Second, through their use in preaching, catechesis, liturgy and formal theological argument the books of both Testaments influenced the Church and the Church influenced the texts in a long process of mutual formation.

It is through some such an account of some sort of mutuality in the relationship between Church and the canon of Scripture, that one is able to create some theological space in what is often an entirely historical discussion – without doing disservice to the history. This sort of account can allow for a sense of the *givenness* of (at least some of) the texts in the canon, a sense that their being called canonical cannot be sufficiently explained by specific reasons such as authorship, use and orthodoxy, although it clearly involves those reasons. Rather, the texts' canonicity derives fundamentally from their very relationship with the Church.

In conclusion, there are two consequences, historical and theological, of the analogy which I have proposed in this article. Historically, the idea of a mutually-shaping relationship between the Church and its texts frees us from

---

70 Hence, Gamble argues: 'the criteria of canonicity are more representative of the ideals which the church held out for scripture than of the actual character of the writings themselves. In particular the principles of apostolicity, catholicity, and orthodoxy were less the effective reasons for canonical recognition than a means of legitimizing the authority that attached to certain documents in virtue of their longstanding use by the church. Therefore, the importance of such principles for the actual history of the canon should not be over-estimated.' (*The New Testament Canon* [see n. 1], p. 71).

the dilemma of seeing 'canonicity' either in terms of a list of criteria thought up by Church, or as the simple fact of the Church's passive inheritance of a traditional collection of texts. Seeing 'canonicity' in terms of a relationship of mutual influence allows the historian to recognise both active and passive factors in the formation of the canon, whilst acknowledging that these may never be totally untangled by historical investigation. Although the reasons for the relationship can be investigated to some degree, there is always going to be a point at which analysis fails – not because there is nothing to know, but because the reality is too complex to know. In a romantic relationship where each partner chooses the other the relationship is created by the complex synergy of the mutual choice. Who can say to what extent one choice is 'caused' by the other? Similarly, the phenomenon of the formation of the canon can never be precisely described: who can say where reception ended and active creation began? The Church fathers' decisions about the canon, their recognition of certain types of Church use and their appreciation of the interrelation of the Scripture and other elements of tradition is evidence of a half-formed realisation that they were to some extent 'creating' and to some extent 'receiving' the canon. Perhaps this is why it is so difficult to draw a neat dividing line in the formation of the canon between the processes of inclusion and of exclusion[71], and why it is so difficult to determine when the canon was formed.[72]

The second consequence of seeing 'canonicity' in terms of the mutual relationship between the texts and the Church is theological: it allows the theologian to avoid the dilemma of a totally naturalistic or a totally supernaturalistic explanation of the term. On the one hand, 'canonicity' is not to be defined by a list of natural qualities seen in the texts (such as authorship by a particular group of people), nor is it to be defined simply as the Church's use of some texts in a particular special way. On the other hand, neither is it to be reduced to a list of supernatural qualities that exist in the canonical texts (and only the canonical texts), which the Church only gradually came to identify. Rather, 'canonicity' lies in the progressive and mutually-forming relationship between certain texts and the Church: a relationship which is complex, historical, but not beyond the bounds of grace.

---

71 Barton stresses that the two processes of growth and limitation are not consecutive, but run in parallel at least from the time of Tertullian (*Spirit* [see n. 3], p. 27).

72 Of course, there came a point at which the Church's determination of the canon became much more explicit: as marriage formalises a relationship, there came a point in the formation of the canon when the relationship settled and became formal, public, and institutionalised. However, like the relationship within a marriage, the mutuality of the relationship between Church and canon did not stop: for, as we have seen, before the process of reception and canonisation had ceased, the mutual process of reception and interpretation had begun.

'A Great and Meritorious Act of the Church'?
The Dogmatic Location of the Canon

by John Webster

1. Introduction

Any attempt to locate the canon doctrinally must do so in the face of two powerful considerations, both of which have contributed to its mislocation:

The first is that, as a consequence of the explanatory successes of the application of critical-historical and comparative methods, the Christian canon has been drawn firmly within the sphere of religious history. As with the theology of the Bible generally, so with the canon: once it comes to be viewed as part of the history of religions, the term 'holy' seems less and less appropriate.

The success of such explanations, of course, depends not only on their intrinsic fruitfulness, nor even on acceptance, tacit or explicit, of the spiritual and intellectual basis of a culture devoted to critical inquiry. It also depends upon the second consideration, which lies deep within the history of modern Christian theology, namely the distortions introduced into Christian theology of Scripture in the post-Reformation era by its *dogmatic* mislocation. In crude shorthand terms, the mislocation occurs when the Christian theology of Scripture is transplanted out of its proper soil – essentially, the saving economy of the triune God – and made to do duty as a foundational doctrine. Scripture, and therefore the canon, share the same fate as the doctrine of revelation. Instead of being a consequential doctrine (consequential, that is, upon logically prior teaching about the prevenience of God in God's dealings with the creation), it shifts to become a relatively isolated piece of epistemological teaching. This process shifts the location of the doctrine, forcing it to migrate to the beginning of the dogmatic corpus and to take its place alongside, for example, philosophical arguments for the existence of God. And the process also modifies its content, as it becomes largely disconnected from its setting in trinitarian, pneumatological and ecclesial doctrine.

The extent to which this process is a natural result of the Reformation insistence upon *sola scriptura* is debatable; it is, I believe, more plausible to see it as the result of the abstraction of *sola scriptura* from the other Reformation exclusive particles *solus Christus, sola gratia* and *solo verbo* (all of which are extensions of the primary principle *solus Deus)*, which, in effect, tied Reformation teaching about Scripture to a wider set of doctrinal materials and thereby ensured its integration into the scope of dogmatics. What is clear, nonetheless, is that as the canon is lifted out of the network of doctrines within terms of which it makes sense, it becomes patent of naturalistic explanation, whether of the more traditional historical-critical variety or of a sociopolitical cast. Moreover, as I shall try to show, most recent attempts to reintroduce doctrinal description of the canon tend to repeat its mislocation by rendering 'canon' as an ecclesial concept, and operating with very minimal appeal to, for example, soteriology or pneumatology.

My suggestion, then, is that if the canon is not to be seen as (at best) an arbitrary or accidental factor in Christian religious history or (at worst) an instrument of political wickedness, it requires careful dogmatic articulation. At the very least, this will involve appeal to a variety of doctrinal materials: an account of revelation as the self-communicative presence of the triune God; an account of the mediation of that self-communication through creaturely forms and activities ('means of grace') including texts, which are annexed and sanctified by God; an account of the church, in particular the doctrinal specification of the processes of 'canonization'; and an account of the sanctified or faithful reader of the canon.

The account which follows is frankly dogmatic. It assumes the truth of the church's confession of the gospel, regarding that confession as a point from which we move rather than a point towards which we proceed. Readers disposed to anxiety about the viability of such an exercise will find little here to still their hearts. *Theologia non est habitus demonstrativus, sed exhibitivus.* In the matter of the canon we are in the sphere of dogmatics: of faith, church, creed, prayer, holiness. Whether it is worth pitching one's tent in such a sphere is something which cannot be argued here; but we can at least try to exhibit some of the benefits of what at first looks very unpromising indeed.

2. The Natural History of the Canon

Adolf von Harnack spoke of the canon as a creative act: 'No greater creative act can be mentioned in the whole history of the Church than the formation of the apostolic collection and the assigning to it of a position of equal rank with the Old Testament'.[1] His words identify what remains a fundamental problem for any doctrinal account of the canon, namely the 'natural' character of the canon and canonization. Four aspects of inquiry into the canon's 'natural history' can be distinguished.

2.1. First, *critical-historical* inquiry into the canon, using the same tools of critical analysis as were developed for looking at individual biblical texts, offers an account of the canon in terms of its *Entstehungsgeschichte*, that is, its religio-historical conditions of possibility, such as the church's response to Marcion. Historians differ as to whether such accounts are merely a necessary or, in fact, a sufficient explanation of the canon, but the effect of such inquiry remains the same: the canon is in some measure de-sacralised, and so shares the same fate as Harnack's other two basic features of catholic, ecclesiastical Christianity – creed and episcopacy: it comes to be seen as a contingent and in some measure arbitrary ecclesial process, and not as part of the providential ordering of the church. The doctrinal effect of such historicisizing of the canon are, clearly, further to erode confidence in the possibility of distinguishing the biblical writings from other texts by the application of the notion of 'inspiration'. Such historical accounts indicate that canonization involves a good deal more than the recognition of some property in the texts: to talk of texts as canonical scripture is not to identify a latent characteristic in certain writings which precedes canonization, but rather to indicate a status acquired through usage and eventual inclusion in the canon. With that admission, the boundary between inspired/non-inspired or apostolic/non-apostolic become very porous. In effect, the canon shifts from the category of 'scripture' to that of 'tradition', precisely because scripture and tradition are so difficult to distinguish with any clarity. And thereby the dogmatic principle of *sola scriptura* becomes increasingly difficult to operate.

2.2. Critical study of the biblical canon draws the canon into the sphere of religious history. Further impetus in this direction is given by *comparative approaches* to canon and canonization,[2] which have reinforced and refined

---

1   A.v. Harnack, *History of Dogma II*, New York: Dover, 1961, p. 62 n. 1.

2   For an overview, see G.T. Sheppard, 'Canon', in: *EncRel(E)* 3 (1987) 62–69. Two collections of texts are important here: J. Assmann/A. Assmann (eds.), *Kanon und Zensur*, Munich: Fink, 1987; A. van der Kooij/K. van der Toorn (eds.), *Canonization and Decanonization*, Leiden: Brill, 1998. In the latter volume, the essays by J.Z. Smith (pp. 295–311) and H.J. Adriaanse (pp. 313–330) are particularly fruitful; the collection also contains a very full annotated bibliography (pp. 435–506). See, further, J.Z. Smith, 'Sacred Persistence: Toward a Redescription of Canon', in: idem, *Imagining Religion. From Babylon to Jonestown*, Chicago: University of Chicago Press, 1982, 36–52; W. Cantwell

the 'immanent' accounts of canonicity found in critical-historical studies of the formation of the biblical canon. Most of all, this has been achieved by specifying that 'canon' is a socio-cultural concept which describes the processes of religious societies rather than intrinsic attributes of texts. Thus, 'being scripture is not a quality inherent in a given text, or type of text, so much as an interactive relation between that text and a community of persons'.[3] Talking of a text as scripture (and therefore as 'canonical') is not to describe the text but its place and use in a community. Hence to elucidate the notion of scripture we have to refer primarily to 'the universe and human life – with the texts as mediating, and in effect secondary'.[4] Crucially, this means that *'There is no ontology of scripture.* The concept has no metaphysical, nor logical, referent; there is nothing that scripture finally "is" ... [A]t issue is not the texts of scripture that are to be understood and about which a theory is to be sought, but the dynamic of human involvement with them ... Scripture has been ... a human activity: it has been also a human propensity, a potentiality. There is no ontology of scripture; just as, at a lower level, there is no ontology of art, nor of language, nor of other things that we human beings do, and are. Rather than existing independently of us, all these are subsections of the ontology of our being persons.'[5] Though Wilfred Cantwell Smith's concern is broader than canonicity, the application of what he has to say to canon is clear enough: the referent of 'canon' is modes of relation between texts and their religious users; no 'metaphysics' of canon is required, in the sense that no account need be offered of any transcendent divine action generating or guiding canonization. Canon is what Jonathan Smith calls human 'repertoire'.[6] In terms of the Christian canon this means, quite simply that '[t]here is no such thing as *the* canon. There are canons, each of them with normative claims which, as a matter of fact, are mostly conflicting with the claims of other canons. Consequently, a canon must be understood as a socio-cultural phenomenon.'[7]

Smith, *What is Scripture? A comparative approach*, London: SCM Press, 1993; and K.W. Folkert's classic analysis 'The "Canons" of Scripture', in: M. Levering (ed.), *Rethinking Scripture. Essays from a Comparative Perspective*, Albany, NY: SUNY Press, 1989, 170–179. P.J. Griffiths, *Religious Reading. The Place of Reading in the Practice of Religion*, Oxford: Oxford University Press, 1999, gives a sharply critical appraisal of some comparativist approaches.

3   Cantwell Smith, *What is Scripture?* (see n. 2), p. ix.
4   Ibid., p. 223.
5   Ibid., p. 237.
6   J.Z. Smith, 'Canons, Catalogues and Classics', in: van der Kooij/van der Toorn (eds.), *Canonization and Decanonization* (see n. 2), 295–311, p. 304.
7   H.J. Adriaanse, 'Canonicity and the Problem of the Golden Mean', in: van der Kooij/van der Toorn (eds.), *Canonization and Decanonization* (see n. 2), 313–330, p. 327.

Neither of these first two factors in the naturalization of the canon necessarily urge the abandonment of the canon; they merely suggest that it may be explained as immanent within communal religious activity. Two other factors, though less directly connected to the study of biblical or religious texts, have a much more critical impact.

2.3. *Socio-political theorists of canon*[8] emphasise that a canon of texts is not simply a bearer of value (aesthetic or religious) but is at one and the same time a product of and a medium for social relations. Canon is 'cultural capital'; giving an account of a canon must therefore involve description of the circumstances and agents of its production, and of its 'institutional presentation'.[9] That is to say, an account of canon which failed to give attention to the socio-political and economic processes of the production and imposition of normative texts would be deficient. For J. Guillory (whose concern is with literary canons) this requires the devotion of critical attention to the school as the site of the canon's invention and reinforcement. 'Canonicity is not a property of the work itself but of its transmission, its relation to other works in a collocation of works – the syllabus in its institutional locus, the school.'[10] And so 'what is required ... is an analysis of the institutional location and mediation of such imaginary structures as the canon in order first to assess the real effects of the imaginary, and then to bring the imaginary itself under more strategic political control'.[11]

So far little attention has been devoted by practitioners of the critical history of Christian doctrine to the analysis of the function of the biblical canon as a normative element in the social imaginary, although *Ideologiekritik* is now an established aspect of much biblical interpretation, whether new historicist or feminist.[12] Such lines of analysis are not unrelated to the work of earlier scholars (W. Marxsen or M. Werner, for example[13]) who argued that the canon, as an aspect of *Frühkatholizismus*, was part of the de-eschatologizing of Christianity and its settlement into normative forms. Recent application of theories of ideology to canonicity turn on more than simply a rather crude dichotomy of charismatic/institutional, and have a much

---

8   The most important text here is J. Guillory, *Cultural Capital. The Problem of Literary Canon Formation*, Chicago: University of Chicago Press, 1993.
9   Ibid., p. ix.
10 Ibid., p. 55.
11 Ibid., p. 37.
12 See D. Jobling/T. Pippin (eds.), *Ideological Criticism of Biblical Texts*, Atlanta: Scholars Press, 1992; R.P. Carroll, 'An Infinity of Traces', *JNWSL* 21 (1995) 25–43.
13 W. Marxsen, 'Das Problem des neutestamentlichen Kanons' (1960), in: E. Käsemann (ed.), *Das Neue Testament als Kanon*, Göttingen: Vandenhoeck & Ruprecht, 1970, 233–246; M. Werner, *The Formation of Christian Dogma*, London: Black, 1957, p. 64ff.

more direct concern with the '*politics* of canonical violence'.[14] That is, the question to put to the text is (in the words of one of the few recent attempts to apply *Ideologiekritik* to the early development of Christian doctrine), 'In whose interest does this text work?', for '[a] surviving text is a successful text ... which means that it has served what turned out to be a successful interest. To understand it fully, we need to be aware of what it does not say, what it controverts, what it represses or suppresses'.[15] And pursuing such questions means, of course, bidding farewell to the *innocence* of the canon; canon is poetics, and therefore politics, and therefore power.

2.4. If ideology critics dissolve the canon's givenness into strategies of power, postmodern repudiations of textual determinacy dissolve the canon into acts of reading – whether through one or other theory of reception, or, more radically, by abandoning the category of 'book' in favour of 'text' or 'intertext'. Both lines of critique assimilate the canon to power, but rather than seeking political oversight of the social imaginary, postmodernism recommends a shift from the book as a stable totality, a presentation of normative authorial meaning, to the text as a shifting field of play:

'Tradition "begins" with speech and "ends" with writing. As "The Ruler of Reality," tradition regulates and regularizes by establishing a normative canon. A κανών is a measuring rod or a rule. A rule, in turn, is a *regula*, which is a straight stick, bar, ruler, or pattern. A canon provides the rule by which to distinguish proper from improper and gives the standard against which to judge anomalies and measure transgressions. Though a tradition can, at least for a time, remain oral, a canon tends to be "fixed" by writing. Canon and book, therefore, are closely related. Once agreed upon, the canon forms the book by which all other books are to be judged and furnishes the rule with which every "lesser" work is measured. In short, the canon constitutes the masterpiece that rules the tradition. As such, it must be the paradigmatic work of a/The Master.'[16]

Once, however, the static metaphysics of origin, intention, presence, 'text-in-itself' are repudiated, then 'canon' loses any force, and is dispersed, for

'without a founding origin and an organizing centre, no work can be a masterpiece. The codependence of texts precludes both the mastery of one text by another and the subservience of one text to another. Scriptural relativity breaks the rule of canon and disperses authoritative tradition. Insofar as canon and tradition extend the circle of the book, the end of one is the dissolution of the other. On the one hand, when the book is breached, canon explodes and tradition shatters. On the other hand, when the rule of canon is broken and the

---

14 D. Jasper, *Readings in the Canon of Scripture. Written for our Learning*, Basingstoke: Macmillan, 1995, p. 9.

15 R. Williams, 'Doctrinal Criticism: Some Questions', in: S. Coakley/D. Pailin (eds.), *The Making and Remaking of Christian Doctrine. Essays in Honour of Maurice Wiles*, Oxford: Clarendon Press, 1993, 239–264, p. 244.

16 M.C. Taylor, *Erring: A Postmodern A/theology*, Chicago: University of Chicago Press, 1984, p. 88.

line of authority disrupted, the book disintegrates. With the unravelling of the book, canon, and tradition, scripture becomes free to drift endlessly.'[17]

The force of all four lines of inquiry is to work against ideas of the canon as a durable *verbum externum* through which the stability of the church can be secured from without. The historicity of the canon, its naturalization or transposition into history, whether the history be that of antique religion, the dynamics of political and economic society or anarchic, undirected freedom, means that it comes to be seen as product, not norm. On the one hand, this attitude can be expressed as a *critical* relation to the canon, which is no longer viewed as bearing an irreducible authority but as a further object for transcendental inquiry. On the other hand, the changed relation can be expressed in terms of a sense that the canon is co-constituted by us; community tradition, or a humanly generated economy of cultural commodities, and acts of reading and reception, are ingredient within the logic of canonicity. In the end, that is, the canon does not transcend us; we transcend the canon. – Where does this leave the possibility of a dogmatic portrayal of the canon?

3. Canon and Community

One obvious response to the naturalization of the canon has been to accept it, abandon any claims to the canon's transcendental status, and envisage the canon as simply an immanent social resource for the construction of common meaning. 'The particular canon we have received is a matter of contingent fact ... But the recognition that its precise contours do not correspond to any set of determinable criteria should not lead us to suggest the abandonment or the modification of the canon as such'. For, first, 'the existence of an agreed canon helps to provide a common sensibility for the Christian community as a whole'; and, second, 'the canon's distinctive status enables it to stand apart in its historic singularity from the changing patterns of Christian belief, and so to serve as a potential source of prophetic correction against the ever-present danger of Christians' being carried along uncritically by the beguiling streams of contemporary thought'.[18] Such accounts fail to satisfy for a couple

---

17 Ibid., p. 179.
18 M. Wiles, 'Scriptural authority and theological construction: the limitations of narrative interpretation', in: G. Green (ed.), *Scriptural Authority and Narrative Interpretation*, Philadelphia: Fortress Press, 1987, 42–58, pp. 53f. For further elaboration of this, see M. Wiles, 'The Uses of "Holy Scripture"', in: *EIT 4*, London: SCM Press, 1979, pp. 73–82. A similar account is offered in: J. Barr, 'The Bible as a Document of Believing Communities', in: *EIT 7*, London: SCM Press, 1980, pp. 111–133.

of reasons. First, their proposal about the functioning of the canon, though correct in linking the canon to community formation, gives only the most abstract depiction of that link, a depiction whose generality is such that it could not count as a rich or persuasive account of how Christian believers view and use the canon in practice. 'Common sensibility' and (for example) 'the mind of Christ' are concepts of a different order. Second, these accounts do not provide any non-arbitrary reasons for the use of the canon by the church. But a canon which is *only* a useful accident, *only* tradition, cannot *rule*. Or if it does rule, its rule is perilously exposed to the charge of – political – caprice.

An initially more fruitful, if in the end insufficient, way forward can be seen in a cluster of recent accounts of the canon which have sought to relocate the notions of canon and canonicity within a theological theory of ecclesial existence, thereby making 'canon' and 'community' correlative concepts. Though these accounts resist the drift to naturalism by retaining some aspects of theological language, the marked tendency to make ecclesiology *the* basic doctrine can introduce some of the dogmatic distortions found in nineteenth-century theologies of moral community, and can thereby find it hard to resist the steady move towards immanence.

An initial example is Charles Wood's admirable study of Christian hermeneutics, *The Formation of Christian Understanding*. Wood – rightly, in my judgment – argues against the domination of Christian theory of interpretation by general hermeneutical principles, suggesting that Christian understanding is 'an understanding whose criteria are informed by the particular aims and interests that motivate it'.[19] The crucial question for Wood is thus not 'what kind of text?' but 'what is the character of Christian understanding?'. The effect of recasting the hermeneutical question in this way is, clearly, to shift the centre of gravity away from the text as a discrete entity, and instead to draw attention to community *use*: 'Theological hermeneutics begins by asking what sorts of abilities constitute the possibility of the distinctively Christian use or uses of these texts, and then goes on to ask how these abilities are gained and strengthened.'[20] The real issue, therefore, is 'the connection between the text and its user or users'. Thus: 'It is crucial to identify the particular use or uses with which one is concerned, and then – recognising that "understanding" always refers to the acquisition or possession of determinate, or at least determinable, abilities with regard to its object – to

---

19 C. Wood, *The Formation of Christian Understanding. An Essay in Theological Hermeneutics*, Philadelphia: Westminster, 1981, p. 21.
20 Ibid.

specify the sort of understanding at issue.'[21] What it immediately striking in such an account is the lack of reference to divine action – to God's use of the text, or, perhaps, God's use of the church's use. None of what Wood says excludes the possibility of such reference. But a worry on this score may be sharpened when Wood goes on to note that Scripture only functions to disclose God 'when it is activated to do so', and that this activation 'depends to a large extent upon the interpreter's readiness to use scripture to that end'.[22] Wood's general proposal is, of course, well taken as a critique of the kind of transcendental hermeneutics in which interpretation is a function of abstractly-conceived mentalist subjectivity, rather than an ability in a context. Nevertheless, it leaves relatively unexplored the question of the relation of the text to God, and precisely thereby it opens up a free space which can be filled by 'community'.

This last problem is especially acute in the strongly functionalist account of the canon offered by David Kelsey in his (aptly titled) *The Uses of Scripture in Recent Theology*, where he proposes that 'to call a set of writings "Christian canon" is an analytic judgment: To say "These writings are the Christian canon" is analytic in "This community is a Christian church".'[23] Accordingly, for Kelsey the primary criterion for canonicity is *use*: 'In declaring just these writings "canon" the church was giving part of a self-description of her identity: we are a community such that certain uses of scripture are necessary for nurturing and shaping our self-identity, and the use of "just these," i.e. "canonical," writings is *sufficient* for that purpose'.[24] On this basis, it is quite natural that the canon be seen as a function of community identity. 'To call [the biblical writings] "canon" is to say that the writings, taken together, no matter what their diversity from one another, function *ensemble* when used in the common life of the church and serve as the sufficient occasion for that presence of God which preserves the church's identity as a single, integral, living reality. No matter how great its inner diversity, this set of writings is to be taken as mirroring in a wholeness of its own the unity of the church's own identity.'[25] Not only does this mean that canonicity is an attribute of scripture derived from its ecclesial deployment rather than from its relation to the revelatory action of God. It also leads to the prioritising of a particular understanding of canonicity. To speak of the canon on this account is to speak of the unity and integrity ascribed to a set of texts by a community engaged in the process of self-identification, rather than of the

---

21 Ibid., pp. 22f.
22 Ibid., p. 38.
23 D. Kelsey, *The Uses of Scripture in Recent Theology*, London: SCM Press, 1975, p. 105.
24 Ibid.
25 Ibid., p. 106.

normativity ascribed to those texts by their relation to an activity of God. 'Canon' advertises ascribed wholeness; and such an ascription is best understood, therefore, as 'a *policy* decision'.[26]

A third example is Rowan Williams' sophisticated restatement of a 'catholic' understanding of the inseparability of church and Scripture in 'The Discipline of Scripture'. The essay proposes that – over against 'closed' accounts of the interpretation of Scripture in which reading is merely a matter of passive reception of already constituted meaning – reading is properly 'dramatic' or 'diachronic'. 'The meanings in our reading,' he writes, 'are like the meanings in the rest of our experience, they are to be discovered, unfolded ... So long as our humanity remains unintelligible except as a life of material change, irreversible movement, it is unlikely – to say the least – that we could establish non-diachronic modes of reading as primary'.[27] Or again: 'Christian language takes it for granted ... that meanings are learned and produced, not given in iconic, ahistorical form. It grows out of a particular set of communal and individual histories, and its images and idioms are fundamentally shaped by this fact.'[28] And so:

'Christian interpretation is unavoidably engaged in 'dramatic' modes of reading: we are invited to identify ourselves in the story being contemplated, to re-appropriate who we are now, and who we shall or can be, in terms of the story. *Its* movements, transactions, transformation, become *ours*...[A] dramatic reading means that our appropriation of the story is not a static relation of confrontation with images of virtue or vice, finished pictures of a quality once and for all achieved and so no longer taking time, but an active working through of the story's movement in our own time.'[29]

'Dramatic' or 'diachronic' reading thus highlights both the *temporal* and the *active* character of our interpretation of texts; they are a matter of 'a complex of interwoven processes: a production of meaning in the only mode available for material and temporal creatures'.[30] The effect on the notion of 'canon' is twofold: first, (as with Kelsey) to construe canonicity as unity, and, second, to make it largely a function of community. '"Scripture" (Jewish as well as Christian) comes to exist as such in a community that says and does identifiable and distinctive things; that has some means of articulating a particular identity. The unity of Scripture has to do with how it becomes part of this articulation, how it establishes itself as a point of reference (a *canon*) for a

---

26 Ibid., p. 177.
27 R. Williams, 'The Discipline of Scripture', in: *On Christian Theology*, Oxford: Blackwell, 2000, 44-59, p. 49.
28 Ibid.
29 Ibid., p. 50.
30 Ibid., p. 55: a statement whose commitment to a certain ontology of history cannot be discussed here.

community with a definite and perceptible historical unity. Its unifying
themes are established according to what is understood as unifying the community.'[31] Williams is quick to point out that '[t]his is *not* to reduce its unity
to something decided upon by the community to suit whatever happen to be
its priorities'[32]; but the grounds for this assertion are opaque, and remain so
without any extensive discussion of – for example – the communicative presence of the risen Christ or the activity of the Holy Spirit.[33]

What are we to make of these several attempts at re-stating the canon,
taken together? There is, doubtless, an immediate attractiveness in giving a
large role to ecclesiology – or, more fitting, perhaps, ecclesiality – namely,
that it is over questions of the nature and activities of Christian communal
life that dogmatics would appear to have the greatest prospects of *rap-
prochement* with the human historical sciences which have done so much to
erode the theological notion of the canon. Deployed in a certain way – as an
ontological *substratum* to everything else which theology wants to say[34] –
ecclesiality can function as the point at which history, socio-cultural and political theory, and theology can intersect. Church construed as human community is patent of both historically immanent and theological explanation.
In terms of our present concern, it appears to offer an idiom through which to
rearticulate Christian claims about the canon without calling into question
what have become established depictions of the canon as natural history.

And other advantages suggest themselves. Paying attention to the canon
as an ecclesial concept may help extract a theological account of Scripture
from giving too formal or juridical an account of the relation of the canon to
the church by stressing that canonicity is best understood in terms of its function in 'establishing and governing certain networks of relationships'.[35]
Moreover, such an emphasis is fittingly linked to a concern for 'regional'
hermeneutics, that is, for an account of interpretation oriented not to common
human experience or universal theories of consciousness, but to the local
practices of specific social-historical traditions.[36] And this is, in turn compan-

---

31 Ibid., pp. 55f.
32 Ibid., p. 56.
33 Some hints in this direction can be found in another essay in the same volume, 'Trinity
    and Revelation', pp. 131–147. And one should note the Christological ramifications of
    Williams' remark: 'Christ is "produced" by the history of the covenant people' (p. 58).
    Incarnation or immanence?
34 On this see the very suggestive essay of C. Ernst, 'The Significance for Ecclesiology of
    the Declaration on non-Christian Religions and the Decree on Missions of Vatican II',
    in: *Multiple Echo*, London: Darton, Longman and Todd, 1979, pp. 137–148.
35 S.E. Fowl, *Engaging Scripture. A Model for Theological Interpretation*, Oxford: Black-
    well, 1998, p. 3.
36 See my essay 'Hermeneutics in Modern Theology: Some Doctrinal Reflections', *SJTh*
    51 (1998) 307–341.

ionable with recent application of the theory of virtue to interpretative activity, with its concern to identify the appropriate dispositions which the Christian reader of the canon finds exemplified in the public practices of the church.[37]

Yet problems remain. In dogmatic terms, the major deficiency is not that of setting the canon in relation to the life-practices of the church; there are, as I hope to show, strong doctrinal warrants for making this move (though only as a consequence of prior dogmatic commitments). The deficiency lies rather in the (largely implicit) notion of 'church' at work here. That notion is characteristically severely underdetermined by other features of the dogmatic corpus: Trinity, soteriology, pneumatology, sanctification. As a result, it often threatens to acquire a generic cast, especially when some of its force is derived from general observations about the functioning of texts in communities rather than from the internal content of Christian self-description. And, furthermore, the implicit notion of church tends to be remarkably modest in its appeal to language about divine action in describing the production, authorization and interpretation of the canon, and heavily freighted towards talk of the church's agency in deciding, ascribing, construing, using, and the like. The question which hangs over all such language is whether it is more appropriate to speak of the people of the book or the book of the people.[38]

It is the presence of these problems which, in the end, distinguishes 'ecclesial' accounts of Scripture and the canon from those in mainstream Roman Catholic theology, despite their apparent similarity in correlating canon and church. In classical Roman Catholic theology, 'church' is a potently dogmatic concept, explicated in terms of the union of Christ as head to the church as his body. To talk of the canon as an 'ecclesial' concept or decision is, on this view, not to identify a feature of texts in communities, but a consequence of the 'pneumatischen Selbstverständnis der Kirche': 'Die Kirche teilt, in ihrer Lebenseinheit mit Christus, seine Schau des Heilshandelns Gottes. Das Selbstbewußtsein der Kirche ist schließlich *das Selbstbewußtsein des*

---

37 See here S.E./Fowl, L.G. Jones, *Reading in Communion. Scripture and Ethics in Christian Life*, Grand Rapids: Eerdmans, 1991.

38 There are many similarities between these ecclesial accounts of the canon and that exemplified in the nineteenth century by Martensen, who argues that 'the notion of a canon in Christianity, be it found in the Bible or in the church, points to a conscious mind *for* which it is a canon. The external canon points to an internal canon, by whose aid alone it can be correctly understood; and that internal canon is the *regenerated* Christian mind, in which the Spirit of God bears witness to the Spirit of man': H. Martensen, *Christian Dogmatics*, Edinburgh: T&T Clark, 1898, p. 41. Ecclesial accounts of canon are less individualist and more corporate: the regenerated Christian mind is the common mind of the church expressed in its practices; but the question remains as to whether such accounts are no less subjective (maybe more so, if they fail to deploy Martensen's language about the Spirit).

ganzen Christus, des Hauptes und Leibes. Jesus Christus ist der Herr der Kirche und darum der Herr der Schrift ... Die Heilige Schrift verweist immer auf diese pneumatische Gemeinschaft ... Die Kanonsbewußtwerdung der Kirche im Lauf ihrer Geschichte ist ein durch den Heiligen Geist geführtes Wachstum ihrer Autopistie.'[39] Roman Catholic rejection of *sola scriptura* in favour of Scripture *and* tradition is thus a corollary of a rejection of the ecclesiological implications of *solus Christus*, not a theory of how groups use texts in the course of forming and sustaining their identity. It is, in other words, a dogmatic, not a sociological, proposal.

The rest of this paper is given over to making an – *evangelisch* – dogmatic proposal about the canon. Dogmatic portrayal of the canon, I suggest, involves a good deal more than offering an ecclesial gloss to a sociology of texts and their uses. It involves an account of the communicative character of the saving economy of the triune God; it involves an account of the sanctification of texts in the complex processes of their history; it involves careful theological specification of the church's act of canonization; and it involves an account of the work of God in shaping the reader of the canon. Like the dogmatic notion of Scripture of which it is a corollary, canon is a plausible notion only within the setting of a range of doctrinal material, each part of which is needed if distortions or misapprehensions are not to creep in. As William Abraham puts it, the notion of canon presupposes 'a complex theological vision of creation and redemption'.[40] We turn to exhibit some aspects of that vision.

4. Canon and Revelation

An account of the canon begins with an account of revelation. Fruitful exposition of this doctrine[41] depends upon successful coordination of a number of concepts and practices. The plausibility of the doctrine of revelation, that is, is a function not only of (for example) a coherent conception of divine action, but also of other factors which furnish the criteria, both intellectual and prac-

---

39 N. Appel, *Kanon und Kirche. Die Kanonkrise im heutigen Protestantismus als kontroverstheologisches Problem*, Paderborn: Verlag Bonifacius-Druckerei, 1964, pp. 376f.

40 W. Abraham, *Canon and Criterion in Christian Theology. From the Fathers to Feminism*, Oxford: Clarendon Press, 1998, p. 1.

41 Properly speaking, revelation is not a 'doctrine', and certainly not a separate dogmatic *locus* (its separation is, in fact, part of the pathology of modern theology). Appeal to revelation is more like a *modus operandi* which pervades the entire dogmatic corpus, and which is a corollary of other primary doctrines (notably, the doctrines of Trinity and salvation).

tical, of such coherence. Hence, an effective doctrine of revelation will be one which is fittingly integrated with more primary Christian doctrines. It will also be one which requires the existence of social traditions – the church – within which appeal to such a doctrine is operative and in which it is expected to carry some weight. And it will be one not unconnected to a certain temper on the part of the theologian, an intellectual and spiritual disposition to the utility of such appeal. Only when all these factors – dogmas; communal context; dispositions – are successfully brought together will the doctrine achieve fruitfulness, plausibility and effectiveness. And the absence of any one factor will in some measure disable the doctrine and its use.[42]

For the purposes of the present argument, our concern is with the fitting integration of the doctrine of revelation with other doctrines as a backcloth to an account of the canon. Theological talk of divine revelation is a corollary of other pieces of Christian teaching; it seeks to identify the consequences for our knowledge of God of the fact that as Father, Son and Spirit, God freely discloses his being and ways to his creatures as part of the saving economy of divine mercy. At the outset this means that a Christian understanding of revelation will be concerned with the *identity* of the self-manifesting God. Only on the basis of an apprehension of God's identity can questions of the mode of revelation be answered with the right kind of specificity; inattention to the identity of the revealer, on the other hand, and especially inattention to the triune character of that identity, leads quickly to the woodenly deistic language of causality which has so afflicted accounts of revelation, biblical inspiration and the canon.

What is required, therefore, is a trinitarian and soteriological account of revelation as the context for talk of the canon. At the heart of such an account is the proposal that revelation is that differentiated action of Father, Son and Spirit in which God establishes saving fellowship with humanity and so makes himself known to us. Revelation is the free work of God in which the mystery of God's will is made manifest and generates the knowledge and obedience of faith. As divine *self*-manifestation, revelation is not merely the communication of arcane information, as if God were lifting the veil on some reality other than himself and indicating it to us. Revelation is an event or mode of relation;[43] it is God's self-presentation to us. As such, its agent is the

---

42 This is why certain kinds of philosophical defence of the doctrine of revelation, however sophisticated and even incontrovertible their argumentation, strike the dogmatician as theologically crude, even beside the point; the prove the wrong thing, or, perhaps, the right thing in the wrong way, and so misshape the doctrine.

43 Over against Francis Watson's argument (cf. F. Watson, 'Is Revelation an "Event"?', *MoTh* 10 [1994] 383–399), I am unconvinced that 'event' is 'a non-relational term with no particular application to the sphere of human relations' (p. 385). Relations are a his-

triune God himself. In revelation, God is outgoing and communicative; revelation is God's eloquence, God's 'speaking out'. The location of this eloquent self-presentation is the history of God with us. That history is the history of the acts in which God establishes saving fellowship with his creatures. It is a history of *fellowship* because at the centre of the history is 'God with us'; it is a history of *saving* fellowship because it is a history which triumphs over the opposition to fellowship with God which is sin. Revelation is therefore reconciliation; indeed, reconciliation is the more comprehensive concept for what is being talked of by revelation.[44]. Saving fellowship is communicative fellowship, in which we come to know the agent of revelation who is also the content of revelation: Father, Son and Spirit. As Father, God is the root or origin of revelation as saving self-manifestation: in him is grounded revelation's sheer gratuity and sovereign freedom. As the incarnate, crucified and glorified Son, God is the agent through whom the saving history of God with us is upheld against all opposition and denial. As Spirit, God is the agent of revelation's perfection, its being made real and effective in the community of the church as the reconciled assembly of the saints. In its entire sweep, from its generation to its fulfilment, revelation is a work of grace.

Scripture, and therefore the canon, are a function of *Deus dixit*, trinitarianly construed as that complex economy of salvation which originates in God's self-knowledge and has its telos in the reconciliation of all things. 'Die Schrift ist nicht der Grund, sondern die Sprachschule des Glaubens: Sie wirkt nicht das Heil, sondern hilft uns, Gottes Heilswirken zu verstehen und uns und anderen verständlich zu machen.'[45] Scripture and therefore the canon are ordered towards this economy; they are elements in a dynamic and purposive field of relations between the triune God and his creatures.[46] This means, accordingly, that Scripture and its properties, including canonicity, can only be rightly apprehended as an item in this economy. Separated from that context, it becomes reified into an independent entity whose nature and operations can be grasped apart from the network of relations in which it is properly located. And like other historical realities within that economy – temple, cult, kingship, sacraments, order – reification means distortion, for, like those other realities, Scripture has its being in its reference to the activity of God. If that reference is damaged or distorted, its true character is obscured. Such

---

tory; history is event.

44 See S. Williams, *Revelation and Reconciliation. A Window on Modernity*, Cambridge: Cambridge University Press, 1995.

45 I.U. Dalferth, 'Die Mitte ist außen. Anmerkungen zum Wirklichkeitsbezug evangelischer Schriftauslegung', in: C. Landmesser et alii (eds.), *Jesus Christus als die Mitte der Schrift*, Berlin/New York: Walter de Gruyter, 1997, 173–198, p. 175f.

46 For what follows, see T.F. Torrance, 'The Deposit of Faith', *SJTh* 36 (1983) 1–28.

damaging of the reference of Scripture to the divine economy of salvation
was one of the chief results of the gradual assimilation of Scripture into theological epistemology in the post-Reformation period; and it has been brought
to its conclusion in the steady drive towards nominalist accounts of Scripture
implicit within both the use of historical-critical methods and postmodern
dissolution of the metaphysics of divine discourse.

There are particular implications here for doctrinal reflection on the
canon. Unless it is set in the larger structure of divine action and its creation
of human response which we call revelation, 'canon' can become *simply*
'rule'; its normative status becomes its own property, rather than a consequence of its place in the divine economy. Above all, reference to divine action falls away, the canon becomes the textualisation of revelation, and the
substance of revelation is resolved into 'a system of truths or a set of normative doctrines and formulated beliefs'.[47] But as a function of revelation, the
canon is not merely list or code; it is a specification of those instruments
where the church may reliably expect to encounter God's communicative
presence, God's self-attestation. It is normative because of what it presents
or, better, indicates (this is part of what it means to have 'apostolicity' as the
criterion for inclusion in the canon). Neither revelation nor the canon' abolish
the mystery of God's freedom, which remains beyond codification. *Because*
it is a function of *deus revelatus*, the canon is also a function of *deus abscon-
ditus*.[48] Because in revelation God remains hidden – that is, because God's
self-communication is his making present of the sheer incomprehensible gratuity of his being and act – a theological understanding of the canon must
always be demarcated from an account of non-referential cultural norms.
Thus the centre of a theology of the canon must be an account of the action of
Father, Son and Spirit, 'the waving hand which imperiously waves the rod,
the canon'.[49]

5. Canon and Authority

The canon is a list of texts. Texts are always, as they say, 'dirty', never ideal;
they are produced and authorised by human agents; they are read, and therefore misread. A dogmatic account of the canon, however, may rather easily

---

47 Ibid., p. 3.
48 Cf. G. Siegwalt, 'Le canon biblique et la révélation', in: *Le christianisme, est-t-il une
    religion du livre?*, Strasbourg: Faculté de théologie protestante, 1984, 39–56, p. 46.
49 K. Barth, *The Göttingen Dogmatics. Instruction in the Christian Religion I*, Grand Rap-
    ids: Eerdmans, 1991, p. 57.

forget the sheer humanity of the canonical texts and the processes of which they form part. The transcendentalist accounts of the biblical writings associated with certain theologies of divine inspiration are a case in point, in that they struggle to retain a sense that the texts of which they speak are just that: *texts*, authored, embedded in the murky traditions and practices of religious groups, inescapably tied to the history of books and their making and reception and (in the case of the canon in its later history) of the making of knowledge through books.[50]

In dogmatic terms, the danger of failing to reckon with the naturalness of the canonical texts is close to hand whenever it is thought that the only way to safeguard those texts' relation to revelation is by denying their naturalness, and instead proposing an immediate relation between God and the texts. Abused in this way, θεοπνευστία as it were short-circuits all historical processes. What is problematic in such accounts is not that the notion of inspiration requires appeal to concepts of divine agency no longer available to us: their purported unavailability is not to be attributed to their rational indefensibility but of a coarsened and cramped notion of rationality.[51] The problem is more a metaphysical problem, a problem about the ontology of texts which perform a function in the divine communicative economy. Post-Reformation accounts of inspiration often fell into the trap of materialism, making the texts of the canon into a single quasi-divine entity which – despite all appearances – does not have a natural history worth speaking of. These kinds of accounts of the texts of the canon are similar to crude notions of eucharistic transubstantiation, in that both assume that material, historical realities can only reliably mediate God if they somehow take on divine properties or even participate in the divine being.

This sort of false ontology of canonical texts can be overcome by spelling out the ontological implications of talk of the canon as a 'witness' or 'means of grace'. At the core of both these notions is an assertion that the texts of the canon are human realities annexed by divine use. By emphasizing that the function of the texts is the clue to their ontology, these notions shift out of the

---

50 For general historical materials here, see B.M. Benedict, *Making the Modern Reader. Cultural Mediation in Early Modern Literary Anthologies*, Princeton: Princeton University Press, 1996; R. Chartier, *The Culture of Print. Power and the Uses of Print in Early Modern Europe*, Princeton: Princeton University Press, 1989; idem, *The Order of Books. Readers, Authors and Libraries in Europe between the Fourteenth and the Eighteenth Centuries*, Cambridge: Polity Press, 1993; A. Johns, *The Nature of the Book. Print and Knowledge in the Making*, Chicago: University of Chicago Press, 1998. On Christian texts, see, for example, H.Y. Gamble, *Books and Readers in the Early Church*, New Haven: Yale University Press, 1995.

51 And besides, we routinely use such language to talk about sacraments, without too much embarrassment or scruple.

quasi-materialist idiom of those accounts which are dominated by a false concept of inspiration.[52] Crucially, however, it is divine, not human or churchly, use which has priority in determining the ontology of the canonical texts. In short: the texts of the canon are human communicative acts which are assumed into the economy of revelation and reconciliation.

On this basis, we may return to Wilfred Cantwell Smith's assertion that 'there is no ontology of scripture',[53] with its implication that the term 'canon' does not draw attention to any properties of the texts so listed. It is true that there are not natural properties possessed by these texts and no others which in and of themselves lead to canonisation. But this does not means that the term 'canon' is purely adverbial, a way of advertising community usage. Rather, recognition of canonicity is recognition of those properties which the texts have acquired as a result of their annexation into the communicative activity of Father, Son and Spirit. The texts *are* that which they are appointed to become, namely instrumental means of gracious divine action. The being of the canonical texts is determined by their divine use.[54]

Alongside talking of the canonical texts as 'means of grace', we might also make use of the language of 'sanctification' to indicate that the texts are segregated by a divine decision to play a role in the divine self-manifestation. To speak of canonicity as sanctification is to affirm both that these texts are natural human historical entities and that they occupy a distinctive place and perform a distinctive role in the economy of salvation. Holiness is properly an incommunicable divine attribute; no created reality, whether person or material object, is intrinsically holy, because God alone, not the creature, is holy. The holiness of any creaturely reality is thus acquired *ab extra*, imputed to that reality by the election of God through which it is separated for a par-

---

52 On the relation of canon and inspiration, see Appendix.

53 Cantwell Smith, *What is Scripture?* (see n. 2), p. 237.

54 Because of this, the category of 'canon' might be said to function analogously to the category of 'genre' (see here K. Vanhoozer, *Is there a meaning in this text? The Bible, the reader, and the morality of literary knowledge*, Leicester: Apollos, 1998, p. 349). To say that a text is of a certain genre is, in part, to say that it is to be read in such-and-such a way because it *requires* so to be read. Genre is, of course, not simply an intrinsic characteristic of a text, but also a function of the construal of the text by readers. But those construals (if they are *construals* and not simply the re-writing of the text) are not wholly independent of texts, which contains features which shape the readers' reading. Canonical status, likewise, is not merely a textual property. This is especially the case because one of the features to which the category of canon draws attention, namely the unity of disparate texts, is by definition not something which can be a property of any one of the texts so collected. Canonical status is partly a construal. But, crucially, as we shall see in the next section, 'construal' in the case of the Christian canon is best understood as recognition of divine use rather than as a proposal for readerly deployment. To view a text as an instance of the 'genre' of canonical writings is therefore to affirm that text's place in a wider soteriological framework which offers the key to its being.

ticular divine purpose. The holiness of people, objects and institutions is always therefore *sanctitas aliena*, a fruit of God's own *sanctitas positiva* in its
external orientation. Accordingly, the holiness of the biblical canon is acquired, and indicates the use of the canonical texts by God as an instrument
of self-attestation. 'Sanctification' here is used to cover the entire range of
processes of which the text is the centre: processes of production (including
tradition and redaction history); processes of canonisation; and processes of
interpretation. Sanctified in this way, the canonical texts are, then, a field of
divine activity.

As a confession of a sanctifying work of God, the canonization of certain
texts means that those texts are not of the same order as other speech-acts of
the church. A confession of canonicity is an acknowledgment that – unlike
homiletic, liturgical or theological speech, for example – these texts are not
merely immanent to the culture of the Christian community. They have, as
we shall come to see, a certain 'over- againstness'. There are two consequences here. One, which here can be mentioned only briefly, is that the
theological notion of canon entails the notion of *sola scriptura*, in that to talk
of canon is to identify the canonical texts as categorically different from other
text- and speech-acts. This is not to render all other text- and speech-acts ille-
gitimate or to seal the canon off from them. It is simply to indicate the force
of the distinction between Scripture and tradition, namely that the relation of
the canon to the self-communicative activity of God is different in kind from
that of all other speech in the church.

A second consequence is that canonized texts have authority. A canon is
thus more than a list or repertoire; talk of the canon is not only enumeration
but also subjugation under and responsibility towards a norm. The norm is
not, of course, merely statutory or legislative; its force is ultimately a function of the canon as means of grace. And its effect is, therefore, to indicate
that all other speech of the church is not arbitrary or sheerly creative, but
normed. As Karl Barth put it:

'With its acknowledgment of the presence of the Canon the Church expresses the fact that it
is not left to itself in its proclamation, that the commission on the ground of which it proclaims, the object which it proclaims, the judgment under which its proclamation stands and
the event of real proclamation must all come from elsewhere, from without, and very con-
cretely from without, in all the externality of the concrete Canon as a categorical imperative
which is also historical, which speaks in time.'[55]

What more might be said of the authority of the canon? The authority of the
canon is its Spirit-bestowed capacity to quicken the church to truthful speech
and righteous action. Confession of the canon's authority is avowal by the

---

55 K. Barth, *Church Dogmatics I/1*, Edinburgh: T&T Clark, 1975, p. 101.

hearing church of that which the Spirit undertakes through the canon's service of the Word, and its proper context is therefore soteriological. From this primary definition flow all other aspects of the canon's authority, such as its role in theological or moral argument, its place in proclamation, or its liturgical presence.

Truthful speech and righteous action are a following of the order of reality, ways of engaging the world which follow its inherent nature and the ends which it displays to us. That which has authority is that which directs us to those ends, and so that which both forms and judges action. Authority is political because it shapes social relations; but true political authority is neither capricious nor arbitrary but *fitting to reality*, potent because it bears the truth to and therefore orders our acts, whether intellectual or practical, in accordance with reality. And so authority cannot be conferred; authorization is not a proposal, but an act of truthful judgement through which authority is acknowledged as that which rightly kindles activity of a specific quality in a specific direction.

That authority is properly a matter for *acknowledgment* is especially important in discussing the nature of the authority of the canon in the church. Very simply, the church is not competent to confer authority on Holy Scripture, any more than it is competent to be a speaking church before it is a hearing church, or competent to give itself the mandate to be apostolic. The authority of canon is not another way of talking about the accumulated *gravitas* which it has acquired through the church's *use*. Acknowledgement of the authority of the canon is not simply an after the event acknowledgement of what the church's custom has come to be in the way it governs its life by a particular set of texts; *de facto* authority is only of any real force if it is grounded in *de jure* authority. If it is not so grounded, then not only does canon become simply tradition, but also it lays itself open to critique as an arbitrary exercise of social power.

The modern historicist critique of authority as only a political postulate has been readily applied to the biblical texts. Most notably was it done so by Immanuel Kant in contrasting the poor benighted 'biblical theologian' working within the confining wall of 'ecclesiastical faith, which is based on statutes'[56] and the rational theologian who strides through the free and open fields of private judgement and philosophy'.[57] The authority of a text, in other words, is for Kant merely 'based on statutes – that is, on laws proceed-

---

56 I. Kant, *The Conflict of the Faculties*, in: A.W. Wood/G. di Giovanni (eds.), *Religion and Rational Theology*, Cambridge: Cambridge University Press, 1996, 233–327, p. 262.
57 Ibid., p. 252.

ing from another person's act of choice'.[58] Of course, we would be foolish to be deaf to the protest against the authoritarian abuse of canonical authority voiced by Kant and his contemporary heirs. But the abuse of biblical authority, its use as a weapon for social wickedness, cannot be countered by stripping the canon of any inherent authority and converting claims about canon into claims about the community. To do that is not to solve the problem of abuse but to repeat it, for canon still remains a function of society, whether that society be the benighted community of ecclesiastical faith or the free enlightened 'learned public'.[59] What is needed, rather, is a dogmatic move: the reintegration of the authority of the canon into the doctrine of God, which will have the effect of decisively redrawing the character of the church's affirmation of the canon's authority, removing that affirmation from the sphere of the politics of invention, and restricting the church's office to the pedagogical one of confessing or testifying attesting that the canon's authority flows from its given place in the economy of grace.

This is not to suggest that the authority of the canon can be abstracted from the life and acts of the church as the place where the saving presence of God is encountered. To lift its authority out of the context of the church would be to formalise that authority by abstracting Scripture from its revelatory and therefore ecclesial setting.[60] Such formalisation often happens if the notion of inspiration is allowed to expand beyond its proper limits in such a way that the authority of Scripture becomes a function of the manner of its (inspired) production rather than of Scripture's service to the authoritative divine Word of revelation. Authority, that is, becomes something derived from a formal property of Scripture – its perfection as divine product – rather than of its employment in the divine service. And the perception of authority does indeed become akin to mute obedience to statute. In the end, this reduces authority to a 'formal supernaturalism'[61] insufficiently integrated into the canon's role as the bearer of the gospel of salvation to the church. An effective account of the canon's authority, by contrast, will place it within a cluster of other affirmations: God as sanctifying, inspiring and authorizing presence; the Spirit as the one who enables recognition of, trust in and glad submission to the claim of Scripture's gospel content; the church as faithful, self-renouncing and confessing assembly around the lively Word of God.

---

58 Ibid., p. 262.
59 Kant, *The Conflict of the Faculties* (see n. 56), p. 261.
60 For an account of this process, see the important essay by Torrance, 'The Deposit of Faith' (see n. 46).
61 E. Schlink, *Theology of the Lutheran Confessions*, Philadelphia: Fortress Press, 1961, p. 10 n. 4.

There is an important consequence here for the manner in which the authority of the canon is apprehended by the church. The church's submission to the gospel is not accomplished simply by notional affirmations of the canon's formal-juridical status in the church. Indeed, such notional affirmations can be the enemy of true spiritual confession, tempting the church to think that confession is a finished business rather than 'a continuous evangelical mandate'.[62] Confession of the canon's authority is part of the church's existence in grateful and repentant acknowledgement of the *benevolentia Dei* through the Spirit's gift. It is not that dull-witted conformity to external ordinance of which Kant was (rightly) contemptuous; nor is it subjection to the letter. It is glad affirmation of the force of *sola gratia* and *sola fide* in the realm of the knowledge of the gospel.

To sum up: the authority of the canon is the authority of the church's Lord and his gospel, and so cannot be made an immanent feature of ecclesial existence. Scripture's authority *within* the church is a function of Scripture's authority *over* the church. The church's acknowledgement of the canon's authority is not an act of self-government, but an exposure to judgment, to a source not simply of authorisation but also and supremely of interrogation. A church in which it makes sense to say: *scriptura sacra locuta, res decisa est* is the antithesis of a stable, statutory human project; it is, rather, a form of common life centred on a confession which subverts. Hence a church of the Word cannot be a closed, static set of relations, a social space characterised by maximal local cohesion and historical durability. It is an 'open' culture. But its openness is not secured by stressing its indeterminacy, or its character as unfinished and unfinishable project, as in some postmodern cultural theory. The church's openness is its subjection to prophecy, its being opened *ab extra* by the interceptive Word of God. What prevents church life from drifting into idolatrous closure is the fact that its 'space' is the economy of God's self-presence, in which it is subject to the interruption of scriptural testimony. 'Revelation is not a development of our religious ideas but their continuous conversion,' said H. Richard Niebuhr;[63] and 'life in the presence of revelation ... is not lived before or after but in the midst of a great revolution.'[64] Part of the office of the canon is to bring that revolution to bear upon the church, and the office of the church to acknowledge this fearsome gift of grace. *Ecclesia non est magistra, sed ministra scripturae; non mater, sed filia; non autor, sed custos, testis et interpres; non judex, sed index et vindex.*[65]

---

62 G.C. Berkouwer, *Holy Scripture*, Grand Rapids: Eerdmans, 1975, p. 36.
63 H.R. Niebuhr, *The Meaning of Revelation*, New York: Macmillan, 1962, p. 182.
64 Ibid., p. 183.
65 D. Hollaz, *Examen Theologicum Acroamaticum* (1741), cited by R. Preuss, *The Inspiration of Scripture. A Study of the Theology of the Seventeenth Century Lutheran Dog-*

6. Canon and Canonization

We may sum up the argument so far with some words from a magisterial essay by T.F. Torrance:

'Jesus Christ is God's self-address to man, but this self-address in order to achieve its end had to penetrate, take form and domicile itself within the address of man to man, as the Word of Christ abiding among men. The reciprocity established between God and man in Jesus Christ had to create room for itself within the reciprocities of human society, and the Word of God which had come 'plumb down from above' had to deploy itself in the horizontal dimensions of human existence in order to continue its speaking and acting throughout history. This involved the formation of a nucleus within the speaker-hearer relations of men, corresponding to and grounded in the communion between God and man embodied in Jesus Christ, as the controlling basis among believers for the extended communication of the Word of God, and the translation of the self-witness of Christ into witness to Christ, answering the normative pattern of His obedient humanity, as the specific form for the proclamation of God's Word to all men.'[66]

What kind of dogmatic depiction is required of those 'reciprocities of human society' which we call the act of canonization? What doctrine of the church is entailed by what has been indicated so far?

The Reformed theologian G.C. Berkouwer is quite correct, I believe, to state that the central issue in this matter (forced upon theology with fresh force by historical accounts of the canon) is 'the relationship between the canon as both norm and authority and the human considerations that can be discerned in the history of the canon'.[67] There can be no recourse to denials of the element of human decision-making in the process of canonization. To make such a move would not only idealise or spiritualise the canon in the way that older theories of inspiration often threatened to do, but also to deny what was proposed in the previous section: that it really is human texts and human textual activity which are sanctified by God. That human activity includes those processes to which we refer in shorthand terms as 'canonization'.[68] What is needed, by contrast, is a theological account of the church's action at this point; we need to give a dogmatic answer to the question of 'the nature of the human activity which can be denoted as the "accepting," the *recipere* of the canon.'[69] Such an answer will provide both a general dogmatic picture of the landscape within which that decision takes place, and a more precise, focussed depiction of the act itself.

---

maticians, Edinburgh: Oliver and Boyd, 1957, p. 98 n. 3.

66 T.F. Torrance, 'The Word of God and the Response of Man', in: idem, *God and Rationality*, Oxford: Oxford University Press, 1971, 137–164, pp. 151f.

67 Berkouwer, *Holy Scripture* (see n. 62), p. 70.

68 It is, of course, important, not to be beguiled into thinking of canonization as a single event or decision: it is more akin to a muddled set of interwoven processes.

69 Berkouwer, *Holy Scripture* (see n. 62), p. 72.

In portraying the larger field which encompasses this decision of the church, it is very important not to begin with the church or with the texts of the Bible. Taking up a hint of Michael Schmaus', Siegwalt properly argues that in the canon we are not dealing with a 'principe-chose' (*Sachprinzip*) but a 'principe-sujet' (*Personprinzip*), such that the crucial issue to be addressed is: 'Comment Dieu se constitue-t-il ... c'est-à-dire se pose, s'impose-t-il (se révèle-t-il) à la conscience humaine dans un sens createur de foi?'.[70] The direction in which theology must move here is thus 'De Dieu au canon ... autrement dit: *du principium essendi au principium cognoscendi*.'[71] Moving in this direction will involve depicting the church's act out of Christology and pneumatology.

Canonization, first, is to be understood in terms of the church's character as assembly around the self-bestowing presence of the risen Christ.[72] In particular, this sct of the church is enclosed within the prophetic presence and activity of Jesus Christ. The primary speech-act which takes place within the church and from which all other churchly speech-acts derive is Jesus Christ's own self-utterance. That self-utterance is mediated through the language of prophetic testimony to which Scripture bears witness and which then forms the basis and norm of the church's public speech. But it is all-important to emphasise that this mediation does not mean that Jesus Christ is replaced as speaker by some human text or official, or that he is mute until the church speaks – any more than the mediation of the *beneficia Christi* through sacraments means that Jesus Christ's saving work is inert until sacramentally realised, or that it is the church's sacramental action which renders Christ present and effective. '[I]n the apostles as the receiving end of His revealing and reconciling activity, Jesus Christ laid the foundation of the Church which He incorporated into Himself as His own Body, and permitted the Word which He put into their mouth to take the form of proclamation answering to and extending His own in such a way that it became the controlled unfolding of His own revelation within the mind and language of the apostolic foundation.'[73]

An account of the canon and canonization is therefore an account of the extension of Christ's active, communicative presence through the commissioned apostolic testimony. And, moreover, an account of the church's canonizing acts has to be rooted in the facts that the church is properly a hearing church before it is speaking church, and that even its speech, when it is prop-

---

70 Siegwalt, 'Le canon biblique', (see n. 48), p. 42.
71 Ibid., p. 44.
72 On the importance of the link between Scripture and the presence of Christ, see I.U. Dalferth, 'Die Mitte ist außen' (see n. 45).
73 T.F. Torrance, 'The Word of God and the Response of Man', p. 152.

erly apostolic, is always contingent upon and indicative of a prior speech-act. Its speech is generated and controlled by Christ's self-utterance. '[T]here exists prior to and above and after every *ego dico* and *ecclesia dicit* a *haec dixit Dominus*; and the aim of Church proclamation is that this *haec dixit Dominus* should prevail and triumph, not only before, above and after, but also *in* every *ego dico* and *ecclesia dicit.*'[74]

Second, therefore, if the church's speech is governed by the self-communication of Christ, the church's acts of judgment (its 'decisions') are governed by the Holy Spirit who animates the church and enables its perception of the truth. The role of pneumatology is primary to 'de-centring' the church's act of canonization, in two ways. Talk of the Spirit is a means of identifying the providential activity of God in the history of the Christian community, including the history of its relation to and treatment of the biblical texts. 'We should,' wrote Friedrich Schleiermacher, 'conceive of the Spirit as ruling and guiding in the thought-world of the whole Christian body just as each individual does in his own ... [T]he faithful preservation of the apostolic writings is the work of the Spirit of God acknowledging his own products.'[75] And talk of the Spirit is also a means of identifying that the perception of canonicity derives not simply from the natural *sensus communis* of the church but from the charismatic gift of 'the sense for the truly apostolic'.[76] In this light, what description is to be offered of the 'great and meritorious act' of canonization?

'I wittingly pass over what they teach on the power to approve Scripture. For to subject the oracles of God in this way to men's judgment, making their validity depend upon human whim, is a blasphemy unfit to be mentioned.'[77] – '[A] most pernicious error widely prevails that scripture has only so much weight as is conceded to it by the consent of the church. As if the eternal and inviolable truth of God depended upon the decision of men!'[78]

That it is the proper office of the Church to distinguish genuine from spurious Scripture, I deny not, and for this reason, that the Church obediently embraces whatever is of God. The sheep hear the voice of the shepherd, and will not listen to the voice of strangers. But to submit the sound oracles of God to the Church, that they may obtain a kind of precarious authority among men, is blasphemous impiety. The Church is, as Paul declares, founded on the doc-

---

74 K. Barth, *Church Dogmatics I/2*, Edinburgh: T&T Clark, 1956, p. 801. Cf. O. Weber, *Foundations of Dogmatics I*, Grand Rapids: Eerdmans, 1981, p. 249.

75 F. Schleiermacher, *The Christian Faith*, Edinburgh: T&T Clark, 1928, p. 602; cf. I. Dorner, *A System of Christian Doctrine IV*, Edinburgh: T&T Clark, 1882, p. 247.

76 Schleiermacher, *The Christian Faith* (see n. 75), p. 603.

77 J. Calvin, *Institutes of the Christian Religion IV.9.xiv*, Philadelphia: Westminster Press, 1960, p. 1178.

78 Ibid., I.7.i (p. 75)

trine of Apostles and Prophets; but these men speak as if they imagined that the mother owed her birth to the daughter.[79]

Johannes Calvin's well-known objection to one interpretation of Augustine's dictum that 'I should not believe the gospel except as moved by the authority of the catholic church'[80] is partly, of course, an objection to a certain construal of the authority of the church. But there is something deeper here: what Calvin fears is that to assert that Scripture takes it approbation from the church is radically to misinterpret the character of the church's act with respect to the canon. It is not that he denies that the church does, indeed, 'approve' Scripture, but more that such an act of approval is, properly understood, a receptive rather than an authorising act. Hence two features of the church's act of approval are of critical importance for Calvin. First, it is derived from the Spirit's presence in the church, and therefore by no means autonomous. 'They mock the Holy Spirit' Calvin says, 'when they ask: ...Who can persuade us to receive one book in reverence but to exclude another, unless the church prescribe a sure rule for all these matters?'[81]: hence his development of the doctrine of the *testimonium internum Spiritus Sancti* as a pneumatological replacement for the idea of ecclesial approbation. But, second, the church's act with respect to the canon is an act of faithful *assent* rather than a self-derived judgment. The language of discipleship is not incidental here: affirming the canon is a matter of the church 'obediently embracing' what comes from God, or of the sheep hearing the shepherd's voice; that is, it is an act of humble affirmation of and orientation towards what is already indisputably the case in the sphere of salvation and its communication in human speech. '[W]hile the church receives and gives its seal of approval to the Scriptures, it does not thereby render authentic what is otherwise doubtful or controversial. But because the church recognizes Scripture to be the truth of its own God, as a pious duty it unhesitatingly venerates Scripture'.[82] Once again: none of this is a denial that canonization is the church's act; it is simply an attempt to specify what *kind* of act. The problem with naturalistic accounts of canonization is not that they show that establishing the canon is a matter of policy, but that – like Calvin's opponents – policy becomes arbitrary *poiesis*: whim, judgment, decision, rather than normed compliance. How may this act of compliant judgment be more closely described? Four characteristics can be identified:

---

79   J. Calvin, 'The True Method of Giving Peace to Christendom and of Reforming the Church', in: *Tracts and Treatises in Defence of the Reformed Faith III*, Edinburgh: Oliver and Boyd, 1958, 240–343, p. 267.
80   Augustine, *Contra epistolam Manichaei quam vocant fundamenti* v.
81   Calvin, *Institutes of the Christian Religion I.vii.1* (see n. 77), p. 75.
82   Ibid., I.vii.2 (p. 76).

First, the church's judgment is an act of confession of that which precedes and imposes itself on the church (that is, the *viva vox Jesu Christi* mediated through the apostolic testimony) and which evokes a Spirit-guided assent. The church's 'decision' with respect to the canon is thus 'simultaneously its acknowledgement of something which it is receiving from an authority over it'.[83] Only in a secondary sense is canonization an act of selection, authorization or commendation on the church's part, for 'it is not for us or for any man to constitute this or that writing as Holy Writ, as the witness to God's revelation, to choose it as such out of many others, but ... if there is such a witness and the acceptance of such a witness, it can only mean that it has already been constituted and chosen, and that its acceptance is only the discovery and acknowledgment of this fact.'[84] The 'decision' of the church is not a matter of pure *arbitrium,* but of *arbitrium liberatum.* Put differently: this decision has noetic but not ontological force, acknowledging what Scripture is but not making it so.[85]

Second, this act of confession, the church's judgment with respect to the canon, is an act of submission before it is an act of authority. This is because the authority of the church is nothing other than its acknowledgment of the norm under which it stands. 'The Church has exactly as much authority as it exercises obedience.'[86] Robert Jenson's recent and rather startling account of the canon falls at just this point: it fails to give sufficient theological specificity to the notion of 'decision'. 'The canon of Scripture ... is ... a dogmatic decision of the church. If we will allow no final authority to churchly dogma, or to the organs by which the church can enunciate dogma, there can be no canon of Scripture. The slogan *sola scriptura, if* by that is meant "apart from creed, teaching office, or authoritative liturgy" is an oxymoron.'[87] But does not this subvert the very affirmation it seeks to make, by construing the church's act of judgment as 'a historically achieved commendation by the church as community to the church as association of persons',[88] and not as an act of deference to that which moves the judgment of the church from without? And how may the church resist its persistent desire to be in monologue with itself unless its 'authoritative' decision with respect to the canon is its avowal of a norm beneath which it already stands and beneath which it can only stand if it is to perceive the truth?

---

83 Weber, *Foundations of Dogmatics I* (see n. 74), p. 251.
84 Barth, *Church Dogmatics I/2* (see n.74), p. 473.
85 For this distinction, see Berkouwer, *Holy Scripture* (see n. 62), p. 78.
86 Weber, *Foundations of Dogmatics I* (see n. 74), p. 251.
87 R. Jenson, *Systematic Theology I*, Oxford: Oxford University Press, 1997, pp. 27f.
88 Ibid., p. 28.

Third, as an act of confession and submission, the act of canonization has a *backward* reference. Through it, the church affirms that all truthful speech in the church can proceed only from the prior apostolic testimony. Canonization is recognition of apostolicity, not simply in the sense of the recognition that certain texts are of apostolic authorship or provenance, but, more deeply, in the sense of the confession that these texts are annexed to the self-utterance of Jesus Christ. The canon and the apostolicity (and so the apostolic succession) of the church are inseparable here. 'The apostolic succession of the Church must mean that it is guided by the Canon.'[89] The wider ecclesiological point – so easily obscured in ecclesiologies which take their cues from socio-historical depictions of the immanent dynamics of communities – is that the church and all its acts are *ostensive*, pointing beyond and behind themselves to that which transcends and precedes them. Thus '[t]he canonic decision of the Church is essentially its confession of the norm already given it, the standard by which it was prepared to let itself be measured ... The canon is an expression of the fact that the Church is only in reference backward actually the Church.'[90]

Fourth, as an act of confession, submission and retrospection, the church's judgment with respect to the canon is its pledging of itself to be carried by this norm in all its actions. Canonization is commitment to operate by a given norm, and thereby to have speech and action mastered by that norm. In a very real sense, the canon spells the end of free speech in the church, if by free speech we mean mere *Willkür*; the canon means obligation to appeal to the canon and be ruled by it in such a way that the freedom of the norm is not transgressed but kept in view at every moment as the norm is applied and operated. One consequence here is that the church's *use* of the canon has a distinctively passive character (not usually stated with any clarity in much talk of the 'uses of Scripture'). In an influential essay, Kendall Folkert drew a distinction between a canon of texts which is carried by other religious activity, 'present in a tradition principally by the force of a vector or vectors' and a canon of texts which is the carrier of other religious activities, that is, 'normative texts that are more independently and distinctively present within a tradition ... and which themselves often function as vectors'.[91] A Christian account of the canon is of the latter variety, because canonicity is not a function of use but use a function of canonicity (which is itself a function of divine approbation and use). Affirmation of the canon is thus a commitment to allow all the activities of the church (most of all, its acts of worship, procla-

---

89   Barth, *Church Dogmatics I/1* (see n. 55), p. 104.
90   Weber, *Foundations of Dogmatics I* (see n. 74), p. 252.
91   Folkert, 'The "Canons" of "Scripture"' (see n. 2), p. 173.

mation and ruling) be as it were enclosed by the canon. Worship, proclamation and ruling do not *make use* of the canon, as if it were a catalogue of resources through which the church could browse and from which it could select what it considered fitting or tasteful for some particular occasion; rather, they are acts which are at all points shaped by the canon and what it sets before the church.

Taken together, these four considerations suggest that, theologically construed – construed, that is, with an eye to its place in the history of the saving self-communication of the triune God – the church's act of canonization is properly passive, a set of human activities, attitudes and relations which refer beyond themselves to prevenient divine acts of speaking and sanctifying. For all the historical, human character of the church's judgment and its emergence from within the common life of Christian communities, there can be no question of the 'mutually constitutive reciprocity' of church and canon,[92] but only of the former's acknowledgment that the latter mediates the apostolic gospel. Like any other element in the church – oversight, service, proclamation, prayer, sacraments, fellowship, witness – the canon is a matter of grace, of a divine promise attached to a creaturely reality. And like all those elements, the canon, too, is 'a playground of human self-will'; but it is also 'the sphere of the lordship of Christ', and so

'if we believe that the Lord is mightier than the sin which indisputably reigns in the Church, if we believe that He is the victor in the struggle against grace which is indisputably widespread even in the Church, then we can count on it that a genuine knowledge and confession in respect of the Canon, and therefore a knowledge and confession of the genuine Canon, is not at least impossible in the Church, not because we have to believe in men, but because if we are not to give up our faith we have to believe in the miracle of grace.'[93]

7. Canon and Reading

So far I have attempted to sketch a dogmatic portrait of the Christian canon as an element in the triune – and especially Christological-pneumatological – reality of God's saving self-communication. To speak of the canon is to speak of that means of grace through which the revelatory self-presence of God in the form of sanctified texts reaches the obedient and attentive community, which responds to that presence by an act of assent and acknowledgement. Such a depiction as this does not command much attention in modern theology, partly because the instinctive nominalism of modern cul-

92 G. Lindbeck, 'Scripture, Consensus and Community', in: R.J. Neuhaus (ed.), *Biblical Interpretation in Crisis*, Grand Rapids: Eerdmans, 1989, 74–101, p. 78.

ture tends to doubt the possibility that human products can refer to the divine economy of grace, partly because a proclivity to voluntarism leads us to suppose that the church, like any other society, is a sphere of unchecked invention. The problem of voluntarism extends into the way in which the reader of the canon is often envisaged as somehow co-constituting the text, so that reading and interpreting the canon become what Kenneth Surin calls 'church poetics'.[94]

It is, of course, incontrovertible that the canon may not be neatly extracted from the reading acts of the church. Once again, the canon is a list of texts, and texts are not icons, not merely static locations of fully determinate meaning; they require the activity of readers. Texts are communicative acts, on the part of both authors and recipients; they demand exegesis. At least at this level, textual essentialism does not serve us well, because it assumes that a text is a kind of repository entirely independent of its reception, and thereby extracts the text from the history of the exchanges which it occasions. But if this is so, then – as with the discussion of the church's act of canonization – the crucial task is that of alert theological specification of readerly activity.

Christian reading of the canon is faithful reading, properly exhibiting the fundamental characteristic of all actions of faith, which is self-forgetful reference to the prevenient action and presence of God. Faithful action is *action*; its practitioners are *agents*. But both action and agent are defined by reference to that in the presence of which (of whom) they find themselves and before which (before whom) they are to demonstrate a relinquishment of will. Even in its acts of construing and interpreting, in bringing a communicative interest to bear upon the text, the Christian reading act is a kind of surrender. Above all, faithful reading is an aspect of *mortificatio sui*, a repudiation of the desire to assemble all realities, including texts, including even the revelation of God, around the steady centre of my will. To read – *really* to read – is to submit to the process of the elimination or correction or conversion of false desire, for it is that false desire – sin – which more than anything else is destructive of the communicative fellowship between God and humanity in which the canon plays its part. – Reading the Christian canon is a matter of *epoche*:

'We have to know the mystery of the substance if we are really to meet it, if we are really to be opened and ready, really to give ourselves to it, when we are told it, that it may really meet us as the substance. And when it is a matter of understanding, the knowledge of this mystery will create in us a peculiar fear and reserve which is not at all usual to us. We will

---

93 Barth, *Church Dogmatics I/2* (see n. 74), p. 598.
94 K. Surin, '"The weight of weakness": intratextuality and discipleship', in: idem, *The Turnings of Darkness and Light. Essays in Philosophical and Systematic Theology*, Cambridge: Cambridge University Press, 1989, 201–221, p. 213.

then know that in the face of this subject-matter there can be no question of our achieving, as we do in others, the confident approach which masters and subdues the matter. It is rather a question of our being gripped ... so that it is only as those who are mastered by the subject-matter, who are subdued by it, that we can investigate the humanity of the word by which it is told us. The sovereign freedom of this subject-matter to speak of itself imposes on us in the face of the word as such and its historicity an ἐποχή ... And the knowledge of this mystery will see to it that the work of exposition, which is the goal of all hearing and understanding, at least enters the stage of convalescence from the sickness with which all exposition is almost incurably afflicted, the sickness of an insolent and arbitrary reading in. If the exposition of a human word consists in the relating of this word to what it intends or denotes, and if we know the sovereign freedom, the independent glory of this subject-matter in relation both to the word which is before us and to ourselves, we will be wholesomely restrained, at the very least in our usual self-assured mastery of the relationship, as though we already knew its content and our exposition could give something more than hints in its direction. We shall be at least restrained in our evil domination of the text (even though in this age we can as little rid ourselves of it as we can of our old Adam generally).'[95]

The concerns which the reader brings to the canon are never simply innocent; they are (especially when they are theological concerns!) a source of potential distortion, even an assault on the freedom and dignity of the text and its matter; they are judgments which must be judged, and of which we must repent.[96] Contemporary theories of hermeneutical 'virtues' move us in something of the right direction, especially insofar as they insist that fitting reading of a canonical text requires the acquisition of moral and spiritual habits and not simply right critical technology.[97] But it remains doubtful whether virtue theory can successfully break free of the tug towards immanence; these accounts of hermeneutical activity still threaten to leave us within the relatively self-enclosed worlds of readerly psyches and habit-forming communities. If what has been said so far about the place of the canon in a network of soteriological relations between God and humanity is of any value, then it will require a much more vigorously charismatic-eschatological understanding of habits and their acquisition than has been offered in the quasi-Aristotelian accounts so far produced.

8. Conclusion

Some modern Christian theologians (especially those with heavy ecclesiological commitments) have been tempted to respond to decanonization – and

---

95 Barth, *Church Dogmatics I/2*, (see n. 74), pp. 470f.
96 On the connections of reading and repentance, see D.L. Jeffrey, *People of the Book. Christian Identity and Literary Culture*, Grand Rapids: Eerdmans, 1996, pp. 167–207, 353–373; W.J. Jennings, 'Baptizing a Social Reading: Theology, Hermeneutics, and Postmodernity', in: R. Lundin (ed.), *Disciplining Hermeneutics. Interpretation in Christian Perspective*, Grand Rapids: Eerdmans, 1997, pp. 117–127.
97 See again, Fowl/Jones, *Reading in Communion* (see n.37).

the corollary process of detraditionalization[98] – by pressing the claims of return to a stable, 'locative' style of church and theology as the only cure to the canonical dyslexia which afflicts us.[99] It is very easy for the notion and use of the canon to be caught up in these kinds of dynamics. But the cost is high. Nearly always, such appeals make little use of language about the freedom of God, and tend to take their energy from the fatally attractive mythology of a closed social and intellectual order. But, more than that, they turn the canon into an inviolable possession, even a weapon. The 'canon syndrome'[100] all too quickly lifts the church's life out of temporality and becomes a means of giving material form to the sanctity and safety of the church's mind. It makes indefectibility into something other than a *promise*.

The complicity of the canon in moral evil is undeniable. But one may adopt one of two postures to this state of affairs. The first, dominant in the modern history of freedom, has been genealogical: trace the history, observes the corruptions of producers and their products, and so cast down the mighty from their thrones. No serious Christian theology can afford to be anything other than grateful for some of fruits of this posture. The other, minority, response, has been to talk of the canon dogmatically as that means of grace through which the judgment of the apostolic gospel is set before the church. If the canon is a function of God's communicative fellowship with an unruly church, if it is part of the history of judgement and mercy, then it cannot simply be a stabilising factor, a legitimating authority. Rather, as the place where divine speech may be heard, it is – or ought to be – a knife at the church's heart.

---

98 See P. Heelas (ed.), *Detraditionalization: critical reflections on authority and identity*, Oxford: Blackwell, 1996.

99 To put the record straight, it is important not to link such developments to the work of George Lindbeck, as can already be seen from his earlier essay 'The Sectarian Future of the Church', in: J.P. Whelan (ed.), *The God Experience*, New York: Newman Press, 1971, pp. 226–243.

100 See Adriaanse, 'Canonicity and the Problem of the Golden Mean' (see n. 7).

The Canon as Space and Place

by Paul S. Fiddes

Among the various senses of the term 'canon' is one that arises more from usage than from any strict derivation of the word – that is, the notion of canon as a bounded space. If by canon we mean a 'list' of books, then the list might be portrayed as a boundary or fence, a line of demarcation enclosing within its borders the literature which is specially authorized by a community, marking this off from other material regarded as foreign. 'Boundary' is a spatial metaphor, although the picture of a dividing line has some affinities with more exact meanings of canon such as 'measure' and 'rule'. If by 'canon' we mean the actual content of these authorized writings, then this is like the area which is enclosed by the boundary marker, and it is this image of the canon as a 'space' that I want to explore here.

If we employ this metaphor, it might seem at first sight that the space of the canon will be smaller, narrower and altogether more restricted in scope than the space that lies beyond the boundary. This is certainly how Immanuel Kant regards the relation between the two spaces. The biblical theologian, tied to the canon, is to keep within the protective 'wall of ecclesiastical faith', and has no business to leap over the wall and 'stray into the free and open fields' of reason and philosophy.[1] Canon is local rather than universal, being the inherited statutes of one particular community, whereas a philosopher can explore the truths to which everyone's reason witnesses. We might summarize Immanuel Kant's view by naming the canon as a 'place' (i.e. localized), and the wide-ranging sphere of human discovery as a 'space' (i.e. universal).

The same kind of spatial distinction is operating in the very different thought of Elisabeth Schüssler Fiorenza, who refers to an image sometimes applied to the biblical literature – the metaphor of an enclosed garden. The wall of such a garden, she notes, 'not only protects the garden with its flow-

---

1   I. Kant, *The Conflict of the Faculties*, in: A.W. Wood/G. DiGiovanni (eds.), *Immanuel Kant, Religion and Rational Theology*, Cambridge: Cambridge University Press, 1996, p. 251.

ers and fruits but also separates it from the rest of the fields and meadows.'[2]
Her concern is the patriarchal nature of this wall and enclosure which has
'always served not only to protect women but also to control and limit them.'
Feminist hermeneutic must accordingly 'transgress canonical boundaries'
and discover the extensive world of literature that borders on the garden, and
gives a proper place to the ἐκκλησία of women's experience. An image for
this wider territory is in fact to be found in scripture itself, and is the 'open
cosmic house of divine wisdom':

> 'Her dwelling of cosmic dimensions has no walls; she permeates the whole world. Her invit-
> ing table, with the bread of sustenance and the wine of celebration, is set between seven cos-
> mic pillars that allow the spirit of fresh air to blow where it will.'[3]

Kant thus contrasts the place of statute with the space of reason; Fiorenza
contrasts the place of male domination with the space of the whole human
experience of divine wisdom.

1. The space and the place of the canon

For many reasons, however, it is clear that any simple contrast between place
(canon) and space (all other writings) is simplistic. The area within the canonical boundaries can in fact appear to the interpreter to be limitless, as an
endlessly open field within which to wander. While Schüssler Fiorenza draws
an image from the wisdom literature of the Old Testament (Prov 9:1–3) in
order to express a breadth of knowledge beyond canonical boundaries, it is
this very spaciousness that is transferred to a bounded canon in the latest
parts of the Hebrew Bible, when wisdom is finally equated with Torah. It is
the limited texts of the Torah that are acclaimed as a universe, as 'the whole
[or 'the all'] for humanity' (Qoh 12:13).

   This contraction of the multiplicity of wisdom to the limited span of Torah may well have been a means of dealing with what was increasingly felt to
be the hiddenness of wisdom. As I have argued elsewhere[4], Wisdom was ex-
perienced as something elusive, not because it was a transcendent entity
(dwelling in heaven) but because the sheer extent of the world to be observed
could not be grasped. In face of this baffling diversity, enquirers after wis-

---

2   E. Schüssler Fiorenza, 'Transgressing Canonical Boundaries', in: idem (ed.), *Searching
     the Scriptures. II. A Feminist Commentary*, London: SCM Press, 1995, p. 11.
3   Ibid.
4   See my essay '›Where Shall Wisdom be Found?‹ Job 28 as a Riddle for Ancient and
     Modern Readers', in: J. Barton/D. Reimer (eds.), *After the Exile. Essays in Honour of
     Rex Mason*, Macon: Mercer University Press, 1996, 171–190.

dom should content themselves with the scope of what was to hand in Torah (cf. Job 28:28). Yet the result was to make the Torah itself into a cosmos whose dimensions were always expanding and where exploration could never come to an end. The most striking image for this experience is provided by Ben Sirach who describes the covenant book, now identified with wisdom, as being like a fertilizing river flowing through the landscape, finally becoming an ocean which fills the world (Sir 24:23–29; NEB):

All this is the covenant-book of God Most High,
the law which Moses enacted to be the heritage of the assemblies of Jacob.
He sends out wisdom in full flood like the river Pishon
or like the Tigris at the time of firstfruits;
he overflows with understanding like the Euphrates
Or like Jordan at the time of harvest.
He pours forth instruction like the Nile,
like the Gihon at the time of vintage.
No man has ever fully known wisdom;
from first to last no one has fathomed her;
for her thoughts are vaster than the ocean
and her purpose deeper than the great abyss.

The same claim is later to be applied to another canon, the fourfold books of the Islamic faith. The Koranic interpreter Iqbāl speaks in his *Jāvīdnāma* of 'the world of the Koran' which reveals more and more possibilities every time one opens the book.[5]

In earlier times, this expansion of meaning was achieved through such exegetical devices as midrash, allegorization and spiritualization. In hermeneutics of the present day, openness of meaning is more likely to be traced to the interplay between the reader and the text in various forms of 'reader-response' theory, or to the establishing of meaning through the 'difference' of words from each other in an endlessly proliferating network of signifiers. While, for instance, Schüssler Fiorenza has found open space for the liberation of women only through 'transgressing canonical boundaries', Mary McClintock Fulkerson has found it within the canon itself. Concerned to include the reading practices of all women, not just those usually selected as exemplars of liberation, she observes that no texts in themselves are either oppressive or liberating. Texts which derive from a patriarchal culture can still be found to be liberating for some readers in their own social setting; it is reading practices that can 'create emancipatory space and widen the realm of God's kingdom'.[6]

---

5   Cited in A. Schimmel, *Deciphering the Signs of God. A Phenomenological Aproach to Islam*, Edinburgh: Edinburgh University Press, 1994, p. 164.
6   M. McClintock Fulkerson, *Changing the Subject. Women's Discourses and Feminist Theologies*, Minneapolis: Fortress Press, 1994, p. 164.

Of course, there can be a considerable difference between older and newer forms of resisting closure of meaning in a text.[7] Modern critical practices may assume the total absence of the author from a text, incapacity of a text to represent anything outside it, a lack of any correspondence between the world of the text and the everyday world, and so the relativization of all meaning. Most notably, the death of the author echoes the more impressive funeral of God, while exegesis in the early church assumed that the final authorship of scripture was – in some sense – divine. It was this latter conviction that provided the impetus to find new levels of meaning; a text that made no sense when read literally must have been intended by God for some useful purpose. Moreover, there was the general theological perspective that since God was infinite and unbounded, the words of God must likewise be uncramped by space and have infinite meanings. I suggest, then, that our own enquiry into the nature of the canon must, similarly, have a theological basis.[8] In pursuing our image of the 'space' of the canon we cannot avoid questions of revelation and the relationship between human words and the Word of God.

The openness of meaning or 'spaciousness' of a text might, it seems, be linked to divine revelation in two ways. In the first place, someone might concentrate on the actual letters of the text, and find expansiveness within them in the manner of a code to be cracked. If the very words have been transmitted by God, then the infinity of God inheres in them; they are multivalent signs because of their immediate divine origin. The human words are equated with divine words and their lack of limits. Thus, Origen as a biblical exegete was determined to derive meaning from every letter of the biblical text.[9] The Islamic tradition of exegesis takes a similar view of the Koran, affirming 'the mystery of the letters' to such an extent that translation from Arabic into other languages is regarded with suspicion as undermining the true meaning of the scriptures. *Sūra* 18:109 echoes the image of the sea of wisdom in Sir 24, but relates it to the marks on the page: 'If the sea were ink for my Lord's words, verily the sea would be exhausted before the words of my Lord ...' Above all the letters of the divine name form a kind of 'refuge' (*hirz*) or sacred space which one can enter and find a world of knowledge.

---

7   This is not to deny similarities. For instance, when Origen draws an analogy between interpreting scripture and making music, he envisages the response of the reader as actively contributing to the meaning by 'learning to strike the strings at the right moment' (*Philokalia* 6.2.1–20).

8   This is advocated strongly by W. Abraham, *Canon and Criterion in Christian Theology. From the Fathers to Feminism*, Oxford: Clarendon Press, 1998, pp. 20–23.

9   Origen, *Philokalia*, 2.4.24.

But alongside this concept of divine word, and already implied by the image of 'refuge', is another in all the major religious traditions; that is, the words of the text are a place where encounter with the Word of God can happen. In the immediate last century it was Karl Barth who most thoroughly drew out the implications of revelation as 'the person of God speaking' (*Dei loquentis persona*, a phrase borrowed from John Calvin).[10] As witness to the Word, the scriptures are also the occasion for meeting with the Word; they are a sacrament or icon in which the God who is speaking comes to presence. So Origen set alongside his view of verbal inspiration the need for encounter with the Spirit of God who breathes through the text.[11] Since Islam is often typecast as holding only a 'literal' view of revelation (as identical with the letters), it is worth recording one of the *hadīth qudsī* which says 'Someone who reads the Koran is as if he were talking to Me and I were talking with him'.[12] In more modern times the Moroccan Islamic scholar 'Aziz Lahbabi has expressed himself in this 'Barthian' way: 'Not the text in itself is the revelation but that which the believer discovers every time afresh while reading it.'[13] In this dynamic view of the divine word, openness or spaciousness of meaning comes from sharing in an ongoing conversation with the God who expresses God's self in an unlimited and never-to-be exhausted way. In this case, there need be no identification between the human word (written text) and the divine word (self-expression of God), and it may well be appropriate for the human word to share in all the frailty, problems and errancy of human life; as with the loaf of the eucharist and the paint and wood of an icon, God takes a piece of created and fallen matter as a place of encounter and a means of grace.

While these two views of the Word have often been run together, if we are to prevent the canon of scripture becoming either an idol or (to use a spatial metaphor from Friedrich Schleiermacher) a mausoleum, we should resolutely adopt the second view on its own.[14] But we must accept the conse-

---

10 K. Barth, *Church Dogmatics I/1*, transl. and ed. T.F. Torrance/G.W. Bromiley (1936–75), p. 304. Barth acknowledges the debt in *Christliche Dogmatik*, I.4.3: see G. Sauter (Hg.), *Karl Barth. Gesamtausgabe. Die Christliche Dogmatik im Entwurf. I. Die Lehre vom Worte Gottes, 1927*, Zürich: Theologischer Verlag, 1982, p. 66. The reference is to Calvin, *Institutes of the Christian Religion*, I.7.4.

11 Origen, *De Principiis*, 4.3.14 (ed. Butterworth, pp. 310-11).

12 *Ahādīth-i Mathnawi*, 39 (ed. Badī'uzzāman Furūzānfar, Tehran: University of Teran Press, 1955; cit. Schimmel, *Deciphering* (see n. 5), p. 157. The *hadīth qudsī* is a collection of sayings regarded as divine words revealed outside the Koran.

13 Cit. Schimmel, *Deciphering* (see n. 5), p. 165.

14 There remains, in my view, some question about whether Barth was resolute enough about this. The parallel he draws between the presence of the divine word in the flesh of Christ and in the written word of scripture is a hazardous one, despite his intention to

quences: this will mean that there can be nothing about *the text itself, in its own characteristics*, that distinguishes it from other literature; the implications of this for a notion of canon I intend to unravel later. For the moment I want to suggest that we have a dialectic here between 'space' and 'place', not on either side of a boundary (Kant, Fiorenza), but within it. On the one hand, canon marks out an area in which there is a spaciousness to wander, in which to meander, to play verbal games, to be imaginative and even – if the inclination strikes one – to do historical-critical exercises. On the other, at some point within this open space, the text becomes a 'place', a specific point of disclosure where we find ourselves drawn into conversation with the God who is speaking. Indeed, in a Christian theological vision, created persons are invited to participate in a conversation that is already going on within the Trinity, to share in movements of love and justice which are (by analogy) like a child speaking in obedience to a parent and a parent speaking to commission a child for a task ('as the Father has sent me so I am sending you'; John 20:21).

There is a dialectic here, because without the space there could be no place, and when we find the place the new insight gained makes it into a space. An appropriate biblical image is the naming of places as sacred sites by the Patriarchs; as Jacob exclaims: 'Truly the Lord is in this place and I did not know it' (Gen 28:16). The particular location of Bethel ('House of God') then takes on cosmic dimensions, as a ladder between earth and heaven.

2. Standing in the place of the other

In such an encounter the reader finds the text to be salvific in the sense of promoting wholeness and enabling a 'flourishing' of life. One way of spelling out this 'encounter' would be to say that the reader finds himself or herself reading 'as another'. This has some affinity with the proposal of Günter Bader, when he writes[15] that:

'Holy Scripture is a predicate to be attributed to those texts which, on the basis of certain indications, one assumes an author has written as himself [or herself] and as a wholly Other. *And the act of reading corresponds to this.*'

---

    deny any 'confusion of natures'; he himself notes that there can be no unity of person in
    the latter case: *Church Dogmatics I/2* (see n. 10), p. 499.
15 In an earlier version of his article (my translation and italics).

Bader is following a literary critic, Klaus Weimar[16], in affirming that all literary texts can only be read properly in so far as the reader reads them 'as
himself [or herself] and as another.' He modifies Weimar's insight, however,
by proposing that in the case of the canon of scripture, we read not only as
another but as 'a wholly Other'. While Bader himself seems to follow Weimar in understanding 'reading/writing as another' to mean wearing masks
and adopting roles in an imaginative way, it is hard to see what reading as a
'wholly Other' might mean unless this goes beyond mask-wearing into empathy with and interiorization of the 'Other' in the self. We can hardly play the
role of a wholly Other, but we can participate in the life and fellowship of
this Other.

Indeed, even with regard to the human 'other' of the writer(s) of the text,
I prefer to follow Paul Ricœur here, in his reflections on *Oneself as Another*.
Ricœur perceives that an authentic encounter with a text occurs when the
reader meets with another: 'hermeneutics is thus, explicitly or implicitly,
self-understanding by means of understanding others.'[17] For Ricœur, this is
embedded in knowledge of persons in general, so that selfhood only flour-
ishes by internalizing the other. The self cannot be posited immediately, but
only through a reflexive process involving signs, narratives and other people.[18] This is 'the self as another', but in his work strictly as a philosopher
Ricœur leaves open what the status of 'the other', the one who makes demands upon our responsibility, might be:

'Perhaps the philosopher as philosopher has to admit that one does not know and cannot say
whether this Other, the source of the injunction, is another person whom I can look in the
face or who can stare at me, or my ancestors for whom there is no representation. ... Or God
– living God, absent God – or an empty place. With this aporia of the Other, philosophical
discourse comes to an end.'[19]

While Ricœur in his role as a philosopher (he speaks otherwise as a believer)
cannot commit himself to name the Other as God, he has identified an 'aporia
of the Other' which encounters us in all relationships and in all our narratives, and he urges that we cannot rule God out in facing this impasse.

Reading scripture, then, we gain the impression that the authors have
been writing 'as themselves and as a wholly Other'. When the text becomes
an occasion for revelation, we read *both* as the human other and as the wholly

---

16 K. Weimar, *Enzyklopädie der Literaturwissenschaft* (UTB 1034), Tübingen/Basel: Fran-
cke, [2]1993, § 168.
17 P. Ricœur, *The Conflict of Interpretations. Essays in Hermeneutics*, Evanston: North-
western University Press, 1974, p. 17.
18 P. Ricœur, *Oneself as Another*, Chicago/London: Chicago University Press, 1992, p. 4.
19 Ibid., p. 355.

Other, internalizing the author and *being* internalized by the gracious act of the triune God. We stand in the place of the other – historian, prophet, poet, priest or wise man – and we find ourselves in the place which God has made for us within God's own self.

But if we follow Ricœur in his view of the 'aporia of the Other' which meets us in all relationships and narratives, we cannot construe the difference between the canon of scripture and all other texts as being that while we read the latter 'as others', we read the former alone 'as the wholly Other'. Rather, we meet the aporia of the Other in all texts. Moreover, we may find support for this in two other considerations. The first is the nature of revelation itself: if revelation is the disclosure of a self-revealing God, then the question arises as to whether this God is free to unveil the divine Self (= utter the divine Word) through a variety of textual media, as God wills. A second reason emerges from the phenomenology of personal relationships. Once the 'other', including the 'other' we meet in literary texts, is understood in an ethical way as making an *unlimited* demand upon us and upon our responsibility for others, then we touch at least a trace of the 'wholly Other' in and through all others, and in all 'faces'.[20] This is a point to which I intend to return in thinking about the practices which a text produces.

In many texts, then, whether inside or outside the biblical canon, we shall find ourselves in the place of reading both 'as another' and 'as a wholly Other'. Likewise there will be a dialectic between space and place in all literature. These are not therefore characteristics that will provide an answer to the question as to *why* the Christian church should regard a certain body of literature as normative for its life. The answer cannot lie in finding certain marks – whether of inspiration, beauty (stressed especially by exegetes of the Koran) or revelation – in one text that will distinguish it from others, but rather in a theological perspective on Christ and the Church. In the first place, it is simply a fact that these writings are closely bound up with the event of Jesus Christ and the birth of the Christian Church. The New Testament writings, assuming and largely incorporating the view of God and the world developed over a long period of time in the Hebrew Bible, witness in a firsthand (though not necessarily eye-witness) way to the life, death and resurrection of the one in whom Christians find the fullest disclosure of the nature and purposes of God. The canon is a 'norm' for the Church because it is 'normed' by the story of Jesus. As Ignatius of Antioch expresses it, 'for me records are Jesus Christ; the sacrosanct records are His cross and death and

---

20 On the infinite summons to responsibility in the 'face' of another, see E. Levinas, *Otherwise than Being*, The Hague: Martinus Nijhoff, 1981, 114–126.

His resurrection ...'[21] Second, Christian scripture happens to be the collection of writings to which the Church has appealed over the years to shape its beliefs and practices; the community has found it to be a means of grace, and in an interactive way it has both formed the canon and been formed by it. As long as we count ourselves members of this community, our identity depends on sharing in this formation.

I am offering here an integration of what might be called 'theological' and 'social-cultural' explanations for the normative position of scripture in the acts of reading of the church. The first concerns the self-revelation of God, and the second relies on contingency ('Christian scripture happens to be ...'). The two are not casually yoked together, however, but relate to a doctrine of a God who exposes God's own self to contingency in creating. The contingent is part not only of our lives and identity, but can be understood to be a factor in the divine life through the self-limitation of a creator God[22]; this God, we may say, takes and uses material which has been formed outside God's absolute control, though not without divine influence.

These two reasons do, of course, raise further questions. With regard to the first, for instance, do the exact boundaries of the canon matter, since other literature might be included either as 'first-hand' material with regard to the New Testament, or as necessary background to the event of Jesus with regard to the Old Testament? Again, how can we escape subjectivity in interpreting scripture by 'the story of Jesus', especially since there is a diversity of New Testament witness and any number of problems concerning faith and history? I hope at least to touch on answers to these questions, but to do so by exploring further the image of canon as 'bounded space'. With regard to the second factor of contingency, *how* do demarcated boundaries of text help to construct identity? Given the fact that there can be a 'spaciousness' within such bounds, what is the advantage of establishing frontiers at all? We can, I suggest, discern three effects of drawing limits to a body of literature. These observations apply in principle to any canon of material (e.g. 'the canon of western literature since the renaissance'), but take on a particular character with regard to the canon of scripture. The canonical boundary, I suggest, (a) imposes obligations; (b) enables deconstruction, and (c) establishes a point of comparison.

---

21 Ignatius of Antioch, *Philad.* VIII:2.
22 Further on this, see my *The Creative Suffering of God*, Oxford: Oxford University Press, 1988, pp. 66–70.

3. Boundary as obligation

A community which holds its identity through a certain body of material has an obligation to engage with it. It cannot ignore it. The boundary marks out an area, sets up a space, in which exploration is required. A community of literary critics dealing with western poetry since the Renaissance develops a 'canon' of literature: they may disagree about the extent to which the members of the canon are 'models' or 'classics' to be imitated, but they are clear that the subject cannot be researched without taking account of them. With regard to the Christian community, as long as we count ourselves part of it we have a demand laid upon us to read, interpret and wrestle with its canon in a manner that no other texts ask from us. Other literature – whether the apocrypha, the writings of St John of the Cross or the poetry of Gerard Manley Hopkins – can produce the impression upon us that they have been written by the author 'writing as himself/herself and as a wholly Other', but we are not obliged to study them and draw them into our lives.[23]

The obligation is *not* to accept the words of the writers of scripture as correct or infallible, but to enter into relation with them. It is to stand where they stand, to attempt to enter with empathy into their 'otherness' from us (using the historical-critical method as well as imagination wherever possible), and to hear the Word of God *with* them. This is the point of the image of 'place': the text becomes an *occasion* where we encounter the Word, which is the self-unveiling of God and God's purposes for human life here and now. To some extent this will be what John Macquarrie calls 'repetitive revelation'[24], or what Barth identifies as the 'contingent contemporaneity of the Word'[25], where the Word of God spoken in the past is re-actualized in the present. But the openness of God to human response within divine purposes, and God's continual creative originality, means that the Word will also take new form and new direction in new times. Nor does the belief that an 'event of the Word' lies behind the written text, and is witnessed to by the text, mean that all narrative must refer to some kind of event in history, as Barth proposed in

---

23 My argument here is that the boundary of the canon itself lays an obligation on members of the community to enter it; we do not need to find a particular theme or motif in the canonical material which has a binding force, whether this is (for example) 'covenant' or 'the coming Kingdom of God'; for the latter, see H.-J. Kraus, *Systematische Theologie im Kontext biblischer Geschichte und Eschatologie*, Neukirchen-Vluyn: Neukirchener Verlag, 1983.

24 J. Macquarrie, *Principles of Christian Theology. Revised Edition* London: SCM Press, 1977, pp. 90–96.

25 Barth, *Church Dogmatics I/1* (see n. 10), p. 145–149.

preferring the term 'saga' to 'myth'.[26] The event of the word may have happened in the very *writing* of the text, at a particular moment in national or personal history; this must anyway certainly be the case with such literary genres as laments, law-codes or wisdom sayings.

The 'place' which we enter to hear the Word will be filled with various kinds of tensions, oppositions and contrasts to which we need to be sensitive. Gerhard Sauter has proposed that in reading the text we ought to be aware of certain distinctions, such as the difference between law and gospel, demand and consolation, promise and fulfilment; to know these well is to have a kind of set of rules which 'build a structure of perception into the faithfulness of scripture', but not by allotting the two sides of the contrasts to particular texts in any fixed or schematic way.[27] Rather, the livingness of the scripture as bearer of the promise of God means that we cannot know in advance when any text will address us as – for instance – law or gospel, which means judgement or salvation; it may address us in different ways in different circumstances. We are to keep faith with scripture by trusting that there is a congruence (Miteinander) of the text rather than contradiction; the Word will be heard in the midst of the 'inner tension' of the text, and in this place of reading 'God will break us open for God's own self'. Here I want to extend this perception in a way that the image of 'place' allows. The judgement of the Word does not just reach the *reader* through the tensions, but the *written human word* of scripture itself is subject to the same judgement of the divine Word. As the text becomes a 'place' of disclosure in which the reader is standing, the Word may be heard sounding in accord or discord with the sentiments in the text.[28] This means that no text in the canon may be dispensed with, none dealt with by cutting it out. It is only through the obligation to stand with the writer and enter into his or her feelings, arguments, vision, mistakes and prejudices that the Word of promise can be heard.

This is the advantage of a boundary enclosing texts: no corner of human life can escape from the judgement of the Word. The very existence of a boundary implies an obligation to pass within it. Attempts to find a 'canon within the canon' which operate by making a selection from among canonical texts (with Marcion as the prime exponent of this method) have an attractive

---

26 Barth, *Church Dogmatics III/1* (see n. 10), pp. 81–87.

27 G. Sauter, '„Schrifttreue" ist kein „Schriftprinzip"', in: J. Barton/G. Sauter (Hg.), *Offenbarung und Geschichten*, Frankfurt a.M.: Peter Lang, 2000, pp. 43–49.

28 The perception that it *may* accord with the text means that the Old Testament, for instance, is not to be read simply as an account of human failure, as suggested by R. Bultmann, 'Prophecy and Fulfilment' in: C. Westermann (ed.), *Essays on Old Testament Interpretation*, London: SCM Press, 1963, 50–75, p. 72: 'an inner contradiction pervades the self-consciousness and hopes of Israel and its prophets'.

honesty about them, in being willing to criticize passages for falling short of the love and justice of God. But a canon is then being made in the image of the selector; what is lost is the 'otherness' of texts which, in their very strangeness of culture, challenge us to reconsider our own.

How then shall we listen for the Word, how be enabled to hear its verdict on human experience? Since the final unveiling of the Word is in the person of Jesus Christ, all human words will be measured by this Word incarnate, by the shape of his story which reflects the character of God and God's project in creation. Moreover, since in Christ the true purpose of human life finds fulfilment, the words of the text will stand under what Fiorenza calls an 'ethics of accountability'.[29] That is, the biblical reader will ask what the ethical consequences of interpreting a text in various ways *has* been in the past and what it is likely to be in contemporary socio-political contexts. What human values will be promoted by the text when read in one way rather than another? Similarly, Fulkerson asks us to observe the ways in which texts, in various social situations, have produced human subjects who make objects of others.[30] When we ask how we shall read this text, remembering our responsibilities in the face of others, this also is reading the text 'as another'; the 'other' whom we confront through the text is not only the original writer(s), but the many who are our neighbours.

To make this reading practice concrete, let us take three examples of how the Word *might* be heard, without being dogmatic or prescriptive. A history-writer of Ancient Israel presents Samuel as claiming to have heard 'the word of the Lord' calling for holy war against the Amalekites (1.Sam 15:2–3, 22–23), and the form of the narrative implies that the writer thinks Samuel to be a true prophet. The reader, however, is not obliged to give the same weight to the ethical insight that 'to obey is better than sacrifice' (V. 22) and to what we would now regard as incitement to a war crime or even genocide (V. 3). Both commands stand under the judgement of the divine Word, and it would not be inconsistent to find one expressing the divine character and the other an all-too human spirit of nationalism and racism. Unlike this notorious Old Testament passage, Luke's account of Pilate's repeated declaration of the innocence of Jesus might seem to be less problematic (Luke 23:4,14,22); but a reader may hear a divine word of judgement on an anti-Jewish bias in this concern to exonerate the Roman authorities, while also hearing the note of God's vindication of Jesus through the narrative. Readers may think that

29 E. Schüssler Fiorenza, 'The Ethics of Biblical Interpretation: Decentering Biblical Scholarship', JBL 107 (1988) 13–15.
30 Fulkerson, *Changing the Subject* (see n. 6), p. 25.

Paul's words about the 'weakness of God' in the cross of Jesus (1.Cor 1:18) are not problematic at all, and get so close to the heart of the revelation of God's nature and purposes in Christ that the human word here is simply equivalent to the divine Word. However, a reader may still hear a word of judgement upon the way that Paul weaves this insight into a rhetoric that at times gets dangerously close to manipulating his readers.

We may differ about how we hear the Word of God in and through these examples. The point is the validity of the process, which neither validates the text as the Word of God in itself, nor discards it as useless for hearing the Word. Unless we were obliged by the boundary of the canon to enter a place where human feelings of national pride and the human tendency to dominate break the surface, we would not hear the Word of judgement on human life, and would not know about human obedience, the meaning of Christ's death and the vulnerability of God. None of these concepts, whether in the text or in the mind of the reader, are – of course – revelation in themselves, as if they were simply propositions communicated by God. They are human response to the self-unveiling of God, or human words which flow from engagement in the divine conversation. But they may be understood as being prompted or enabled by the impact of God's self-disclosure, so that (as Karl Barth puts it), 'revelation seizes the language'.[31] We may believe that human words can be *appropriate* to the reality of being immersed into the interweaving movements of giving and receiving in love that we call 'Persons of the Trinity'.[32]

Finding this appropriateness depends, to be sure, on being able to measure the text by the 'canon' of Christ, as the one who is himself the 'canon within the canon'. Given the diversity of witness to Christ in the writings of the New Testament, and the shaping of this witness by situation and theological intention, how can we have such a criterion at all? Perhaps it might be safer to follow the direction of recent 'canonical criticism', and find a criterion in the shape of the canon itself, taken as a whole.[33] Following our spatial metaphor, we might call this the 'lie of the land', or the profile of the landscape, and we should certainly be aware of this general configuration of the space bounded by canon. However, while this approach seems to promise greater objectivity, since it is the canon of the Church it hardly escapes de-

---

31 Barth, *Church Dogmatics I/1* (see n. 10), p. 430
32 For this idea of Persons as 'movements of relationship', see my book, *Participating in God. A Pastoral Doctrine of the Trinity*, London: Darton, Longman and Todd, 2000.
33 B.S. Childs, *Introduction to the Old Testament as Scripture*, London: SCM Press, 1979, pp. 72–83.

pending in the end upon the criterion of Christology.[34] There is also a worry-
ing possibility that a 'biblical theology' might float free of historical criticism, and so of history itself. I suggest that any theological view of canon
cannot be detached from Christology, and this means being committed to the
ongoing incarnation of Christ in the Church as 'the Body of Christ'. The
'story of Jesus' cannot then be held as an individual possession, but must always be tested out against the picture of Christ held by the universal Church,
by the community in which (as Schleiermacher perceived) the Redeemer is
present. We must seek for at least a minimal consensus about the story of Jesus, held within the whole Church, in every time and space. This is also part
of our commitment to the community which is shaped by the canon of scripture.

Irenaeus, then, was on the right track with his insistence on a 'canon of
faith' or 'canon of truth', followed by the *regula fidei* of Tertullian. Some
short summary of the story of Jesus is required, though I suggest that it an
open question whether this is to be culled from historic creeds and confessions of the historic Church, or to be an aim of ecumenical cooperation in
every age. Irenaeus' own canon, that God the Father of Jesus Christ is also
the one Creator of all things, is marked in its formulation by dispute with the
gnosticism of his times. There is at least one test we can apply to such a
summary: it must be *capable* of making sense of the whole diversity of biblical witness, or having a good 'fit', while it will at the same time be deepened
and broadened by investigating this witness, including taking the risks of historical criticism.

The images of 'space' and 'place' thus allow us to develop a theology of
the Word which takes account of both its human and divine dimensions. The
canonical boundary *obliges* us to enter a wide-ranging space of human experience, offering 'places' where revelation can happen. In these places we
stand alongside witnesses to the Word from the past, though their very witness is always subject to judgement from the Word itself. In reading the text
'as another' we enter into their experience, and although the nature of the
'place' is certainly not limited to authorial intention, their voice is a means
through which we can hear and enter the divine conversation. Recent critical
theory has stressed that the act of writing distances authors from their creation, and even interrupts their proximity to themselves.[35] While this critical

---

34 Cf. J. Barr, *Holy Scripture. Canon, Authority, Criticism*, Oxford: Clarendon Press, 1983,
    pp. 79ff.; Barr judges that Childs is continually ambiguous about whether by 'canon' he
    means the inner organic development of the collection of texts, or the final form of the
    canon of the church.
35 See J. Derrida, *Writing and Difference*, transl. A. Bass, London: Routledge 1993, p. 183.

insight has sometimes led to the 'death' of the authorial subject, with the entire exclusion of the author's intention from the meaning of the text, it is true that the author is absent from a text in a way that is not true of the living voice. While 'traces' of the author's presence remain, the text is open to use and re-use beyond his or her control. Deconstructive criticism has thus often contrasted the 'oppression' of a voice with the freedom offered by writing.[36] However, if we are to read 'as another', there is an advantage in recovering some element of voice. This need not be oppressive for at least two reasons: the human voice is itself under judgement from the Word, and the divine 'voice' is inviting us into conversation, not issuing unilateral mandates.

Reading a text aloud in the context of liturgy may well help to recover the sense of 'place'; the liturgy can recover the voice which has been partly lost in writing, and further lost in our own cultural tradition of mainly reading silently. William Abraham, in his study of canon, reminds us that in the earliest church oral material from the Apostles was held in higher esteem and trust than written material.[37] As Papias puts it: 'I did not think that what was to be gotten from the books would profit me as much as what came from the living and abiding voice.'[38] In the terms employed by Emmanuel Levinas, there is a priority of 'the saying' over 'the said'.[39]

Here the Christian tradition may learn from the Islamic, where listening to the *sound* of the Koran interweaves with seeing the calligraphic art on the page. Revelation happens, Islamic teachers say, through the mysterious relations between seeing the words (signs), hearing the sound and knowing the content: 'To listen to the Koran means to listen to God; hearing becomes seeing, seeing becomes hearing, knowing turns into action ...'[40] The recitation of prayers which contain passages of the Koran opens a sacred space, allows the worshipper/reader to enter a place of dialogue which has already been initiated by God's speaking of the Word. The use of a prayer mat with its boundaries symbolizes this place of encounter, the entering of the 'refuge' constructed by reciting the words of scripture.

---

36 See, e.g., J. Derrida, *Speech and Phenomena, and Other Essays on Husserl's Theory of Signs*, transl. D.B. Allison, Evanston: North Western University Press, 1973, pp. 129–140.
37 Abraham, *Canon and Criterion* (see n. 8), pp. 32–33.
38 Papias, quoted by Eusebius, *Hist. Eccl.* III:39:3f.
39 Levinas, *Otherwise than Being* (see n. 20), pp. 5–7, 9–20.
40 *Die Gaben der Erkenntnisse des Umar as-Suhrawardī*, übers. u. eingel. v. R. Gramlich, Wiesbaden: Steiner, 1978, p. 41.

4. Deconstruction and comparison

If a canonical boundary marks out an area we are obliged to enter, it also defines a body of material which can be subverted in the interests of truth and
creativity. In recent 'deconstructive' biblical criticism, the diversity and inconsistencies within scripture have not been regarded as a matter to be regret-
ted and excused (if not actually harmonized), but rather *celebrated* as evidence that the text is undermining itself. Whenever there is a danger of a
closed system of thought building up, it is argued, the network which is
formed by the 'difference' of signifiers from each other can be broken open
for new and endless meaning. Moreover, the text itself can give clues to this
openness, this undermining of dogma, by offering a little piece that does not
fit in and which inverts or subverts the pattern of the whole. Closure is always being resisted by the text itself.

The deconstructive interpreter, suggests Mark Taylor, is wandering along
an 'unstable border', since such criticism is both inside and outside the area
of thought that it is questioning.[41] Deconstruction is parasitic, depending
upon the system or hierarchy that it is subverting. The critic is 'in the mid-
dest', walking along 'a boundary that knows no bounds', caught in a cease-
less play of opposites, in a 'middle kingdom'. While Taylor himself does not
align this liminality or marginality with the boundaries of the canon, there is
an evident connection. The line which encloses the 'normative' literature is
also touching on adjacent territory, the area 'outside' the canon. The deconstructive critic is always, as it were, walking the frontier of the canon, leaning
both ways. The boundary seems to set up an 'either/or' contrast, but the critic
may at times want to say 'neither/nor' or even 'both/and'.

A deconstructive approach can be a useful tool of criticism for the biblical
interpreter, though taken to the extreme it can end in a total relativization of
meaning and truth. Deconstruction is valid in so far as the interpreter can
never reach the mystery of God to which the written text points, yet cannot
literally describe, and in so far as even the human personality eludes complete analysis. Human language about the infinite will always fail, and deconstructive criticism can usefully pick up the points where it falls short.
With regard to canonical boundaries, literature which lies beyond the borders
can be too easily polarized with canonical material as if they are mutually
exclusive (one thinks of the facile distinctions made between 'Greek and Hebrew ideas of time' in some biblical theologies). It is important to continually

---

41 M.C. Taylor, *Erring. A Postmodern A/theology*, Chicago: University of Chicago Press,
    1984, pp. 10–12.

ask the question, with William Blake, as to whether there can ever be progression without contraries.[42] At least we ought to be continually suspicious
about why alterities are being excluded. It may be that confronting an alterity
to an established dogma will alert us to the judgement of the Word on the text
itself.

As an example to illuminate this abstract discussion, we might do worse
than return to the difficult passage in 1.Sam 15, in which the intransigent
prophet Samuel finishes Saul's job for him (as the prophet sees it) and hacks
Agag to pieces in front of the altar of Yahweh in Gilgal. For whatever reasons, Saul has failed to carry through the 'ban' on the Amalekites, and has
received the verdict from Samuel that 'Because you have rejected the word of
the Lord/ he has also rejected you from being king.' I have already suggested
that it is the reader's responsibility to discern what *actually might be* the
'word of the Lord' in this situation, and have raised the possibility that it
might – despite authorial intention – be a word of judgement on self-
preservation driven by nationalism. It would be interesting to consider, with
the help of such tools as the historical-critical method and redaction criticism,
whether this might have been the Word of God at the time of the period of
early kingship in Israel when a fairly recent collection of tribes was establishing its identity among its older neighbours, or at the time of the writing of the
court history when Judah was facing different problems with superior powers
in the region, or whether it is only the Word of God here and now when a
new spirit of nationalism has appeared in our global village. Anyway, it is a
word heard in the 'place' offered by the text, discordant with what the historian himself apparently thinks to be the divine word which Saul has rejected.
What I now want to stress is that the figure of Samuel in this narrative bol-
sters up the rejection of Saul with a comment on Yahweh's character: 'The
Glory of Israel will not recant or change his mind; for he is not a mortal that
he should change his mind.' (V. 29). This is a text that, out of context, has
been appealed to frequently in the history of biblical interpretation as support
for the philosophical concept of the immutability of God. Whether in the intention of the original historian, or in the minds of interpreters, a contrast is
drawn between the Hebrew depiction of a consistent God, and the gods of
other mythologies in the Ancient Near East and in Ancient Greece who
change their minds in an arbitrary way, and who consequently treat human
beings with an unpredictable cruelty.

---

42 See W. Blake, *The Marriage of Heaven and Hell*, Plate 3, in: G. Keynes (ed.), *Blake.
Complete Writings*, London: Oxford University Press, 1966, p. 149.

Such latter narratives are beyond the canon, and must apparently be held in antithesis to the canonical picture of God. Yet this very passage concludes by undermining its own declaration about a non-repentant, inflexible God: 'Samuel grieved over Saul, and *the Lord was sorry* that he had made Saul King over Israel' (V. 35, echoing V. 11). It seems that the God who cannot change his mind over Saul's rejection *could* change his mind over Saul's selection. We might regard V. 35 (with V. 11) as a mere, unthinking contradiction of V. 29, arising from the historian's careless use of his sources, or V. 29 might be excluded as a late redaction to the passage.[43] But we could instead read the passage as a whole and find here a hint, an incentive, to deconstruct the narrative with its entire picture of God, including a national deity who wages holy war.[44] This might then lead us to look again at other ancient mythologies, not simply to polarize the 'wholly Otherness' of the God of Hebrew religion with the gods of other literatures who are beset by human pathos and emotions.

A deconstructive approach thus involves comparison with other literatures beyond the canon, but the canonical boundary invites such comparison even when subversion of the canonical text is not immediately in view. The enclosure of a certain body of material by a community may privilege it, not for reading in *exclusion* from other texts, but always for reading in *relation* to others. The notion of canon obliges us, not only to explore the material so marked off, but to bring it into conjunction with other territories. It is as if *all* writings are near neighbours, all lie on the immediate further side of the boundary, and their proximity cannot be ignored.[45] Correspondingly, any comparison between them must always involve the canon as one member. There will be myriad ways of inter-connecting the different members of the world-archive of texts; the claim of canon is always to be included where this involves the 'flourishing' of human life. Until quite recently this has been the position of the canon of the Hebrew-Christian scriptures in the west; it has been, in the words of William Blake, 'the great code of art'.[46] Similarly, within the medieval Islamic world, Koranic exegesis provided the basis for almost all scholarly undertakings. As the canon of western literature cannot

---

43 So P. Kyle McCarter, *1 Samuel* (AncB 8), New York: Doubleday, 1980, p. 268, judging that 'the contradiction is so blatant that we must question its originality', and suggesting a late addition perhaps derived from Num. 23:19.

44 R.W. Klein, *1 Samuel* (WBC 10), Waco, TX: Word Publishers, 1983, p. 156, does not recognize a deconstructive aspect, but does take a positive approach to paradox: 'Perhaps the paradox expresses the real truth: he never changes his mind, and yet he does".

45 Given the history of the Christian church, there is a particular need to read the Christian canon alongside later Jewish texts.

46 See N. Frye, *The Great Code. The Bible and Literature*, London: Ark, 1983, pp. xii–xvi.

be understood without reference to the Bible, all literature in Arabic and other Islamic idioms is, to this day, permeated by allusions to the Koran. Alongside Blake's phrase may be set what Paul Nwyia has called 'the Koranization of the memory'.[47]

Perhaps now an answer can be glimpsed to the question I raised earlier, about the exact limits of the boundary of canon. Given that other candidates might be advanced for the criterion of 'nearness of witness' to Christ and his cultural cradle in Judaism, how much does the *exact* composition of the list matter? Must a Protestant Christian really think that the content of *Ecclesiastes* (Koheleth) is obviously superior in quality to that of *Ecclesiasticus* (The Wisdom of Jesus Ben Sirach)?[48] Would it have been disastrous for the life and faith of the Christian Church if the *Epistle of James* or the *Book of Revelation* had failed to make it into the canon and the *Didache* had? We will only become anxious about this if we have some theory of revelation that isolates it within the canonical texts, and so differentiates these from all other others as the only media of revelation. My argument has been that in all literature there is a 'place' for the word of God to be heard (or a place into which the Spirit can breath, as the wind blows through an area in the world)[49], as well as an open 'space' for expansive meaning; my occasional references to the Koran and other Islamic writings throughout this paper have been a deliberate exemplification of this view. However, this does not cancel the importance of having canonical boundaries, which are essential for (at least) the three reasons I have urged. The Christian church holds its canon of scripture as witness to Christ, who is the final authority for faith and practice; as long as the witness we have is adequate for salvation – that is, for the flourishing of human life and its divinization in the life of God – then the exact path taken by the boundary line of the canon is not critical. Other literature is not excluded from use in comparison and deconstruction; had the *Epistle of James* not been included in the canon, we can be sure that it would still be useful and frequently used in offering a critique of Pauline theology and in illuminating the wisdom sayings of the Gospels.

---

47 P. Nwyia, Ibn 'Atā' Allāh et la naissance de la confrérie Šadilite, Beirut: Dar el-Machreq, 1972, p. 46.

48 It may be significant that a recent question in the BBC Radio4 quiz 'Brain of Britain' attributed Ecclesiastes 12:1-8 to 'Ecclesiasticus' without a squeak of protest from any contestant or member of the audience.

49 This is surely the dynamic sense of θεόπνευστος ('breathed into by God') in 2.Tim 3:16.

5. Christ as space and place

The normative function of the canon of Christian scripture depends entirely on its relation to Christ, and so it is not surprising that spatial imagery is applied within the scriptures to Christ himself. As the 'canon within the canon', Christ is the essential place where the Word of God can be heard, and contracts into himself the cosmic spaciousness of wisdom. When the author of the Fourth Gospel writes that 'the word became flesh and dwelt (or 'pitched his tent') among us' (John 1:14), he is recalling the Exodus story of making a tent or tabernacle for God to dwell among the people of Israel (Ex 25:8-9), which had become an eschatological image for God's final dwelling on earth (e.g. Joel 3:17, Zech 2:10). At the same time the Greek verb σκηνοῦν ('to pitch a tent' or 'to dwell'), has an assonance with the Hebrew root שׁכן, used in the Old Testament for the 'dwelling' of God among his people, and from which was later derived the term *shekinah* in Rabbinic theology as a reverent periphrasis for the divine presence. Thus, as Raymond Brown summarizes it, 'we are being told that the flesh of Jesus Christ is the new localization of God's presence on earth, and that Jesus is the replacement of the ancient tabernacle.'[50] But there are also echoes here of passages in the wisdom writings about the dwelling of personified Wisdom among human beings, and notably the song of Wisdom in Sir 24:8-10:

'He that created me decreed where my tent should be.
He said, "Let your tent be in Jacob
and your inheritance in Israel."
.... In the sacred tent I ministered in his presence,
and so I came to be established in Zion.'

As I have already suggested, in Hebrew wisdom literature Wisdom is not hidden because it has disappeared to heaven, but because of its inexhaustible scope; it is too extensive for comprehension, because the God to whom wisdom belongs has an infinite capacity for life and creative action. This Johannine Prologue is thus affirming that the divine word/wisdom is incarnate in Christ because this Son comprehends in himself the multiplicity of God's works and attributes. In 'one' Son (V. 18) there is the 'fullness' of the many (Vv. 14, 16), just as Wisdom is 'unique' yet also 'multiple' (Wisdom 7:22). In case we miss this idea that the complexity of divine wisdom has been contracted into a human person, the author of the Prologue makes reference immediately to Torah: 'the law indeed was given through Moses; grace and

---

50   R.E. Brown, *The Gospel According to John I-XII* (AncB 29), London: Geoffrey Chapman, 1971, p. 33.

truth came through Jesus Christ.' Wisdom was thought to be made accessible by being contracted into the bounds of the Torah; indeed, the song in Sir 24 about Wisdom 'tenting' in Zion and its temple, which is echoed in John 1:14, goes on to affirm that wisdom dwells in 'the covenant-book of God most High'. As we have already seen, this leads to a belief about the spaciousness of Torah: since wisdom's thoughts are 'vaster than the ocean', and 'from first to last no one has fathomed her', the Torah 'pours forth wisdom in full flood' (Sir 24:23-29).

The πλήρωμα which is in Christ (V. 16) is therefore not an early reference to the Gnostic cosmos, but to the way that one human son makes known the many aspects of God. This God, like the divine attribute of wisdom, is hidden because human minds cannot get a grasp on the complexity and inexhaustibility of the divine life, love and creativity through which 'all things came into being' (V. 3) and which fills all things. We can only know this God through the focussing of the many in the one person. Christ is normatively the 'place' where we hear the Word of God and are drawn into the place which God opens up within God's self.

The diversity and variety of the canon is well exemplified in the different Gospel portrayals of Jesus, which make clear that Christ transcends all witnesses to him, and cannot be acquired as a possession by any party of group. In his reflections on Christology, John Milbank comments on this elusiveness of the person of Jesus in the Gospel records, and the multiple metaphors to which the narratives resort in order to identify him: 'Jesus is the way, the word, the truth, life, water, bread, the seed of a tree and the fully grown tree, the foundation stone of a new temple and at the same time the whole edifice'. Milbank notes that these metaphors are essentially spatial:

They suggest that Jesus is the most comprehensive possible context: not just the space within which all transactions between time and eternity transpire, but also the beginning of all this space, the culmination of this space, the growth of this space and all the comings out and in within this space.[51]

Milbank's own conclusion is that Jesus is the 'comprehensive space' and 'our total situation' in the sense that the total shape of his actions and words can be realized again and again in new situations.[52] Divine personhood is 'an instruction to go on re-narrating and re-realizing Christ.'

In accord with this insight, we may consider further the claim that *both* the Old and New Testaments are canonical in so far as they witness to Christ.

---

51 J. Milbank, *The Word Made Strange. Theology. Language, Culture*, Oxford: Blackwell, 1997, pp. 149–150
52 Ibid., p. 156f.

This might be taken in the weaker sense that while the New Testament witnesses to Christ, it *assumes* generally the Old Testament presentation of the
nature and acts of the God whom Christ reveals. The theological approach to
the canon which I have been urging, and which involves 'places' in which
the Word can be heard, seems however to demand a more integrated link between Christ and the Hebrew Scriptures, if the Word or self-expression of
God is to be identified with Christ himself. Here we may pick up on a long
history of exegesis, by proposing that every 'place' of revelation is a 'type'
of the place which is Christ. By this I do not mean a kind of predictive typology, in which features of an Old Testament narrative or character are seen by
ingenious allegory as being reproduced in the person or acts of Christ, and
which may be appealed to as 'messianic proofs'. I mean that every place of
revelation will be Christ-shaped in so far as Christ fulfills the hopes and ex-
pectations of typical human experience, and in so far as the pattern of his life
embodies what have been recognized in many places as gracious acts of
God.[53] If the divine Word judges human life, whether approving or contradicting it, then this Word can be seen as finally 'fleshed out' in the 'total
shape' of Jesus' actions and words. We have then a hermeneutical circle, but
not an unreasonable one: to enable us to hear the Word in a place in the text,
we apply the criterion of the story of Jesus, while God's purpose for human
life which the text discloses can be seen as realized in that same story. Con-
fronted then by this purpose in our own context, we hear the Word as an ethical demand in the face of 'the other'.

If we now work out the implications of the relationship of the Christian
canon to other literatures through deconstruction and comparison, and follow
through the general view of revelation I have been propounding, we are
bound to open up a wider theological perspective: other places in other texts
outside the canon must also be able to function as 'types' of the place which
is Christ.[54] In this sense Rudolf Bultmann was on to something when he proposed that many kinds of literature in the ancient world could act as a first
Testament or preparation for the New Testament. [55] Nevertheless, the two

---

53 Cf. G.v. Rad, 'Typological Interpretation of the Old Testament', in: Westermann (ed.),
   Essays (see n. 28), 17–39, p. 36; also G.W.H. Lampe, 'The reasonableness of typology',
   in: idem/K.J. Woollcombe, *Essays on Typology*, London: 1957, pp. 29–31.
54 Cf. J. Moltmann, *The Church in the Power of the Spirit*, London: SCM Press 1975, p.
   162: 'There were Jewish reasons for believing Jesus to be the Christ ... Today we shall
   have to enquire into Hindu, Buddhist and Islamic reasons for faith in Jesus ... they will
   be given a messianic direction towards the kingdom.'
55 R. Bultmann, 'The Significance of the Old Testament for Christian Faith', in: B.W.
   Anderson (ed.), *The Old Testament and Christian Faith*, London: SCM Press, 1964, pp.
   8–35, pp. 17, 34.

factors I have already adduced – nearness to the event of Christ and the identity of the community – mean that it is only the Hebrew Bible which we are *obliged* to regard as the Christian Old Testament. As Barth put it, though on a slightly different issue, 'If the question what God can do forces theology to be humble, the question what is *commanded* of us forces us to concrete obedience.'[56]

---

56 Barth, *Church Dogmatics I/1* (see n. 10), p. 55.

The New Testament Canon of Scripture and Christian Identity

by Robert Morgan

1. The Problem of Diversity

Discussions of unity and diversity within the New Testament are driven by the recognition of differences (e.g. between the four gospels, noted as early as the second century[1]) coupled with the traditional role of scripture, sharpened and perhaps overestimated by Protestantism, in defining what is Christian and what is not. This function requires agreement (where it matters) between the different biblical witnesses. Major differences between the Old and New Testaments are to be expected in any view of revelation unfolding through history, and here the New determines what remains valid in the Old, but within the New Testament itself a far greater degree of agreement is expected. Even differences of chronology in Jesus' ministry have proved embarrassing, and perhaps even cast doubt on John's gospel[2], though the sense of 'where it matters' and a certain skill in harmonisation were sufficient to overcome these difficulties. The disagreement between Peter and Paul at Antioch (Gal 2:11–14) was troubling[3] because apostolic unity was from Irenaeus onwards represented as foundational for the church, but until the modern critical historical investigation of the Bible, pioneered in the eighteenth century, made its decisive breakthrough in the 1830s and 40s the traditional picture of apostolic unity held firm. Prior to that, even when orthodox christol-

---

1 See H. Merkel *Die Pluralität der Evangelien als theologisches und exegetisches Problem in der Alten Kirche* (TC 3), Bern/Frankfurt a.M.: Peter Lang, 1978. The popularity of Tatian's *Diatessaron* is well-known and see later Augustine's *De consensu evangelistarum*.

2 This is probably why Gaius of Rome rejected John's gospel (as well as the Apocalypse) at the beginning of the third century. So H.v. Campenhausen, *The Formation of the Christian Bible*, London: Adam & Charles Black, 1972, p. 240.

3 E.g. Augustine's disagreement with Jerome's denial that there was any real disagreement. Cf. F. Overbeck, *Ueber die Auffassung des Streits des Paulus mit Petrus in Antiochien (Gal. 2,11ff.) bei den Kirchenvätern* (1877), Darmstadt: Wissenschaftliche Buchgesellschaft, 1968.

ogy and traditional supernaturalism began to crumble in the Enlightenment the diversity within early Christianity was scarcely perceived as a serious problem undermining the protestant appeal to scripture as normative for Christianity.

When in 1835 D.F. Strauss' *Life of Jesus* shattered the illusions of har-monisers and made notions of scriptural inerrancy finally incredible, only a false view of scripture was destroyed, not the possibility of its giving clear theological guidance as to what constituted authentic Christianity. However painful to piety[4], the destruction of belief in inerrancy (long since abandoned by some) was not where the serious theological challenge of this epoch-making book lay. The historicity of the gospels and the contrast between the history of Jesus and the post-resurrection christology of the gospels was far more important, and began a new phase in modern theology, but there was no need to follow in Strauss' left-wing hegelian steps. His account of the gospels was seen as a challenge to further historical work and new christology rather than a subversion of the possibility of basing Christian theology on the Bible. The differences and conflicts which his teacher F.C. Baur found among the New Testament witnesses, on the other hand, posed a more fundamental challenge. In disputing the theological unity of these writers[5] it raised doubts about the capacity of scripture to function as a norm of authentic Christianity, and so define and preserve its identity.

These doubts have persisted as New Testament scholarship has continued along lines pioneered by F.C. Baur, correcting his historical reconstruction at many points but accepting and enlarging his view of the diversity in early Christianity. Scripture remains the main *source* of Christian faith and theol-ogy, but (in the view of many) can no longer function as a *norm*, because it does not speak with one voice or yield a single theology. Far from a harmo-nious symphony we find conflict and disagreement in the first as in every generation of Christianity.

As the New Testament itself has come to be seen as a selection made in the interests of the emerging catholic orthodoxy of the second century the diversity in early Christianity has been seen to be wider than that within the New Testament itself, and it is natural for liberal theologians to demand that witnesses once suppressed be again heard, especially as speculative recon-

---

4   'Piety turns away with horror from so fearful an act of desecration ...' (D.F. Strauss *The Life of Jesus Critically Examined* [1835], ed. P.C. Hodgson, London: SCM Press, 1973, p. 757).

5   Initially in 1831, working from 1 Cor 1:12, 'Die Christuspartei in der korinthischen Ge-meinde, der Gegensatz des petrinischen und paulinischen Christenthums in der ältesten Kirche, der Apostel Petrus in Rom', *TZTh* 1831/4, 61–206 = idem, *Ausgewählte Werke in Einzelausgaben I*, Stuttgart-Bad Cannstatt: Frommann, 1963, 1–146.

structions of these may be found to support contemporary concerns such as the place of women in Christian leadership or accounts of Christianity uninfluenced by Paul. That task of tentative reconstruction is plainly a duty of historical research and if carried out responsibly it may well in principle have theological repercussions, posing a challenge to the canonical selection of texts which constitutes the New Testament. In practice the speculative hypotheses sometimes proposed about the Gospels of Thomas[6] and Peter[7], or about the supposed sources of the canonical gospels[8] pose no real threat to the canon, but the diversity among the New Testament witnesses themselves (as opposed to their sources) is another matter. Critical historical research has destroyed old ideas of the canon's doctrinal unity[9] and compelled Christian theology to understand any such unity in new ways.

That there be some kind of theological unity to scripture is a prerequisite of scripture functioning as a norm defining Christianity, but any account of this must do full justice to the diversity visible to historical investigation. Despite the tendency of some New Testament scholars to exaggerate the differences and conflicts it is not hard to find a large measure of agreement among this handful of Christian authors writing in Greek within two or three generations of each other, between 50 and (say) 130 A.D. There is no denying significant diversity, but there is also a large measure of agreement within this selection of texts chosen as representing a single emerging religion. Any modern believer who chooses to be religiously and theologically formed, as opposed to being merely historically informed, by texts which were deliberately excluded from the defining collection of texts is a decision against the consensus of the second-century and subsequent church. It would require a wide following before it succeeded in changing the contours of the canon or the character of Christianity. Other roads to revolution, such as reducing the importance of scripture or constructing alternative narratives of Jesus, are more effective ways of breaking with traditional Christianity, where that is the agenda.

---

6   Although a second-century gnostic writing, several scholars argue that it is independent of the synoptic gospels and contains earlier traditions of some sayings and parables. It is grossly overweighted in Robert Funk's 'Jesus Seminar' and J.D. Crossan makes it pivotal to his reconstruction of the historical Jesus (*The Historical Jesus*, Edinburgh: T&T Clark, 1991).

7   J.D. Crossan argues unconvincingly for a very early passion source in this second century document (*The Cross that Spoke*, San Francisco: Harper and Row, 1988).

8   For sober accounts of Q see C.M. Tuckett, *Q and the History of Early Christianity*, Edinburgh: T&T Clark, 1996; D.R. Catchpole, *The Quest for Q*, Edinburgh: T&T Clark, 1993. Theories about different strata in this unavailable document remain popular but also contested in North American scholarship.

9   E.g. R. Bultmann, *Theology of the New Testament II*, London: SCM Press, 1955, p. 237.

Liberal Christians might regret that the larger diversity in Christian origins has been to some extent suppressed, but Christians have consented to be defined by this collection, and even without a doctrine of inspiration the appeal to centuries of experience now provides grounds for remaining with the existing canon. There is no need either for theories of apostolic authorship to support the church's decision to read and expect Christian identity to be largely defined by these texts. How this defining takes place, however, granted the diversity among the New Testament witnesses, remains a question insufficiently addressed, perhaps because the issue has lost its burning interest for liberals who dislike burning heretics and in any case now accord less weight to scripture. They see the problems posed for Christian identity by historical research and are not worried, whereas the problems remain unseen or denied by many conservative Christians.

The conclusion of this article's argument will be that New Testament theologies, properly conceived and articulated, contain the potential to allow 'scripture' to function as a *norm* which protects the identity of Christianity, as well as helping it remain the main *source* of Christian faith (and so theology) that it plainly is every day and in every congregation. Anxiety about the identity of Christianity admittedly seems faithless to some, and it is surely true that God may be calling the world to a radically different future. Religious and theological experimentation is therefore always to be welcomed and tested. But until new truth clearly replaces the old, religious communities are wise to remain loyal to the truth they have received and live by, developing it at the edges rather than subverting it at the centre. New Testament theologies will therefore have an important ecclesial role if they reinforce the central structures and help define the boundaries of a Christianity that can be called true to scripture.

The Old Testament (whether larger Greek or smaller Hebrew) occupies a quite different position from the New when it comes to defining Christianity. That it was taken over by the church is of fundamental importance for the definition of Christianity (in particular against gnosticism and Marcion). The New Testament is not rightly understood except on this presupposition and the identification of God which it involves, but the Old Testament writings are not themselves a defining norm of Christianity, and the Bible or scripture as a whole is only such a norm when this is explained in a way that clearly differentiates between the roles of the Old and the New Testaments. That is an argument for separate Old and New Testament theologies, fulfilling different ecclesial tasks, rather than *gesamtbiblische Theologien.*

What it means to be a catholic[10] Christian has always been defined by reference to the God of Israel decisively revealed in Jesus Messiah as witnessed to by the writings of the New Testament and subsequent tradition normed by scripture. How this self-construal has worked in practice is complex and open to debate. There are some disagreements between Roman Catholics and Protestants, and also within the different denominations themselves, about how it should work today. The dissolution of rationally untenable views of scripture (notably inerrancy) and perhaps even of the protestant scriptural principle itself,[11] has posed a problem for those who still insist that scripture must provide a *norm* of Christian faith and theology, as well as a *source*.[12]

The question seems more urgent for Protestants than for Catholics, who have an alternative norm (however problematic) in the magisterium, and Anglicans, who have appealed to the creeds and reason alongside scripture, and oddly insisted on bishops as belonging to the essence, while actually being normed (until recently) more by liturgical uniformity imposed by the political establishment. However, the primary role of scripture (at least in theory) within Catholicism and Anglicanism means that the problem is equally urgent for them, and in fact the protestant appeal to scripture may also involve all those other factors (church tradition, worship, teaching office, reason). The point of the protestant scriptural principle was to establish a bottom line. When authorities conflict, what is decisive? At this point most Anglicans prior to John Henry Newman knew they were Protestants, and offence was caused when the Oxford movement repudiated that label. A more appropriate Anglican position would be to deny the oppositional character of Catholicism and Protestantism.[13] It can be argued that Martin Luther's appeal to scripture is (as intended) authentically catholic, and that only ecclesiastical perversions and other political factors prevented its acknowledgement as such; and that neo-protestantism's appeal to scripture in isolation from the life of the church was as much a break with classical Protestantism as with Catholicism. The primacy of scripture was recognized within Roman Catholicism when Vatican II abandoned Trent's language of 'two sources' of revelation, and protestant theologians now recognize the importance of tradition in seeking to un-

---

10 'Itzie Lieberman used "the Catholics" in its broadest sense – to include the Protestants' (P. Roth, 'The Conversion of the Jews', in: idem, *Goodbye, Columbus*, London: Penguin 1986,   127–145, p. 127). I.e. excluding eccentric developments which owe much to Christianity, but would not define themselves primarily by reference to the Old and New Testament scriptures.

11 Cf. W. Pannenberg, 'The Crisis of the Scripture Principle', in: idem, *Basic Questions in Theology I*, London: SCM Press, 1970, pp. 1–14.

12 See G. Ebeling 'Sola Scriptura and Tradition' (1963), in: idem, *The Word of God and Tradition*, Philadelphia: Fortress Press, 1968, pp. 102–147.

13 E.g. Baur, *Christuspartei* (see n. 5).

derstand the Christian meaning of scripture. There is still disagreement about where the magisterium is located and how it should function. A sometimes tense relationship between bishops and theologians may be better than either having too much power.

This sixteenth-century inner-Christian debate about the right ordering of authorities has been relativised in the modern period by a far deeper division between those who read the Bible as their scriptures (however they relate its authority to other factors) and those who study it with no such religious interest, or with only a residual religious interest in this important cultural artefact. That new chasm has been largely concealed for about 200 years because most biblical studies have been pursued in such ecclesial environments as German theological faculties (Roman Catholic as well as Protestant), seminaries, nineteenth-century Oxbridge, and English non-conformity. Even the French 'independents'[14] have been heavily dependent on their German protestant neighbours. Since the 1960s and especially in North America, that has dramatically changed with the strong and welcome participation of Jewish biblical scholars in university education, and also the emergence of a more truly secular environment for biblical studies.

In retrospect the roots of this secularization of biblical scholarship can be traced back to the Enlightenment and the new historical methods which make no Christian assumptions about the inspired character or divine subject-matter of these texts. It was only the beliefs of the practitioners which kept the discipline theological, not the texts themselves. Now that many biblical scholars are not clergy and some not believers it is not surprising that fewer claim to be writing *theology*, or talking of God through their exegesis and interpretations, however valuably their historical and exegetical scholarship contributes indirectly to that confessional and hermeneutical task of Christian theology.

To much contemporary biblical scholarship (outside Germany where the ecclesial link of the theological faculties is still remarkably strong) the question of its relationship to contemporary Christian belief and practice is often a matter of indifference or even polemic. The roots of this fissure can be seen in late nineteenth-century liberal protestant scholarship. A notable example is provided by William Wrede's criticisms of the New Testament theologies of B. Weiss, W. Beyschlag and H.J. Holtzmann.[15] What is revealing in this monograph is how much Wrede can take for granted as agreed by himself

---

14 See A.H. Jones, *Independence and Exegesis*, Tübingen: Mohr Siebeck, 1983.
15 W. Wrede, *Über Aufgabe und Methode der sog. Neutestamentlichen Theologie* (1897), in: G. Strecker (ed.), *Das Problem der Theologie des Neuen Testaments*, Darmstadt:

and Holtzmann and other liberals, and how self-evident most of what he says appears to New Testament scholars today.

The agreement was deceptive then, and now involves rejecting K. Barth's and R. Bultmann's reassertion of biblical scholarship's theological and confessional interests. Many today prefer W. Wrede's program[16] and sometimes seem unaware of the differing aims of biblical scholars who share the same methods. That could be made clearer by the difference between New Testament *studies* and New Testament *theology* (which still largely overlap) being analysed. Wrede is such a good historical critic, and the historical paradigm of biblical scholarship has so dominated twentieth-century biblical studies that modern biblical scholars can agree with him while overlooking matters which he too easily took for granted. For example, his remark that 'No New Testament writing was born with the predicate "canonical" attached' (p. 70) is certainly true, possibly even witty. It contains an important point about historians' evaluation and use of sources, but it does not say everything that biblical interpreters may want to say about these texts. Their inclusion in the Christian canon of scripture makes a claim about their subject-matter which historians bracket off, and gives them (for some) a privileged status which historians of Christian origins must resist. But most New Testament scholars are more than historians of Christian origins and Wrede's redefinition of 'New Testament theology (so-called)' as 'the history of early Christian religion and theology'[17] was a category mistake. Admittedly the development of the discipline from G.L. Bauer (1800–04) to H.J. Holtzmann (1896) offered some support for Wrede's view, and Holtzmann's reply was weak,[18] but a closer reading of the history of this largely descriptive but also hermeneutical discipline reveals theological as well as historical interests.[19] Rather than regretting these as distorting elements, and abolishing the discipline along with the label,[20] it would be

---

Wissenschaftliche Buchgesellschaft, 1975, pp. 81–154; English tr. by R. Morgan, *The Nature of New Testament Theology*, London: SCM Press, 1973.

16 Notably H. Räisänen, *Beyond New Testament Theology*, London: SCM Press, 1990 [2]2000.

17 Wrede, *Problem* (see n. 15), p. 153f. (English tr. p. 116).

18 In the second edition of his *Lehrbuch der Neutestamentlichen Theologie* (Tübingen: Mohr Siebeck, 1911) he concedes Wrede's argument for considering extra-canonical writings (p. 23).

19 See G. Ebeling 'What does the phrase "Biblical Theology" mean?', in: idem, *Word and Faith*, Philadelphia: Fortress Press, 1963. Also my articles 'New Testament Theology', in: S.J. Kraftchick/C.D. Myers, Jr./B.C. Ollenburger (eds.), *Biblical Theology: Problems and Perspectives*, Nashville: Abingdon Press, 1995, p. 104–130, and *AncBD* 6 (1992) 473–483. Also A.K.M. Adam, *Making Sense of New Testament Theology*, Macon, GA: Mercer, 1995, and H. Boers *What is New Testament Theology?*, Philadelphia: Fortress Press, 1979.

the label,[20] it would be more true of what biblical scholars and others think and write, to distinguish the different (though overlapping) *tasks*, and also the different *aims* of historical description and theological interpretation, even where they share the same exegetical *methods*.

The kinds of theological interpretation which abandon the constraints of historical exegesis do not concern us here because the argument will be that only historically disciplined New Testament theologies can contribute directly to enabling scripture to function as a *norm*, clarifying the identity of Christianity. Much as Aquinas implied that only the literal meaning of scripture was relevant in doctrinal argument[21] it seems that only respect for authorial and textual intention will restrict the range of possible meanings and make possible the conversation that is necessary if scripture is to provide direct guidance about the true identity of Christianity. Modern literary readings of scripture, unconstrained by historical exegesis and context, might well (like figural interpretations in the past) inflame the passions and make scripture a constant source of faith, and so indirectly of theology, but the normative function of scripture demands a more sober exegesis. It is from this more limited range of meanings that New Testament theologies have been constructed. The discipline has been subject to historical controls from nontheological biblical scholarship. Insisting on these is not to denigrate the more free-ranging styles of scriptural interpretation written from such important perspectives as liberation theology and feminism. Different kinds of biblical study are legitimate and the boundaries between them are not always clear, but aims and methods can be clarified. A broad view of what is legitimate New Testament interpretation includes all sorts of possible 'readings', and some of these may clarify Christian talk of God, but only if New Testament theologies properly so-called remain bound by historical exegesis will they help the church to read its scripture as a norm of its faith and life.

2. Locating the Scriptural Norm

In view of the theological diversity of scripture, even the New Testament scripture, many doubt whether this can be decisive in defining or preserving Christian identity. It clearly remains the main *source* of Christian faith, but its function as a *norm* is in question. Our suggestion is that while New Testa-

---

20   As Wrede does (*Problem* [see n. 15], pp. 153f. (English tr. p. 115f.), – rightly, if the discipline is identified with historical description.
21   S. Th. I.1.9.

ment theology in general, interpreting any text in the light of the gospel to which it bears witness and so with a view to contemporary Christianity enables scripture to be a *source* of faith and theology, only complete New Testament theologies, a genre familiar from G.L. Bauer's *Biblische Theologie des Neuen Testaments* (4 vols., 1800–04) to the recent crop represented by P. Stuhlmacher, H. Hübner, A. Weiser, and J. Gnilka, interpret this scripture as a whole and enable scripture to be in principle the defining *norm* of Christianity. The norm is scripture but scripture is operative as a norm only when it is interpreted theologically, i.e. with reference to what believers claim is its essential subject-matter, the saving revelation of God in Jesus. Every satisfactory New Testament theology contains in outline its author's theological interpretation of the New Testament as a whole (and so something of this interpreter's understanding of Christianity), and implies a view of the Old Testament as speaking of and identifying the same God. One reason for modern biblical and systematic theologians holding in mind if not writing up a complete New Testament theology is that their interpretations of scripture as a whole clarify and preserve the identity of Christianity as normed by scripture through all this religion's changes in different ages and cultures.

Church history consists crucially in the interpretation of scripture[22], and in most of this reading and living scripture provides a *source* of faith. But there is also the more specialist task of defining boundaries and saying where a development seems to part company with the essentials of Christian faith and community. This requires a sense of the Christian meaning of scripture and the tradition as a whole, and that sense is developed by theologians and other church leaders implicitly constructing their own (unpublished) New Testament theologies and systematic theologies. F.D.E. Schleiermacher's programme for theological education takes longer (and costs more) than many are willing to countenance.

New Testament theologies based on historical and exegetical study differ among themselves. It is therefore only in the on-going conversation between them that the scriptural norm of Christianity is perceived and so operational. That means that scripture is fortunately quite a 'soft' norm. On-going discussion of what scripture means is the life-blood of Christian community, but far from wanting a hard and sharp norm by which to exclude people the church wants the conversation to continue until the heterodox see the error of their ways (or in all conscience exclude themselves). Let a thousand New Testament theologies bloom. The conversation deepens and enlarges believers'

---

22 So G. Ebeling 'Church History is the History of the Exposition of Scripture', in: idem, *Word of God* (see n. 12), pp. 11–31.

understanding of the faith by which they live and continues as long as there is a Christian church.

Instead of arguing this case from the history of the discipline, it will be instructive to consider two of the most interesting and important writers on the canon from the past sixty-odd years, E. Käsemann and B.S. Childs. For all his disagreements with his teacher, Käsemann represents the Bultmann school (and behind him M. Luther), whereas Childs is influenced by K. Barth (and behind him J. Calvin). They thus represent the two main strands of twentieth-century protestant theological interpretation of Christian scripture. Both have strengths where the other is defective and both are concerned with the identity of Christianity. Childs is surely right (with J. Calvin and H. Küng)[23] to be guided by the canon of scripture as a whole, but Käsemann is surely right that the canon or scripture as such is not precise enough to serve as the norm identifying authentic Christianity, and also right to welcome the contributions of modern historical scholarship to the theological interpretation of scripture. Our suggestion will be that Childs' canonical orientation and Käsemann's insistence on a christological criterion guiding the critical theological interpretation of scripture should be combined in the kind of New Testament theology which enables scripture to function as a norm of Christian identity.

The differences of generation and academic context between E. Käsemann and B.S. Childs should be noted at the outset. In the more secular context of the late twentieth-century American academy Childs has in a remarkable series of writings since *Biblical Theology in Crisis* (1970) fought for a specifically Christian theological interpretation of scripture. That is one reason why he has won a sympathetic hearing among scholars who disagree strongly with the arguments and specific proposals of his 'canonical criticism'. He has touched the conscience of a discipline that until recently was, and in ecclesial locations still should be, a *theological* discipline.

Writing in the far more confessional theological environment of German theological faculties fifty years ago, E. Käsemann could take Christian theological aims for granted while pressing the problems raised for his own protestant theology by his radical historical criticism with its roots in the rationalism of the Enlightenment.

E. Käsemann and B.S. Childs dominated the two main debates about the canon in European theology since the Second World War. Both were concerned with theological interpretation of the Bible in the Christian church, but

---

23 'Der Frühkatholizismus im Neuen Testament als kontroverstheologisches Problem', *ThQ* 142 (1962) 385–424, reprinted and discussed in E. Käsemann (ed.), *Das Neue Testament als Kanon*, Göttingen: Vandenhoeck & Ruprecht, 1970, pp. 175–204.

focus on two different, though related, meanings to the word 'canon', a weak one and a theologically stronger one. The word can (and usually does) refer merely to a *list* of writings accepted as somehow authoritative – so that the 'canon of scripture' (often called 'the canon') can simply mean 'scripture', as in J.S. Semler's *Abhandlung von freier Untersuchung des Canon* (1771–75) and C.F. Evans' unpublished phrase 'the curse of the canon' in raising the question later published as *Is 'Holy Scripture' Christian?* (1971). Canon as *list* is in these contexts synonymous with scripture.

But the word 'canon' in the New Testament itself (at Gal 6:16 cf. 2.Cor 10:13–16), and in the second-century phrase translated 'canon of truth', and referring to the 'rule of faith', means measuring-rod or rule, and in tune with this the word 'canon' often refers to the function of scripture as a *norm* of Christian faith and theology.[24] This theological meaning was always implicit in the literary one: one function of the *list* was somehow to act as a *norm*, and the 'list' meaning is present when the norm is in view. Whatever was invoked as a norm, whether a creed, or a particular text, or the *regula fidei*, was derived from scripture as a whole and guided its interpretation. But the idea that scripture is the 'norm' that defines correct Christian belief became more prominent when the Reformers appealed to scripture against tradition and the magisterium. They still interpreted it within the church and so in the light of tradition, but made it more prominent, and Luther in particular gave it a sharper critical edge. Whether and how scripture can or should still work in this way is an open question. E. Käsemann proposes a 'canon within the canon' but the phrase is sometimes misunderstood, and the theory itself can perhaps be strengthened by the contribution of Childs – surprisingly, since B.S. Childs is himself deeply hostile to Käsemann's approach.

Both these protestant theologians assume that scripture is a *source* of Christian faith and theology. E. Käsemann's emphasis on the New Testament as a *norm* is evident in his collection and annotation of fifteen contributions to the debate: *Das Neue Testament als Kanon* (1970), and in his provocative phrase 'the canon within the canon'.[25] The weaker use of the word to mean simply the total list of writings read as 'scripture' can be seen in the title of his famous article, 'The Canon of the New Testament and the Unity of the

---

24 As in the older protestant dogmatics, where scripture is *norma normans* and tradition *norma normata* – by scripture.

25 See I. Lönning, *"Kanon im Kanon"*, Munich: Chr. Kaiser, 1972, for a full discussion of Käsemann's thesis and its background. Also H.-J. Schmitz, *Frühkatholizismus bei Adolf von Harnack, Rudolf Sohm, und Ernst Käsemann*, Düsseldorf: Patmos, 1977, pp. 190–201.

Church' (1951)[26] and the section on 'the canon' in 'Is the Gospel Objective?'
(1952/53), but both these essays are about the diversity in the New Testament
and the need to discriminate in hearing the gospel. Luther's dialectic between
scripture and the gospel is Käsemann's model, and it implies a canon (critical
norm) within the canon of scripture. Even those who (with K. Barth) are re-
luctant to use this as Käsemann and R. Bultmann insisted, to 'distinguish the
spirits' within the New Testament itself, can learn from Käsemann that Christian theological interpretation of scripture requires a christological norm or
rule of thumb (or rule of faith) to guide it: a canon in the narrow sense, but
drawn from scripture itself. Käsemann does not (like Marcion) reduce scripture (the canon in the broad sense of list of scriptural writings) to those writings which best reflect the christological criterion. Recognition of theological
diversity in the New Testament makes that a tempting option but it both mis-
understands and destroys scripture, which is a document of history where the
gospel has been heard, not a textbook of pure doctrine.[27] Theological criticism of scripture may on occasion be necessary, but it had better not become
a hatchet. Käsemann continued to interpret the whole New Testament theologically, despite disapproving of parts he labelled 'early catholic'.

This earlier German debate was mostly about how scripture could continue to function as 'canon', i.e. as a critical *norm*, in the modern world
where radical historical criticism has caused a 'crisis of the scriptural principle' (see n. 11). The *auctoritas causativa* of scripture had long been challenged by the modern recognition of its human character, and restated without the doctrine of inerrancy. But more serious than this, the theological contradictions within scripture highlighted initially by F.C. Baur seem to undermine its *auctoritas normativa*.[28] Historical understanding of the church's
formation, and recognition of diversity within the canon, have surely weak-
ened the appeal to scripture against ecclesiastical tradition. As the scriptural
basis of protestantism crumbled, nineteenth-century liberal theology provided
philosophical, experiential, and historical substitutes. Doubting whether these
communicated the gospel of God adequately, the dialectical theology of the
1920s mounted a neo-Reformation return to the theological interpretation of
scripture on which Protestantism had been founded. It resolved in new ways
the tensions between this gospel-oriented interpretation and the insights of
modern critical historical studies.

---

26 The German title makes Käsemann's question clearer: 'Begründet der neutestamentliche
    Kanon die Einheit der Kirche?', *EvTh* 11 (1951/52) 13–21. Both essays are translated in
    idem, *Essays on New Testament Themes*, London: SCM Press, 1964.
27 So Käsemann, *Essays* (see n. 26), p. 410.
28 Baur, Christuspartei (see n. 5). – On this see C.H. Ratschow, *Lutherische Dogmatik zwi-
    schen Reformation und Aufklärung I*, Gütersloh: Gerd Mohn, 1964, pp. 106–116.

This was remarkably successful in revitalizing the church's use of scripture as a *source* of its faith (as a preaching text), but initially little effort was made to show how scripture could also function as a *norm*, as it apparently had in the past. One reason for this is perhaps that the dialectical theologians were criticising liberals who would not be persuaded to rethink by appeals to scripture as such. It was therefore wiser simply to engage in theological interpretation (using scripture as a *source* of faith and theology) and let the scriptural *norm* assert itself against liberal protestant versions of Christianity by the production of more persuasive interpretations of scripture and the gospel. That might still be the best way forward, but Käsemann's sharp eye for problems (and his delight in theological dispute) led him into an area where his own protestant commitments seemed vulnerable. His solution to the problem, summed up in the phrase 'canon within the canon', is worth revisiting at a time when the alternatives are less attractive than ever. If both a biblicism tending towards fundamentalism, and the traditional Roman Catholic reliance on the magisterium are incredible (or lack muscle) today, the classic protestant appeal to critical theological interpretations of scripture in defining authentic Christianity need to be heard afresh.

The ambiguity in the word 'canon' meant that 'Kanon im Kanon' was and still is open to misunderstanding, as though the *list* meaning were intended in both parts of the phrase, rather than 'a *norm* within the *list* of canonical scriptures'. It could seem as though scripture was being reduced to a list within the list, and this impression was reinforced by the common appeal to the 'canon criticism' of Luther's Prefaces and September Testament (1522/23), where four New Testament writings were not quite taken off the list, but placed below the line.

This step toward exclusion was soon abandoned. It was always an unfortunate gesture, because it distracted attention from the act of theological criticism to one possible result, and from Luther's sense of the christological content of scripture guiding any Christian theological interpretation, to his less important privileging of one part of scripture over another. That is an inevitable consequence of interpreting scripture in the light of what it is essentially about, but the important point is his positive christological orientation, not his unhelpful remarks on the Epistle of James. Luther's point was that the gospel is what scripture is about: scripture is there to preach Christ, and parts of it do so more powerfully than other parts. For the purpose of defining Christianity some passages are therefore more central, and the real norm or criterion is the gospel itself: Christ heard in scripture, rather than scripture as such. One might say that the living Christ is the canon within the canon, and an interpretation aiming to communicate this gospel might on occasion be critical of

the letter of scripture (as K. Barth conceded) – precisely in order to clarify
the true Christian meaning of scripture as a whole, which is clear enough.

M. Luther's canon criticism thus provided twentieth-century critical theologians with a weapon against the biblicism which remains strong in conservative evangelicalism. It is the gospel, not scripture as such, which identifies
Christianity. But applying it against biblicism by appealing to Christ or the
gospel against scripture is always open to the counter-charge of subjectivism,
because 'Christ' or 'the gospel' criterion is not something objectively
'given'. It is located in the understanding of the theological interpreter and is
applied intuitively. The interpreter's understanding of Christ has to be defended rationally by reference to scripture and tradition and experience, but
that is rarely conclusive because these are always open to conflicting interpretations and the casting vote about 'what proclaims Christ' seems to be in
the hand of the modern interpreter rather than to depend on the weight of the
scriptural evidence. This explains K. Barth's refusal to agree with R.
Bultmann about the necessity of *Sachkritik*, even though (as Bultmann
pointed out) Barth's theological interpretation was also critical, i.e. itself involved judgments about what the gospel is (see n. 52).

K. Barth's suspicions of R. Bultmann's more than residual liberalism, and
his refusal to allow in principle the unbridled use of a weapon sharp enough
to cut off the branch on which he was sitting, was shrewd. Luther's 'what
preaches Christ' is more use as a positive criterion of what is central in scripture than as a negative one for putting down James and Jude, much less Hebrews and the Apocalypse (which preach Christ rather powerfully, even if
defectively), or for removing them from the list. M. Luther's animus against
James is understandable. In chapter 2 James probably criticises what he
thinks Romans is saying. In that case he probably misunderstood Paul. It is
also possible that he is criticizing someone else's misunderstanding of Romans, which would reduce the disagreement between these New Testament
writers, though not those within early Christianity. Certainly the apostles
could disagree (Gal 2:11–14), but this did not prevent Paul from claiming
that they proclaim the same crucified and risen Christ (1.Cor 15:1–11). There
is substantial agreement about what is essential to authentic Christianity and
it is well summarized at Eph 4:4–6.

E. Käsemann does not cut parts of the canon out,[29] but he is so critical of
some major New Testament writers (Matthew, John, and especially Luke)

---

29 As Marcion did. Käsemann's willingness to 'break a lance' for Marcion acknowledges a
    certain affinity (while rejecting of course his two gods); cf. *Essays* (see n. 26), p. 356.
    But it is because the New Testament is not a textbook of pure doctrine that excision is
    fundamentally mistaken, he adds (p. 410).

that he gives the impression of being guided by his historical and religious perception of Paul and Jesus, rather than by the witness to God in Jesus heard in scripture as a whole. His interpretations of the New Testament, like F.C. Baur's, find divisions where one might expect a non-Hegelian biblical theologian to emphasize the unity which is also present among the various witnesses. Some parts of scripture are surely more central than others to the gospel *Sache*, but where *Sachkritik* (criticism in the light of the *Sache*) is practised without restraint[30] a theology is no longer shaped by the canon, i.e. scripture as a whole and excluding apocryphal writings. R. Bultmann's existential interpretation can be questioned from this perspective, and E. Schüssler Fiorenza's feminist interpretation offers a clear example.[31]

E. Käsemann proposed Paul's doctrine of justification of the godless as the 'canon within the canon' and this has looked like tribute to his Lutheran tradition, an obvious criterion only from that perspective. It may or may not have been central to Paul, but is scarcely mentioned elsewhere and was not much taken up in the early church before Augustine, except by Marcion. But some criticisms of Käsemann have been based on a misunderstanding, as though he were arbitrarily preferring one part of the New Testament and making it his criterion. That is wrong. In the Lutheran *sola scriptura* stands the *sola fide*, *sola gratia*, and above all *solus Christus*. For Käsemann as for Luther, Christ, not the church, is the criterion of Christianity. The issue is how this is most appropriately expressed. In a noteworthy corrective to the liberals' hostility to 'doctrine' or church teaching expressed in fixed formulae, he argued that reference to the 'Christ event' without defining this doctrinally and also mirroring the historical reality of Jesus' teaching, work, and cross was not a sharp enough criterion of 'what preaches Christ', and that Paul's doctrine expressed the gospel present in Jesus' attitude to sinners most clearly.[32] It is this reference to the historical figure of Jesus which makes Käsemann's interpretation of the New Testament broadly convincing to many, but it was not as prominent in his earlier discussions of the canon as it later became. It perhaps needs to be spelled out today in ways that make his later emphasis on discipleship of the Crucified One more explicit at the methodological level. Käsemann's christological criterion was always implic-

---

30 This tendency of Käsemann's procedure is explicit in S. Schulz, *Die Mitte der Schrift*, Gütersloh: Gerd Mohn, 1976.

31 *In Memory of Her*, London: SCM Press, 1983, and many subsequent publications. For some excellent critical discussion see A.C. Thiselton, *New Horizons in Hermeneutics*, London: Harper Collins, 1992, pp. 442–452. Fiorenza's feminist commentary *Searching the Scriptures II*, London: SCM Press, 1964, with its introduction 'Transgressing Canonical Boundaries', is anti-canonical, with several late non-canonical writings making up nearly half the volume.

32 *Essays* (see n. 26), pp. 404–410.

itly a matter of praxis more than doctrine, even though he thought the theologian's task was precision, and therefore proposed formulae and other oversharp formulations.

E. Käsemann's corrective to the liberals' bias against doctrine is constructive, but it leads him into the problem with 'doctrine' that the old liberals (and perhaps Jesus himself) disliked: its use as a weapon of exclusion. Käsemann's insistence on the centrality of christology, and a christology which reflects the teaching, work, and cross of Jesus, can be given a less adversarial form than it receives in his and Luther's doctrine of justification. Theologians like precision and definition, but a sharp criterion is necessary only if the aim is to exclude alternatives. It is usually better to let them wither on the vine, on the Gamaliel principle. Instead of Käsemann's pauline scalpel one might propose as the scriptural criterion of Christianity something less precise: the 'Jesus magnet' portrayed by the gospels, drawing all and sundry to himself when he is lifted up on the cross and to the Father (John 12:32), alluring individuals from different tribes, confessions, and theologies into fellowship with him in a discipleship that acknowledges the one God and no other.

This magnet can be identified in the 'historical Jesus' (so-called) of E. Käsemann and A.v. Harnack and L.E. Keck, in the 'biblical Christ' of M. Kähler and A. Schlatter, in the Jesus of W. Thüsing, and in H. Schürmann's 'Gestalt and Geheimnis' of Jesus, to name only a few of the most distinguished theological writers on Jesus. It draws some into a simple imitation of Jesus, others into mystical interpretations of the Johannine language of mutual indwelling. Critical theological questions can be raised about both, but neither is *prima facie* excluded. Within the community more or less adequate accounts of believers' relationship to God in and through Jesus can be discussed and qualifications agreed to be necessary, but the basic criterion of what counts as Christian needs to be made as broad as possible. Relationship with God in the Spirit through the crucified and risen Jesus may suffice.

This metaphor of Jesus as magnet gives a more inclusive indication of the christological centre of scripture than any doctrinal criterion and although it is less sharp it can provide the christological hermeneutical key to the scriptures functioning as the norm of Christianity. A 'norm' can say what is normal without hastening to exclude the abnormal. Even what F.D.E. Schleiermacher called 'diseased' versions of Christianity can be given time to heal, as the whole body offers resistance to some poison, not removed by premature recourse to surgery, as has often happened in church history, for political more than religious reasons.

Christological definition of the 'Jesus magnet' visible in the gospel story of God's self-giving love was soon thought necessary, but the need is not obvious. A church which interprets in its life and thought the whole New Testament witness to God's engagement with the world in Christ knows what is authentic Christianity without depending much on phrases designed to exclude rivals from the loving community. Theologians will still coin phrases designed to help others see the light of Christ, and when these formulations conflict theological argument is necessary. Some theological arguments are not quickly resolved and do not need to be. Competing formulations can coexist for centuries without leading to confessional divisions. Meanwhile theological conversations and even liturgical experiments continue. Bishops and synods authorize one form rather than another for normal Christian worship and teaching without hastening to condemn what others find helpful. And the most common form such conversations and experiments take is the on-going theological interpretation of scripture.

The second-century church began to define the person of Christ doctrinally, and also appealed to a 'rule of faith' and creeds to guide the interpretation of scripture. The early christological titles, the gospel narratives, and other apostolic (and pseudo-apostolic) writings were not felt sufficient to define its faith in the face of new questions and developments. It retained its Jewish scriptures and produced new ones, but these always had to be understood in the light of its faith, and that required compact expression, to give immediate guidance and sense of direction. Creeds were no more a substitute for scripture than a rudder is substitute for the engine that drives a ship forward, or the charts indicating the direction and goal of the voyage. Both images correspond to the theological roles of scripture which go beyond its religious roles in nourishing and expressing faith. Neither the scriptural engine and charts nor the credal rudder make the theological task of interpretation unnecessary. Charts, engine and rudder are only instruments in the hand of a pilot, helping the pilot or interpreter steer in the right direction, and ensure (so far as possible) that the ship called the church keeps on course for its goal while all its crew (and passengers) fulfil their life tasks together as a loving and serving community. Without this guidance by wise pilots with a hand on the tiller the power of the engine might become misdirected and the ship go round in circles or capsize. The christological formula is a rudder which fits the ship as well as the scriptural engine does. It is constructed from the same materials and is fitted to the task it fulfils in the hand of theological pilots who study the scriptural charts, see that the engine is running, and steer in the right direction.

For scripture to fulfil its theological task of communicating and correcting Christian faith some such guide to assist its interpretation is needed. Credal statements are not the kernel of Christianity out of which theology is un-

folded, but regulative principles based on a sense of the gospel heard in scripture, and so guiding both the interpretation of scripture and theological elaboration. The rudder image suggests only how the christological criterion functions. A related but more important question is its character, and the ship with
its motley crew on its voyage to an eschatological goal does not need a surgi-
cal knife which cuts out diseased members, except in a mutiny. The summary
account of Jesus it needs is more like a magnet which draws the pilgrim people of God into the unknown future and closer to the heart of the mystery in
whom and with whom the community lives.

Another analogy to describe the character and role of the christological
criterion or rule of faith which guides Christian interpretation of scripture is a
baton in the conductor's hand, enabling this leader to draw from the various
instruments and players in the orchestra a harmonious symphony corresponding to the script or score that the theological leader has learned. Each New
Testament witness can be played by interpreters to create all sorts of attractive and unattractive sounds, but the conductor or New Testament theologian
directs herself as exegete to draw from each New Testament writing a sound
that is true both to that instrument and also to the Christian gospel being performed. The metaphor of a musical score being performed implies that this is
done time and again by the same and by different interpreters and that a full
complement of instruments (the various New Testament witnesses) is desirable. The christological criterion is merely an instrument in the hand of the
interpreter who knows the script and draws from every leading instrument a
tune which is recognizably part of the same symphony. We learn little about
the symphony from a little drum like Jude, but quite a lot from the gospel
strings and the pauline brass.

E. Käsemann's canon within the canon was a christological criterion of
authentic Christianity. He protested vehemently against H. Schlier and H.
Conzelmann when he thought they understood early creeds and confessions
in a way that might by-pass the kerygma,[33] but he thought that a christological criterion, expressed in doctrinal language, was necessary if scripture is to
function as a norm of Christian faith and theology. That view seems to coin-
cide with how the creeds and scripture have together guided Christian faith
and theology, from the beginnings and throughout history. It is one reason
why Anglicans have emphasised the historic creeds. The use of a creed or
christological criterion does not contradict the *sola scriptura* so long as this

---

33 *New Testament Questions of Today*, London: SCM Press, 1964, p. 32; 'Konsequente
    Traditionsgeschichte?' (*ZThK* 62 [1965] 137–152). My defence of the Anglican use of
    the creeds and of the second-century 'rule of faith' is to be sharply distinguished from

means (as it always has) *scripture interpreted within the church*, and so long as the creeds considered essential are interpreted in the light of scripture and understood to summarize the gospel proclaimed in scripture.

Calling it a 'canon within the canon' was neat, provocative and misleading, but Luther's phrase about the article on which the church stands or falls is exactly what the christological criterion should be. Justification by faith, on the other hand, has become a shibboleth, just as the ὁμοούσιον was intended as a shibboleth at Nicaea. That was appropriate if christological definition and the exclusion of alternatives was necessary at that early point in the history of Christianity, and inappropriate if driven by political considerations, or as a century later by ecclesiastical rivalries. E. Käsemann's 'justification of the ungodly' was not chosen for political or ecclesiastical reasons, any more than Luther wanted to exclude Catholics. Its weakness is that the norm ought to be self-evident, and ought to promote unity. Lutherans value it in part because it has marked Lutheran identity over the centuries, but it has been a barrier against communication with other Christians, preserving Lutheran identity more effectively than Christian identity. Perhaps any norm will be open to misinterpretations. The historic creeds can sound like a bundle of myths until properly interpreted. But at least the creeds are obviously talking about Jesus as the saving revelation of God whereas that reference to Jesus remains implicit in *iustificatio impii*, giving the impression that the gospel is more about human sin and wretchedness than the glory of God in the face of Jesus Christ. Protestantism exaggerated some Augustinian aspects of its medieval heritage, and there is nothing more medieval than the doctrine of justification. Paul would surely have marvelled at what his commentators have made of him, though perhaps less at Käsemann's understanding of justification, which is aligned with his historical understanding of Jesus. But that shows that the criterion is more ambiguous than Käsemann thought. Its negative edge (not by works) is more valuable in prophetic criticism of the church than as a general criterion or norm, identifying Christianity and guiding the Christian interpretation of scripture.

Doctrinal definitions of authentic Christianity have usually been formulated in opposition to some view considered defective. Christological description of the crucified and risen Jesus as Lord and Christ, helped to communicate the gospel, but even New Testament christology is sometimes directed against opinions deemed unsatisfactory, and that is more clear later in the process of doctrinal elaboration. Paul's language of justification on a basis of faith not Torah-observance, on the other hand, was intended to *persuade* op-

---

what Käsemann is criticizing, *viz* substituting the 'historical Jesus' or an early creed for the gospel as the christological criterion of scripture and Christianity.

ponents by scriptural argument that Jews and Gentiles alike were included in what God was now doing, and included on the basis of their faith in Christ, not any Jewish religious practice. The religious power of his language lies in its personal appeal (e.g. Gal 2:19f.). Its theological power lies in its antithetical formulations which are clearly excluding an alternative theological opinion, but not driving anyone out of the church. It was not false doctrine which led Paul to call for excommunication of an offender at 1.Cor 5. It is not entirely clear what Paul's phrase 'works of the law' in Galatians and Romans denies are necessary for membership of the church and salvation. This unclarity allowed his antitheses to be directed against new opponents (Pelagian moralism and the Catholic religious system), even on occasion against morality and against natural theology, as well as against Paul's original opponents, the judaizers in Galatia. But these exegetically dubious extensions of Paul's meaning and consequent exclusions have come to look unjustified to historically-schooled exegetes. Even Augustine and Luther are more persuasive when they are being positive about Christ and grace and faith than when they are being negative about Pelagians or Catholics. It is possible to welcome Luther's use of Paul's language in prophetic criticism of the medieval church without making it the universal norm of authentic Christianity.

Paul's positive language about God's grace revealed in Christ and responded to in faith expresses the *foundation* of Christianity (cf. 1.Cor 3:11) and is a scriptural *source* of Christian faith and theology. His zeal in excluding false understandings of Christ and the gospel perhaps echoes his zeal as a pharisee, but in fact is his attempt to persuade. His rhetoric was on occasion misleading (cf. Gal 5:2)[34] and could invite the kind of misunderstanding we see in James 2:14–26. In his defence one might argue that he was excluding exclusiveness, and that in those first few years more definition was needed than subsequently. Either Paul was right to include Gentiles as Gentiles, without requiring Torah-observance, or he was wrong. Those who agree with him about not circumcising Gentiles can welcome his definition of Christianity, and even the scriptural argument by which he defended it, without making the latter into their own preferred definition of the gospel, or accepting unconditionally the ways it was applied and extended by Augustine and Luther.

Helpful as Augustine found Paul's language to criticize moralistic distortions of the gospel of grace, one may question whether he needed to exclude Pelagians rather than simply confute and correct them. In any case his use of Romans for this purpose is now exegetically implausible in the light of E.P.

---

34 It is hardly necessary to insist that Paul is not here excluding anyone from the church by this incautious remark, since Jewish Christianity as such would then be excluded.

Sanders' explanation of Paul's actual aims.[35] Paul's rhetoric has inspired millions for centuries and communicated the gospel of Christ more effectively than most New Testament witnesses. He surely understood it more profoundly than any of them, but his abstruse argument against 'works' probably convinced nobody in Galatia, Antioch, Jerusalem, or Rome (if indeed anyone understood it), and illuminated Marcion only when distorted out of all recognition. It served Augustine and M. Luther well only when reapplied against targets the apostle would scarcely have recognised. Paul's antitheses are rhetorically powerful, but his own targets did not survive, which is why his language was not much echoed in the early church until directed at new targets. Since these new applications cannot be exegetically defended today they seem off-target when used as appeals to scripture to justify dividing the church by excluding those who understand the gospel differently, instead of continuing the conversation about the meaning of scripture and continuing that discussion within the one Christian church. Augustine's doctrine of grace, drawn largely from Rom 5–7, can and must still do battle with Pelagian moralism, and it may now find new support in the historical study of Jesus, but this is a debate that continues within the church. Pelagius should not be excommunicated or even lose his *venia legendi*. He has as many New Testament shots in his sling as Augustine does. That does not make him right, but he has a right to be heard.

Similarly E. Käsemann's interpretation of Romans still has considerable power, assisting scripture to function as a *source* of Christianity. But if his account of justification by faith alone is exegetically out of focus this is not a convincing proposal for a christological *norm* excluding false versions of Christianity. Even if Käsemann had got Paul right on this point (as he has on many others) justification would not be a satisfactory summary of Paul's gospel of the crucified and risen Lord. Paul himself did not use his scriptural argument about justification as either an epitome of his gospel,[36] or as a christological norm. He developed it as an argument to persuade his readers that he was right about what the gospel involved and did not involve for Gentiles.

If E. Käsemann's choice of norm is open to question, the roots of the trouble lie behind him in K. Barth's *Romans*. The Reformers had applied

---

35 *Paul, the Law and the Jewish People*, Philadelphia: Fortress Press, 1983. This was anticipated by F.C. Baur, inaugurated by Krister Stendahl, and independently supported by H. Räisänen, F. Watson, and J.D.G. Dunn among others.

36 Rom 1:16f. has often been wrongly read as such, because it states his subsequent argument thematically. Even here the '*all* (Jews and Gentiles) who believe' should be emphasised, not simply the contrast to be introduced at 3:20ff. between justification by faith and by works.

Paul's powerful dialectic to their sixteenth-century target and Barth reapplied this to his own. His rhetoric had enormous religious and theological power, speaking of God positively in a way that owed much to Paul and the Reformers, but his negation of 'religion' and natural theology was never exegetically convincing and has proved theologically questionable. F.D.E. Schleiermacher and the liberals were surely right to suppose that in a secular culture the gospel is more likely to be heard in a dialectical relationship to 'religion' than in a dialectical negation of it. Both Barth and Käsemann could use Paul's language of justification as prophetic critique within the Christian community, but to attack 'religion' wholesale overshoots this target. M. Luther knew that sacraments, morality, true religion are good in themselves, and that the gospel is unlikely to be heard, let alone take root without them, even though it transcends them as God's grace transcends all human efforts. When religion is corrupt it needs reforming, but in a materialist culture it is usually worth nurturing, not tearing down. F.D.E. Schleiermacher was positive about 'religion' even when rejecting the Enlightenment natural religion, including I. Kant's 'religion' of reason. Much modern religiosity requires criticism for its narcissism and its acceptance of an intolerable *status quo* – but not for being religion. Religious experience and the search for God are taken seriously in Acts 17, and even the 'scientific study of religion' which brackets off the question of God can provide material for apologetics and natural theology. The pauline dialectic of law and gospel is not the place to look for the christological identity of Christianity[37] and the early Barthian interpretation of this in terms of a critique of 'religion' was merely theological shock tactics.

Some christological definition of Christianity remains necessary, but it needs to be drawn from more than Paul. To be scriptural the christological criterion needs to give some account of scripture as a whole or at least of the New Testament (which presupposes the Old) as a whole. At this point B.S. Childs offers a possible corrective to the incisive but one-sided biblical theology of E. Käsemann. Accepting with Käsemann (and against Childs) the need for a 'canon' (measuring-rod) which speaks of Jesus and ensures that he is the measure of Christian interpretation of the canon of scripture, the corresponding emphasis upon scripture as a whole can be clarified by some brief and critical attention to Childs' 'canonical criticism'.

---

37 Cf. A.v. Harnack's remark that 'Paulinism has proved to be a ferment in the history of dogma; a basis it has never been' (*History of dogma*, New York: Harper and Row, 1961, p. 136).

3. The Canon as 'tota scriptura'

Like the canon debate re-ignited by E. Käsemann after the second War, this later debate about the canon and biblical theology is also part of twentieth-century theology's adjustment to modernity, but it stemmed from the then more conservative American debate about biblical theology, which owed much to K. Barth but had little in common with the more radical side of German biblical studies and hermeneutical theology. R. Bultmann and his pupils had continued the older liberals' historical research, combining it with Barth's neo-Reformation impulses in a kerygmatic theology. Here it was the preached Word, the living voice of the gospel, rather than the written word that mediates God's revelation. Scripture is indispensable tradition, interpreted in proclamation so that revelation might happen. The canon of scripture contains more than 'the gospel'; only its 'centre' is definitive of contemporary Christian belief and practice. By contrast B.S. Childs and his theologically conservative allies call the Bible Word of God and hope to find in the canon of scripture as such a *solution* to the crisis caused by modern rationalist biblical criticism: attention to the canonical shape of scripture is seen as a new remedy for the disease of reducing scripture to historical sources or seeing in it a cacophony of conflicting voices. Whereas the kerygmatic theologians' answer to these problems preserved their critical history-of-traditions roots, Childs broke with this paradigm for biblical scholarship and incidentally pointed the theological study of scripture towards the now fashionable literary paradigm suggested by the notion of canon as collection or list of approved literature. He himself, however, resisted the secularising tendencies present elsewhere in this shift to a more literary interest in the Bible, retaining traditional theological descriptions of the Bible.

Both discussions have had things to say about the unity of the Bible and it is clear why this is so important to Protestantism and such a central theme in the biblical theology on which protestant Christianity depends. A religious anthology might serve as a source and resource, but to serve as a norm it needs to be construed as a unity. Diversity and contradictions have to be incorporated within a theory of unity conceived at some more general level. However, the two debates have discussed this from different perspectives. The New Testament debate was conducted by scholars acutely aware of the diversity in this small collection, and was concerned with the question of scripture (in effect the New Testament plus what this includes of the Old) as a norm. The unity within or behind the variety of literary forms and diversity of theologies was the issue here. In the later debate, conducted mainly by Old Testament theologians, the question was more the relation of these Jewish

writings to Christianity, or the Old Testament to the New. Christian theologians and biblical scholars have always asked about the unity of the two Testaments in one Bible,[38] and this question has assumed different shapes and
received different answers since the Bible has been studied historically. G.
von Rad[39] insisted on its importance for Old Testament theology, and even if
Part III of his second volume was little followed he still looms large in the
background of the most recent discussions by Old Testament scholars. B.S.
Childs has actually written a *Biblical Theology of the Old and New Testaments* (1992) which contains 'theological reflection on the Christian Bible'
(sub-title). He has also written *The New Testament as Canon: An Introduction* (1984), expecting his 'canonical approach' to overcome or at least soften
the theological diversity among the New Testament witnesses which has ex-
ercised historically critical New Testament theologians like E. Käsemann.

It is certainly possible (and desirable) to take a less adversarial view of
the New Testament witnesses than E. Käsemann and his hero F.C. Baur did,
but the fatal step in B.S. Childs' theological interpretation of the New Testament is to allow his vision of the canon to come into conflict with well-
grounded historical judgments and overcome them. Since authentic letters of
the historical Paul are included in the canon, Paul is one of the witnesses to
be heard. He is not to be suppressed by the so-called 'canonical Paul', even if
that was intended by the makers of the collection. Certainly the pauline pseu-
depigrapha are also to be heard and evaluated in their own right, but they
cannot be allowed to determine how Paul's authentic letters are read. Childs'
move is not only implausible, it subverts the use of the New Testament as a
norm by reading part of it (Paul) against his own intentions. For the New
Testament to function as a norm all its witnesses must be heard (so far as
possible) in accord with their authorial intentions, as happens in most New
Testament theologies.

The emphasis that B.S. Childs (and J. Calvin and K. Barth) bring against
E. Käsemann (and M. Luther and R. Bultmann) is to insist that the identity of
Christianity be defined by the whole of scripture being interpreted theologically. Nothing is excluded from the canon (list) even if the canon (norm) is
clearer in some parts of scripture than in other parts. This emphasis pays
more serious attention to the Old Testament as Christian scripture than liberal
theologians like F.D.E. Schleiermacher, A.v. Harnack, and (if they will par-

---

38 E.g. twenty-three essays in: C. Dohmen/T. Söding (eds.) *Eine Bibel – Zwei Testamente*,
    Paderborn: Schöningh, 1995; H. Seebass, *Der Gott der ganzen Bibel*, Freiburg: Herder,
    1982.
39 *Old Testament Theology*, 2 vols., Edinburgh: Oliver and Boyd 1962/65 (German 1957
    and 1960).

don the label) Bultmann and Käsemann did.[40] The New Testament assumes much Old Testament belief and practice, and a theological interpretation of the whole New Testament (typically a New Testament theology) needs to reflect this. To treat the two Testaments in the same way, on the grounds that both are Christian scripture, is biblicist, but to underestimate the Old Testament is to misunderstand the New. All scripture is there to be read, however rarely and critically some parts are read in practice, but when it comes to defining Christianity in an age that takes authorial intention seriously, the New Testament witnesses (who presuppose the witness of the Old while accepting only more or less of its contents) are relevant in a way the Old Testament is not. The alternative strategy of abandoning textual determinacy and historical context enabled second-century Christians to retain the Old Testament, but to apply that strategy to the New Testament today would (apart from being implausible) lose the possibility of this scripture defining Christian faith.

Like most biblical theologians most of the time Childs seems more concerned with scripture as a *source* of Christian faith than as a *norm*, but his notion of 'canonical shape' contains the germ of a suggestion about how scripture might function as a norm which is very different from E. Käsemann's doctrinal (or credal) proposal. But it comes into such conflict with historical reason that it seems better to explore the more rational proposal of enabling the New Testament to clarify the identity of Christianity (function as a norm) by being interpreted theologically in New Testament theologies which are guided by constant reference to Jesus of Nazareth. Such properly carried out *theological interpretations* of *all* the *New Testament witnesses* include what these all presuppose about God from their Jewish theological matrix, and also what they presuppose of the life, death and resurrection of the Messiah Jesus and the gift of the Spirit. These complete 'theologies of the New Testament' (published or unpublished) contribute to the theological task of defining Christian identity today.

Scripture functions as a *source* of faith in all biblical theology. Even the interpretation of a single passage from either Testament can evoke a faith response if the rest of the religious system is in place. The aim to serve this religious goal is what distinguishes biblical theology from a biblical scholarship which need not be interested in the question of God or contemporary Christianity. But even Christian theologians disagree over whether, how, or how far, scripture can also serve as a *norm*, contributing to the *definition* of

---

40 The first three are notorious for undervaluing the Old Testament. See F. Watson, *Text and Truth*, Edinburgh: T&T Clark, 1997, pp. 128–176. Käsemann can hardly be excepted, even though it was a sermon on Is. 26:13 which in 1937 landed him in Gestapo detention.

Christianity today – not only by identifying elements which should be present, and suggesting how they are related, but also by putting into question versions of Christianity which are (in F.D.E. Schleiermacher's word) diseased.

Only complete New Testament theologies can hope to fulfil this role, and that is arguably their main theological function. The canonical shape of the Christian Bible cannot of itself perform this task, despite containing some guidance for the Christian interpretation of scripture. What is important in the canonical shape of scripture can be reflected in the structure of a New Testament theology. Writing and discussing these works help clarify which contemporary forms of Christianity are true to the witness of scripture. There cannot be a single normative New Testament theology, because theological interpretations like all interpretations are historically conditioned, valid in a particular time and place and subsequently retrieved, reactualised – or consigned to Schleiermacher's 'lumber-room of history', but the debate about and between them will clarify what is scriptural and what is not.

Defining Christianity is an on-going process of interpreting scripture as a whole and in its parts, undertaken by both biblical and doctrinal theologians. One biblical scholar's New Testament theology is only that one theologian's reading of these texts at a particular time and place, and that theologian's implicit proposal for reinforcing and correcting contemporary Christianity. Any such proposal is based on an array of historical and exegetical judgments organized with a view to clarifying the essential content of the whole. In this on-going debate about individual texts and broader swathes of tradition, historical hypotheses are proposed and new concepts explored. New Testament theologians thus make a direct contribution, assisted by their own and other biblical scholarship, to the definition of Christian faith and life today. Their New Testament theologies are more than aggregates of historical and exegetical conclusions covering the whole New Testament. Granted the status and authority of the New Testament for Christians, theological interpretations of it are also contemporary theology, advancing or at least implying proposals concerning the doctrinal, moral, and religious identity of Christianity today, and showing that the diverse New Testament witnesses can be understood to cohere and support this, rather than subvert it by contradicting one another. It thus helps the church to read the New Testament as scripture with a view to correcting (norm) as well as informing (source) its own faith and practice.

This textbook genre is not the most common form taken by New Testament theology. Christian theological interpretation of scripture is usually focused on individual writings or passages, enabling a part of scripture to be a source of Christian faith. But the textbook genre is the form which most naturally enables the New Testament as a whole (together with all it implies from the Old) to function as a norm. It has to be interpreted in the light of its *Sache* or christological centre, and this requires a *hermeneutische Maßstabe*, whether Käsemann's or some other.

New Testament *theology* and New Testament theologies are therefore essential for the life of the church. They are not, however, the only way that New Testament *scholarship* contributes to the task of Christian theology. Systematic theologians may draw on a wider range of biblical studies than biblical theology and see New Testament scholarship as an auxiliary discipline. Christian biblical scholars who do not claim to be theologians can agree with this account of their role within theology. It is, however, quite damaging for Christianity if it claims that only non-theological interpretations are true because only these are *wissenschaftlich*. Against this, E. Käsemann and B.S. Childs agree that biblical studies should embrace not only historical, linguistic and literary scholarship, but also theological analysis and construction.[41]

4. Defining Christianity from Scripture

We have distinguished two meanings of 'canon', corresponding to two Christian theological uses of scripture: as source and norm. As a product of the dialectical theology, E. Käsemann could take the first use of scripture, as a *source* of Christian faith and theology, for granted. It was the second use meaning *norm* that led him to develop Luther's 'canon criticism' and christological criterion for theological criticism of the New Testament. As it stands this canon or list of texts is too diverse and questionable to serve as a norm. A canon (norm) within the canon (scripture) is therefore needed, by which even scripture can be theologically criticized (*Sachkritik*). Whether that model is preferable to the way the 'rule of faith' in the second century and the creeds in Anglicanism have functioned to guide the interpretation of scripture may be questioned, but the suggestion has been that this is how Käsemann's norm functions in his own theological practice, rather than as a Marcionite knife cutting out the parts of scripture which seem not to accord with a particular theologian's understanding of the gospel. The role of justifi-

---

41 Käsemann spoke of the 'thoroughly misplaced modesty' of exegetes who 'suppose that they merely do the historical donkey work for the systematic theologian' (*New Testament Questions* [see n. 33], p. 7).

cation within Lutheranism (analogous to the creeds in Anglicanism) supports this interpretation of Käsemann's responsible use of the necessary *hermeneutische Maßstabe*, even if he sometimes gave the impression of wanting to use it like Jack the ripper or the Red Queen.

By contrast, B.S. Childs' 'canonical approach' to biblical interpretation, no longer even called 'canonical *criticism*', is not critical of the canon. It does not need to be because it does not expect scripture to provide so direct, concise and usable a norm as E. Käsemann wanted. It is the shape of the whole rather than theological interpretation of scripture guided by a credal or doctrinal formula which is supposed to inform Childs' faith and theology, whether or not this is really the case. His 'canonical approach' or theological interpretation of scripture reflects the other meaning of the word 'canon' (i.e. list) and *scripture* is rightly preferred to 'canon' in his title *Introduction to the Old Testament as Scripture* (1979). Perhaps because he is an Old Testament theologian, and the Old Testament as such never has been a 'norm' of Christian faith, except to the extent that it has contributed to the New Testament norm, what Childs has written is less about the *auctoritas normativa* of scripture, than about its prior *auctoritas causativa*, as the source and foundation of Christian faith and theology. But here the word 'scripture' is more appropriate, and in fact Childs has found most agreement on matters covered by the notion of *scripture*, and least where he discusses what the fact of a canon and its shape require of the Christian theological interpreter.

The debate he has stimulated is, however, relevant to our focus on the task of defining Christianity, (the old 'essence of Christianity' or identity of Christianity question) and therefore on scripture as *norm* for the following reasons: 1) the use of scripture as a *norm* presupposes the notion of 'scripture' which B.S. Childs like K. Barth has done much to revive within biblical scholarship. – 2) It also presupposes the theological use of scripture as a *source*; the two are intertwined. – 3) the Christian canon of scripture contains two Testaments; it is therefore impossible to argue for a New Testament theology fulfilling the norming function of scripture without showing how it includes or relates to what is essential in the Old Testament. The relationship of the two Testaments has to be clarified even by biblical theologians who think *gesamtbiblische Theologien* mistaken in principle. – 4) Childs' emphasis upon the canon directs attention to the biblical *texts* rather than to the *history* behind them. This is the primary focus for all theological use of scripture, contrary to the residually Hegelian New Testament theologies of the late nineteenth century and beyond which found the theological meaning of scripture in the history behind the texts. – 5) Childs has attended to the Christian Bible as a whole, and to each Testament in its integrity, as is appropriate in the theological use of scripture. Even if he exaggerates the theological significance of the 'canonical shape' of scripture, beyond the broad question of the relation of the Old and New Testaments, his synthesisings supply a deficiency in the earlier debate about scripture as a norm. The Christian Bible as such cannot function as a norm unless interpreted with the help of a christological criterion, but to be *scriptural* this needs to be based on the New Testament as a whole, together with as much of the Old Testament as these early Christian writers consider essential to the definition of Christianity.

B.S. Childs' entirely proper interest in the Bible as Christian scripture follows Barth's recognition that the church's understanding of its scripture as witness to God's saving activity has often been excluded in principle by a critical historical approach to the texts which has no place for confessional talk of God. That problem had engaged German Old and New Testament theology for fifty years before Childs passed his negative verdict on the Anglo-American biblical theology movement and began to develop his own alternative route to the same goal. In view of the polemical tone of some of this debate[42] it is important to recognize the common ground shared by Childs, his generally unsuccessful American predecessors, his relatively successful teachers and contemporaries in German Old and New Testament theology, and his equally theologically-minded critics. They all recognize (as some do not) that the biblical witness to God is foundational to the existence and life of the church, and that Christians need a theological interpretation of their scriptures which articulates this witness rather than obscuring it.

Many theologians as well as literary critics would also agree with Childs that it is 'the final form of the text' (which is what the religious community reads) that scholars should interpret. A textual critic can point out weaknesses in this formulation,[43] and it does not in any case justify a ban on what might be exegetically helpful and theologically fruitful explorations of the prehistory of the texts, but the general point can be supported by more than a merely pragmatic argument.[44] However, this valid point is met by the notion of *scripture*. The notion of *canon* evokes historical discussions of its forma-

---

42 E.g. J. Barr, *Holy Scripture: Canon, Authority, Criticism*, Oxford: Oxford University Press, 1983. See also idem, *The Concept of Biblical Theology*, London: SCM Press, 1999. M.G. Brett, *Biblical Criticism in Crisis?*, Cambridge: Cambridge University Press, 1991, provides an excellent discussion of Childs' programme into the 1980s.

43 D.C. Parker points out that strictly speaking there is no such thing (*The Living Text of the Gospels*, Cambridge: Cambridge University Press, 1997).

44 P. Stuhlmacher *Biblische Theologie des Neuen Testaments II*, Göttingen: Vandenhoeck & Ruprecht, 1999, 325 has given the uncertainty of historical judgments about earlier stages of the tradition as the reason ("Da") for seeing the 'main task of critical biblical interpretation' as explaining the canonical final form in which the texts have come down to us.

tion and boundaries. It directs attention to the form of scripture rather than to its content, and some of the conclusions which Childs draws from the 'canonical shape' of scripture fly in the face of common sense.[45] In his earlier (1983) critique of B.S. Childs James Barr doubted 'that the idea of the canon is of first-rate importance for biblical Christianity. Scripture is essential, but canon is not. Canon is a derivative, a secondary or tertiary concept, of great interest but not of the highest theological importance. It is unlikely in face of the biblical evidence that it can be made into the corner-stone of any convincing biblical theology'.[46] In support of this it might be added that systematic theologians have discussed 'the doctrine of Holy Scripture', not 'the doctrine of the canon', and this preference naturally extends to discussions of theological interpretation, as in D. Kelsey's admirable work, *The Uses of Scripture in Modern Theology* (1975). Even the German canon debate, focussed on the question of a norm within the New Testament, became a discussion of 'the centre of *scripture*'.[47]

The ecclesial context and aim of most theological interpretation of the Bible is expressed in both words, but the ecclesiastical word 'canon' does have the merit of being less bland than the conventional word 'scripture'. It also emphasizes the *whole* of scripture, which is salutary, since most theological interpretation of scripture is inevitably selective. The discredited 1940s versions of biblical theology contained valid impulses as well as serious defects and Childs deserves credit for trying to meet that movement's goals in a less vulnerable way. But this background also accounts in part for major differences between his work and the earlier German New Testament debate where the canon of scripture was seen as a problem on account of its history and some of its contents. E. Käsemann stood firmly with R. Bultmann against K. Barth advocating a *critical* theological interpretation of scripture. The difference of emphasis is between those who like J. Calvin and Barth are concerned for the scopus of scripture as a whole, and those who like M. Luther and Käsemann are willing with Luther to 'urge Christ against scripture'. The latter suspect the former of biblicism, the former the latter of subjectivism – both with some justification. The two sides need each other as a brake and warning against dangers in their own theory.

---

45 The pseudonymous writings of the New Testament lead him to play off 'the canonical Paul' against the historical Paul. See below, n 55.
46 Barr, *Holy Scripture* (see n. 42), pp. 63f.
47 C.K. Barrett refers to Käsemann's *Kanon* collection with the remark that the question of the 'canon within the canon' is 'not far removed from the "centre of the NT"'. 'The Centre of the New Testament and the Canon', in: *Die Mitte des Neuen Testaments. FS Eduard Schweizer*, Göttingen: Vandenhoeck & Ruprecht, 1983, pp. 5–21, p. 19 n. 3. The collocation is also clear in B. Ehler, *Die Herrschaft des Gekreuzigten. Ernst Käsemanns Frage nach der Mitte der Schrift* (BZNW 46), Berlin: Walter de Gruyter, 1986.

The reason why New Testament theologies are the most appropriate form for a theological interpretation of Christian scripture intended to clarify the identity of Christianity is that these give an account of the whole New Testament. In doing so they see that some texts are central, others peripheral. They constantly make theological judgments about the witnesses being heard, i.e. the texts being read, and do so on a basis of the interpreter's own provisional understanding of the gospel, which can be summarized in a simple formula. That critical theological interpretation of all the New Testament witnesses (not their sources) does not mean being unsympathetic. E. Käsemann accepted that 'early catholicism' is what was needed to express and defend the gospel in the second century, but denied that it should be normative for the twentieth.

B.S. Childs' proposals have been criticized by some who nevertheless share his concern for a theological interpretation of the church's scriptures at a time when the scholarly community's literary and historical analyses of the Bible have become largely independent of the religious community's theological reflection. In opposing or again failing to communicate the religious testimony of these texts some biblical scholarship has been party to the decline of the churches which depend on that. The religious deficit of a purely historical and literary scholarship was addressed in Britain and America by the earlier biblical theology movement. Since the decline of this movement Anglo-American scholarship has expanded into a healthy pluralism, and this has sometimes included an aggressive secularism. It is a measure of Childs' theological ambition that like Barth he not only sounded an alarm but attempted to turn the tide of historical-critical readings of the Bible. In doing so he parted company not only with atheological and anti-theological trends in biblical scholarship, but also with the liberal theological project (continued in German Old and New Testament theology) of combining the traditional theological aims of scriptural interpretation with the new historical methods and results. He thus isolated himself from many of his natural conversation-partners and lost sight of the necessary contribution made by historical study to the use of the Bible as a norm.

The need to reassert and recover a genuinely theological interpretation of scripture does not justify an onslaught on historical criticism. Attention to the biblical literature in the form in which it is available does not preclude enquiry into its pre-history. This sometimes solves problems in the texts as we have them, and may contain lessons for theology. To brush it aside is to make common cause with fundamentalism. Bible-readers, including Christians, may learn from the hypothetically reconstructed Amos as well as from the way his editors understood and arranged the collection of his oracles, imposing their own interpretation on the prophetic heritage. More importantly, the historical study of Jesus may possibly offer some guidance for Christians, stimulating reflection by challenging the evangelists' imperfect presentations.[48]

One might with M. Kähler and K. Barth finally resist that argument, but it demands consideration. The prophets, apostles, and above all the messiah echoed in scripture have some claim to be heard in their own right even though the form in which their teachings have survived focuses readers' attention on the work of anonymous later editors also. It remains the witness of *scripture* that the church hears, expecting to be addressed by its essential content, the gospel of Christ or saving revelation of God in the crucified and risen Jesus, and that justifies Childs' emphasis upon the final form of the text, if not his exclusion of other relevant questions. If there is a correct insight in the notion of the 'canonical shape' of the Christian Bible and the New Testament, it will emerge in considering the appropriate shape for a New Testament theology, but to bring the canonical form of scripture into conflict with historical reason is to invite the comment of I. Kant that 'a religion which rashly declares war on reason will not be able to hold out in the long run against it.'[49] One may also in a post-modern world reverse that dictum. An Enlightenment rationality which declares war on religion instead of merely criticizing its evils and abuses will fail to fulfil the necessary task of a rational theology. Neither fundamentalism nor Kant's religion of reason are authentic accounts of Christianity, as F.D.E. Schleiermacher and K. Barth both insisted in ways which remain paradigmatic for modern Christian theology.

5. An Inclusive Christological Criterion

This discussion of B.S. Childs and E. Käsemann on the canon as scripture (list) and as norm has yielded the following points:

Firstly, support for their advocacy of *Christian theological interpretation of scripture*, i.e. interpretations typically (but not necessarily or exclusively) undertaken by believers and aiming to speak of God who is known to the Christian community as Saviour in the life, death and resurrection of Jesus,

---

48 I argue this in 'Towards a Critical Appropriation of the Sermon on the Mount', in: *Christology, Controversy and Community:* New Testament Essays in Honour of David R. Catchpole, Brill: Leiden, 2000, pp. 157–191.

encountered through the witness of these texts. Both these Christian theologians subscribe broadly to the programme contained in K. Barth's successive Prefaces to his *Romans*. Rather than dig doctrinal information or revealed truth from an authoritative scripture or merely describe ancient religions, they read this God-given collection of literary texts on the presupposition that they speak of the God of Israel revealed in Christ, interpreting them in their more or less final form, i.e. our best approximation to author's autograph.[50] E. Käsemann also investigated the history of traditions behind scripture and interpreted the christological hymns etc. in their own terms as well as understanding the New Testament authors in the light of their use of earlier materials. He interpreted these earlier materials theologically, and saw great theological significance in historical Jesus research. He did not publish a complete New Testament theology and yet was the most influential theological interpreter of the New Testament in his generation. Historical analysis assisted his theological penetration of the New Testament and contributed to the on-going discussion of these texts. Despite its hypothetical character this should not be dogmatically excluded from theological interpretation, as B.S. Childs proposes, but welcomed as possibly enriching our understanding of scripture.

Secondly, this interpretation of the texts in order to hear and communicate their witness to divine revelation does not preclude accepting their fallible human character. This has been clarified by historical study and that may result in historical criticism not only contributing to theological interpretation (*Sachexegese*) but also becoming an instrument of theological criticism (*Sachkritik*).[51] However, it is clear that theological criticism of a biblical author needs to be tentative and sparing if the interpreter's own prejudices are not to override the witness of scripture. Christians have often reserved judgment or interpreted problematic passages in the light of the larger witness of scripture rather than be negative about any part of scripture, but this is neverthless silently to engage in *Sachkritik*.[52]

---

49 Preface to first ed. of *Religion within the Limits of Reason Alone* (1793), New York: Harper & Row, 1960, p. 9.
50 Historical and text-critical judgments are essential here. Thus Mark's witness is interpreted without reference to Mk 16:9–20, and John's without reference to John 7:53 – 8:11, though both these passages deserve an appended note. If a New Testament theologian considers Rom 7:25b and 16:25–27 to be glosses, despite lack of manuscript support, it is necessary to say so and bracket them because the aim is to interpret the text in as close a form as possible to the original.
51 I argue this in: 'Expansion and Criticism in the Christian Tradition', in: *The Cardinal Meaning*, ed. by M. Pye/R. Morgan, The Hague: Mouton, 1973, pp. 59–101.
52 As R. Bultmann in his review articles argued K. Barth was doing, both in *The Epistle to the Romans* and in *The Resurrection of the Dead* (cf. *Faith and Understanding I*, London: SCM Press, 1969, pp. 66–94, esp. 72,81,86,92f.

Thirdly, the whole of scripture is to be read, though some parts contribute more to its essential theological subject-matter than other parts. The Old Testament as a whole identifies for Christians as well as Jews who God is, and is therefore indispensable and foundational for any theological interpretation of the New. Christian knowledge of God in Christ is based on the witness of the New Testament, but this includes and must be shown to include whatever of the Old is essential to understanding and accepting this witness. The Old Testament faith in God as Creator and Judge, the Spirit and the future hope in particular are constitutive of Christian witness to God in Christ, and much else in the Old Testament is expressive of it. But the Old Testament is never Christian scripture without the Gospel proclaimed in the New, and it is to be interpreted in Old Testament (i.e. Christian) theology from a Christian perspective, i.e. as open to the New, without damaging its own integrity as a pre-Christian collection of texts. Other modes of interpreting these texts, e.g. as contributing to the history of religion, i.e. from a non-Christian perspective, can be welcomed by theologians for any insights they yield and as a control against the frequent vagaries of theological interpretation, but they are no substitute for historically responsible Christian Old Testament theologies like G. von Rad's.

Fourthly, while any part of the Christian Bible might provide a springboard for theological interpretation and so be a *source* for faith, only the New Testament writers (who were intending to express Christianity) can in a historically-conscious age provide a *norm*, defining Christianity. But these witnesses assume the Old Testament faith of Israel. They understand its prophetic witness and their own gospel of the Christ in the light of each other, insisting on continuity and fulfilment, and generally minimizing the discontinuity. The Old Testament thus contributes to the scriptural *norm* which identifies Christianity as well as to the scriptural *source* of Christian faith and theology, but does so (and always has done so) only as *Vetus Testamentum in Novo receptum*,[53] or (better) in *Evangelio, in Christianismo receptum*. Read with due regard to its original, pre-Christian context, its contribution to defining Christianity is thus limited, but it is essential and foundational.

Fifthly, while Christian theological appropriation of the Old Testament is selective, the same cannot be said of the New Testament, as all these texts are early Christian writings, chosen for their agreement about what the second-century church considered essential and deliberately made part of a canon intended to define Christian identity alongside and determining the interpretation of the Septuagint. To interpret only one's preferred parts of the New

---

53 Borrowing the phrase from H. Hübner, *Biblische Theologie des Neuen Testaments*, 3 Vols., Göttingen: Vandenhoeck & Ruprecht, 1990–95, but refocusing it.

Testament theologically is no longer to be guided by the canon, i.e. by scripture as a whole. Such selectivity gives the modern interpreter more freedom in respect of the tradition than is compatible with loyalty to scripture (*Schrifttreue*). Selectivity with respect to the Old Testament is compatible with this insistence on the whole of the New if it corresponds to what the New Testament authors and subsequent Christian orthodoxy took over from the Jewish scriptures and into their definitions of Christianity. Used in this way, in conjunction with the New, the Old Testament scriptures remain valuable in teaching Christian morality, spirituality, worship, and trust in the God of Abraham and Jesus, as well as essential for understanding New Testament faith in God.

Sixthly, for the New Testament as a whole to be a norm defining Christianity, its diverse witnesses with their different theologies have to be seen to proclaim the same gospel[54] and evoke the same faith. Only a complete New Testament theology can make that argument, and it will do so only when guided by, i.e. in dialectical relationship with, a summary christological formula which can be seen to derive from scripture, to be true to all its witnesses, and to summarize authentic Christianity. If such a *Kanon im Kanon* or *hermeneutische Maßstäbe* can be found (and E. Käsemann's particular proposal was questioned) it may provide a rule of faith and rule of thumb for measuring modern theological proposals, however radical, for their faithfulness to historical Christianity, which is one test of their authenticity. Such a summary definition would be one way in which the New Testament canon of scripture contributes to maintaining Christian identity. It requires the conversation of New Testament theologies to make good its author's claim to represent the shared convictions of the New Testament writers while acknowledging (and celebrating) the diversity. There can be no question of forcing these witnesses into a procrustean bed, but they must be described in such a way as to show that the christological rule of faith selected is true to them all.

Seventhly, while this christological criterion must be true to all the New Testament authors, it need not be true to all their (hypothetical) sources. It does not claim to embrace the full diversity of early Christianity, only the theological diversity of the New Testament canon, which already excludes some early developments.[55] It must plausibly reflect what is central to each

---

54 On this H. Diem, *Dogmatik* (1955), München: Chr. Kaiser, [2]1957, is valuable. Insisting that the rule of faith, creed, or christological formula guides its interpretation might suggest that this (drawn from scripture) is the real norm. That would be wrong, ignoring where the formula is drawn from, but it is true that the rule of faith acts as a rule of thumb in assessing theologies for their scriptural character or orthodoxy.

55 Even if it once existed Q was not included in the canon of scripture as an independent voice, only as integrated into the theologies of Matthew and Luke. Paul was included as

author's Christianity even though some of the shorter writings provide insufficient data to establish this beyond doubt. The theological interpreter needs to be alert to what each author can presuppose, and here the apparent relationship between one text and another will help fill in the picture. Suggesting how each author understood Christianity on the basis of short texts which are pursuing a more limited aim is uncertain, but all that is needed are plausible suggestions, not historical demonstration. Some New Testament writings are peripheral to the definition of Christianity. They undermine the unity of the canon only if they reject or oppose the definition proposed, as M. Luther thought the Epistle of James contradicted his own pauline canon within the canon.

The final issue which this discussion poses is what formula or rule of faith best summarizes what Christians see as central to the scriptural witness. Is there a scriptural norm which will help maintain Christian identity? The norm itself would remain scripture, but a rule of faith or creed or christological formula that summarizes the central thrust of Christian scripture would guide its interpretation. Any such criterion is bound to be christological because it is in the crucified and risen Jesus that Christians see the decisive saving revelation of the God of Israel and Creator of the world, the Judge and Saviour. Whether it need be a *doctrinal* criterion is less obvious, especially because the revelation of God was for all, according to Jesus and Paul. There are different ways of speaking of Jesus as the saving revelation of God, and the New Testament narratives prioritize inclusiveness over precision.

Doctrinal definitions such as the ὁμοούσιον were usually intended to exclude false teaching. In the New Testament the denial of Jesus' humanity is condemned as false christological doctrine (1.John 4:2f.). However gently the community treats its naively docetic members (perhaps a silent majority throughout most of church history) it cannot authorize anyone to teach this error. Even F.D.E. Schleiermacher must be challenged over his account of Jesus' sinless humanity and M. Kähler joined in thanking even the liberal lives of Jesus for echoing in their own way 'Luther's statement that we can never draw God's Son deep enough into our flesh, into our humanity.'[56] But

---

Paul, through his authentic letters, even if the pseudo-paulines were intended to influence how Paul was heard and read. Here critical judgment overrules canonical shape. To include Q as an independent witness allows critical judgment to overrule the canonical writings. That is necessary in historical reconstruction of early Christianity, but intolerable in theological interpretation. It leads to Kähler's nightmare, a papacy of professors (led by those with the best public relations).

56 F.C. Baur criticized F.D.E. Schleiermacher's christology as early as 1827, and D.F. Strauss more famously in *The Christ of Faith and the Jesus of History* (1865); English tr. Philadelphia: Fortress Press, 1977. For M. Kähler, see *The So-called Historical Jesus*

not even Paul, who passionately *argues* with believers who understand the truth of the gospel and what it implies about church membership differently from himself excludes anyone (despite Gal 5:2, cf. n. 34) on doctrinal grounds. John draws a clearer doctrinal line but in the gospel he draws it against the opponents of Jesus, not believers. At John 6:60–66, disciples who reject his high christology withdraw themselves and reveal themselves never to have been believers (v.64, cf. 1.John 2:19); they are not (so far as we can see) excommunicated. John of Patmos seems to have been a more divisive figure, but it is no longer possible to identify the Nicolaitans or Jezebel, or to be sure what was at issue between the Presbyter in 3 John and Diotrephes. On the whole the New Testament aims to be inclusive of all believers, even when sending warning signals about deviations (Acts 20:29f.). That does not make the second-century construction of orthodoxy a mistake, but it counsels caution about excluding any christological error except denial of the humanity of Jesus among those who confess him the risen Lord and Christ (Acts 2:36 etc.). Denial of Jesus' vindication by God seems not yet to have been entertained as a possible Christian standpoint.

Second-century catholicism excluded Marcion and some forms of Christian gnosticism as evidently incompatible with first-century faith as now defined by the New Testament. That judgment seems in retrospect an inevitable and right application of the christological criterion. The situation becomes more ambiguous after that and it is possible that some of the exclusions were premature. Christian orthodoxy was defined in terms of the divinity (as well as the humanity) of Jesus Christ, the crucified and risen Lord. The argument of this essay implies that this is defensible only if that definition is true to all the New Testament writers. Or to put that in another way, the doctrine of the divinity of Christ must be understood in a way that is compatible with the faith of these witnesses – whom it claims to interpret.

Locating the unity of the New Testament and the formula summarizing Christianity, and guiding Christian theological interpretation of scripture in the doctrine of the divinity (and humanity) of Christ corresponds to the Anglican use of the creeds as the hermeneutical key to scripture. The proposal needs defending as true to all the New Testament writers. Only so (i.e. when understood in a way that is true to them) is it a *scriptural* criterion, rather than one imposed on the interpretation of the New Testament by later orthodoxy. That view might be defended by some Roman Catholic theologians as what is meant by the church controlling the interpretation of scripture. A liberal catholic Anglican who subscribes to the Reformation scriptural principle,

and the Historic, Biblical Christ (1892), English tr. Philadelphia: Fortress Press, 1964, p. 46.

on the other hand (as many Roman Catholic theologians do also), must show that this hermeneutical criterion is itself scriptural, i.e. true to the whole New Testament.

It is evidently true to John's gospel, and when we analyse what John meant by calling Jesus 'my Lord and my God' (20:29) or 'the Word made flesh' it is clear that the doctrine of the Son's divinity must be interpreted in revelational terms. Jesus is the revelation of God (cf. 1:18; 8:19; 12:44; 14:9). K. Barth's formulation, that in having to do with Jesus we have to do with God[57], might seem a minimal interpretation of the doctrine of the divinity of Christ, but it seems to say what John intends and what all the New Testament writers would want to say. This formula is not a sharp knife for excluding heretics, but it does exclude christologies which see Jesus as no more than a religious teacher and which give no account of his resurrection.

A church which defines itself by a dogmatic belief in the divinity of Jesus interpreted in a way that every New Testament writer and most subsequent Christians (including liberal Anglicans) could accept, defines its faith as a relationship to God determined by a knowledge of Jesus Christ crucified and risen. Jesus is identified by the story of his life and teaching and death in the gospels, but the church's memory of him is shaped by the conviction (reflected in the last chapter of each gospel) that God vindicated him and that believers' lives are transformed by his life and death, his real presence and influence, and by confidence about the future disclosed by his resurrection. In other words, Christian knowledge of Jesus involves speaking of the Spirit (e.g. 1.Cor 15:45) and was soon found to require speaking of God as Trinity.

There are thus limits to even a generous orthodoxy, but the imprecision of the 'having to do' formulation is an attempt to be inclusive. Docetists can still be challenged by it because their Jesus is not the human historical Jesus of Nazareth of the gospels, and versions of Christianity which deny the mystery of the resurrection and any doctrine of the divinity of Christ and so the Triune God are hard pressed to claim continuity with the New Testament witness. By contrast, most of the later patristic christological arguments concerned better and worse ways of articulating this shared faith in Jesus of Nazareth as the decisive saving revelation of God. Like the theological arguments between Lutherans and Calvinists they did not need to be matters dividing the church.

---

57 See *Church Dogmatics II/1*, Edinburgh: T&T Clark, 1957, pp. 206–211. See also p. 251, that what is aimed at here is 'not a christological article ... but Jesus Christ Himself.' Reference to the divinity of Christ as the christological criterion is not to one article of

John's doctrine of the divinity of Jesus has to be distinguished from the mythological form he gave it in his language of descent and ascent or return to the Father.[58] Where he came from (above) and who he is (the man from heaven who is in heaven: John 3:13) project the claim that he can and does reveal God, and that in responding to him by believing, one enters into relationship with God and is caught up in the life of God (John 13–17). Pre-existence is not a necessary corollary of the *doctrine* that Jesus is the revelation of God, but this mythological idea, now so misleading, once helped communicate that claim.[59] It is an important constituent element in the particular theology of this gospel which is different from other theologies in the canon, but a unitary theological system is not the level at which the unity of the New Testament is to be found. The statement of John 1:14, the climax of the Prologue and the epitome of the whole Gospel, gives only one possible conceptual expression to the confession of Jesus as Lord (and Saviour, rare though that word is) which is normative for orthodox Christianity, and was held in common by all the New Testament witnesses. The unity of the New Testament is a *Verkündigungseinheit* (1.Cor 15:11), and *Glaubenseinheit* summarized in the acclamation of Eph 4:5f. – a text which identifies the four components of our 'having to do' formula. Johannine specifics such as pre-existence and the Logos concept are not essential to the formula. This 'in having to do with Jesus we have to do with God' speaks of faith and of Jesus: the Risen Lord is the crucified Jesus of Nazareth. It also speaks of God, the God of Israel, the Creator, who chose a people and then through Jesus' life, death and resurrection brought Gentiles also into a covenant relationship with Godself. It implies the community which 'we' entered by 'one baptism' (Eph 4:5), receiving the Spirit that is sometimes scarcely distinguished from the risen Christ. These elements of the 'having to do' formula constitute the unity of faith shared by all the New Testament witnesses, and subsequent Christian orthodoxy.

The specifically Johannine presentation of Jesus reflects on this shared faith more profoundly than most, but is also open to theological criticism despite being true to our (Johannine) interpretation of the *vere Deus, vere homo*. It is arguably less attractive than the synoptic pictures, and that is one reason for resisting the literalism that wants to insist on John's historical accuracy. Historical Jesus research may contribute to a cautious theological criticism

---

faith among others but a pointer to the revelation of God that holds all Christian faith and theology together.

58 I argue this in 'St John's Gospel, the Incarnation, and Christian Orthodoxy', in: *Essentials of Christian Community: Essays in Honour of Daniel W. Hardy*, Edinburgh: T&T Clark, 1996, pp. 146–159.

59 See K.-J. Kuschel, *Born Before All Time?*, London: SCM Press, 1992.

(*Sachkritik*), however often it has been theologically misused to construct an 'alternative narrative' to replace traditional Christian perceptions of Jesus. The way John's Jesus talks about 'the Jews' is intolerable to those who have been convinced about its anti-semitic potential. The outrageous charge of deicide has roots in John 19:16, followed first, perhaps, by Lk 23:25, as well as by Mt 27:25. John's theology has been adjudged individualistic, his ethics minimal, his ecclesiology sectarian, his christology tending towards docetism, his dualism problematic. But these charges are debateable. John 1:14 contradicts 6:63 and is anti-docetic. Christian orthodoxy fastened on this text and softened John's dualism. The gospel of John has been interpreted in different ways and the debate continues both in secular university contexts and within the theological community of those who seek to understand their faith by wrestling with and arguing about scripture. Different exegetes will differ about whether theological criticism is necessary but most modern interpretations,[59] like most ancient ones, accept that John assumes the humanity as well as the divinity (interpreted revelationally) of Jesus.

In the context of the rest of the Prologue, and of the narrative which follows, John 1:14 identifies the human being who is the revelation of God – not merely the revealer, but himself the revelation. The final verse of the Prologue causes surprise (despite 20:28) by calling him (in the earliest manuscripts) 'the only-begotten God' (contrast only-begotten *Son* at 3:16,18; 1.John 4:9; and in later mss of v.18; and also contrast 1:14c). But this final verse 1:18 confirms that *revelation*, not cosmology, is the category by which to understand 1:14 and indeed the whole Prologue with its Wisdom echoes – and the whole gospel with its preference for the language of 'agency' or sending: the agent speaks with full authority for the king who sent him. The language of descent and ascent used later in the gospel to express this event of revelation in pictorial form (mythologically) is no surprise after a Prologue which introduces Jesus as the revelation of God. It resists any reducing of the gospel story to those elements which can be historically verified.

Revelation requires recipients as well as a sender, and it requires some (however elusive) content. Epitomising the gospel as a whole John 1:14 reports an appropriate response – beholding the glory of God in the incarnate Jesus Christ (cf. 2.Cor 4:6), i.e. believing on him (cf. John 2:11), and these plurals (cf. 3:11) insist on the community dimension of this inescapably individual response. There is no revelation without reception, negative as well as

---

60 E. Käsemann's account of John's 'naïve doceticism' in his *The Testament of Jesus*, London: SCM Press, 1968, was justly criticized by G. Bornkamm ('Towards the Interpretation of John's Gospel' [German 1968], in: J. Ashton (ed.), *The Interpretation of John*, Edinburgh: T&T Clark, [2]1997, pp. 79–98.

positive. The story of Jesus includes the gathering of disciples and opposition. Alongside christology the main themes of New Testament theology are accordingly ecclesiology (discipleship) and eschatology (judgment), both of which speak of God and Jesus.

This is not the place to summarize Johannine christology in detail, relating it to what is said about the Spirit-Paraclete and showing how the later doctrine of the Trinity is adumbrated in the Farewell Discourses. Neither is there space to show how the doctrine of the divinity of Christ, understood in this revelational way, corresponds to the convictions of the other New Testament writers. These are tasks for a New Testament theology. It is most important here to defend our inclusive christological criterion (which implies, but does not explicate, the claim that Jesus saves) against those who want its soteriological dimension made more specific, even at the cost of making it more exclusive.

Any formulaic summary must speak of God in Christ and so of salvation in and through him. That is why definitions of the essence of Christianity are usually doctrinal. For example: Christianity is essentially distinguished from other monotheistic faiths belonging to the teleological type of religion 'by the fact that in it everything is related to the redemption accomplished by Jesus of Nazareth'.[61] One might question 'by', and prefer 'in', since God is the subject of God's saving activity and Jesus the place where this happens, as well as himself God's eschatological agent. 'God in Jesus' is the briefest summary of Christianity, but since this religion is about human flourishing it is better to say 'salvation from God in Jesus'.[62]

How redemption or salvation is effected is a matter of theological theory, secondary to the dogmatic claim that it has been accomplished. To make some particular theory of the atonement, such as Jesus' death as a sacrifice, part of one's norm, (as Stuhlmacher does)[63] is initially plausible because this sacrificial theory is very early (pre-pauline) and was probably presupposed by all the New Testament witnesses, even if some of them (Luke and John in particular) apparently attached little importance to it. But it locates the unity of the New Testament at a *level* at which the diversity is quite clear, the level of theological theory. Even if this particular theory is quite general in early Christianity it is secondary to the centrality of Jesus as the saving revelation of God, and it was over a thousand years before it became (in the West) a matter for profound theological elaboration. It is not part of the essential doc-

61 F.D.E. Schleiermacher, *The Christian Faith* (1831); English tr. Edinburgh: T&T Clark, 1928, § 11.
62 So E. Schillebeeckx, *Jesus: an Experiment in Christology*, London: SCM Press, 1979.
63 Stuhlmacher, *Biblische Theologie II* (see n. 44), pp. 310–312.

trinal norm of Christianity. It excludes, and in the hands of a Württemberger
pietist would probably be intended to exclude, theological liberals, even those
who would accept the doctrine of the divinity of Christ as defined above,
such as F.D.E. Schleiermacher, R. Bultmann, and E. Käsemann. These would
all argue that their christologies imply a soteriology, but that they do not need
to repristinate the one preferred by P. Stuhlmacher, for all its biblical pedigree.

Every worked-out christology implies a soteriology. The christological
criterion proposed here, the divinity of Christ interpreted to mean that Jesus
is the saving revelation of God, is not a worked-out christology (i.e. a theologically articulated belief), but (perhaps like Chalcedon's *vere Deus vere
homo*)[64] a kind of christological grammar stating what any worked-out christology needs to conform to in order to be orthodox, i.e. essentially continuous
with the New Testament witnesses. It does not develop a christology and so
does not imply a particular soteriology, but it does imply the need for both.
To look for the unity of the theologically diverse New Testament in a particular christology or soteriology is to look in the wrong place. Even the category
of messiahship, accepted by all the witnesses, is open to different interpretations. How in Jesus God saves must also be open to different elaborations.

The 'having to do with Jesus' formula has the merit of reaching behind
the New Testament witnesses and giving a plausible account of the ministry
of Jesus, and his disciples' response to his authority. The evidence is not
strong enough to provide the foundations for a christology, and any foundation which said nothing about the resurrection of Jesus would be unsatisfactory in any case. But some coherence between Jesus' aims and his disciples'
response during the ministry on the one hand, and the disciples' and their
successors' post-resurrection faith on the other is surely appropriate, and it is
entirely credible that Jesus thought he was sent by God and in some sense
God's agent (regardless of the title Messiah), and that in following him the
disciples thought they were in some sense responding to God. If Mk 9:37 is
authentic, Jesus may have seen himself as God's representative acting and
speaking with the full authority of God. One might say more about structural
correspondences between the activity of Jesus and post-resurrection christology[65] but more is not needed to support the christological formulation chosen
to summarize Christian belief and guide Christian theological interpretation
of the New Testament.

---

64 My recourse to this formula in 'Can the Critical Study of Scripture provide a Doctrinal
    Norm', *Journal of Religion* 76 (1996) 206–232, insisted that this does not endorse the
    terms in which patristic and later christology articulated it.

.   A more important question about the formula chosen is whether it is not too loose to be called a doctrinal norm at all. The way it speaks of Jesus (the revelation of God), and Christian response to Jesus ('having to do with') speaks of discipleship rather than doctrine. It identifies the man from Nazareth as a magnet drawing those who are attracted by him into relationship with God. Again, precision is lost, and it becomes harder to exclude followers of Jesus on account of their heterodoxy if this 'having to do with Jesus' is made normative, but that might be an advantage today. A generous orthodoxy is more attractive and surely more true to Jesus himself than a narrow one.[66] It is still the person of Jesus that is decisive, not his teaching, and the possibility of 'having to do' with him as the living Lord today presupposes his resurrection (however understood) and a doctrine of the Spirit. It also presupposes the community of his disciples, and that requires the guidance and correction of an ecclesiology which subordinates disciples to their Lord. And in this unjust world, still very largely subject to the powers of evil, it must include the Christian hope of a better world already operative wherever the Lord is present in his disciples.

Although E. Käsemann made *iustificatio impii* his canon within the canon, he came to insist very strongly that discipleship of Jesus is what mattered most. The Lutheran concern with pure doctrine, and the right preaching of word and sacrament, remain important, especially for theologians, i.e. ministers of the word who have to try to speak truly of God in Christ. But what makes their preaching credible (or otherwise) is in part their own discipleship, and for most purposes a christological criterion that is slow to exclude any disciple of Jesus is more use than the sharpness of a narrow orthodoxy. Interpreting the doctrine of the divinity of Christ by K. Barth's 'having to do with Jesus' formula allows it to be understood in terms of discipleship, and invites us to interpret the New Testament theologically in accord with that norm. It is hard to doubt that a programme carried out on those lines, i.e. lives lived in discipleship to the crucified Jesus, would make the identity of Christianity sufficiently clear. It would also point the interpretation of the New Testament in a New Testament theology in the right direction, and so inform and instruct Christian preaching.

---

65   E.g. W. Thüsing, *Die neutestamentlichen Theologien und Jesus Christus I*, Münster: Aschendorff, [2]1996, pp. 68–112.

66   Cf. E. Käsemann, *Jesus Means Freedom*, London: SCM Press, 1969, ch. 1: 'Was Jesus a "liberal"?'.

Der Kanonbegriff in Biblischer Theologie und evangelischer Dogmatik

von Caroline Schröder-Field

1. Annäherung im Namen des „Kanons"

Dem Kanonbegriff bzw. Kanonproblem wird von verschiedenen Seiten Interesse entgegen gebracht. Doch auch wenn sich im „Kanon" die einzelnen Disziplinen der Theologie und anderer Wissenschaften treffen, ist damit noch nicht entschieden, dass sie mit ihren Worten dasselbe meinen oder mit dem Kanonischen des Kanons dieselben Erwartungen verbinden. Die Situation erinnert an eine Beschreibung, die Otto Weber 1955 in seinen Grundlagen zur Dogmatik bietet. Damals fiel der Verzicht auf die Klärung des Kanonproblems ins Auge. Man hatte den Kanon nicht angetastet, aber die Gründe vermutet Weber weniger in einer Hochschätzung des Kanons als in dessen Vernachlässigung bzw. Umgehung:

„Es ist auffällig, dass ... bisher kaum jemand die Forderung erhoben hat, den Kanon neu zu fassen. Die Ursache liegt *erstens* wohl darin, dass die historische Forschung, von der die für die heutige Problemlage maßgebenden Einsichten ausgegangen sind, als *historische* überhaupt keinen *verbindlichen* Kanon kennt. Sie kennt die einzelnen Schriften und interpretiert diese als Quellen für die Ur- und Frühgeschichte des Christentums. Sie kennt ferner den Kanon als eine geschichtlich gewordene Zusammenstellung ohne verbindliche Kraft. Das *theologische* Problem des Kanons ist in der historischen Forschung erst sichtbar geworden, seitdem sich diese wieder als *theologische* Disziplin begriff. *Zweitens* wird das nahezu völlige Fehlen eines Begehrens nach Änderung des Kanons darauf zurückzuführen sein, dass auch in der *Dogmatik* auf weiteste Strecken bewusst oder unbewusst ein ‚Kanon im Kanon' herrscht. Daher ist auch in der Dogmatik das *Problem* des Kanons erst in neuester Zeit wieder aktuell geworden."[1]

Die Situation hat sich seither geändert. Die Exegese kümmert sich längst nicht mehr nur um einzelne Schriften, die als „Quellen für die Ur- und Frühgeschichte des Christentums" dienen und man fragt auch hier nach der Entstehung und Lokalisierung von Verbindlichkeit. Die Dogmatik andererseits

---

1   O. Weber, Grundlagen der Dogmatik I, Neukirchen-Vluyn [7]1987, 289.

orientiert sich nicht mehr vorwiegend an einem „Kanon im Kanon", sondern hat die Frage nach einem schriftgemäßeren Umgang mit biblischen Texten in die Reflexion ihre Begründungsproblematik aufgenommen: auch sie will sich der Weite und dem Reichtum biblischer Texte aussetzen und sei es, dass sie dabei das Risiko eingeht, einiges von ihrem ererbten Material grundstürzend zu revidieren oder gar zu verlieren. Im Zuge dieser veränderten Interessenslage wendet man sich dem Kanon zu – oder vielmehr, man rekurriert auf den Kanonbegriff in unterschiedlicher Weise und mit den verschiedensten Erwartungen. In der Exegese erscheint das Kanonproblem als Experimentierfeld einer methodischen Neuorientierung. In der evangelischen Dogmatik bemüht man sich, nicht erst in jüngster Zeit, um eine Neubestimmung des Verhältnisses von Bibel, Kirche und Lehre und verwendet in diesem Zusammenhang die Begriffe „Kanon" und „Schrift" nahezu synonym.

Dies ist das *tertium comperationis* mit der Situation, die Otto Weber vor Augen steht: Der Kanonbegriff und seine Stellung innerhalb der Theologie, gewissermaßen als ihr Bindeglied, ist nach wie vor *klärungsbedürftig* – auch und gerade wenn alle davon reden. Wenn im Interesse der Kanonsproblematik eine Annäherung der theologischen Disziplinen geschehen soll, dann bedarf es einer gründlichen Ansicht des Begriffs und der mit ihm verbundenen Erwartungen.

2. „Kanon" – Ein Gegenstand fächerübergreifenden Interesses

H. Graf Reventlow stellt das Kanonproblem als Teil der Biblischen Theologie vor.[2] In dem Unternehmen „Biblische Theologie" sind die unterschiedlichsten Interessen und Perspektiven versammelt. Als Seitenzweig der Exegese ist sie nicht unumstritten, und auch die Dogmatik sieht sich von ihrer Zielsetzung in Frage gestellt.[3] In ihrem Rahmen wird die Frage nach dem

---

2   „Im ganzen lässt sich die Kanonsfrage nur im Zusammenhang mit dem Gesamtproblem einer Biblischen Theologie würdigen; das wiedererwachte Interesse am Kanon hängt aufs engste mit der Wiederbelebung der Diskussion um diesen umfassenden Aspekt zusammen" (H. Graf Reventlow, Hauptprobleme der Biblischen Theologie im 20. Jahrhundert, Darmstadt 1983; zum Kanonproblem: S. 125–137, Zitat S. 135).

3   Friedrich Mildenberger beschreibt das „charakteristische[s] Dilemma" der Biblischen Theologie: „Entweder führt sie ihren historischen Ansatz konsequent durch; dann verliert sie ihren Gegenstand, eben die Biblische Theologie, und tauscht sich statt dessen ein Stück Vergangenheit ein ... Oder sie revidiert ihren emanzipatorischen Ansatz und bestimmt ihr Verhältnis zur Dogmatik nicht nur negativ; dann wird freilich ihr Selbstverständnis, in dem sie sich im Rahmen moderner Wissenschaft als ‚theologische Aufklärung' ihren Ort zugewiesen hat, problematisch werden" (F. Mildenberger, Biblische Theologie als kirchliche Schriftauslegung, JBTh 1 [1986] 151–162, S. 151).

Kanon vor allem von Alttestamentlern bedacht[4], während sie unter Neutestamentlern weniger Resonanz erfährt.[5] Die Vertreter und Vertreterinnen der alttestamentlichen Exegese müssen sich beispielsweise fragen lassen, ob sie es mit der Hebräischen Bibel oder mit dem Alten Testament zu tun haben. Können sie sich den Schriften des Alten Testaments ohne Rücksicht auf deren Aufnahme durch die Schriften des Neuen Testaments und der Kirche zuwenden? In welchem Ausmaß soll das gegenwärtige Judentum und seine Auslegungstraditionen in ihrer Arbeit Berücksichtigung finden? Wie verhält sich die alttestamentliche Forschung zu der Behauptung, dass der christliche Kanon erst durch das Neue Testament zum Abschluss kommt?

Nun ist auch das Interesse der alttestamentlichen Exegese an der Bibel als Kanon bzw. an biblischen Texten als kanonischen Texten nicht selbstverständlich. Es indiziert eine Verschiebung innerhalb der exegetischen Methodenlehre. Bevor sich die Exegese dem Kanon als einem Gegenstand eigenen Interesses zuwenden konnte, bedurfte es einer gewissen Distanzierung von der literarkritischen und der überlieferungsgeschichtlichen Schule, die die ältesten literarischen Schichten für maßgeblich hielten, zu der redaktionsgeschichtlichen Methode, die sich um die Nachgeschichte oder *relecture* der Texte bemühte. Im Rahmen dieser Methode – so Reventlow – sei es möglich geworden, „den Bibelgebrauch im synagogalen und frühkirchlichen Gottesdienst" zu berücksichtigen.[6] So gelte es nicht mehr nur, die ursprüngliche Verfasserintention zu rekonstruieren, auch sei es nicht damit getan, mit Hilfe analytischer Methoden die vorliegenden größeren Zusammenhänge aufzusprengen, sondern die Aufmerksamkeit der Bibelwissenschaft richte sich vielmehr darauf, den Prozess der Synthese, das Werden des Kanons aufzudecken. In diesem Sinne plädiert J.A. Sanders für die Methode des „canonical criticism":

---

4 So kann man das Interesse am biblischen Kanon von einem Interesse an einer gesamtbiblischen Theologie präludiert sehen, und hier wird es „nach dem barbarische[n] Angriff des Nationalsozialismus gegen alles Jüdische und damit auch gegen alles Alttestamentliche, aber auch Christliche" vor allem um die Wiedergewinnung des Alten Testaments „für die Theologie und Praxis" gehen, „und zwar nicht nur in der bloß duldenden Haltung, daß es nicht abgeschafft werden kann, sondern in der des Hörers: ‚Er weckt alle Morgen, er weckt mir das Ohr, daß ich höre wie ein Jünger' (Jes 50,4)" (H. Seebass, Der Gott der ganzen Bibel. Biblische Theologie zur Orientierung im Glauben, Freiburg/Basel/Wien 1982, 24).

5 Diese Beobachtung gilt auch für die theologische Gesprächslage in den USA: „Ein auffälliges Merkmal der Kanondiskussion, das gleich zu Anfang erkannt werden sollte, ist die Konzentration des Interesses vor allem auf das Alte Testament bzw. die Feststellung, dass die Diskussion vor allem intensiver im Bereich des Alten Testaments und unter Alttestamentlern als innerhalb der neutestamentlichen Wissenschaft geführt worden ist" (P. D. Miller, Der Kanon in der gegenwärtigen amerikanischen Diskussion, JBTh 3 [1988] 217–239, S. 218).

6 Reventlow, Hauptprobleme (s. Anm. 2), 129.

„Im Mittelpunkt des canonical criticism werden nicht die Einleitungsfragen nach Quellen und Einheitlichkeit stehen, die die Traditionsgeschichtler so sehr beschäftigt haben, sondern vielmehr die Fragen nach Wesen und Funktion der aufgenommenen Tradition. Wenn eine Tradition in einer bestimmten Situation zugrunde gelegt wird, müssen wir davon ausgehen, dass sie in dieser Lage als dienlich empfunden wurde: Sie sollte eine Aufgabe erfüllen, und aus diesem Grund nahm man sie auf. Im Zentrum des canonical criticism stehen die Fragen nach dem Wesen der Autorität und nach der Hermeneutik, der gemäß diese Autorität in der Situation, in der sie gebraucht wurde, eingesetzt wurde. Welcher Art waren die Bedürfnisse der Gemeinschaft und wie wurde ihnen begegnet?"[7]

Dieser Wertewandel von der Hochschätzung des Früheren als des Ursprünglichen zur Anerkennung des Späteren, Gewachsenen bzw. Prozessualen[8] erlaubt auch eine Revision und Modifikation der vielgeschmähten Inspirationslehre. So lassen sich Inspiriertheit und Irrtumslosigkeit der Schrift sozial verstehen, nämlich als Nötigung, zum rechten Verständnis eines biblischen Textes prinzipiell alle am Entstehungsprozess Beteiligten zu berücksichtigen; die dogmatischen Prädikationen können nicht einzelnen Schriftstellern oder Büchern zugeschrieben werden, sondern gelten für die Schrift im ganzen, das Neue Testament eingeschlossen.[9]

„Kanon" ist das Resultat, dem Vorgänge zugrunde liegen, die in unterschiedlicher Weise von Interesse sein können: die Entstehung des Kanons, die Kanonisierung, beruht einerseits auf „konziliare[n], offizielle[n] oder inoffizielle[n] Entscheidungen"[10] der Kirche; andererseits auf dem von diesen Entscheidungen und ihren Trägern relativ unabhängigen faktischen Gebrauch der Texte und Traditionen innerhalb der gottesdienstlichen Gemeinschaft. – Dies sind nicht nur Varianten einer historischen Fragestellung: Je nachdem, für welchen Vorgang man sich interessiert, verrät man etwas darüber, wo man innerhalb der kirchlichen Hierarchie die Selbstdurchsetzung des Gotteswortes ansiedelt.

---

7   J.A. Sanders, Adaptable for Life. The Nature and Function of Canon, in: Magnalia Dei. The Mighty Acts of God. Essays on the Bible and Archaeology in Memory of G. Ernest Wright, Garden City, NY 1976, 531–560, S. 543f.

8   Brevard S. Childs, an dessen Veröffentlichungen (Biblical Theology in Crisis, Philadelphia 1970; Introduction to the Old Testament as Scripture, Philadelphia 1979; The New Testament as Canon. An Introduction, Valley Forge 1985; The Old Testament Theology in a Canonical Context, Philadelphia 1986; Biblical Theology of the Old and New Testament. Theological Reflection on the Christian Bible, Minneapolis 1993) die Diskussion des Kanonproblems nicht vorbeigehen kann, sieht es anders als Sanders. Er ordnet dem Interesse an der Entstehungsgeschichte des Kanons das Interesse an dessen Endgestalt vor.

9   Der soziale Charakter der Inspiration sei auf katholischer Seite von J. McKenzie (Social Character of Inspiration, CBQ 24 [1962] 115–124) und von J. McCarthy (Personality, Society and Inspiration, TS 24 [1963] 553–576) herausgearbeitet worden; Norbert Lohfink halte zudem die wissenschaftliche Exegese dazu an, das Neue Testament als letzten Hagiographen des Alten Testaments zu beachten; Reventlow, Hauptprobleme (s. Anm. 2), 130f.

10 Miller, Kanon (s. Anm. 5), 225.

Die Beiträge des „Jahrbuchs für Biblische Theologie" *Zum Problem des biblischen Kanons* sowie jüngere Publikationen in der Zeitschrift „Evangelische Theologie" zeigen, wie sehr Vertreter aller theologischen Disziplinen an dem Projekt „Biblische Theologie" beteiligt sind – auch der Kanonbegriff scheint einen jeden über die Grenzen seines Faches hinauszuführen. Das mag sich schlicht dem Umstand verdanken, dass „Kanon" die ganze Bibel meint, und dass die Bibel in ihrer Ganzheit, d.h. in ihrem Zusammenschluss von Neuem und Altem Testament unter zwei Buchdeckeln, alles andere als selbstverständlich ist. Es muss immer wieder und wohl angesichts verschiedener Anfragen immer wieder neu bedacht werden, worin die Ganzheit, wenn nicht gar die Einheit, der Bibel besteht. Keine theologische Disziplin wird dies für sich allein bedenken können.

Was verspricht man sich im einzelnen von einer Beachtung des Kanons bzw. des Kanonischen in den verschiedenen theologischen Disziplinen? – Die Antwort muss lauten: ‚höchst Verschiedenes!' – Dazu einige Beispiele:

Norbert Lohfink spricht von „kanonischer Schriftauslegung" und versteht unter Kanon dezidiert den christlichen Kanon. Daher ist mit der „kanonischen Schriftauslegung" der Anspruch verbunden, alttestamentliche Texte für die Gemeinde auszulegen, d.h. unter Berücksichtigung ihrer Aufnahme in den Schriften des Neuen Testaments und ihres Bezugs auf Christus. Erst so, und indem aufgezeigt wird, inwiefern die Gemeinde Anteil am Geschick Christi erhalte, werde der alttestamentliche Kanon „voll ausgelegt".[11]
Unter dem Stichwort „'kanonischer' Zugang" bedenkt *Ingo Baldermann*, wie die Kanonizität der Bibel für den Unterricht fruchtbar gemacht werden kann. Der Anlass ist die Verdrängung des biblischen Unterrichts durch den problemorientierten Religionsunterricht und die damit verbundene Reduktion der Bibel zu einer „Randexistenz im Unterricht" – diese Entwicklung stehe im Widerspruch zu dem reformatorischen Schriftprinzip, das „ja alles andere als eine autoritäre Vorgabe dogmatischer Inhalte und ihres Wahrheitsanspruchs" sei.[12] So versteht Baldermann „Kanon" als Ermöglichung von Lernprozessen, die nicht ohne Auseinandersetzungen auskommen. Der Kanon fördere Prozesse *gemeinsamen* Lernens. Dieses Kanonverständnis entspricht einem didaktisch (der Gegenbegriff ist „dogmatisch") verstandenen Schriftprinzip – maßgeblich ist die Orientierung am „Prozess der Einsicht".[13] Dabei verschränkt Baldermann Schriftprinzip und Kanonbegriff, sieht letzteren durch ersteres interpretiert und nimmt vor allem die Regel auf, dass sich die Schrift selbst auslegt.[14]

---

11 N. Lohfink, Was wird anders bei kanonischer Schriftauslegung? Beobachtungen am Beispiel von Ps 6, JBTh 3 (1988) 29–53.

12 „Systematiker und Exegeten stimmen darin überein, dass allein schon die immense Widersprüchlichkeit biblischer Aussagen verbietet, die Bibel in solcher Weise zur norma normans zu machen. Das Schriftprinzip formuliert vielmehr das bleibende Recht der kritischen Rückfrage gegen den autoritären Anspruch sich verfestigter Traditionen. Wie es dazu kommen konnte, dass das Schriftprinzip selbst dazu dienen musste, die traditionelle Lehrautorität zu verfestigen, und dies nicht nur in der Katechetik, sondern auch im interkonfessionellen Dialog, bleibt das große Rätsel seiner Wirkungsgeschichte" (I. Baldermann, Didaktischer und „kanonischer" Zugang. Der Religionsunterricht vor dem Problem des biblischen Kanons, JBTh 3 [1988] 97–111, S. 99).

13 Baldermann, ebd., 100.

14 „Mit der Bezeichnung der Schrift als sui ipsius interpres beschreibt Luther tatsächlich die Binnenstruktur des Kanons als eine didaktische und dialogische Struktur. Die bibli-

Rolf Rendtorff versteht unter „Kanon" die Hebräische Bibel, die Juden und Christen gemeinsam ist und der gegenüber sie beide grundsätzlich in derselben Position sind. Daher seien sie zur „gemeinsame[n] Beschäftigung mit unserer gemeinsamen Hebräischen Bibel" genötigt. Gleichzeigt überträgt er jedoch auf diesen – aus christlich-traditioneller Sicht verkürzten – Kanon die reformatorische Regel der Schriftauslegung: „Die Hebräische Bibel ist selbst ein theologisches Buch, das aus sich selbst heraus theologisch interpretiert werden kann und soll."[15] – Rendtorff antwortet in seinem Aufsatz auf den im selben Heft der EvTh abgedruckten Essay von Jon D. Levenson, in dem dieser erklärt, warum jüdische Bibelwissenschaftler kein Interesse an Biblischer Theologie aufbringen können.[16] Die Erwartung, die Aufnahme der Kanonsproblematik im Rahmen einer Biblischen Theologie könne das jüdisch-christliche Gespräch beleben, könnte durch Levensons Aufsatz etwas gedämpft werden.

Schließlich gibt es neben der Beachtung des Kanons als dem Corpus verbindlicher Schriften für Juden und Christen bzw. für die Kirche noch das *Interesse an einem „Kanon im Kanon"*. Es lebt, wenn auch umstritten, unter Vertretern und Vertreterinnen aller Disziplinen, auch der Exegese, immer wieder auf. So findet *Walter Dietrich* den roten Faden des Alten Testaments im Gerechtigkeitsverständnis findet, ein Faden, der bis zum Neuen Testament und darüber hinaus wohl bis zur Reformation reicht. Seine Ausführungen zeigen ihn als Theologen, der sich sowohl der refomatorischen Tradition als auch dem jüdisch-christlichen Gespräch verpflichtet weiss.[17] Auch *Ferdinand Hahn* möchte zeigen, dass Gottes Gerechtigkeit und die

---

schen Schriften nehmen ausdrücklich Bezug aufeinander und wollen in solchem Zusammenhang gelesen sein. ... Die Außenseite des biblischen Kanons, die ihn zum entscheidenden Maßstab für alles theologische Reden, auch im Unterricht, erklärt, ist nur die Außenseite des Schriftprinzips; seine Innenseite ist die durch und durch dialogische Struktur des Kanons. Dass überhaupt ein Kanon entstand, ist ein Zeichen für die Notwendigkeit eines verbindlichen Maßstabs; dass der Kanon aber diese Gestalt annahm, die Gestalt einer Zusammenfügung so unterschiedlicher Stimmen, ist ein Zeichen dafür, dass die Verbindlichkeit nicht autoritär in dogmatischen Setzungen gesucht wurde, sondern im Dialog" (Baldermann, ebd., 107f.)

15 R. Rendtorff, Wege zu einem gemeinsamen jüdisch-christlichen Umgang mit dem Alten Testament, EvTh 51 (1991) 431–444, S. 440.

16 J.D. Levenson, Warum Juden sich nicht für biblische Theologie interessieren, EvTh 51 (1991) 402–430 (vgl. auch den Bezug auf diesen Aufsatz im Beitrag von M. Wolter in diesem Band [s.o. S. 50ff.]). – Levenson zufolge ist der Umstand, dass sich jüdische Wissenschaftler nicht für eine biblische Theologie interessieren, nicht als Defizit zu verstehen. Im Gegenteil, das Interesse christlicher, d.h. aber vor allem protestantischer Bibelwissenschaftler an biblischer Theologie sei folgerichtiges Symptom einer Überspanntheit – die Überspanntheit apokalyptischer Höchsterwartung an die eigene Gegenwart; die Überspanntheit des jüngeren Geschwisterkindes, das seine Zugehörigkeit legitimieren muss; hinzu komme die Überspanntheit derer, die die Traditionsprozesse auf das historisch Ursprüngliche durchstoßen wollen („Ad fontes!") und daher den Ausstieg aus der Kontinuität der Tradition demonstrieren müssen. So betrachtet erscheint das Phänomen einer biblischen Theologie eher als ein Krankheitsphänomen. Oder anders gesagt: Die alttestamentliche Exegese wird eigentlich erst durch außerbiblische, vor allem christlich bzw. protestantisch theologische Konstruktionen zu ihrer Bemühung um eine Theologie des Alten Testaments gedrängt; fallen diese Konstruktionen weg, dann gibt es eigentlich auch keinen Anlass, eine Theologie des Alten Testaments anzuvisieren.

17 „Sie ist mindestens so sehr Evangelium wie Gesetz – wenn sie auch das eine nicht ohne das andere ist. ... Die gesamte paulinische Rechtfertigungslehre ist im Alten Testament präludiert ... Gewiss, die Christusgestalt fehlt noch, aber auch sie ist präludiert: in Propheten etwa, die sich bei Gott für die Ungerechten verwenden, oder in dem Gottesknecht, der durch sein ʼLeiden ʼVielen zur Gerechtigkeit hilft" (W. Dietrich, Der rote Faden im Alten Testament, EvTh 49 [1989] 232–250, S. 248). „Nicht, dass die geschichtlich gewachsenen und in der späteren Geschichte immer wieder bedeutsam ge-

Rechtfertigung des Menschen für das Urchristentum insgesamt von Interesse sind. Er spricht von einer „Traditionslinie", die „vom Alten Testament und Frühjudentum her" über Jesu „Botschaft von der anbrechenden Gottesherrschaft" die vorpaulinische Überlieferung, Paulus und die nachpaulinischen Schriften erreicht hat. Die neutestamentliche Heilsbotschaft könne zwar nicht auf die Rechtfertigungsaussagen reduziert werden, sie bilden jedoch ihren Mittelpunkt.[18] Anders verteidigt *Werner H. Schmidt* die Mitte des Alten Testaments, die er in der „Ausschließlichkeit des Glaubens" bzw. im Ersten Gebot findet.[19] Zudem habe die Exegese „Altes und Neues Testament miteinander zu lesen". „Vielleicht darf man urteilen ... : Nach dem Alten Testament kann sich Gott menschlich – im Menschen und wie ein Mensch – zeigen, nach dem Neuen Testament als Mensch."[20]

Unter dem Stichwort „Kanon" wird von Vertretern aller theologischer Disziplinen die Frage bzw. das Problem des Normativen aufgegriffen. Für die Exegese bedeutet das eine Modifikation ihres Selbstverständnisses. Jedoch sollte man nicht übersehen, dass auch außerhalb der Kanonsdiskussion Exegeten nicht unbelastet vom reformatorischen Schriftverständnis arbeiten. Will man etwa die Geschichte der historisch-kritischen Forschung erzählen, so empfiehlt es sich, genau hier einzusetzen: bei einem Kapitel über das protestantische Schriftprinzip.[21] Exegese kann sich gar als Bemühung um normati-

---

wordenen Unterschiede zwischen Altem und Neuem Testament hier einfach beiseitegeschoben werden sollen; dennoch dürfte es im Blick auf die von vielen Seiten angestrebte Biblische Theologie nicht unerheblich sein, wenn die hier behauptete Mitte des Alten Testaments so nahe an die seit der Reformation oft für das Neue Testament reklamierte Mitte von der Gerechtigkeit Gottes und der Rechtfertigung des Menschen heranführt" (ebd., 249). „An ihm [dem Leitfaden „Gerechtigkeit"] entlang lassen sich die Inhalte des Alten Testaments so entfalten, dass sie als Fundament jüdischer wie christlicher Glaubensinhalte, ja auch innerjüdischer und innerchristlicher Glaubensunterschiede – und zugleich doch als Grundlage gemeinsamen Glaubens an den einen Gott und gemeinsamen Handelns nach seinem Willen begreiflich werden" (ebd.).

18 „Als Ausdruck der an keine Voraussetzung gebundenen Zuwendung Gottes und der Erneuerung des Menschen ist die Rechtfertigungslehre eine zentrale Ausformung der Grundbotschaft des Neuen Testaments. Sie ist insofern nicht ein Thema neben anderen, sondern sie ist Grundthema schlechthin, unabhängig davon, ob die Rechtfertigungsterminologie gebraucht wird. In diesem Sinn haben die Reformatoren, vor allem Martin Luther, mit gutem Grund die Rechtfertigungslehre als ‚Mitte und Grenze' (Ernst Wolf) verstanden. Daran hat eine evangelische Theologie, sofern sie im reformatorischen Sinn schriftgebunden bleibt, auch heute festzuhalten" (F. Hahn, Gerechtigkeit Gottes und Rechtfertigung des Menschen nach dem Zeugnis des Neuen Testaments, EvTh 59 [1999] 335–346, S. 346).

19 W.H. Schmidt, Zur Theologie und Hermeneutik des Alten Testaments. Erinnerungen und Erwägungen zur Exegese, EvTh 62 (2002) 11–25.

20 Schmidt, ebd., 25.

21 So H.-J. Kraus, dessen *Geschichte der historisch-kritischen Erforschung des Alten Testaments* (Neukirchen [4]1988) mit dem Kapitel „Das protestantische Schriftprinzip und die Anfänge der Bibelkritik" beginnt. Auch J.D. Levensons Stellungnahme zur Biblischen Theologie arbeitet mit der Voraussetzung, dass sich diese nicht nur dem in der Renaissance laut werdenden Ruf „Ad fontes!", sondern vor allem der reformatorischen Lehre von der Schrift verdankt. Levenson spricht von dem „niemals endende[n] protestantische[n] Streben nach Wiederherstellung des Ursprünglichen, das diese intensive Beschäftigung mit der christlichen Bibel erzeugt". So sei der Gegensatz von Schrift und

ve Aussagen verstehen; sie ist nicht weniger als Dogmatik auf der Suche nach dem Verbindlichen – biblische Texte greifen unmittelbar in das Leben der Kirche ein, sofern diese sich „in reformatorischer Weise vom biblischen Zeugnis bestimmen lässt".[22]

Über das Ausmaß, in dem Exegeten sich in ihrer Arbeit reformatorischer Lehre verpflichtet sehen können, kann jedoch auch ein heftiger Streit entbrennen. Beispielhaft ist die scharfe Auseinandersetzung zwischen Klaus Berger und Hans Weder.[23] Im Zuge dieser Auseinandersetzung beruft sich Berger auf den Kanon zur Profilierung der exegetischen Arbeit. Diese habe sich in Loyalität zum Bibelwort zu vollziehen, von dem die Kirche bezeugt habe, dass es am nächsten an Jesus heranführt. Loyalität zum Bibelwort bedeute, der Fremdheit und Vielfalt des biblischen Wortes Rechnung tragen, und dies sei mit einer Reduktion der biblischen Schriften auf das seit der Reformation Bekannte nicht vereinbar. Der Streit zwischen Berger und Weder ist insofern symptomatisch, als hier deutlich wird, wie sehr auch die Exegese sich mit ihrer Verpflichtung weniger dem Kanonbegriff als vielmehr dem reformatorischen Schriftverständnis gegenüber auseinandersetzen muss. Auch die Exegese hat zu fragen, inwiefern es ihr um Normatives im Sinne evangelischer Theologie geht: Dieses ist in gewisser Weise tatsächlich immer dasselbe. Daher der Unmut des einen, der der ständigen Wiederholung überdrüssig ist und zur differenzierteren Wahrnehmung mahnt, und die Beharrlichkeit des anderen, der bei aller Differenziertheit auf dem Gemeinsamen als einer nicht konstruierten, sondern entdeckten Gegebenheit insistiert.[24]

Die Entwicklung innerhalb der Bibelwissenschaft, die Empfindlichkeit und zugleich die Aufmerksamkeit für das Normative, kann als ein Indiz dafür verstanden werden, dass die Frage nach der Autorität der Bibel – bei aller

---

Tradition, die „innerprotestantische Dynamik ... die Mutter der biblischen Theologie" (Warum [s. Anm. 16], 416).

22 So folgert P. Stuhlmacher in einer Auslegung von Mt 28: „Unser Einblick in Tradition, Redaktion und Konsequenzen von Mt 28,16–20 erlaubt es, noch pointierter [als Martin Hengel] zu formulieren: Eine Kirche, die sich in reformatorischer Weise vom biblischen Zeugnis bestimmen lässt, kann und darf sich aus christologischen Gründen nicht von dem Missionsauftrag lösen, der in Mt 28,16–20 bezeugt ist" (P. Stuhlmacher, Zur missionsgeschichtlichen Bedeutung von Mt 28,16–20, EvTh 59 [1999] 108–130, S. 129).

23 Ausgetragen in EvTh 52 (1992) 309–336.

24 Berger gegen Weder: „H. Weder scheint zu den Exegeten zu gehören, die zwischen Paulus und Luther, zwischen dem Evangelisten Johannes, Calvin und dem eigenen Bekenntnis auch nicht die Spur einer Differenz zu sehen imstande sind. Das führt leicht zu einer undifferenzierten Einheitsdoktrin, die dem Reichtum der Schrift und der Verschiedenheit der Rezipienten in gleicher Weise nicht gerecht wird" (a.a.O. [s. Anm. 23], 334). – Weder gegen Berger: „Der Unterschied von Gesetz und Evangelium ist sowohl bei Jesus (sachlich, nicht terminologisch), als auch bei Paulus und Johannes (terminologisch und sachlich) ein Sachverhalt, den die Reformation nicht erfunden, sondern entdeckt hat" (a.a.O. [s. Anm. 23], 336).

Vorsicht bzw. Skepsis gegenüber dogmatischen Aussagen über die Bibel als Schrift – über kurz oder lang nicht ausgeblendet bleiben kann.

So ist in der Exegese in jüngerer Zeit die Frage nach Wirksamkeit und Autorität der Bibel in Anlehnung an literaturwissenschaftliche Beschreibungen aufgenommen worden.[25] Auch dies ist ein fächerübergreifender Ansatz.[26] Mit Hilfe solcher Anregungen von außerhalb theologischer Aussagezusammenhänge lässt sich der Umstand, dass die Bibel Menschen in Anspruch nimmt, weniger autoritär erklären: Wenn von „Intertextualität" und „intertextuellem Spiel" die Rede ist, lassen sich die Freiheit und Kreativität des Lesens und Verbindlichkeit des Gelesenen und Zu-Lesenden gleichermaßen denken;[27] wenn man Texte als „Bezugstexte" versteht und von einem „an-

---

25 Zum folgenden vgl. Peter Müllers Darstellung der „Literaturwissenschaftliche[n] und exegetische[n] Perspektiven", in: Verstehst du auch, was du liest? Lesen und Verstehen im Neuen Testament, Darmstadt 1994, 128–147, bes. 146f.: „Die Kanonisierung hat den Schriften dazu verholfen, auf vielfältige Weise gelesen und in vielen Dimensionen rezipiert zu werden, Bezugstexte zu bleiben. In diesem Sinne hat der Kanon, obwohl er gleichzeitig andere Schriften ausschloss, die Intertextualität durchaus gefördert. Im Übrigen gilt dies nicht nur für die biblischen Schriften. In einer ganzen Reihe von Texten haben Menschen verschiedener Generationen und Epochen wesentliche Erkenntnisse, Wertvorstellungen und Hoffnungen zum Ausdruck gebracht. Dass dies in bestimmten Texten auf offenbar grundlegende Weise geschehen ist, bemisst sich an dem andauernden Rückbezug auf sie. Denn bei allem Pluralismus: es gibt zweifellos Texte, nicht nur die Bibel, auf die immer wieder Bezug genommen wird, während andere im intertextuellen Spiel unbedeutend bleiben. ... Solche Texte und die in ihnen zum Ausdruck gebrachten Vorstellungen ‚unterliegen einer historisch gewachsenen Unbeliebigkeit, sie wollen unumkehrbar sein'. Auch wenn sie weitergedacht werden, bleiben sie beispielhaft. Sie gehören in eine Geschichte hinein, die sie hervorgebracht hat, die aber von diesen Schriften im weiteren Verlauf zugleich mit geprägt wurde. Diese Wirksamkeit bestimmter Texte gibt ihnen Besonderheit."

26 Das fächerübergreifende Interesse manifestiert sich gelegentlich in einer Person: So ist Peter Müller Neutestamentler und Religionspädagoge.

27 Bemerkenswert ist der Einfluss der Literaturwissenschaft auf die Exegese. Sie hilft erklären, wie Lesen funktioniert. Solche Erklärungen können das Lesen beeinflussen, ändern: sie regen die Konstruktivität des Lesens an und bewältigen die Bedrohung durch den Pluralismus – in der konstruierten Welt ist Raum für viele Stimmen! (vgl. U. Bail, Von zerstörten Räumen und Barfußgehen. Anmerkungen zu Text-Räumen der Enge in der Hebräischen Bibel, EvTh 61 [2001] 92–101). Der Artikel beginnt mit „[m]ethodische[n] Überlegungen zum lesenden Reisen durch Raumtexte und Texträume" (101): „Das lesende sequenzielle Abschreiten der Worte, Sätze, Zeilen und Seiten, mit denen die Imagination des Lesers sich den Raum erschafft, der im Text entworfen wird, korrespondiert mit der lokalen Bewegungslosigkeit des Exegeten, der Exegetin beim Schreiben über den Raum. Über den Raum nachdenken bedeutet immer das gleichzeitige Durchschreiten mehrerer Räume: das ‚Verlassen' des Schreibtisches beim Eintritt in die imaginativen Raumfluchten der biblischen Texte, das Durchqueren der Seite Zeile für Zeile von oben nach unten, die Schaffung eines Textraumes beim Schreiben der exegetischen Beobachtungen und Überlegungen, das Reisen in und durch die Räume der biblischen Texte – ‚Lesen bedeutet, woanders zu sein, dort wo wir nicht sind, in einer anderen Welt'. Lesen ist eine Reise zu imaginierten Räumen und bedeutet mindestens an zwei Orten gleichzeitig zu sein" (94). „Durch die kooperative Interaktion zwischen Le-

dauernden Rückbezug" spricht, mag man sich ungezwungen an dogmatische
Beschreibungen erinnert fühlen, nach denen die Kirche auf ihren biblischen
Kanon als auf das Zeugnis ihres Ursprungs *zurückblickt*. Und wenn man zudem noch sieht, dass es auch außerhalb des biblischen Kanons „Kanonisches" gibt, sofern auch außerhalb der Kirche „bei allem Pluralismus" Texte
entstehen, die einer „'historisch gewachsenen Unbeliebigkeit'" unterliegen,
die also in hohem Maße invariant und beispielhaft sind, dann lässt sich beides
miteinander in Einklang bringen – dass „Kanon", und daher auch der biblische Kanon etwas Besonderes ist, und dass das Verhältnis „Kirche-Kanon"
nichts allzu Besonderes darstellt: Die Entstehung eines Lesekanons aus einer
Lesegemeinschaft bzw. einer Lesegemeinschaft aus einem Lesekanon ist ein
durchaus vergleichbarer, also einsehbarer Vorgang, zu dessen Erklärung man
weder auf übernatürliche Ursachen rekurrieren muss noch auf ein explizit
theologisches Vokabular angewiesen ist. In diesem Sinne kann man auch an
umstrittenen Modellen der Autoritätsregelung vorbei die Autorität biblischer
– und anderer – Texte erklären und bestätigen: „Im Rahmen solcher Lese-
und Interpretationsgemeinschaften kann auch die Autorität der Texte ,be-
kannt' werden, nicht im Sinne einer Setzung, sondern als Lesen, Hören und
Diskutieren, als Erzählung von Beziehungen, als Weitererzählen, als Bekanntmachung und Einladung."[28]

Nimmt man derartige Anregungen auf, könnte man Kirche zwar noch als
„creatura verbi" verstehen, sofern sie als „Lese- und Interpretationsgemein-
schaft" lebendig bleibt. Sofern ihr Tun bzw. Verhalten in Bezug auf die ihr
gegebenen Schriften jedoch als „Lesen, Hören und Diskutieren, als Erzählung von Beziehungen, als Weitererzählen, als Bekanntmachung und Einladung" verstanden wird, entspricht der Intertextualität biblischer Texte ein
hohes Maß an Interaktivität zwischen Lesegemeinschaft und Lesekanon. Das
ginge vielleicht auf Kosten der parallel formulierten Grundsätze, dass sich
der Kanon selbst legitimiere und dass sich die Schrift selbst auslege. Dafür
bedarf es dann nicht mehr der strengen Einseitigkeit eines kerygmatischen
Theologie- und Bibelverständnisses, um die Autorität der Bibel befestigen.
Die Bibel stellt zwar einen Sonderfall innerhalb der Literaturgeschichte dar,
aber eigentlich nur, sofern religiöse Texte der Antike mit anderen Erwartungen konfrontiert werden, als „literarische[n] Werke dieses oder des letzten
Jahrhunderts, und zwar insofern, als sie sich selbst nicht als fiktionale Texte
verstehen".[29] Wichtig ist, dass diese Relativierung der Bibel bei gleich-

---

senden und dem linearen Diskurs des Textes entsteht eine mögliche Welt, ein multidi-
mensionaler Raum, in dem viele Stimmen anwesend sind" (95).

28 Müller, „Verstehst du auch ...?" (s. Anm. 25), 160.
29 Müller, ebd., 144.

zeitiger Berücksichtigung ihres Sonderstatus auf die unrevidierten Zuschreibungen des altprotestantischen Schriftverständnisses verzichten kann – und diesbezüglich besteht zwischen Exegeten, Vertretern der Praktischen Theologie und Dogmatikern eine weitgehende Einigkeit.

Neben dieser nun möglichen, vielversprechenden Einigkeit gibt es jedoch noch ein gemeinsames Desiderat – die Frage, ob „Kanon" und „Schrift" sich so ohne weiteres aufeinander beziehen lassen, ob sie etwa tatsächlich in entsprechender Weise auf das für die Kirche Normative verweisen, wird wenig beachtet.[30] Gerade die Dogmatik ist diesbezüglich, wie sich zeigen wird, wenig vorbildlich.

3. Nach dem Kanon fragen und die Schrift meinen: Die Dominanz des Schriftbegriffs in der evangelischen Dogmatik

Für die evangelische Dogmatik sollte „Kanon" ein mit Vorsicht zu genießender Begriff sein. Er markiert die Autorität der biblischen Schriften im Verhältnis zur Kirche – und ihrem Lehramt – nicht zwingend auf reformatorische Weise. Auf katholischer Seite bedeutet der Kanonbegriff eine Subordination der biblischen Schriften unter die Autorität des kirchlichen Lehramtes, das einen unmittelbaren Zugang zur göttlichen Offenbarung hat. Aufgrund dieses Zugangs versteht sich das kirchliche Lehramt auch über die Inspiriertheit der biblischen Schriften informiert und autorisiert, diese zu umgrenzen und zu erklären.[31] So verstanden, ist der Kanonbegriff der reformatorischen *sola*

---

30 Der historischen Frage nach der Entstehung des alttestamentlichen Kanons ist die Unterscheidung von „Schrift" und „Kanon" jedoch nicht fremd. So weist P.D. Miller auf zwei Arbeiten (Leiman und Sundberg) hin, für die die Differenzierung der Begriffe Kriterium des historischen Urteils ist (Kanon [s. Anm. 5], 223f.).

31 In diesem Sinne äußert sich Karl Rahner: „Wie alle Heilstaten Gottes uns durch göttl. Offenbarung, die durch das Lehramt der Kirche authentisch verkündigt u. interpretiert wird, bekannt sind, so gilt das auch von der durch die Inspiration gegebenen göttl. Urheberschaft der Heiligen Schrift. Dass ihre Bücher inspiriert u. so kanonisch sind, wissen wir unmittelbar durch die kirchl. Lehrverkündigung, die die göttl. Offenbarung als ursprüngl. Quelle dieses Wissens bezeugt. Die Kirche hat in diesem Sinn sich immer das Recht der Umgrenzung des K. zugeschrieben, indem sie Apokryphen als solche kennzeichnete u. dieses Recht in den Erklärungen über den K. der Hl. Schrift ausgeübt hat" (K. Rahner, Art. Kanon. B. Dogmatisch, LThK² 5 [1960] 1283). – In Anlehnung an Rahner schreibt Hans Waldenfels: „Somit ist die Heilige Schrift in dem Akt, in dem Gott die Kirche will und setzt, als ein diese Kirche konstituierendes Moment mitgewollt und mitgesetzt. Die Inspiration ist in das göttliche Wollen der Kirche eingebettet. Die Heilige Schrift nimmt am göttlichen Ursprung der Kirche teil. Als grundlegendes Moment der Sammlung der Christusgläubigen ist sie selbst Wirksamwerdung des Geistes Christi. ... In der Rahnerschen These wird aber dann auch ein denkbares Konkurrenzverhältnis zwischen Kirche und Schrift aufgelöst. Die Schrift ist – strenggenommen – keine Instanz,

scriptura-Forderung, der hermeneutischen Regel *scriptura suipsius interpres* sowie dem evangelischen Selbstverständnis der Kirche als *creatura verbi* diametral entgegengesetzt. Vielleicht ist dies der Grund, warum in evangelischen Dogmatiken zwischen „Kanon" und „Schrift" kaum unterschieden wird. Sofern im dogmatischen Kanonbegriff das Thema „Kirche" immer schon angelegt ist, kann und darf „Kanon" eigentlich nichts anderes meinen als das, was im Rahmen der Lehre von der Heiligen Schrift zur Bibel und zum Bibelgebrauch gesagt werden kann!

In den *Grundlagen der Dogmatik* entfaltet Otto Weber innerhalb von § 2 „Die Heilige Schrift und die Kirche" die Kanonthematik. Gleich zu Beginn, in dem Abschnitt „Die Autorität der Kirche als Übung des Gehorsams"[32], arbeitet er das spezifisch reformatorische bzw. evangelische Bibelverständnis heraus. Auf diese Weise ist der Kanonbegriff in den Schriftbegriff sowie in das evangelische Kirchenverständnis eingebunden. „Kanon" indiziert die Gehorsamshaltung der Kirche gegenüber den ihr anvertrauten Schriften. Die Überschrift kündigt das Thema „Kanon" an, und indem dieses in Abgrenzung von katholischen Implikationen eingeführt wird,[33] ist immer wieder von der „Schrift" die Rede.[34] Dabei kann Weber auch vom „Schriftkanon" sprechen.[35]

An Webers Darstellung des Kanonproblems lässt sich beispielhaft das Wechselverhältnis von „Kanon" und „Schrift" herausarbeiten. Die Begriffe werden nicht grundsätzlich voneinander unterschieden; es wird auch nicht bei

---

die der Kirche gegenübersteht, so dass umgekehrt diese sich der Schrift gegenüber als Instanz aufspielen könnte. Die Heilige Schrift ist Gottes Wort *als* Wort der Kirche. Insofern kann und muss die Kirche dieses *ihr* Wort autoritativ interpretieren und bleibt doch selbst an die Schrift in derselben Weise gebunden, wie sie an ihre erste und grundlegende, von Gott in Christus gebildete Phase gebunden ist" (H. Waldenfels, Kontextuelle Fundamentaltheologie, Paderborn u.a. 1985, 435).

32 O. Weber, Grundlagen der Dogmatik I, Neukirchen-Vluyn [7]1987, 274f.

33 „Die Kirche wird nicht mehr primär als göttlich begründete Lehrinstitution, sondern als Stätte der Verkündigung verstanden. Das schließt ihre Anstaltlichkeit nicht aus. Es schließt aber die Vorstellung aus, als sei die Kirche die Spenderin und Verwalterin eines supranaturalen Heilsschatzes, der ihr zur sakralen Verfügung überlassen und anvertraut sei, und als gehörte das Schriftwort zu diesem Heilsschatz hinzu" (Weber, ebd., 275f.).

34 Vgl. Weber, ebd., 274–277, die Abschnitte: „Die Autorität der Kirche als Übung des Gehorsams" und „Die bevollmächtigte Darbietung der Schrift durch die Kirche" sowie besonders die Formulierung zur Selbstlegitimation bzw. Selbstkanonisierung der biblischen Schriften: „Welche Schriften zum Kanon gehören, das lässt sich einzig an diesen Schriften selbst erkennen. ... dass die kanonischen Bücher kanonisch sind, das geht der kirchlichen Feststellung der Kanonizität logisch voraus ... Das Zeugnis des Heiligen Geistes kann sachlich nur das an der Schrift *selbst* sich bekundende ist; es ist von der Selbstevidenz der Schrift nicht unterschieden. ... Damit aber werden wir für die Frage, *was* kanonisch sei, auf die *Schrift* selber zurückverwiesen" (ebd., 284). Man beachte hier die Unbefangenheit, mit der Weber von „Schriften" zu „Schrift" und „Kanon" bzw. „kanonisch" wechselt.

35 Weber, ebd., 277.

der Frage eingesetzt, mit welchem Recht man sie aufeinander beziehen kann. Die Zuordnung erfolgt vielmehr selbstverständlich und ohne Rücksicht auf möglicherweise unterschiedliche Prägungen. Diese lassen sich nur indirekt erschließen, und diese Undeutlichkeit hat weitreichende Konsequenzen:

a) Der dezidierten konfessionellen Einbindung des Kanonbegriffs, dem ständigen Verweis auf die theologischen Einsichten der Reformatoren, aber auch auf die Gefahr einer Annäherung an tridentinische Konzeptionen[36] kann man kaum noch entnehmen, dass man „Kanon" auch anders verstehen kann.

b) Die enge Verknüpfung des reformatorisch gefassten Kanonbegriffs mit bestimmten Autoritäts- und Normierungserwartungen lässt wenig Raum für die Frage, ob die Bibel als Kanon nicht auch andere Formen der Autoritätsregelung zulässt. Wie nah steht etwa der dem Kanonbegriff inhärente Autoritätsanspruch dem „sola scriptura" der Reformation?

c) „Kanon" erscheint dem Schriftbegriff *untergeordnet*. So wirft etwa Webers Darstellung von Kriterien der Kanonbildung ein Licht auf das Ausmaß dieser Unterordnung.[37] Denn dies sind explizit theologische Kriterien,

---

36 Vgl. den Passus innerhalb der Revision des Originalitätskriteriums: „Im *zweiten* [die Reduktion des Kanons auf die „in sich selbst widerspruchslose, sachförmige Wahrheit"] Fall träte das wohl noch Schlimmere ein ... es würde mit einer auf das Cohaerenzkriterium aufgebauten Neufassung des Kanons genau das Kanonsverständnis des Tridentinums eingeführt" (Weber, ebd., 294f.).

37 Aus dem Apostolizitätskriterium der Alten Kirche wird das Originalitätskriterium: „Der Kanon ruft die Kirche zu ihrem Ursprung zurück. Wir können daher, ohne Wesentliches zu verkürzen, das Kriterium der Apostolizität als Kriterium der *Originalität* verstehen: kanonisch sind die Schriften, die den jederzeit Anerkennung fordernden Ursprung der Kirche aussagen" (Weber, ebd., 285). „Ohne Wesentliches zu verkürzen" – woran könnte dabei gedacht sein? Was könnte durch diese Auslegung von „Apostolizität" unterschlagen werden? Weber weist darauf hin, dass die reformatorische Rezeption des Kanonbegriffs zu gravierenden Veränderungen geführt hat. „Die Alte Kirche hatte Originalität mit Apostolizität identifiziert und die letztere literarisch verobjektiviert aufgefasst. Indem die *Reformatoren* ihr Augenmerk allgemein von der formal-objektiven Gegebenheit auf die Sache der Verkündigung lenkten, bahnten sie auch einer Verinhaltlichung des – von ihnen literarisch im allgemeinen noch geteilten – Apostolizitätskriteriums den Weg. Original und apostolisch konnte nur das sein, was das reine *Evangelium* aussagte. Von da her konnte sich ein *materielles* Kriterium für die Kanonizität ergeben: das vielerörtete ‚Was Christum treibet' *Luthers*" (ebd., 286). Wenn man demgegenüber Apostolizität als Verfasserschaft versteht, räumt man die Möglichkeit ein, die in Frage stehenden Schriften auf die autorisierten, weil inspirierten Lehrer der Kirche zurückzuführen. Dann wäre es möglich, die „Lehre" der Bibel vorzuordnen, und zwar nicht materialiter, sondern als Ausübung jenes kirchlichen Amtes, das die Kirche zusammenhält, indem es ihr die Bibel gibt – sowohl in der ursprünglichen Verschriftlichung als auch im kontinuierlichen Prozess der Auslegung. Die Konsequenz ist eine Relativierung des Normativen: So wie die Bibel ohne Lehramt nicht zustande gekommen wäre, so kann sie ohne dieses Amt gar nicht gelesen und verstanden werden. – Deutlicher noch lässt sich die reformatorische Prägung des zweiten Kriteriums „das wir das *Cohaerenzkriterium* nennen wollen" erkennen (ebd., 286). Diesem Kriterium werden sowohl Luthers Unterscheidung von Gesetz und Evangelium als auch die calvinistischen Ansätze einer Föderaltheologie zugeordnet. Auch lässt sich von diesem Kriterium her die – wiederum von

die den biblischen Kanon in seinen Grenzen bestätigen, indem sie über diese Grenzen – und über sich selbst – hinausweisen: auf die „Einheit Gottes-in-seiner-Offenbarung"[38], auf den „*faktische[n] Ursprung*", der durch den „*faktisch* [nicht prinzipiell] geschlossenen *Kanon* repräsentiert"[39] wird. Der Kanon lässt sich, so wie er ist, nicht umgehen – er ist „die Zusammenfassung des verbum externum"[40] – und doch besteht die Nötigung, über ihn hinauszugehen: als „'Text für die Verkündigung'"[41] weist der Kanon „selbst über sich hinaus, aber eben nicht auf die Kirche, sondern auf ihren Herrn, und auf diesen in seiner (freilich vom Zeugnis der Schrift nicht ablösbaren) Geschichtlichkeit"[42].

d) In dieser Bestimmung ist der Kanonbegriff theologisch „aufgeladen", keineswegs konfessionsneutral, sondern mit den dogmatischen Topoi der Eklesiologie, Christologie und Rechtfertigungstheologie verbunden. Man kann aber auch sagen, dass er vom Schriftbegriff absorbiert wird. Ein Blick auf die gegenwärtigen dogmatischen Entwürfe bestätigt diesen Eindruck. Es scheint, dass, wenn evangelische Theologen in Deutschland von der Bibel reden, sie eher von „Schrift" als vom „Kanon" reden. Oder anders: wenn dogmatisch nach dem Kanon gefragt wird, wird unversehens von der Schrift gesprochen.

So dominiert in der evangelischen Theologie nicht der Kanon-, sondern der Schriftbezug. Bestimmend für die evangelische Dogmatik sind das reformatorische Schriftverständnis mit seinen richtungsweisenden Formeln *scriptura sui ipsius interpres* und *viva vox evangelii*. Diese Formeln regeln in spezifischer Weise die Autorität bzw. die Akzeptanz der Autorität der biblischen Schriften. Die Erwartung, die Schrift lege sich selbst aus, impliziert den Abbau der Autorität, die dem Lehramt und der Tradition zugeschrieben

---

den Reformatoren geleistete – theologische Kritik einzelner biblischer Schriften verstehen.

38 Weber spricht hier von „geschichtlicher Cohaerenz" (ebd., 292) bzw. von „'personaler' Einheit", die nicht die „Permanenz eines Gedankens" ist, sondern „allein in der ‚Person' Jesu Christi offenbar" wird (ebd., 293). In diesem Zuammenhang lässt sich zwar auch von einer „Mitte der Schrift" und von einem „Kanon im Kanon" reden, aber so wenig wie sich dieser „Kanon im Kanon" kanonisieren ließe, so wenig lassen sich bestimmte biblische Schriften mit Hilfe eines inhaltlich konzis spezifizierten Kohärenzkriteriums ausscheiden. Weber sieht in der Handhabung des Kohärenzkriteriums noch ein anderes Kriterium am Werk: „das Kriterium der *Treue*" – „Und das dürfte wohl auch ein kirchliches Kriterium sein" (ebd., 294).

39 Weber, ebd., 294.

40 Weber, ebd., 292.

41 In Anlehnung an Hermann Diem. Dieser versteht die „*Geschichte der Kanonsbildung ...* als die *Geschichte des Predigttextes*" (H. Diem, Die Einheit der Schrift, EvTh 13 [1953] 385–405, S. 393).

42 Weber, Grundlagen I (s. Anm. 32), 291.

wird. Die Erwartung, dass die sich selbst auslegende Schrift im gesprochenen Wort des Evangeliums, in der aktuellen Wortverkündigung, zur Geltung kommt, gibt den Prediger bzw. die Predigerin und die hörende Gemeinde als den eigentlichen Ort des Verstehens zu erkennen.[43]

Der Begriff „Schrift" ist unvermeidlich mit den Konstituenzien der reformatorischen Rechtfertigungslehre verknüpft. Hier muss auf zwei Gefahren hingewiesen werden: Die eine besteht darin, dass das Schriftwort von dem aktuellen Verstehen gar nicht unterschieden werden kann bzw. dass eine Auseinandersetzung mit dem Text, welche sich den entsprechenden theologisch geprägten Formulierungen gegenüber auf Distanz hält, prinzipiell als defizient angesehen wird. Die andere Gefahr hat mit dem Umstand zu tun, dass der Singular von „Schrift", weit mehr als der Singular von „Kanon", die Einheit der biblischen Schriften bzw. Texte suggeriert: Es entsteht der Eindruck, als müsse in ihrer Zuspitzung auf die Verkündigung des Evangeliums immer dasselbe gesagt werden („was Christum treibet"). Dies kann beengend oder erstickend wirken, zumal wenn man der Vorstellung keinen Raum gibt, dass auch „dasselbe" höchst differenziert und spannungsvoll sein kann.

Zudem ist der Schriftbegriff und das ihm zugeordnete Kanonsverständnis von einer merkwürdigen Ambivalenz: Sofern er im Faktum der biblischen Schriften die einzige maßgebliche Autorität kirchlichen Lebens sieht, verbindet er sich mit dem Bestreben, diese Autorität so gründlich wie möglich zu sichern (altprotestantische Lehre von der Heiligen Schrift und der Verbalinspiration). Sofern er pragmatisch/seelsorglich auf die Rechtfertigungsbotschaft ausgerichtet ist, zeigt er eine Tendenz dazu, das Faktum der Verschriftlichung aufzuheben. Der Schrift liegt das mündlich und persönlich gesprochene Wort zugrunde; die Schrift kommt eigentlich erst im mündlich und persönlich gesprochenen Wort zum Ziel[44] – in dem Wort, das als Gesetz

---

43 Gerade hier zeigt sich auch Diems Kanonbegriff reformatorisch geprägt: „Die Kirche ... kann nur sagen, dass sie tatsächlich in all diesen Zeugnissen in ihrer ganzen Verschiedenheit die Stimme des einen Christus gehört hat und deshalb auch wir sie hören können und sollen. Oder anders gesagt: *indem die Kirche uns den Kanon gab, steht sie dafür ein, dass die ganze Schrift sich predigen lässt*" (Diem, Einheit [s. Anm. 41], 391.

44 Auch Wilfried Härles Dogmatik kann als Beispiel dafür angesehen werden, wie selbstverständlich in der evangelischen Dogmatik reformatorische Lehrer und Lehren herangezogen werden, um sich dem Thema „Kanon" anzunähern. In dem Abschnitt, in dem er die „geschichtliche Notwendigkeit der Kanonbildung" bedenkt, wird zudem die beschriebene Ambivalenz von Schrift/Kanon sehr deutlich. „Diese zweifache Überlieferung [Erzählung sowie Unterweisung und Lehre] geschieht (in der Regel) zunächst in *mündlicher* Form. Und das ist – wie insbesondere Luther immer wieder betont hat – auch dem Gehalt der Gottesoffenbarung in Jesus Christus, als dem *Evangelium*, ganz angemessen. Die schriftliche Fixierung, in der die Lebendigkeit einer menschlichen *Stimme* eliminiert ist, stellt im Blick auf das Evangelium einen Notbehelf dar. Aber im Blick auf das drohende Verblassen der Erinnerung und mit dem Auftauchen von irritierenden Abweichungen wächst das Bedürfnis nach *Verschriftlichung*, durch die das Überlieferte

oder Evangelium gehört werden kann, ein Potential, das nicht auf einer text-inhärenten Qualität beruht.[45] So gesehen ist das Interesse einer am sog. Schriftprinzip orientierten Theologie an den Quellen der biblischen Schriften nicht ganz deutlich. Auch wird zwar im allgemeinen zugestanden, dass der Kanon als die verschriftlichte Kunde von Gottes Offenbarung den Blick der Kirche rückwärts, zu ihrem Ursprung hin, bindet.[46] Andererseits meinen „Schrift" und der von ihr her verstandene Kanonbegriff nichts anderes als die Lebendigkeit – die Konkordanz[47] – biblischer Stimmen in ihrer gemeinsamen Ausrichtung auf gegenwärtiges Hören.

Was wäre nun, wenn man die Trennung von „Schrift" und „Kanon" voll-zöge? Ist eine solche Trennung überhaupt denkbar, und unter welchen Vor-aussetzungen wäre sie möglich? Wäre der Kanonbegriff alle oder auch nur einige Konnotationen des reformatorischen Schriftbegriffs los, würde er Au-torität vielleicht auf andere Weise regeln. Wie könnte man sich dies vorstel-len? Zunächst könnte es schlicht um die Verbindlichkeit des Schriftcorpus als Summe bzw. Liste der biblischer Schriften in ihrer Pluralität gehen. Der Ka-nonbegriff bedeutete zwar eine Abgrenzung bestimmter Schriften, verzichtete aber darauf, diesen Schriften theologisch auf den Grund zu kommen. Die Abgrenzung reflektierte schlicht ihren faktischen Gebrauch an den wesentli-chen Orten kirchlichen Lebens, also vor allem im Gottesdienst – und damit nicht in ausschließlichem Bezug auf die Predigt. Durch die Einführung des Kanons, könnte man sagen, werde die Entwicklung und der Umgang mit

---

festgehalten, vor Verfälschungen (besser) geschützt und weiterverarbeitet werden soll [hierzu bemerkt Härle in einer Fußnote: „Dem *Gesetz* ist die Schriftlichkeit ganz ange-messen"]. Wegen der schlechthin grundlegenden Bedeutung der geschichtlichen Gottes-offenbarung ist dieses Bemühen um Sicherung der Überlieferung für die Glaubensge-meinschaft von größter Bedeutung. ... Das ‚sola scriptura' ist deshalb nicht zu verstehen als eine *Konkurrenz* zum ‚solus Christus', sondern als dessen *Konsequenz* angesichts der Notwendigkeit geschichtlicher Überlieferung" (W. Härle, Dogmatik, Berlin/New York 1995, 112f.).

45 „Als theologische (nicht formgeschichtliche) Unterscheidung will sie keine zwei Textsorten, nämlich Vorschriften und Zusprüche, voneinander abgrenzen. Sie besagt vielmehr, dass *jedes biblische Wort uns als Gesetz oder als Evangelium begegnen* kann" (G. Sauter, Die Kunst des Bibellesens, EvTh 52 [1992] 347–359, S. 357).

46 „Der Kanon ist Ausdruck dafür, dass die Kirche jeweils nur im *Rückbezuge* Kirche ist" (Weber, Grundlagen I [s. Anm. 32], 278).

47 Diem bezieht sich auf die Studie von G. Eichholz, Jakobus und Paulus. Ein Beitrag zum Problem des Kanons (TEH NF 39), München 1953, der der Frage nachgeht, was Jakobus und Paulus einander zu und „was sie *miteinander uns* zu sagen haben". In Anlehnung an diese Frage fordert Diem ein „Konkordanz*hören*", an dem Exegeten und Dogmatiker gleichsam beteiligt sein sollen. „So schützt der Kanon mit dieser Forderung des Mithö-rens nicht nur die einzelnen Zeugen gegenseitig, sondern er schützt auch den Ausleger davor, dass dieser nicht durch seine eigenen Deutungskategorien daran gehindert wird, in den verschiedenen Zeugnissen das Zeugnis von Christus zu hören, den alle diese Zeu-gen gemeinsam bezeugen wollen" (Diem, Einheit [s. Anm. 41], 403).

kirchlicher Tradition in doppelter Weise geregelt. Die Entwicklung von Tradition werde zwar keineswegs unterbunden, aber sie geschehe in einer gewissen Ausrichtung, d.h. im Bezug auf und im Dialog mit der als ursprünglich gedachten Traditionsbildung, die einerseits begrenzt und andererseits von größtem, vielleicht gar unerschöpflichem Reichtum ist. Denn wenn neue Texte ihre Legitimität durch ihren Bezug auf eine begrenzte Anzahl älterer Texte gewinnen, werden diese immer wieder neu gelesen, immer wieder neu gehört und gewähren gewissermaßen immer wieder neue Einsichten. So wäre aller weiteren Traditionsbildung – auch den Äußerungen und Entscheidungen eines kirchlichen Lehramtes – ein hohes Maß an Intertextualität auferlegt. Die Ausrichtung aller weiteren Tradition auf den Kanon wäre jedoch nicht punktuell bzw. konzentriert, sondern eher diffus. Man verzichtete auf den Versuch einer konsequenten Harmonisierung und Vereinheitlichung und unterstriche so nur den Reichtum bzw. die Irreduzibilität, gewissermaßen auch die Inkommensurabilität der biblischen Aussagemöglichkeiten.

Lassen sich „Schrift" und „Kanon" trennen? Wo geschieht eine solche Trennung? Was verspricht sie, und was sind ihre, möglicherweise nicht einkalkulierbaren Folgen? – Ein von den Konnotationen des Schriftbegriffs relativ unbelastetes Kanonverständnis könnte reizvoll sein im Rahmen eines Versuches, einen von konfessionellen Streitigkeiten ungestörten Zugang zur Bibel zu gewinnen.

Wir stellten die Frage, ob sich die Begriffe „Schrift" und „Kanon" voneinander trennen lassen. Dass es, wie wir gesehen haben, Ansätze zu einer solchen Trennung gibt, dass der Zugang zur Bibel von einem literaturwissenschaftlich geprägten Kanonbegriff her eine größere Freiheit gegenüber explizit theologischen Einsichten ermöglicht, mag von den unterschiedlichen theologischen Disziplinen verschieden aufgenommen werden. Für die meisten gegenwärtigen dogmatischen Entwürfe gilt jedoch, dass „Schrift" und „Kanon" austauschbare Begriffe sind – wichtig ist, dass sie sich beide auf die Bibel als Ganze beziehen, auf ihre Autorität, auf ihren Anspruch, Norm theologischer Urteilsbildung und kirchlicher Identität zu sein, auf ihre Einheit und Vielstimmigkeit, und auf das, was in dieser Vielstimmigkeit immer wieder zu gemeinsamem Hören anregt. So interessiert man sich in der dogmatischen Diskussion, wie sie in den neueren Entwürfen festgehalten wird, mehr für die Frage, wie sich theologische Urteilsbildung zur Bibel verhalten kann bzw. muss. Nicht der Kanon als solcher ist das Problem, sondern die Frage, wie sich die Dogmatik in der Gewinnung ihrer Aussagen sinnvoll an biblischen Texten orientieren kann.

4. Vier mögliche Wege einer Verhältnisbestimmung von Bibel und Dogmatik

Dogmatik könnte man als Lesehilfe[48] verstehen für die vielfältigen biblischen Texte, an denen Glaube entsteht und sich in unvermeidlicher Komplexität entfaltet – etwa in dem sie Regeln aufspürt bzw. an die womöglich notorisch vernachlässigten Regeln erinnert, nach denen gemeinsames Lesen und Hören biblischer Texte geschieht.

Man könnte einwenden, dass die Dogmatik in dieser Hinsicht längst abgelöst worden ist von den exegetischen Diszplinen der theologischen Wissenschaft, von einem, wenn auch strittigen Methodenkanon der historisch-kritischen Forschung. Die Dogmatik als Lesehilfe oder gar Gebrauchsanweisung für biblische Texte in Anspruch zu nehmen, wäre dann vermessen, ließe den Streit der Disziplinen aufleben und schürte alte Vorurteile. Dogmatische Arbeit erscheint gleichbedeutend mit vorurteilsbelasteter Forschung, also gerade das Gegenteil von dem, was man in der Exegese anstrebt. Die Dogmatik muss ihr Recht verteidigen, auf die Texte der Bibel so zurückzugreifen, dass sie im Gespräch mit ihnen die elementaren Einsichten gewinnen und formulieren kann, aus denen die Gestalt des Glaubens erwächst, wie sie ihn in ihrer Systematik – oder besser: in ihren Zuordnungen – auszusagen bestrebt ist. Diese defensive Lage bestimmt auch ihren Umgang mit der Bibel als Kanon und mit den durch die Reformation gewonnenen Regeln, der besonderen Autorität biblischer Texte gerecht zu werden.

---

48 Otto Weber rät in seinem Vorwort zum Heidelberger Katechismus, vor allem die biblischen Texte zu lesen und zu meditieren, auf die sich die Fragen und Antworten des Katechismus als eine Art Auslegung beziehen. Nur so werde man der Intention des Katechismus gerecht: „Es ist aber heute wichtig, dass der Katechismus nur eine antwortende Verarbeitung der biblischen Stellen sein sollte. Daher kann man den Katechismus nur verstehen, wenn man die erwähnten biblischen Stellen *vorher* liest. An ihnen will der Katechismus gemessen sein, und es wäre leichter, einen ‚Katechismus' allein aus den Bibelstellen zu bilden, als den Katechismus ohne die zugrunde gelegten biblischen Texte zu verstehen" (O. Weber [Hg.], Der Heidelberger Katechismus, Gütersloh ⁵1996, 14). Nun ist ein Katechismus zwar keine Dogmatik, aber es gibt doch gewisse Ähnlichkeiten: die Zusammenhänge des christlichen Glaubens werden sprachlich dargestellt, so dass die Adressaten zum Mitsprechen eingeladen werden. Im Fall des Katechismus geschieht dies in sehr komprimierter Weise. Der Form nach einem Dialog nachempfunden, lässt er freilich keinen Raum zu Gegenrede, Rückfragen oder argumentativer Entfaltung. Eine Dogmatik muss dagegen die Komplexität der theologischen Gesprächslage berücksichtigen. Aber letztlich ist zu fragen, ob nicht das, was Weber zum Umgang mit dem Katechismus anmerkt, auch für Funktion und Gebrauch einer Dogmatik gilt: im Blick auf die biblischen Texte ist sie schlicht eine Lesehilfe – eine verzichtbare?

4.1. Die Geschichtsbewussten

Evangelische Dogmatiken sind sich mehr oder weniger dieser Problemlage bewusst, sie greifen sie in sehr unterschiedlicher Weise auf. Da gibt es zunächst diejenigen, die in Anlehnung an die klassischen Prolegomena mit einer Grundlegung der Theologie, ihres Gegenstandes und ihrer Methoden beginnen und hier auch den Tagesordnungspunkt „Bibel" verhandeln. Sie orientieren sich an den historisch gesehen maßgeblichen Stationen des protestantischen Schriftverständnisses (!) und prüfen deren charakteristische Optionen, indem sie ihre „Wahrheitsmomente" bedenken (G. Ebeling, W. Joest, W. Härle, W. Marquardt/M. Klaiber). Der Weg, den das protestantische Schriftverständnis von der Reformation über Orthodoxie und Aufklärung gegangen ist, erweist sich nach diesen Darstellungen teils als Gratwanderung, teils als Holzweg – jedenfalls erscheint ein unbefangener Umgang mit biblischen Texten durch die Fehler der Vergangenheit kaum mehr möglich oder jedenfalls sehr beschwerlich. Der Dogmatik – so scheint es – kommt die Aufgabe zu, in einem gesonderten Kapitel die Erinnerung an diese Wegstrecke mit ihren tückischen Fallen wach zu halten, und im übrigen ihrem eigenen Duktus zu folgen. Daher sieht es so aus, als könne man das Problem „Bibel" in einer Art Einleitung ablegen, um dann ungehindert zur Tagesordnung überzugehen – und diese wird zusehends von anderen Dingen bestimmt. Was bleibt, ist vielleicht noch eine Art „Sachkriterium" des Bibellesens, wie es auch für die Dogmatik relevant ist. Es ist bei aller Vielfalt biblischer Zeugnisse und dogmatischer Themen gut handhabbar, weil es sich in einer Formel niederschlägt und in die unterschiedlichsten Aussagezusammenhänge transportieren lässt.[49] Das Problem ist dann jedoch, dass es in einer solchen Loslösung eigentümlich blass bleibt – oder, wie D. Ritschl sagen würde, dass es eine so große Reichweite hat, dass es sich nicht mehr spezifizieren lässt[50].

An der Art und Weise, wie in kompendienhaften Dogmatiken die Prolegomena-Pflichtübungen verrichtet werden, übt F.-W. Marquardt Kritik. Hier werden „weniger problematisierend als beschreibend Einleitungsfragen der Dogmatik genannt und ihr Stellenwert (wird) aus der Geschichte der dogmatischen Wissenschaftsdisziplin erörtert". An diese Art der Darstellung sei die

---

49 Entsprechend wird auch die Autorität der Schrift als eine abgeleitete verstanden – entscheidend ist als „Grund des christlichen Glaubens ... die Selbstoffenbarung Gottes in Jesus Christus" (Härle, Dogmatik [s. Anm. 44], 111. Ähnlich heißt es bei Wilfried Joest: „Die biblische Schriftensammlung wird ... in einem besonderen, gerade ihr zukommenden Zusammenhang mit dem Geschehen der Selbstbekundung Gottes in Jesus Christus gesehen" (W. Joest, Dogmatik I, Göttingen ³1989, 57).
50 D. Ritschl, Zur Logik der Theologie. Kurze Darstellung der Zusammenhänge theologischer Grundgedanken, München ²1988, 112.

Frage zu richten, „ob jeweils genug bedacht ist, was man tut, wenn man die christliche Lehre ... immer wieder aus dem Fragebestand ihrer Geschichte erarbeitet".[51] Im Blick auf die Grundlagen der Dogmatik und hier besonders in Bezug auf das sog. Schriftprinzip scheint eine geschichtsbewusste Würdigung wirksamer theologischer Einsichten, ihres kritischen und belebenden Potentials, aber auch ihrer Problemzonen und Fehlleistungen, nicht hinreichend: weder das Kanonische am Kanon noch das reformatorische *sola scriptura* lassen sich durch eine bloß rückblickende Berichterstattung geltend machen. So läuft wohl auch die Behauptung, dass die Bibel mehr oder anderes ist als Tradition, immer Gefahr, selbst zu einem Traditionsstück zu werden.

4.2. Ausblendung und Unterordnung des Themas

Auf der anderen Seite stehen Entwürfe, für die der Umgang der Dogmatik mit der Bibel überhaupt kein Thema mehr ist, mit dem ein dogmatischer Entwurf beginnen müsste (E. Schlink, W. Pannenberg).

Für E. Schlink ist nicht etwa Gottes Handeln, wie es uns in den biblischen Schriften bezeugt wird, der Gegenstand der Theologie, sondern die Christenheit in ihrer Einheit, Komplexität und Vielfalt, wie sie uns gegenwärtig mit all ihren Spannungen, Divergenzen und unterschiedlichen kulturellen Zusammenhängen vor Augen tritt. Schlinks Dogmatik soll der ökumenischen Gesprächsfähigkeit der großen Kirchen dienen, und im Schatten dieser Absicht ist der dogmatische Rekurs auf die Schrift nicht zu problematisieren, sondern so zu präsentieren, dass sich eine Art Minimalkonsens anbietet, in den sich jeder und jede mehr oder weniger leicht einfinden kann und nach dessen Erweiterungen dann gefragt werden darf. Daher beginnt Schlink mit der Frage nach dem „Einsatz", die er sogleich mit einer Zusammenfassung des Evangeliums beantwortet: was „Evangelium" bedeutet, lässt sich im direkten Zugriff auf einschlägige neutestamentliche Texte umreißen, so dass wir bereits auf der dritten Seite ganz bei der Sache sind. Bezeichnender Weise wird der biblische Kanon erst wieder innerhalb der Ekklesiologie zum Thema, und zwar unter dem Aspekt der „Erhaltung" bzw. der „Unzerstörbarkeit der Kirche".[52]

Ganz anders motiviert finden wir in W. Pannenbergs *Systematische[r] Theologie* kein eigenes Kapitel zum Thema „Bibel" bzw. „Schrift" – dieses

---

51 F.-W. Marquardt, Von Elend und Heimsuchung der Theologie. Prolegomena zur Dogmatik, München ²1992· 173.
52 E. Schlink, Ökumenische Dogmatik. Grundzüge, Göttingen 1983 = 1993, 626ff.

wird innerhalb eines Rückblicks auf die Geschichte der Prolegomenathemen verhandelt; der Begriff „Schriftprinzip" erscheint nicht einmal im Register. Die Geschichte evangelischer Prolegomena liefert für Pannenberg den Beweis, dass ein unmittelbarer und autoritativer Rückgriff auf biblische Texte längst nicht mehr möglich ist und dass statt dessen der Religionsbegriff in den Vordergrund der Prolegomenaüberlegungen treten muss. Die Dominanz des Religionsbegriffs entspricht der Auflösung der „alte[n] Gleichung von Schrift und Wort Gottes"[53]. Pannenberg kann sich dem Ergebnis dieses Auflösungsprozesses nur anschließen: er widmet darum ein ganzes Kapitel einer Rehabilitation der Religionsproblematik als des noch unentschiedenen Streites der Götter bzw. Religionen in der Geschichte.[54]

4.3. Die Krisenbewussten

Von besonderem Interesse ist m.E. ein dritter Typ dogmatischer Entwürfe, der einen Neuansatz dogmatischer Arbeitsweise intendiert und sich auf einen veränderten Umgang mit den biblischen Schriften beruft. Kurz gesagt: Das Verhältnis zwischen Bibel und Dogmatik ist nicht in Ordnung und muss sich ändern. Was man vermeiden möchte, ist vielerlei – etwa der missbräuchliche, weil verkürzende und verzerrende Umgang mit biblischen Texten als *dicta probantia*. In diesem Sinne will F. Mildenberger aus den Fehlern der Dogmatik lernen. Er möchte sie aus den Höhen ihrer Abstraktion holen und an eine Lebenswirklichkeit heranführen, die 1. einer bestimmten geistigen Tradition entstammt und daher auch deren Brüche und Umbrüche mitträgt, die 2. durch die Vermittlung des kirchlichen Sprachraums zum ständigen Umgang mit biblischen Texten angeregt wird, und die 3. in einem für die Theologie ganz wesentlichen Sinne Widerfahrnissen ausgesetzt ist, die von diesen Texten nicht bereits vorgeprägt sind, sondern die ihrerseits Einfluss auf eine neue Erschließung der Texte haben. Will die Theologie die Konstitutionsmerkmale dieser Lebenswirklichkeit beachten, darf sie weder von biblischen Texten noch vom geistlichen Leben abstrahieren. Statt dessen muss sie deren lebendiger Verschränkung nachgehen und wird sich dann davor hüten, den Eindruck zu erwecken, etwas „Fertiges", „Abgerundetes" bieten zu wollen. Die Dogmatik muss zwar das Dogma in seiner Vollständigkeit im Blick haben. Doch um dies zu gewährleisten, schlägt Mildenberger in Anlehnung an den Sprachgebrauch der Alten Kirche die Unterscheidung von Theologie und Ökonomie vor. Die Prämissen sind: a) dass Gott „nie isoliert Gegenstand des

---

53 W. Pannenberg, Systematische Theologie I, Göttingen 1988, 47.
54 Pannenberg, ebd., 133ff.

dogmatischen Denkens" ist, sondern „nur in der Vermittlung durch ...
welthafte Wirklichkeit"[55] b) dass Gott sich „in seinem Heilshandeln" auf „die
Welt des von Gott abgefallenen sündigen Menschen" anders bezieht: „Auch
so wird also Gottes Beziehung zur Welt gedacht." Der springende Punkt ist
m.E. dieses „auch so": es markiert einen Bruch, der es gerade der Systemati-
schen Theologie verwehrt, „systematisch" im Sinne einer Prinzipentfaltung
zu sein, und es erhöht ihre Aufmerksamkeit gegenüber der Vielfalt biblischer
Redemöglichkeiten.

In einem anderen Sinne strebt H.-J. Kraus in ausdrücklicher Orientierung
an den Schriften des Alten und Neuen Testaments einen Ausbruch aus herkömmlicher Dogmatik an: Systematische Theologie beziehe sich auf die Bibel, sofern sich in ihr die ersten Zeugen des kommenden Gottesreiches auf
eine Weise geäußert haben, die bleibenden Verbindlichkeitscharakter hat. Für
die Gestaltung theologischer Arbeit tritt eine Art Sachkriterium hervor, das
aus der eschatologischen Stoßrichtung biblischer Texte gewonnen wird: es
bringt die Vielfalt ihrer Stimmen in einen gewissen Gleichklang. So hält sich
Kraus an „die Perspektive des kommenden Reiches Gottes", gesteht dem
Alten Testament „eminent kategoriale Bedeutung" zu und bringt den „Dialog
mit dem Judentum in die systematische Darstellung" ein. Daher sieht er sich
genötigt, Biblische Theologie systematisch zu rezipieren und umgekehrt
*„Systematische Theologie im Kontext biblischer Geschichte und Eschatolo-
gie"* darzustellen. Einer solchen Konzeption entspreche „ein kritischer Dialog
mit der traditionellen Dogmatik"[56] – was bleibt, sind trinitarische Ausrichtung und ein entsprechender Aufbau.

Radikaler sieht es F.-W. Marquardt: angesichts des Elends christlicher
Theologie, d.h. ihrer Mitschuld an der Shoa, müsse auch die Dogmatik ganz
von vorne anfangen – mehr als je zuvor ist sie dabei auf das Gespräch mit
Juden und mit den Zeugnissen jüdischen Glaubens angewiesen. Marquardt
strebt eine Lesart biblischer Texte an, die sich zutraut, ihnen „im Zweifelsfall
eine neue Wirkungsgeschichte zu öffnen".[57] Er versteht seine Prolegomena
als „Evangelische Halacha", für die „Lebensverbindlichkeit" ein Leitgedanke
ist. Dies bedeutet u.a., dass „wir zuallererst das ‚Gesetzesjudentum' neu sehen lernen müssen".[58] So richtet sich Marquardt gegen vieles, was in evangelischen Dogmatiken unbestrittene Geltung gehabt hatte, etwa gegen die luthe-

---

55 F. Mildenberger, Biblische Dogmatik. Eine Biblische Theologie in dogmatischer Perspektive. I. Prolegomena: Verstehen und Geltung der Bibel, Stuttgart 1991, 32.
56 H.-J. Kraus, Systematische Theologie im Kontext biblischer Geschichte und Eschatologie, Neukirchen-Vluyn 1983, v.
57 Marquardt, Elend (s. Anm. 51), 99. Dies versucht er etwa durch eine Auslegung der sog.
   „Ur-" und „Vätergeschichte" der Genesis sowie des Epheserbriefes.
58 Marquardt, ebd., 166.

rische Unterscheidung von Gesetz und Evangelium mit ihren Nachwirkun-
gen: „Das Denken in zwei Reichen verwehrt ihm [dem protestantischen
Theologen der Tradition] auch nur Versuche, den religiös-politischen Dop-
pelsinn des jüdischen Gesetzesgehorsam zu verstehen. Entweder Religi-
onsgesetz – oder evangelische Freiheit, lautet die Losung. Dass auch einer
der neutestamentlichen Zeugen, Jakobus, von einem ‚Gesetz der Freiheit‘
sprechen kann (Jak 2,12) verschlägt nichts: Er steht seit einem Verdikt Luthers sowieso im Zwielicht. Vom Entweder-Oder der Verkündigung her –
Gesetz oder Evangelium – wurden aber im Protestantismus die historischen
Begriffe gebildet.“[59] Marquardts Prolegomena fügen sich nicht in die Auseinandersetzung zwischen historisch-kritischer Exegese und Dogmatik, sie
konfrontieren vielmehr sowohl den Methodenkanon der Exegese[60] als auch
die begrifflichen Vorgaben der Dogmatik[61] mit der jüdischen Auslegungstradition und ihren Regeln. Die Geschichte der Theologie mit ihren Verurtei-
lungen müsse kritisch ins Visier genommen werden, so dass die Rehabilitation des Vernachlässigten oder gar „Häretischen" eine reale Möglichkeit darstellt.[62] „Wir bestreiten damit der Geschichte ihren gesetzlichen Anspruch auf
unsere Arbeit.“[63] Welches Verhältnis die Dogmatik zur Bibel hat, ist ihr nicht
mehr vorgegeben. Im Sinne Marquardt ist es durchaus möglich, und angesichts des schuldhaften Verhältnisses zum Judentum notwendig, sämtliche
Konzeptionen kritisch zu befragen, mit denen christliche – protestantische –
Theologie ihr Bibelverständnis bzw. ihr jeweils aktuelles Hören auf biblische
Texte reglementiert hat.

---

59 Marquardt, ebd., 201f.
60 Auch sie könne sich nämlich nicht dem Vorwurf entziehen, in ihrer zweihundertjährigen
    Geschichte Israel bzw. die jüdische Bibelauslegung als Gesprächspartner ignoriert zu
    haben. Zudem störe sie die Unbefangenheit, mit der die Bibel als Einheit gelesen wird,
    und schließlich habe auch sie in ihrer Quellenscheidung unbiblische Schemata ange-
    wandt, die sich dem Geist der Aufklärung verdanken (universalgeschicht-
    lich/partikulargeschichtlich; Urgeschichte/Vätergeschichte) (Marquardt, ebd., 288f.).
61 Die Dogmatik sei jedoch an den „Materialverdrängungen und -vergewaltigungen" in
    besonderem Maße schuldig, und obendrein sei sie rückständiger: sie arbeite „nach Inhalt
    und Form dem Judentum gegenüber traditionell noch verschlossener ... als ihre wissen-
    schaftlichen Nachbarn" (Marquardt, ebd., 179).
62 Es ist bezeichnend, dass sich Marquardt immer wieder an der „‚ersten Reformation‘
    (z.B. der Böhmischen Brüder)" orientiert: „Ich glaube, dass die frühesten Protestanten in
    den Waldenser-Tälern Piemonts und in Böhmen einigen Fragen, die sich den ökumeni-
    schen Kirchen heute stellen, näher waren als manche Fragen und Antworten (‚bür-
    gerlichen‘) Städtereformation in Deutschland ... In bezug auf das berühmte ‚Theorie-
    Praxis-Verhältnis‘ z.B., dessen Bedenken m.E. heute mehr als je zur Aufgabe von Prole-
    gomena zur Dogmatik gehört, sind sie uns vorbildlich voraus. Jedenfalls ist es dieser
    vorlutherische Protestantismus, von dessen inneren evangelischen Voraussetzungen her
    unsere Theologie die jüdische Herausforderung deutlicher als eine eigene Sache erfahren
    kann" (ebd., 9).
63 Marquardt, ebd., 174.

Auch D. Ritschl zufolge sollten „wir christliche Theologie immer so
betreiben, als schaute uns ein Jude dabei über die Schultern", und wo immer
es gilt, das Gegenstandsfeld der Theologie in Augenschein zu nehmen, müsse
man „von ‚Juden und Christen‘, der Synagoge und der Kirche" sprechen.[64]
Jedoch verwahrt sich Ritschl gegen die Fiktion einer Biblischen Theologie,
da er die Übertragbarkeit der „theologischen Inhalte" der Bibel in spätere
Zeiten grundsätzlich bezweifelt[65] – als einzige Ausnahme nennt Ritschl die
Weisheitsliteratur. Dagegen orientiert er sich an den phänomenologisch gewonnenen Begriffen von „story" und „regulativen Sätzen". Ihrer Leitungs-
funktion traut er die für ethische Fragen notwendige Theoriebildung zu. Das
für die Dogmatik grundlegende Problem, „dass die biblischen Schriften sich
nicht zur Erstellung eines Lehrgebäudes hergeben wollen" ist durch die von
den biblischen Wissenschaften erzeugte „Vielfalt exegetischer Ergebnisse"[66]
gleichsam potenziert worden. Vor diesem Hintergrund bieten sich die iden-
titätsbildenden Konzeptionen von story und story-Trägern als einziger Aus-
weg an. Es entspricht diesen Konzeptionen, das *sola scriptura* durch ein *sola
traditione* abzulösen. Nicht zufällig spricht sich Ritschl am deutlichsten gegen die Schaffung des biblischen Kanons aus: „Die Entscheidung der Kirche,
mit der Feststellung des Kanons biblische Schriften von späteren Büchern
ähnlichen Inhalts qualitativ abzugrenzen, hat ein Problem geschaffen, das erst
in den letzten 200 Jahren voll ins Licht gerückt ist: historisch geurteilt besteht
kein Unterschied zwischen der Transmission und Rezeption von Tradition
innerhalb der biblischen Schriften und in der späteren Kirchengeschichte,
theologisch geurteilt wird aber an einem Unterschied festgehalten. Ein heim-
licher Deismus ist in diesem Konzept unverkennbar."[67] Das eigentlich Unbe-
friedigende bestehe dabei in der Voraussetzung, dass die Wahrheit „ausschließlich in der Vergangenheit"[68] liegt. Ihr könne nur die Reduktion der
Schriftauslegung auf die hermeneutische Methode entsprechen, die ihrerseits
unter der verräterischen Frage steht: „Wie kann dieser alte Text für mich heute neu und relevant werden?"[69] Dagegen hebt Ritschl die Bedeutung der
Patristik hervor. Für die Frage nach dem rechten Umgang mit den biblischen
Schriften jenseits von Fideismus, Fundamentalismus und Offenbarungsposi-

---

64 Ritschl, Logik (s. Anm. 50), 97.
65 „*Theologie im Sinn einer Theoriebildung auf regulative Sätze hin liegt in den biblischen
    Schriften höchstens in Annäherung vor. Die Erwartung an die Bibel, eine Sammlung
    einheitlicher, greifbarer und direkt verwendbarer theologischer Lehraussagen im Sinn
    einer ‚biblischen Theologie‘ zu erhalten, ist eine Fiktion*" (Ritschl, ebd., 98; Hervorhe-
    bung im Original).
66 Ritschl, ebd., 99.
67 Ritschl, ebd., 100; im Original kursiv.
68 Ritschl, ebd., 101.
69 Ritschl, ebd., 102.

tivismus habe sie Vorbildcharakter, weil in dieser Zeit bislang unüberholter Ökumene die biblische Botschaft mit „Doxologie und Ethik verbunden"[70] war, weil parallel zu ihr mit der Entstehung des Talmuds die Blütezeit jüdischer Schriftauslegung anzusiedeln ist und da diese Zeit der gegenwärtigen in besonderer Weise verwandt ist: schließlich war auch damals die Kirche genötigt, „in lebendiger Auseinandersetzung mit einer nicht-christlichen Umwelt"[71] zu bestehen. Ritschl mag sich hier einem Typ Dogmatiker zugehörig zeigen, der neben dem biblischen Kanon – oder statt dessen – bestimmte Meilensteine bzw. Epochen der Theologiegeschichte als wegweisend annimmt: vielversprechend erscheint die Kontaktaufnahme zu dem geistigen Klima einer bestimmten Zeit , in der „Fülle" vorhanden war, eine Fülle, von der man auch heute noch ernten kann. Nur dass diese Fülle eben nicht wie selbstverständlich in der Reformationszeit oder in der Zeit der „Urkirche" zu suchen ist!

Es ist zu fragen, ob nicht auch in solchen dogmatischen Entwürfen, die an dem prinzipiellen Unterschied zwischen Kanon und Tradition festhalten, die ausdrückliche Orientierung an den biblischen Schriften als Autorität kirchlichen und geistlichen Lebens von der Hochschätzung ganz bestimmter Zeiten theologischen Entdeckens oder Umdenkens begleitet wird – von Zeiten also, in denen Entscheidendes deutlich geworden ist, was lange im Dunkeln gelegen hatte. So mag Ritschl anderen Entwürfen in der Einschätzung des biblischen Kanons fern stehen, hinsichtlich der Beobachtung, dass sich biblische Texte zu Gehör bzw. in Erinnerung bringen, steht er dagegen weniger im Abseits. Vielleicht hat sich der Tonfall geändert, etwa gegenüber einer Auffassung, nach der die Kanonizität der biblischen Schriften in ihrer Effizienz begründet ist.[72] Ritschl spricht dagegen von einer „Verifikation durch Wiedererkennen" und sieht in der durch „Anlässe" („occasions") ausgelösten „spontane(n) Erkenntnis" – d.h. im „,Wiedererkennen' von Traditionselementen, die im Gedächtnis der Kirche ruhen" – sowohl den „Moment der ‚Offenbarung'" als auch die Nötigung zu einer Anbindung des Bibellesens an konkretes Leben.[73] Die Regel des Wiedererkennens aufgrund von Anlässen macht beides deutlich, erstens dass die Auffassung einer besonderen Wirksamkeit biblischer Schriften auch bei dem Kritiker der Kanonskonzeption

---

70 Ritschl, ebd., 105.
71 Ritschl, ebd.
72 Vgl. Joest, Dogmatik I (s. Anm. 49), 61: „Was die Geltung der Schrift begründet, ist das Geschehen ihrer Wirksamkeit." Oder Kraus, Systematische Theologie (s. Anm. 56), 45, These zu §18: „Die Umgrenzung und Herausstellung der biblischen Schriften in der Form eines Kanons entspricht der Erfahrung der Kirche hinsichtlich der kerygmatischen Effizienz dieser Dokumente".
73 Ritschl, Logik (s. Anm. 50), 106f.

nachwirkt, und zweitens dass die protestantische Orientierung allein an der
Schrift der Einebnung aller Schriften in einen unüberschaubaren Tra-
ditionsraum bzw. in das abgründige „Gedächtnis der Kirche" gewichen ist.
Angesichts dieses Gedächtnisses – das sich im übrigen kaum von einem Kulturraum unterscheidet – ist das gelegentliche Hören auf biblisches Material
ein vergleichsweise kleines Wunder: es bedürfe nur „der direkt oder auch
vage erinnerten Story der Juden und Christen".[74] Trotz dieser Entmy-
thologisierung der Bibel und ihrer Wirksamkeit gibt es aber noch eine gewisse Nische, in der sich ein anderer Geist als der menschlicher Traditionen vielleicht noch ein wenig bewegen kann, eine Spur göttlicher Vorsehung, könnte
man meinen, aber so zurückhaltend angedeutet wie etwa durch ein *passivum
divinum*: „Man wird kaum im voraus planen können, welche Ereignisse zu
Anlässen des Wiedererkennens und welche nicht dazu führen können. Aber
wer Anlass-los lebt, sich der Dynamik und Tragik konkreten Lebens entzieht,
der wird die Tradition und die Bibel nicht verstehen, sollte er sie auch noch
so intensiv studieren. ... Im spontanen Wiedererkennen ... sortiert sich das
Traditionsgut sozusagen ‚von selbst', d.h. durch Anlässe, ‚occasions'."[75]

4.4. Von der Möglichkeit dogmatischer Schrifttreue

Neben diesen Bemühungen, Dogmatik und Bibel in neuer Weise aufeinander
zu beziehen, und zwar so, dass die terminologischen Rahmenbedingungen
der Dogmatik gesprengt und eine Neuordnung des Materials notwendig wird,
gibt es schließlich noch den Versuch, im Rahmen herkömmlicher Dogmatik
– oder vielleicht besser: mit Rücksicht auf bewährte Strukturen dogmatischen
Denkens – die Bibel zu Wort kommen zu lassen, ohne sie auf *dicta probantia*
zu reduzieren. G. Sauter zufolge muss sich der rechte Umgang mit biblischen
Texten an die „Schrifttreue" halten: Diese ist zunächst nicht eine Tugend des
Theologen oder der Theologin, sie ist vielmehr „*die Treue der Schrift, der
wir trauen*", das heißt: „auf die Treue der Schrift hin können diejenigen, die
gemeinsam hören auf das, ‚was dir gesagt ist', Treue zueinander wahren."[76]
Die Grundregel, dass die Schrift nicht hintergangen werden solle, entspreche
der Orientierung am Literalsinn. Dazu gebe es „dogmatische Regeln für das
Bibellesen", zu denen die Unterscheidungen von Geist und Buchstabe, Gesetz und Evangelium, Verheißung und Erfüllung zählen. Dass diese „*ein
Wahrnehmungsgefüge für Schrifttreue*" aufbauen, bedeutet, dass sie dem

---

74 Ritschl, ebd., 108.
75 Ritschl, ebd., 107f.
76 G. Sauter, Zugänge zur Dogmatik, Göttingen 1998, 290.

Miteinander biblischer Texte mehr zutrauen als ihrem Gegeneinander, dass sie in diesem spannungsreichen Miteinander die sich selbst auslegende „Schrift" erfahren, deren Lebendigkeit sich Gottes verheißungsvollem Handeln verdankt, und dass die einzelnen Texte in diese Lebendigkeit auf eine Weise hineingenommen werden, die es nicht erlaubt, im voraus sagen zu können, wie sie uns begegnen werden. So bilden die Unterscheidungen keine Schematismen, nach denen etwa die Einheit der Schrift in geistvolle und geistlose, in fordernde und aufrichtende Texte oder in solche aufteilen, in denen Versprechungen und Prophezeiungen gemacht und solche, in denen die Erfüllung solcher Versprechungen und Prophezeiungen festgehalten wird. Dies wäre ein Missverständnis, das den Blick durch biblische Texte auf Gottes Handeln und Gottes Gegenwart verstellen müsste. Die genannten Unterscheidungen seien Regeln des Bibellesens, des erwartungsvollen Vernehmens, das dem polyphonen Klang der Texte nachgeht, anstatt ihnen etwa ein Fazit zu entnehmen. Diesen Regeln kann nur im Zusammenklang mit den Texten, aus denen sie vernehmbar werden, sinnvoll gefolgt werden; d.h. man weiß nicht bereits vorher oder zu irgendeinem Zeitpunkt unabhängig von der „Schrift", was „Evanglium" oder was „Gesetz" bedeutet, etc.[77]

Dies führt zu einer anderen Sicht der Kanonsthematik bzw. zu der Frage, welche Art Einheit die Bibel bezeugt – und welche Art Einheit für die Kirche sowie für die Gestaltung des Verhältnisses zwischen den Konfessionen von der Schrift her maßgeblich sein müsste.[78] Maßgeblich sei die _Vielfalt von Erwartungsperspektiven_: „Perspektiven, die sich weder aufeinander zurückführen lassen noch aufeinander abgebildet werden können, die derart ineinandergreifen, dass die Wahrnehmung nie zu einem Ende kommt und nicht auf eine Reihe zu bringen ist".[79] Diese Einsicht ist wegweisend, sofern sie nicht nur zu einem Umgang mit der Bibel jenseits von Dogmatismus und

---

77 Vgl. den Zusammenhang von Rechtfertigungslehre und Schrifttreue: „Gottes unverdiente Gnade wird uns nirgendwo anders als im biblischen Wort mitgeteilt, und umgekehrt hängt die Rechtfertigung aus Gnaden und allein im Glauben (sola fide) an der Erwartung des Handelns Gottes, die uns zur ‚Schrift' leitet und uns in ihr suchen lässt" (Sauter, ebd., 282).

78 Zur Parallelisierung der kanonischen Vielstimmigkeit und des konfessionellen Pluralismus gibt es seit E. Käsemanns Aufsatz (Begründet der neutestamentliche Kanon die Einheit der Kirche?, EvTh 11 [1951/52] 13–21) eine Vielzahl von Äußerungen. So W. Härle in Abgrenzung von Käsemann: „Die komplexe Bedeutung des biblischen Kanons wird angemessener beschrieben, wenn man sagt, dass er als solcher in der Vielzahl der Konfessionen bzw. kirchlichen Richtungen die Einheit der _Kirche_ (sing.!) bewahrt. ... Weil der Kanon das grundlegende, ursprüngliche Zeugnis von diesem Glaubensgrund enthält, _darum_ und _insofern_ bewahrt er die durch das Christusgeschehen begründete Einheit der Kirche. Da der Kanon diesen Glaubensgrund aber auf vielfältige, spannungsvolle, teilweise sogar widersprüchliche Weise bezeugt, begründet er _zugleich_ die Vielzahl der Konfessionen" (Härle, Dogmatik [s. Anm. 44], 134).

79 Sauter, Zugänge (s. Anm. 76), 291.

Biblizismus weist, sondern vor allem weil sie ermöglicht, ohne Reduktions-
bestrebungen die Umrisse von Gottes Handeln auszusagen. Wenn sich Dogmatik an diese Einsicht hält, sagt sie von Gott etwas aus, das sie nicht erfin-
den kann (oder erfunden haben kann) und das sie, wenn sie es gefunden hat,
gleichsam von allen Seiten betrachten und beschreiben muss. Dass dies vor
dem Hintergrund bestimmter Erfahrungen mit der Schrift und mit Hilfe von
Gedächtnisstützen (wie dem Kirchenjahr) geschieht, sollte für eine Verhält-
nisbestimmung von Bibel und Dogmatik Berücksichtigung finden.

5. Zwischenüberlegung

„Für das Verfahren der Dogmatik hatte das Schriftprinzip ... die seltsame
Folge, dass die Schrift zwar reichlich zum Belegen dogmatischer Aussagen
diente, das Auslegen biblischer Aussagen jedoch keine dogmatischen Folgen
hatte. Die zementierte Autoritätsstellung der Bibel diente der Zementierung
der Dogmatik und in gewisser Weise deren Abschirmung gegen die Bibel."[80]
Was G. Ebeling hier als Charakterzug der altprotestantischen Orthodoxie ver-
merkt, scheint das Selbstverständnis der Dogmatik bis in die Gegenwart zu
belasten. Es ist geradezu Konsens geworden, das *sola scriptura* als ein Traditionsstück anzusehen, durch das das eigene Wort der Bibel mehr schlecht als
recht lebendig gehalten werden kann.

   Verbindlichkeit und Lebendigkeit scheinen zwei Zuschreibungen biblischer Texte zu sein, die sich nicht so recht festhalten lassen – weder durch
eine Inspirationslehre, über deren Versagen weitgehend Einigkeit besteht,
noch durch die weitgehend unreflektierte Verschränkung von Schrift- und
Kanonbegriff. Sauters Bemühung, in Anlehnung an theologische Unterscheidungen Regeln des Bibellesens zu bestimmen, kann als ein Versuch einge-
schätzt werden, dies beides festzuhalten: Verbindlichkeit und Lebendigkeit
biblischer Texte. Bemühungen dieser Art werden jedoch in der gegenwärtigen Debatte von einem Problembewusstsein überlagert, das sich zu unterschiedlichsten Rücksichten genötigt sieht. Sofern es nicht ganz auf das *sola
scriptura* verzichtet[81], läuft es zumeist auf eine Erstarrung hinaus, die nicht

---

80 G. Ebeling, Dogmatik des christlichen Glaubens I, Tübingen [3]1987, 33.
81 Etwa, indem man auf das sola verzichtet und Ergänzungen anregt. So G. Ebeling, der
    dem *scriptura* die *experientia* zur Seite stellt und zugleich das *sola scriptura* mit Hilfe
    des *sola experientia* festhalten möchte. „Es wäre widersinnig, von Schrift und Erfahrung
    als zwei einander addierbaren oder einander einschränkenden, jedenfalls als zwei von-
    einander unabhängigen Quellen zu reden. Die hermeneutische Überlegung zeigt, dass die
    Schrift nur dann in ihrer Geschehensbewegung vom Wort zum Text und vom Text zum

mehr erlaubt, über bestimmte regulative Einsichten hinauszugehen. Diese haben jedoch selten die Kraft, zu Regeln zu werden, durch die die Schrift heute zu uns sprechen kann – die Antwort auf die Frage, wo und wie Gott heute handelt, wird durch sie oft eher verstellt als angebahnt.

Im Umgang mit der Bibel lässt sich diese Frage jedoch nicht verdrängen. Weder der Schrift- noch der Kanonbegriff lassen sich vollständig enttheologisieren. In der Dogmatik sind sie ohnehin zumeist wechselseitig aufeinander bezogen, auch wenn hinsichtlich ihrer legitimen theologischen Implikationen der Konsens bereits im Zerbrechen begriffen ist. Man kann sie revidieren, indem man sie aus ihrer Verschränkung löst und zur reformatorischen Theologie auf Distanz geht, sich dezidiert um ökumenischen Weitblick bemüht oder an andere Epochen der – gemeinsamen – Kirchengeschichte bzw. der Geschichte von Kirche und Judentum hält. Man kann versuchen, die Wirksamkeit und Autorität der Bibel mit Hilfe von Modellen zu beschreiben, die theologisch weniger aufdringlich erscheinen. Aber man unterschätzt dabei die Bibel als ein „in selbstverständlicher Weise ‚bekanntes' Buch", das selbst da, wo es eben nur noch als Buch betrachtet wird, Wirkung zeigt: „Offenbar hat man ... etwas an der Bibel schon allein dadurch, dass man sie hat." – Man muss sie nicht einmal mehr lesen.[82]

Vielleicht ist dies Ausdruck dafür, dass neben und mit den gravierenden Auflösungserscheinungen der kirchlichen Präsenz im gesellschaftlichen und persönlichen Leben die Reste christlichen, evangelischen Bewusstseins noch eine Weile fortleben. Dann müsste man nur noch ein Weilchen warten und die Frage nach Wirksamkeit und Autorität der Bibel würde sich von selbst erledigen. Vielleicht wird in dieser unreflektierten Hochschätzung der Bibel

---

Wort erfasst wird, wenn das Wort nicht am Leben vorbeigeht, sondern in das Leben eingeht, wenn es also mit Erfahrung zu tun hat in der Weite menschlicher Lebenserfahrung." Diese wird übrigens sehr weit gedacht, „außerordentlich überdehnt(en)", wie Ebeling zugibt: hierzu gehöre die dogmatische Tradition, die eigene Lebenserfahrung einschließlich möglicher Impulse durch Religion, Philosophie, Literatur und Kunst sowie die wissenschaftliche Welterfahrung. In dieser Weite will auch die Ausschließlichkeit der Schrift verstanden werden: „Ohne dass sich dabei sozusagen alle Schleusen Himmels und der Erde öffnen und in weitesten Dimensionen ein Ringen um das Wort des Lebens und damit der Streit um das wahre Leben entbrennt, hat die Dogmatik offenbar das sola scriptura nicht ernst genommen. Es ruft geradezu nach dem sola experientia" (Ebeling, ebd., 42).

82 Müller, „Verstehst du auch ...?" (s. Anm. 25), 147ff. In diesem Zusammenhang sollte der Umstand Beachtung finden, dass die Bibel nicht nur eine Auslegungs-, sondern auch eine Wirkungsgeschichte hat; vgl. H. Räisänen, Die Wirkungsgeschichte der Bibel. Eine Herausforderung für die exegetische Forschung, EvTh 52 (1992) 337–347. Räisänen weist hier auf ein Desiderat der Bibelforschung hin. Die Wirkungsgeschichte der Bibel ist weiträumiger, zum Teil wohl auch folgenreicher – und ihre Folgen sind schwerer kontrollierbar – als die Auslegungsgeschichte. Inwieweit haben sie mit der Hochschätzung der Bibel als Kanon zu tun?

jedoch eine kaum mehr ausgesprochene Erwartung festgehalten, nämlich dass in ihr „Anrede und Selbstmitteilung Gottes"[83] geschieht, dass sie „Wort Gottes" ist und also der besondere, der unvergleichliche Zusammenhang, in dem sich die Frage nach Gottes gegenwärtigem Handeln überhaupt stellen kann. Sollte dies so sein, hätte eine Zurückhaltung oder gar Vorenthaltung expliziter theologischer Urteile in der Frage nach dem Zugang zur Bibel bzw. nach dem rechten Umgang mit ihr weitreichende Folgen. Denn die Bibel wird – ob als Kanon oder als Schrift, ob mit oder ohne geistliche Leitung durch ein Lehramt – gelesen. Und wenn nicht, dann finden zumindest gelegentlich Bücher über sie reißenden Absatz. Und wenn sie auch da, wo sie nicht mehr gelesen wird, noch Beachtung findet, dann gleichsam als Stellvertreter für ein nebulöses Fragen nach Gottes Gegenwart. Der kirchliche – vielleicht sogar überkonfessionelle – Umgang mit der Bibel als Schrift bzw. als Kanon hat dieses Fragen zu präzisieren gewusst und ist ihm nicht ohne Rekurs auf die biblischen Texte nachgegangen. Vielleicht kann man diesbezüglich eine Einigkeit innerhalb der theologischen Diskussion vermuten, die bei aller Uneinigkeit im einzelnen, nicht unterschätzt werden darf. An ihr wird deutlich, woraufhin überhaupt von Wirksamkeit und Autorität der biblischen Schriften – in ihrer Begrenztheit und in ihrer Vielstimmigkeit – geredet werden kann: nämlich hinsichtlich der Präzisierung des Redens von Gott, der als Gott der ganzen Bibel gegenwärtig wird. Umgekehrt wird deutlich, dass man sich weit außerhalb der vermuteten Einigkeit befindet, wenn man ein Reden von Gott an der Bibel vorbei, ohne Rücksicht auf ihre Grenzen und ihre Stimmen wagt. D.h. die Frage nach Gott bzw. Gottes Handeln und die Frage nach Wirksamkeit und Autorität der biblischen Schriften gehören zusammen, verweisen aufeinander. Dies ist jedoch eine theologische Einsicht, die, wie alle theologischen Einsichten, bestritten werden kann. Man kann den Versuch machen, die beiden Fragen voneinander zu lösen. Die Bibel hat ein Ansehen, das ohne die explizit theologischen Regeln der Schriftautorität wirksam werden kann. Dazu zwei Beispiele:

6. Kontraste – regellose Nachwirkungen der Schriftautorität?

6.1. Im ökumenischen Dialog spielen die Mormonen eine eher untergeordnete Rolle. Die „Kirche Jesu Christi der Heiligen der Letzten Tage" versteht sich nicht einmal als christliche Kirche. Der unüberbrückbare Abstand, in dem sie sich zu dieser verhält, wird durch ein Buch markiert, für das die reli-

---

83 Sauter, Kunst (s. Anm. 45), 355.

giöse Gemeinschaft der Mormonen den Anspruch göttlicher Offenbarung erhebt. Verfasser dieses Buches Mormon ist Joseph Smith (1805–1844), ein mäßig gebildeter Bauernsohn aus dem westlichen Staate New York,[84] der von phantastischen Ideen umtrieben und mit dem Unternehmergeist der *frontier-people* in kurzer Zeit eine Fortsetzungsgeschichte des Alten Testaments niederschrieb, laut eigener Darstellung als Übersetzung eines Originals, das sich in ägyptischen Hieroglyphen auf goldenen Tafeln befand. Zu der „Übersetzung" wurde er durch den Engel Moroni angeleitet, der ihm als technische Hilfsmittel die „Urim und Thumim" aushändigte. Was bei dieser Übersetzung bzw. Offenbarung herauskam, war ein Brückenschlag zwischen dem alttestamentlichen Volk Israel und den nordamerikanischen Ureinwohnern als den verlorenen Stämmen Israels, war außerdem die Einbeziehung der eigenen Gegenwart in diese Geschichte der Etablierung des Gottesreiches in einem von Feinden umlagerten, aber von Gott verheißenen Land. Auf der Grundlage einer neu empfangenen „Schrift" konnten die Gründerväter der Mormonenkirche alttestamentliche Verheißungen nach Amerika verpflanzen und in der Konfrontation mit den politischen Bedingungen der Zeit aktualisieren, sie konnten eine Gemeindeordnung errichten, die sich von der christlichen Tradition an dem empfindlichen Punkt des Eheverständnisses und der Sexualethik unterschied, und sie konnten sich in einem von Europäern noch nicht eingenommenen Landstreifen Nordamerikas ein Utopia aufbauen, in dem sie die frisch angeeigneten biblischen Verheißungen eingelöst sahen. Was aus europäischer Sicht wie eine kuriose Wildwestgeschichte anmutet, hatte immerhin kirchengründende Folgen und sollte in den USA einen beachtlichen Kulturraum gestalten: den Staat Utah mit Salt Lake City als einem neuen Jerusalem. Es ist aber deutlich, dass sich diese religiöse Bewegung nicht mehr im Rahmen christlicher Lehre und Tradition befinden konnte – bei aller möglichen Häresie könnte es keiner christlichen Kirche einfallen, der Bibel ein zweites Buch an die Seite zu stellen, zumal eines, zu dessen Niederschrift man sich nicht bereits in etwa zweitausendjährigem Abstand wissen musste. Dem Christentum gegenüber stellt die „Kirche Jesu Christi der Heiligen der Letzten Tage" eine Neuerung dar, die mit der gemeinsamen Grenze der Schrift auch den „alten" Lehrbestand hinter sich gelassen hat: „Joseph's was no more dissenting sect. It was a real religious creation, one intended to be to Christianity what Christianity was to Judaism: that is, a reform and a consummation."[85]

---

84 Der Staat New York galt damals als „burnt-over-district", als eine Gegend, die von den unterschiedlichsten religiösen Bewegungen heimgesucht war.
85 F. Brodie, No Man Knows My History, New York 1945, viii.

Es ist unter christlichen Kirchen manches strittig, aber es ist weitgehender Konsens, dass die biblischen Schriften des Alten und Neuen Testaments erstens eine normative Grundlage außerordentlichen Ranges darstellen und dass sie zweitens im Sinne ihres Textbestandes mehr oder weniger abgeschlossen sind. Beide Aspekte bedingen einander, und sie können in gewissem Maße fragwürdig werden – die Schrift als Norm wird von der „regula fidei" begleitet, ihr Verhältnis zur kirchlichen Tradition wird ihr als Konstitutivum zugerechnet, so dass sie eben niemals allein durch sich selbst begegnet; andererseits lässt sich exegetisch nicht so recht von einem abgeschlossenen Textbestand reden, und auch unter theologischen Gesichtspunkten muss es offen bleiben, inwiefern der biblische Text abgeschlossen ist – ob im Sinne einer Vorgabe oder im Sinne einer Erstarrung oder, schöner gesagt, Kristallisierung. Obwohl also Normativität und Definität des biblischen Kanons immer wieder der Explikation bedürfen, bleibt doch deutlich und unstrittig, worauf man sich bezieht, wenn man vom biblischen Kanon spricht, und diese Bezugsgröße ist gleichsam die Konstante, auf die man sich im Streit um die Bedeutung und Tragweite von Kanonizität stillschweigend geeinigt hat. Eine weitere Offenbarung, die zu einer zweiten Bibel führen würde, wäre eine kirchensprengende Absurdität, und der Rekurs auf sie könnte unmöglich im Rahmen eines innerkirchlichen Diskurses geschehen. Die Umgrenzung der biblischen Schriften entspricht der Sorge um kirchliche Identität.[86]

6.2. Auch in Nordamerika, aber in einem anderen Sinne als bei Joseph Smith, ist vor einigen Jahren der Bestseller *The Bible-Code* verfasst worden. Auch hier geht es darum, die gegenwärtige Zeit mit ihren großen geschichtlichen Einschlägen in Verbindung mit dem biblischen Text zu bringen – in diesem Fall mit dem Text der hebräischen Bibel. Es geht darum, in der alttestamentlichen Geschichte des Gottesvolkes Auskünfte über die Menschheitsgeschichte in ihren letzten Tagen zu entdecken. Auch hier werden bislang völlig unbekannte und von den Kirchen unbeachtete Buchstabengefüge entschlüsselt, allerdings nicht wie bei Smith mit Hilfe von Urim und Thumim, sondern mit Hilfe eines mathematischen Dekodierungsverfahrens – das also allen kirchlichen Auslegungsgewohnheiten weit überlegen ist. Was dabei herauskommt, sind zu einem großen Teil bereits eingetroffene Weissagungen

---

86 Man könnte hier auch an andere kirchliche Gemeinschaften denken, die sich entschieden primitivistisch auf die Bibel berufen und sich von allen späteren, „unbiblischen" Lehrentwicklungen distanzieren. Die Norm wird auf den Kanon beschränkt, eine *regula fidei* sei nicht nötig, oder anders gesagt, der Kanonsgrenze werde man allenfalls durch eine Biblische Theologie gerecht, die die Bibel mit ihren eigenen begrifflichen Mitteln erschließt, nicht aber mit einer Dogmatik, deren Sprache eine völlig andere Herkunft und Verpflichtung bezeugt.

von Geschehnissen politischer Relevanz (wobei die Geschichte der USA wiederum eine herausragende Rolle spielt). Auch hier wird die Kanonsgrenze umgangen, aber nicht durch die Entdeckung eines zweiten Geschichtsbuches, sondern durch die vom Geiste der Wissenschaft geleitete Schaffung eines neuen Textbestandes, der kaum oder nur gelegentlich mit dem ursprünglichen Textbestand in Verbindung steht, wie er von Juden und Christen jahrtausendelang gelesen wurde und in Gebrauch war. Außer den bereits eingetroffenen Weissagungen, die die Methode dieser „Schriftauslegung" bestätigen sollen, finden sich aber auch solche, deren „Eintreffen" noch aussteht, zum Beispiel die Aussicht auf einen atomaren Weltkrieg. Hier spielt ausnahmsweise der ursprüngliche Text, in dem die betreffende Weissagung gefunden wird, eine Rolle: das „Sch^{e}ma Jisrael" (Dtn 6,4f), das Herzstück der hebräischen Bibel. So absurd uns dieser Zugang zum biblischen Text auch erscheinen mag, er ist gewissermaßen ein später Ausläufer jenes Umgangs mit der Bibel, der ihre Autorität und Normativität vor allem in der übernatürlichen Fähigkeit gesehen hatte, Geschichte im voraus anzukündigen oder anzudeuten. Da er über die Sinneinheiten des Textes weitgehend hinwegsieht, kann man ihn kaum als eine Ergänzung etwa des vierfachen Schriftsinns oder der halachisch-haggadischen Auslegungstradition verstehen, und da er den Text in eine Buchstabenfolge auflöst, die in völlig neuer Weise lesbar gemacht werden soll, hat er wohl auch nichts mit dem sensus litteralis zu tun, auf den sich die reformatorische Theologie im Unterschied zu einer traditionsgeleiteten Theologie beruft – es sei denn, man verstehe „Buchstabe" buchstäblich als Buchstabe.

6.3. Die beiden Beispiele zeigen, dass man die Kanonsgrenze auf sehr unterschiedliche Weise hintergehen kann, gerade dann, wenn man die eigene Schöpfung als Fortsetzung des biblischen Textbestandes versteht. Sie zeigen außerdem, dass wir hier gleichsam spontan um die Absurdität solcher Fortschreibungen wissen. Wir fühlen uns auf einen Umgang mit der Bibel verpflichtet, der uns von solchen abenteuerlichen Unternehmungen klar und deutlich trennt. Für uns bedeutet die Kanonizität der Bibel, dass wir zwar viele Bücher und viele Texte haben, aber doch nur diese eine Sammlung alttestamentlicher und neutestamentlicher Schriften, deren Geltung für uns trotz aller Strittigkeit mit keinem anderen Text vergleichbar ist.

Die Kanonizität der Bibel ist eine Grenze, die für uns als Kirche von Bedeutung ist. Das heißt auch, dass wir als Kirche gewissermaßen ein Gespür dafür haben, wie die Bibel zu lesen ist – und wo der Umgang mit biblischen Texten absurd wird. Dieses Gespür besteht in der Vertrautheit der Kirche mit den biblischen Schriften, die ihr nie ganz verloren gehen kann.[87] Sie hat ein mehr oder weniger intensives und umfangreiches Wissen davon, was ihr Text ist und wie sie in ihn einsteigen bzw. wie sie von ihm eingeholt werden kann. Kanonizität der Bibel bedeutet also, dass die Kirche sich zwar nur an *einem* Buch in äußerster Verbindlichkeit orientieren wird, dass sie diese Orientierung aber von vielen Stimmen – und sicherlich auch in zahlreichen Kontexten – gelernt hat und sich von diesem fortgesetzten Lernprozess nicht dispensieren kann, weder durch den Rekurs auf eine himmlische Eingebung noch durch einen „mathematisch-wissenschaftlichen" Eingriff in die Textgestalt. Was in der Frage nach der Kanonizität der Bibel auf dem Spiel steht, ist nicht bloß die Zuordnung von Bibel, Kirche, Lehre und Tradition. Auf dem Spiel steht die Notwendigkeit eines Gegenübers (und die möglichen und wirklichen Folgen eines Verzichtes auf dieses Gegenüber) – nicht zu verwechseln mit der Frage nach Kontinuität und Diskontinuität, Vergleichbarkeit und Inkommensurabilität der in Frage stehenden Größen. Nun ist das Festhalten an diesem Gegenüber nicht eine Geschmacksfrage hinsichtlich der geeigneteren Präposition, es hält vielmehr eine Reihe von Themen wach, die der Kirche aufgegeben bleiben: z.B. die Geltung und Erfüllung von Verheißungen für unsere Wahrnehmung von Welt und Geschichte, oder anders gefragt: Wo entsteht unsere Frage nach Gottes Handeln, und wie bleiben wir an diese Frage gebunden?

7. Der zerbrechliche Konsens evangelischer Dogmatiken: Kirche als creatura verbi

Die skizzierten Beispiele bringen uns auf die Spur eines kirchlichen Konsens, der jedoch, wenn wir an die vorliegenden dogmatischen Entwürfe denken, zerbrechlich ist. Regulative Einsichten lassen sich in übersichtlicher Zahl repetieren, aber sie werden mit Rücksichten und Intentionen angereichert, sie werden umgedeutet, entschärft und in Schach gehalten, und trotz gleichlautender Formeln lassen sich hier und da Keile ansetzen, die zu Spaltungen führen müssten, sobald man den Versuch macht, die verschiedenen Auffassungen des biblischen Kanons miteinander ins Gespräch zu bringen. Bleiben wir aber zunächst bei dem Gemeinsamen – im einzelnen werden sich die Ausnahmen jeweils in Erinnerung bringen!

---

87 Selbst einem Joseph Smith ist diese Vertrautheit nicht ganz verloren gegangen; vgl. die Beobachtung, dass das Buch Mormon eine starke Anlehnung an die alttestamentlichen Geschichtsbücher zeigt und so originell im Grunde nicht ist.

Im Unterschied zur katholischen Auffassung besteht auf evangelischer Seite ein weitgehender Konsens darüber, die Kirche konsequent als *creatura verbi* zu verstehen: Kirche und Bibel stehen einander gegenüber, jedoch in einem Gefälle, d.h. die Bibel hat der Kirche das Entscheidende zu sagen, die Kirche hat also von der Bibel das Entscheidende zu vernehmen. Diese theologische Einsicht darf sich durch die historischen Erkenntnisse in die Entwicklung des biblischen Kanons nicht irritieren lassen, auch wenn sie diese Erkenntnisse in der Darstellung des Lehrtopos „Schrift" bzw. „Kirche" berücksichtigen muss. Die Kirche ist dem Kanon der biblischen Schriften untergeordnet – an dieser Unterordnung ändern die Einsichten in die Kanonbildung grundsätzlich nichts, etwa dass der Kanon seinen Ursprung in der gottesdienstlichen Versammlung hat. So wird vielfach betont, dass der Kanon von der Kirche abgegrenzt, aber nicht geschaffen wurde. Also kann das kirchliche Handeln in bezug auf die Bibel insgesamt nicht als Autorenschaft charakterisiert werden, sondern als rezeptiver Akt der Anerkennung.[88]

Die Kirche blickt auf den biblischen Kanon wie in einen Spiegel: seine kirchengründende Funktion bleibt als korrigierende, aber auch affirmative Wirksamkeit erhalten, etwa in der Frage, inwieweit der Kanon ein Dokument des innerkirchlichen und theologischen Pluralismus ist und daher zulässt, bestätigt und im Blick auf ein Ganzes miteinander vermittelt, worunter die Kirchen in ihrer Vielfalt und in ihrem Getrenntsein leiden. Noch schärfer wird der biblische Kanon als Mittel kirchlicher Identitätssuche aufgefasst, wo man ihn erstens thematisch innerhalb der Ekklesiologie unterbringt und dort den unversöhnlichen Gegensatz zwischen Kirche und Welt zum Schauplatz der Kanonisierung erklärt. So verfährt E. Schlink, der in dem Dreigestirn „Kanon, Dogma, Kirchenrecht" – denen jedoch nicht dieselbe Invarianz eingeräumt wird – die Mittel zur Erhaltung der Kirche sieht. Schlink spricht von der „Unzerstörbarkeit der Kirche", die ihrerseits eine „Störung dieser Welt" sei: Kirche und Welt befinden sich in einem erbitterten und kompromisslosen Kampf gegeneinander. „In diesem Kampf ist das Ziel der Welt die Vernich-

---

88 Vgl. Schlink, Dogmatik (s. Anm. 52), 632ff. oder W. Marquardt/M. Klaiber, Gelebte Gnade. Grundriss einer Theologie der Evangelisch-methodistischen Kirche, Stuttgart 1993, 56f.: „In seinem Grundbestand ist der Kanon der Kirche zugewachsen ... Zunächst wurde einfach anerkannt, was sich für das Leben der Kirche als maßgebliches Zeugnis herausgestellt hattte, und daraus hat man dann Kriterien gewonnen, mit denen man in den wenigen Zweifelsfragen eine Entscheidung für die Abgrenzung des Kanons treffen konnte ... Sie (die Kirche) erkannte – bewusst oder unbewusst – damit an, dass sie ein Gegenüber brauchte, an dem sie sich orientieren musste und an dem sie auch gemessen werden konnte. Natürlich ist das entscheidende Gegenüber für die christliche Kirche Jesus Christus als ihr erhöhter Herr. Aber wie kommt er im Leben der Kirche zu Wort, und wo ist sein aktueller Wille zu hören?"

tung der Kirche".[89] Angesichts dieser lebensbedrohlichen Lage ist die „Abgrenzung der Kirche im Kampf mit der Welt" die vornehmliche Aufgabe des biblischen Kanons – sowie der ihm zur Seite gestellten Kampfmittel Dogma und Kirchenrecht. Denn die Tücke der Auseinandersetzung zwischen Kirche und Welt bestehe gerade darin, dass sich die Welt in die Kirche gleichsam einschleichen will, um sie weniger von außen, als von innen zu zerstören – und wo der Feind gleichsam im Innern zu suchen ist, bedarf es wiederholter Grenzziehungen und fortgesetzter Selbstreinigung, verbunden mit der „Ausscheidung von nur scheinbaren Gliedern": Auch dafür steht nun der Kanon. Erschreckend scharf klingt es, wenn es bei Schlink heißt, dass „das im Wortlaut Festgelegte zunehmend die Bedeutung eines Schutzes und Haltes der Kirche für ihr Bleiben auf ihrem geschichtlichen Grund" erhalten habe[90] – dies etwa im Vergleich mit Härle, der ebenfalls in der Verschriftlichung des Wortes und in der Kanonisierung der biblischen Schriften einen notwendigen Akt kirchlicher Identitätsbildung und -wahrung sieht. Bei Schlink wird diese Identitätswahrung jedoch als anhaltende Kampfhandlung der Kirche „und ihres Vorstoßes in die Welt"[91] verstanden. Die militärische Sprache mag befremden, und die mit dem Kanon verbundene Forderung nach Selbstreinigung mag inquisitorisch klingen, vielleicht zeigt sich hier aber die Verbindung von Kanon und Kirchenzucht, die ja nur da einleuchtet, wo sich die Kirche gefährdet sieht durch die Fremde, in der sie sich befindet und die sie andererseits nur schwer erkennen und benennen kann. Vielleicht müsste bei dieser Zuordnung des biblischen Kanons zum „Kirchenkampf" deutlicher werden, was Schlink eingangs erwähnt, nämlich dass die „Unzerstörbarkeit der Kirche" nichts anderes ist als Gottes Verheißung, die sich Menschen nicht durch selbstgeschmiedete Waffen sichern können. Dann würde dem Kampf die Bitterkeit genommen, und der Kanon müsste nicht Waffe und Machtmittel sein, sondern wäre Wüstenbrot, Lebensmittel der Kirche an einem ungastlichen Ort.

Der Kanon als Mittel der Identitätswahrung kann aber auch anders zur Sprache gebracht werden. W. Joest sieht die Bestimmung der für die Kirche geltenden Normen von der Frage geleitet, „wie im geschichtlichen Fortgang kirchlicher Glaubensverkündigung ... das in Jesus Christus gesprochene Wort Gottes in seiner Identität bewahrt bleiben kann; bzw. wie das Wort der Kirche im Weitersagen dieses Wortes erhalten wird".[92] Verbindet man diese Frage mit dem ekklesiologischen Thema, so könnte man sagen: die Kirche

---

89 Schlink, Dogmatik (s. Anm. 52), 626.
90 Schlink, ebd., 629.
91 Schlink, ebd., 630.
92 Joest, Dogmatik I (s. Anm. 49), 87.

sorgt sich am besten um ihren eigenen Bestand, wenn sie sich um die Erhaltung des ihr anvertrauten Wortes sorgt.

Es fällt nun auf, dass sich die vorliegenden Dogmatiken überwiegend vorsichtig oder gar kritisch zur Bibel als Kanon verhalten (G. Ebeling, D. Ritschl). Andererseits bemüht man sich, das protestantische Schriftprinzip aufzunehmen. Dabei ist man sich jedoch darin einig, dass die Historizität der biblischen Texte – in ausdrücklicher Abgrenzung gegen die altprotestantische Inspirationslehre – mit der reformatorischen Orientierung an der Schrift vermittelt werden müsse. Hier kommt es nun zu ganz unterschiedlichen Gewichtungen der regulativen Einsichten. Besondere Hochschätzung genießt die „viva vox Evangelii" (G. Ebeling, F.-W. Marquardt). Die Exklusivpartikel – das *sola* – werden dagegen nicht mehr besonders ernst genommen: viel zu vielschichtig sind die Prozesse des Bibellesens mit dem, worauf Menschen „sonst noch" hören, verwoben, als dass sich ein *sola* noch sinnvoll behaupten ließe. Auch klassische Unterscheidungen wie die zwischen Gesetz und Evangelium sind mit Vorsicht zu genießen (zu genießen: G. Sauter; aber mit Vorsicht: H.-J. Kraus, F.-W. Marquardt). Eine Möglichkeit, Verbindlichkeit und Lebendigkeit biblischer Texte zu erfahren, besteht darin, diese auf die Frage nach Gottes Willen zuzuspitzen. Dass diese Möglichkeit alles andere als uniform ist, macht sie so vielversprechend – auch wenn hier zunächst wieder die Divergenzen im Vordergrund stehen. So sehen W. Marquardt/M. Klaiber an der Frage nach Gottes bindenden Willen den Gegensatz zwischen fundamentalistischer und liberaler Theologie aufbrechen. Dabei nehmen sie diesen Gegensatz ernst genug, um das eigene Bibelverständnis mit seiner Hilfe als Mittelweg zu positionieren. Der Suche nach Gottes Willen nimmt sich auch F.-W. Marquardt an, wenn er seine Bemühungen um „Evangelische Halacha" an der Frage orientiert „Was sollen wir glaubend tun?" Noch einmal anders klingt es bei G. Sauter, der für die Irreduzibilität des Willens bzw. des Handelns Gottes plädiert und daher auch die verschiedenen Regeln des Bibellesens rehabilitiert sehen will: Durch sie werde eine Spannung erzeugt, die die Bibellesenden ein Leben lang begleitet – es ist dies wohl nichts anderes als die Spannung des geistlichen Lebens.

Mit gemischten Gefühlen blickt man auf die Kanonisierung als notwendige kirchliche Selbstvergewisserung und als Verlust der viva vox Evangelii zurück – überspitzt gesagt wird sie zum unvermeidlichen Sündenfall der Kirche. Schlimmer noch ist es um die altprotestantische Inspirationslehre bestellt: sie kann sich nicht so leicht auf Unvermeidlichkeit berufen, ist sie doch erst die zweifelhafte Schöpfung des nachreformatorischen Zeitalters evangelischer Theologie und daher eine Verfallserscheinung. Die Inspirationslehre muss gegen ihren Strich gelesen werden, wenn man das Gute aus ihr noch herausholen möchte. Sie wird jedoch trotz aller Kritik auch immer wieder zu einer Quelle gegenwärtiger Theologie, sofern sie daran erinnert, wie das in den Prolegomena verankerte Schriftprinzip pneumatologisch zugeordnet werden müsste – diese Zuordnung kann allerdings nur als Desiderat dogmatischer Arbeit festgestellt werden. Insgesamt zeigt sich, dass die Dogmatiken auch am Ende des 20. Jahrhunderts das Problem ihrer Herkunft verarbeiten müssen. Von ihrer Struktur, ihrem Aufbau, ihrem Vokabular verdanken sie vieles den Dogmatiken des 17. Jahrhunderts, aber diese sind gleichsam eingekeilt zwischen Reformation und Pietismus bzw. Reformation und Aufklärung. Von allen Seiten hagelt es Kritik, die es zu berücksichtigen gilt: der reformatorischen Ursprünglichkeit gegenüber fühlt man sich des Rückfalls in die Scholastik schuldig, dem Pietismus gegenüber fühlt man die eigene Blutleere, die Erfahrungsarmut; begriffliche Differenziertheit wird als Spitzfindigkeit gesehen; der Aufklärung gegenüber muss man einen alle loci durchziehenden Supranaturalismus zugeben, auf den man, gerade wenn man sich an der Bibel orientiert, auch verzichten kann (oder vielleicht nicht?; vgl. Ritschls „Verifikation durch Wiedererkennen"). Hinzu kommen Erschütterungen neueren Datums, die den Rückgriff auf Bewährtes ganz grundsätzlich in Frage stellen und dazu drängen, die ausgetretenen Pfade theologischen Arbeitens ohne wehmütige Rückschau zu verlassen. Kann es der Dogmatik überhaupt gelingen, Regeln für den Umgang mit der Schrift zu formulieren, ihr, die sie doch die Inspirationslehre auf dem Gewissen hat? Kann es ihr gelingen, die Bibel anders zu gebrauchen denn als *dicta probantia* – etwa so, dass sich Dogmatik und Exegese begegnen, sei es, dass sie einander ins Wort fallen, sei es, dass sie einander zustimmen? Kann Dogmatik einen Beitrag dazu leisten, dass die Bibel ihr eigenes Wort sagt (und zwar durchaus im Sinne des Literalsinnes) bzw. dass sie in ihrer Ganzheit und Einheit vernommen wird, ohne dass sich an Ganzheit und Einheit falsche Erwartungen knüpfen? Die m.E. schwierigste Frage, in der sich viele Aspekte des Kanonproblems bzw. des sog. Schriftprinzips sammeln, ist folgende: *wie entgehen wir der Erstarrung, wie bleiben wir lebendig* und wodurch lässt sich diese Lebendigkeit nur scheinbar und kurzfristig erreichen (etwa durch grundlegende Kritik an Begriff und Lehre)?

Noch einmal: Was in der Frage nach der Kanonizität der Bibel auf dem Spiel steht, ist – über die Zuordnung von Bibel, Kirche, Lehre und Tradition hinaus – die Notwendigkeit eines Gegenübers. Daher hält sie eine Reihe von Themen wach, von denen sich die Kirche nicht dispensieren kann: Wie lassen sich Welt und Geschichte wahrnehmen, wenn wir uns an der Vielfalt und Ordnung biblischer Worte orientieren? Wie wird dabei unsere Frage nach Gottes Handeln angeregt bzw. gebunden – gerade im Unterschied zu dem, was Menschen tun können, was sie voraussehen und bewirken, verkennen und erleiden?

Die Inspirationslehre der altprotestantischen Orthodoxie sollte den göttlichen Ursprung der biblischen Schriften so festhalten und deutlich machen, dass Text und Kanon rückwirkend und daher auch für alle Zukunft von dem verfälschenden Zugriff menschlicher Kreativität geschützt blieben. Durch definitive Zuordnungen des Menschlichen und des Göttlichen ließe sich, so könnte man meinen, das vom reformatorischen Schriftverständnis anvisierte Gegenüber am besten darstellen und wahren. Jede Entdeckung einer Verzahnung oder Verschränkung kann dagegen wie ein Angriff auf das Gegenüber erscheinen, so dass eine klare und verbindliche Orientierung an der Schrift und dem Schriftgemäßen unmöglich gemacht würde. Auch die Festlegung kirchlichen Handelns bzw. biblischer Autorenschaft auf ihren jeweiligen geschichtlichen Kontext – selbst wenn man ihren Produkten zugesteht, über die Grenzen ursprünglicher Intentionen hinaus wirksam zu sein, und im Zuge eines solchen Zugeständnisses diese menschlicherseits ungeahnte Wirksamkeit Gott bzw. Gottes Geist zuordnet – kann als ein solcher Angriff auf das grundlegende Gegenüber der Kirche verstanden werden. Es ist möglich, das Gegenüber zu „retten", indem man zunächst auf die Gleichung Schrift = Wort Gottes verzichtet bzw. indem man einräumt, dass Bibel nicht gleich Schrift ist – dass es hier durchaus eine unübersehbare Vielzahl verschiedener Aussagen gibt, die nicht alle denselben Anspruch auf Verbindlichkeit haben können und haben müssen. Nur wenn man die Menge des Allzumenschlichen und des daher eher Unverbindlichen in der Bibel anerkennt, lässt sich vielleicht noch ein heiliger Rest retten, etwas, das klar und deutlich vom Menschen unerfindbar ist und das sich ebenso klar und deutlich dem Auflösungsprozess menschlicher Kritik widersetzt. Diese Hoffnung auf eine innerbiblische Selbstkritik,[93] in der die Spreu vom Weizen getrennt wird, kann sich auf Luthers „was Christum treibet" berufen[94], auf die sehr unterschiedliche Wer-

---

93 Vgl. W. Härles Hinweis auf den doppelten Genitiv des Begriffs „Schriftkritik": dieser bezeichne „also die von der Schrift geübte und ausgehende Kritik gegenüber aller anderen Lehre"; zugleich werden „die biblischen Schriften ... von der Mitte der Schrift her zum *Gegenstand und Adressaten* der Kritik" (Härle, Dogmatik [s. Anm. 44], 138).

94 „Kanonisch ist es (das biblische Zeugnis), weil und sofern es ‚Christum treibet', und Christum treiben heißt für ihn (Luther): die Rechtfertigung des Sünders allein durch Gottes Tat in Jesus Christus predigen" (Joest, Dogmatik I [s. Anm. 49], 63); vgl. Härle, Dogmatik (s. Anm. 44), 137f., der sich der lutherischen Beschreibung der Schriftmitte aus drei Gründen anschließt: 1. weil „die Mitte der Schrift auf einen Punkt" reduziert und so zu einer „gemeinsamen Aussageabsicht" macht, die „unterschiedlich interpretierbar und unbegrenzter Entfaltung und Differenzierung fähig" ist, 2. weil die Schriftmitte beim Namen genannt wird, so dass in „der Mitte der Schrift ... *der Mensch* (steht), in dem Gott sich zum Heil der Welt geoffenbart hat", 3. weil die Schriftmitte nicht als Lehre oder Lehrsatz, sondern „als ein lebendiges *Geschehen*" charakterisiert wird. Zugleich

tung einzelner biblischer Bücher durch den Bibelübersetzer und Reformator. Sie kann sich den Grundsatz zueigen machen, dass die Schrift ihre eigene Auslegerin ist, und wird dabei den Zugang zu „dunkleren" Stellen von dem Verständnis der „hellen" Texte abhängig machen. Dabei knüpft sie an die Erfahrung jahrhundertelanger Bibellektüre an und verbindet sie zugleich mit dem reformatorischen Fanal, dass es nicht nur dunklere und hellere Texte gibt, sondern dass es Texte gibt, die nicht nur heller, sondern hell sind, zu denen wir ganz unbeschwerten Zugang haben (bzw. die sich wie von selbst gegenüber menschlichen Verstehensbedingungen durchsetzen): und gerade diese seien die wirklich wichtigen, die unverzichtbaren – unverzichtbar für die Kirche, die Gemeinschaft der Bibellesenden, für Sein oder Nichtsein jedes einzelnen, unverzichtbar aber auch für ein Verständnis des biblischen Kanons insgesamt, d.h. für den Umgang mit weniger hellen bis dunklen Texten.

Es ist nun möglich, die Erfahrung mit zugänglichen und unzugänglicheren biblischen Texten mit dem unbedingten Zutrauen in den biblischen Kanon zu dem Prädikat der Suffizienz zu verbinden, und von hierher eine Unterscheidung zwischen Obligatorischem und Fakultativem anzubahnen: Wenn Suffizienz der Schrift bedeutet, dass die Bibel im Blick auf das Heilsnotwendige hinreichend und selbstgenügsam ist, dann ist dieses Prädikat für Texte, die Nicht-Heilsnotwendiges beinhalten, verzichtbar, so verzichtbar, dass sich in diesem Verzicht zwei freundliche bis indifferente Abgrenzungen aussprechen: zum einen die Abgrenzung von wissenschaftlicher, historisch-kritischer Exegese[95], zum anderen von naturwissenschaftlichen Erkenntnisprozessen und den ihnen entsprechenden Weltbildern[96]. Die Problematik dieser Suche nach dem Heilsnotwendigen bildet einen Problemzusammenhang innerhalb des Kanonverständnisses, und zwar nicht nur für den dogmatischen, sondern auch für den exegetischen Umgang mit biblischen Texten. Die umstrittene Idee einer Biblischen Theologie, der immer wieder auflebende Gedanke eines Kanons im Kanon, einer Schriftmitte, eines oder mehrerer Sachkriterien oder Leitperspektiven, aber auch schon die faktische Inanspruchnahme biblischer Texte durch die Kirche – etwa die in der Liturgie

---

spricht sich Härle gegen eine Einengung der Schriftmitte auf die paulinische Rechtfertigungslehre aus.

95 „Bei den Spaltungen der Kirche haben unterschiedliche Schriftauslegungen eine so große Rolle gespielt, dass für den ökumenischen Dialog der Einsatz der differenziertesten und präzisesten Methoden, die die philologisch-historische Forschung entwickelt hat, geboten ist. ... Dieser Forderung widerspricht nicht die alte, durch viele Jahrhunderte hindurch bewährte Überzeugung, dass die Heilige Schrift trotz mancher dunkler Stellen für einen jeden Christen und zwar auch für die Nichttheologen im Hinblick auf alles, was zu unserem Heil nötig ist, klar und verständlich ist" (Schlink, Dogmatik [s. Anm. 52], 638).

beheimatete christologische und trinitarische Lesart des Psalters (bzw. der Verzicht darauf im neuen Evangelischen Gesangbuch) – dies sind Beispiele für die weitreichende Relevanz einer wenigstens hypothetisch unproblematischen Identifikation des Heilsnotwendigen.

Kritik ist gewiss naheliegend, besteht doch die Gefahr einer implizit vorausgesetzten Zuordnung von Zuständlichkeiten – wenn man dies denn als eine Gefahr versteht; die säuberliche Aufteilung von Verantwortungsbereichen und Zuständlichkeiten kann ja auch etwas Beruhigendes haben, jedenfalls solange für die eigene Tätigkeit und Verantwortung noch etwas übrig bleibt. Gefahr besteht auch, wenn der Dogmatiker oder die Dogmatikerin wittert, dass das Heilsnotwendige als das Leichtverständliche dem wissenschaftlich-theologischen Laien zugeordnet wird und er oder sie darüber arbeitslos werden könnte – wenn man dagegen gut dogmatisch an die pneumatologischen Verstehensbedingungen des Heilsnotwendigen erinnert, hat man nicht weniger ein Eigentor erzielt, da ja die Dogmatik die erste theologische Disziplin (und vielleicht auch die letzte) sein muss, die darauf insistiert, dass man Glauben nicht lernen kann (G. Sauter), dass die Gabe des göttlichen Geistes reines Widerfahrnis ist, menschlicherseits unverfügbar und unerschwinglich, und dass es schlechterdings keine pneumatologische Hermeneutik gibt (E. Schlink). Wenn andererseits der reformatorische Grundsatz der Klarheit und Suffizienz der Bibel aufgenommen wird, um die Theologie insgesamt vor der möglichen Irritation durch naturwissenschaftliche Erkenntnisse zu schützen, so kann gerade diese Maxime des „Leben und leben Lassen" als ein Grundsatz nicht gegenseitigen Respekts, sondern gegenseitiger Gleichgültigkeit kritisiert werden. Will man hier den theologischen Diskurs für eine mehr als theologische, wissenschaftlich qualifizierte Beschreibung der Wirklichkeit offen halten, so wird man sich dagegen sträuben, die Vielfalt biblischer Texte auf das Heilsnotwendige zu reduzieren – oder man wird es sich mit der Identifikation des Heilsnotwendigen nicht – etwa unter Berufung auf Klarheit und Suffizienz – leicht machen.[97] Das Unternehmen einer innerbiblischen Kritik muss sich jedenfalls immer wieder die

---

96 „Eine Anwendung für naturwissenschaftliche Erkenntnisse z.B. liegt nicht im Interesse der methodistischen Theologen" (Marquardt/Klaiber, Gelebte Gnade [s. Anm. 88], 62).

97 So nimmt Ritschl die innerbiblische Mythoskritik als Impuls auf, sich mit naturwissenschaftlich angeregten Weltbildern auseinanderzusetzen: *„Die implizite und stellenweise auch explizite Kritik biblischer Bücher an mythologischen Welt- und Menschenbildern ihrer Umwelt macht die Bibel zwar nicht zu einem Buch wissenschaftlicher Welt- und Menschenerklärung, erlaubt aber doch die Folgerung, dass biblisch orientierte Theologie auf eine nüchterne, wissenschaftliche Sicht der Weltwirklichkeit hinstreben und ständig mit ihrer Möglichkeit rechnen soll. Dabei spricht vieles dafür, dass biblischer Glaube damals und heute eine Gesamtperspektive naturhafter und anthropologischer Wirk-*

Rückfrage gefallen lassen, ob sie im Aufspüren dessen, „was Christum treibet", wirklich die Fülle des Handelns Gottes im Blick hat.

8. Ergebnis und Ausblick

Sieht man sich die Inanspruchnahme des Kanonbegriffs in der Exegese und
in der breiteren Diskussion um die Biblische Theologie an, kann man recht
unterschiedliche Eindrücke gewinnen. Da wird der Kanon als Endgestalt zur
Ausgangsstation einer gesamtbiblischen, zumindest potentiell normativen
Theologie; und dann wiederum öffnet der Kanonbegriff den Blick in eine
aufregende Vergangenheit, in die kaum absehbare Weite einander immer
wieder überlagernder und neu formierender Traditionsprozesse. Man kann im
Kanon, nämlich in der Hebräischen Bibel, eine zwar vergessene, aber nun
doch wieder freizulegende und zu beschreitende Brücke zum gegenwärtigen
Judentum sehen; und andererseits kann man im Rekurs auf den Kanon Alten
und Neuen Testaments eine „kanonische Auslegung" fordern, die den christologischen Bezug der alttestamentlichen Texte expliziert und gezielt an die
christliche Gemeinde weitergibt. Man kann sich im Verweis auf den biblischen Kanon für Pluralität stark machen, die nicht doktrinär eingeschränkt
werden darf, wo immer man es mit biblischen Texten zu tun bekommt – sei
es in der biblischen Exegese, sei es im Religionsunterricht. Man kann andererseits versuchen, inmitten der Pluralität die Einheit zu suchen, sei es, indem
man nach einem Kanon im Kanon, einer Mitte der Schrift fragt, sei es indem
man von Axiomen, Leitperspektiven oder gar von einem Geist der Bibel[98]

---

lichkeit zur natürlichen Voraussetzung hat" (Ritschl, Logik [s. Anm. 50], 35; Hervorhebung im Original).
98 So G. Theißen, Die Überzeugungskraft der Bibel. Biblische Hermeneutik und modernes
Bewusstsein, EvTh 60 (2000) 412–431, S. 430f.: „Er [der Geist der Bibel] durchdringt
ihre historischen und unhistorischen Erzählungen, bestimmt realistische und mythische
Aussagen, modelliert ‚facts' und ‚fiction'. Die biblische Zeichenwelt wird durch sie eine
Zeichensprache, die durch eine bestimmte Grammatik geregelt wird, eine kunstvoll konstruierte Welt – gebaut mit Hilfe weniger formaler Axiome. ... Neben ihr stehen andere
‚konstruierte Welten'. ... Die Bibel verstehen, heißt, diesen Geist zu verstehen, ohne dass
man sich deswegen mit diesem Geist identifizieren muss. Aus solchem Verstehen kann
Einverständnis werden, wenn wir für uns die Fragen beantworten: Was ist subjektiv evident? Was ist sachlich notwendig? Was ist dialogfähig? Mit Hilfe der Grundmotive lassen sie sich beantworten: ... Die Bibel überzeugt, wo internalisierte biblische Überzeugungen kontingent durch Erfahrung bestätigt werden. ... Die sachliche Notwendigkeit
der Bibel ist in ihren Axiomen und Grundmotiven begründet, die der biblischen Zeichensprache ein eigenes Zentrum geben: Alles ist hier vom Glauben an den einen und
einzigen Gott und an Jesus Christus her organisiert. In Christus, wie er in der Bibel dargestellt wird, sind die Axiome und Grundmotive ‚inkarniert'. Sie machen die Wirklich-

spricht. In der Fahndung nach Einheit kann man sich ganz auf der Linie traditioneller, reformatorischer Theologie bewegen oder man riskiert im Anschluss an jüdische Auslegung den Ausbruch aus dieser nicht unbelasteten Tradition. Auch im Zusammenhang christlicher Exegese kann man die Frage aufnehmen, inwieweit in der Existenz des biblischen Kanons Autorität wirksam wird. Aber diese Frage ist nur eine unter vielen, während sie in der Dogmatik durch das sowohl vom Kanon- als auch vom Schriftbegriff anvisierte Gegenüber von Bibel und Kirche besonders präzisiert wird.

Dies mag ein wesentlicher Unterschied zwischen dem Umgang mit dem Kanonbegriff in Biblischer Theologie und Dogmatik sein: während erstere den Begriff in vielfältiger Weise einsetzt, so dass sich die verschiedensten, durchaus konträren Interessen damit verbinden können, hat die evangelische Dogmatik den Kanonbegriff so sehr „evangelisch" präzisiert, dass ihm zumindest die konfessionelle Offenheit weitgehend verloren gegangen ist. Hier hat der Kanonbegriff eine dienende Funktion: er ist dem Schriftbegriff zur Seite gestellt, so dass er wie dieser hilft, Wirksamkeit und Autorität der Bibel der Kirche gegenüber zu beschreiben. Im Rahmen dieses Interesses gibt sich die Dogmatik vor allem Rechenschaft darüber, wie sie selbst zum Nutzen der Kirche als *creatura verbi* auf biblische Texte rekurrieren kann bzw. welche – schriftgemäße – Hilfe sie bereitstellen muss, damit Menschen jederzeit mit solchen Texten umgehen können. Bei aller fragwürdigen Identifikation der Begriffe „Kanon" und „Schrift" – und es ist zu fragen, was man durch eine genauere Differenzierung dieser Begriffe erreichen könnte – ist dies der hervorzuhebende Beitrag der Dogmatik: dass sie mit der immer wieder neu zu formulierenden Frage nach Gottes Handeln das Lesen der Bibel vorbereitet und begleitet.

Gerade wenn die Dogmatik mit der Insistenz auf dieser Frage aus dem Rahmen etwa der exegetischen Interessenslage fällt, sollte man auf das hinweisen, worin sich die theologischen Disziplinen einig sind – und vielleicht einmal die Frage wagen, worin diese Einigkeit begründet ist.

Zunächst gilt es daher schlicht festzuhalten, dass sich in der Wahrnehmung biblischer Texte eine Veränderung zugetragen hat: mit dem Marginalbegriff „Kanon" hat die Frage nach dem Normativen erneut Beachtung ge-

keit für Gott transparent. Insofern kann der Glaubende sagen: Durch Christus wird Gott zugänglich. Worin liegt schließlich die Dialogfähigkeit der Bibel? ... Auch wenn Menschen im Alltag streiten, können sie es nach derselben Grammatik tun. Einverständnis mit der Bibel geht über ein allgemeines Verstehen hinaus. Einverständnis bedeutet vom ‚Geist' der Bibel erfassen zu lassen und das eigene Leben und Denken mit ihren Grundmotiven und Axiomen so zu durchdringen, dass der Bibeltext zur Chance einer Dialogaufnahme mit Gott wird. Dieser ‚Geist' der Bibel begegnet nur durch die ‚Buchstaben' der Bibel hindurch, er ist aber nicht mit ihm identisch."

funden. Eine Exegese, die sich um die ursprüngliche Gestalt und Aussageabsicht einzelner biblischer Texte bemühte, musste die vorliegende Gestalt des
Textzusammenhangs aufbrechen. Die Exegese konnte den Kanon nicht un-
versehrt lassen, selbst wenn sie ihn als solchen nicht antastete. Zu den Voraussetzungen, auf die die Exegese in ihrem grundsätzlichen Streben nach
Voraussetzungslosigkeit (die trotz aller Einschränkungen anvisiert wurde)
verzichtete, gehörte zudem auch das Normierende der biblischen Schriften,
und zwar in formaler wie in materialer Hinsicht. Dass die biblischen Schriften insgesamt und im einzelnen Bindendes zu sagen haben, konnte nicht von
vornherein angenommen werden, genauso wenig, wie man meinte, unabhängig von den jeweils zu analysierenden Texten oder gar vor einer sorgfältigen
und unbefangenen Analyse das Normierende formulieren zu können.

Dazu eine abschließende Beobachtung: Die Exegese war einmal von dem
Interesse an dem historisch Ursprünglichen geleitet. Auf diesem Wege musste sie den Kanon in viele kleine Einzelteile aufsprengen. Die Dogmatik, zumal sofern sie sich reformatorischen Gedanken verschrieben sah, konnte sich
den Kanonbegriff nur so zu eigen machen, dass sie in ihm den Platzhalter des
Ursprünglichen (des der Kirche konstitutiv und kritisch Gegenüberstehenden)
sah. Durch den Kanonbegriff wurde die Zäsur zwischen den biblischen
Schriften und der kirchlichen Tradition markiert, eine Funktion, die – innerhalb der evangelischen Theologie – dem Begriff zukommt, unabhängig von
der Frage, inwiefern der Kanon auch als Tradition angesehen werden kann.
Wenn sich Exegeten zunehmend für den Kanon in seiner literarischen Endgestalt interessieren, dann kann man hierin sehen, wie sich Exegese und
Dogmatik aufeinander zubewegen, aber auch, wie unterschiedlich die Konnotationen des Kanonbegriffs sein können.

Exegese und Dogmatik begegnen sich, wenn der Exegese der Kanon
plausibel und der evangelischen Dogmatik, für die der Kanon immer schon
der Garant des Ursprünglichen war, der Kanonbegriff in seiner Verbindung
mit dem reformatorischen Schriftverständnis problematisch wird. Um sich
des gemeinsamen Grundes zu vergewissern, bedarf es vor allem einer Klärung, was mit *Ursprünglichkeit* gemeint ist und wie dieses Ursprüngliche
zugleich bindend und lebendig geblieben ist bzw. bleiben kann.

Kanon und Kirche

von Gerhard Sauter

Herrn Kollegen Günter Bader
zum 60. Geburtstag

1. Die Einheit der Kirche: eine durch den Kanon aufgeworfene und ver- schärfte Frage

„Der n[eu]t[estamen]tliche Kanon begründet als solcher nicht die Einheit der Kirche. Er begründet als solcher, d.h. in seiner dem Historiker zugänglichen Vorfindlichkeit dagegen die Vielzahl der Konfessionen." Diese Einschätzung begründete Ernst Käsemann vor einem halben Jahrhundert erstens damit, dass das Kerygma, die Christusbotschaft, von Anfang an höchst unterschiedlich vermittelt worden sei, sodann mit „der außerordentlichen und das NT übergreifenden Fülle theologischer Positionen in der Urchristenheit und ihrer wenigstens teilweise zutage tretenden Unvereinbarkeit"[1].

Käsemanns Urteil, das auch wegen seiner Zuspitzung immer wieder gern zitiert worden ist, mag den Befund einer *theologischen Pluralität* des neu- testamentlichen Textbestandes zutreffend wiedergeben. Ob daraus auch auf die Vielzahl von Konfessionen geschlossen werden darf, kann dagegen be- zweifelt werden, gerade aus geschichtlichen Gründen. Denn vom modernen Protestantismus abgesehen, nehmen viele christliche Kirchen das Neue Tes- tament eben nicht als Sammelbecken theologischer Positionen wahr, die wie deutsche Universitätsprofessoren miteinander konkurrieren. Unterschiede sol- cher „Positionen" werden von theologischen Forschern noch zusätzlich ver- schärft – vor allem, wenn sie selber einen positionellen Zuschnitt vorzeigen wie Käsemann, der am liebsten auch evangelische Zunftgenossen einer frem- den „Konfession" zurechnen möchte, falls sie andere neutestamentliche Schriften mehr schätzen als er (beispielsweise Oscar Cullmann mit seinem

---

1 E. Käsemann, Begründet der neutestamentliche Kanon die Einheit der Kirche? (1951), in: ders., Exegetische Versuche und Besinnungen I, Göttingen 1960, 214–223, S. 221.

„heilsgeschichtlichen" Interesse am lukanischen Geschichtswerk[2]). Wer –
wie Käsemann – einzig und allein das „Wort vom Kreuz" (1.Kor 1,18) gelten
lässt, und zwar ausgelegt durch *sein,* Käsemanns, Verständnis der paulinischen Rechtfertigungslehre, wird anderslautende neutestamentliche Schriften
nur als abweichend oder gar als Gegensätze vermerken. Doch andere vernehmen die Vielstimmigkeit der neutestamentlichen Zeugen durchaus nicht
als Disharmonie. Denn sie haben eine andere Vorstellung von „Einheit", zumal von „Einheit der Kirche": von einer Einheit, die kein Unisono bietet,
sondern die einer erheblichen Innenspannung, anderen Akzente, Gewichtungen, Perspektiven, Zuordnungen Raum lässt, ohne alles und jedes grenzenlos
gelten zu lassen. Zum Beispiel Rowan Williams:

„Die Einheit der Heiligen Schrift hängt damit zusammen, ... wie sie sich selbst als Bezugs-
punkt (als *Kanon)* für eine Gemeinschaft mit einer begrenzten und wahrnehmbaren historischen Einheit begründet. Ihre Einheit stiftenden Themen werden aus dem gewonnen, was als
einheitsstiftend für diese Gemeinschaft angesehen wird. Das bedeutet *nicht,* ihre Einheit auf
etwas zu reduzieren, das die Gemeinschaft als ein für allemal akzeptabel angesehen hat,
gleichgültig, was immer ihre Prioritäten sein mögen. Dieses bedeutet andererseits: Wenn die
Gemeinschaft ihren Mittelpunkt in dieser oder jener Sammlung von Erzählungen oder Praktiken findet, wenn sie findet, dass genau *diese* ausdrücken, wem die Gemeinschaft sich selbst
für verantwortlich hält, dann werden diese Identitätsmerkmale begründet und erklärt durch
alles, was im Text maßgeblich ist und was demnach in gewissem Sinne den Text für den
Leser im Kontext dieser Gemeinschaft gliedert."[3]

Rowan Williams spricht als anglikanischer Theologe, der inzwischen ein kir-
chenleitendes Amt übernommen und als Erzbischof von Canterbury diese
Leseweise der Heiligen Schrift zu verantworten hat. Die tief gestaffelte Lese-
kultur, für die er plädiert, enthält ein unverkennbar anderes Verständnis
kirchlicher Einheit, als es bei Käsemann durchschimmert. Folgerichtig führt
sie auch zu einem anderen Kanonverständnis und zu einer anderen Lesepraxis. Sie ebnet Unterschiede zwischen biblischen Büchern durchaus nicht ein
und stellt auch keine gekünstelte Übereinstimmung her. Im Gegenteil: Das
Nebeneinander biblischer Texte erzeugt eine *Spannung,* die uns, die Leserinnen und Leser, in eine Auseinandersetzung mit diesen Texten und zugleich
mit uns selber verwickelt. Dies geschieht vor allem dann, wenn Texte, die
ungefähr gleichzeitig entstanden sind, Unterschiedliches oder gar Gegensätz-
liches sagen. Dann sehen wir uns genötigt zu fragen, wo *wir* stehen und ob
wir dort stehen bleiben dürfen – angesichts widerstreitender Direktiven, die
wir vielleicht erst auf anderer Ebene als zusammengehörig erkennen müssen.

---

2 O. Cullmann, Die Tradition als exegetisches, historisches und theologisches Problem,
   Zürich 1954; Ders., Heil als Geschichte. Heilsgeschichtliche Existenz im Neuen
   Testament, Tübingen [2]1967.
3 R. Williams, Der Literalsinn der Heiligen Schrift, EvTh 50 (1990) 55–71, S. 68.

Um solche Differenzen bemerken zu können, müssen wir uns freilich auf die Bibel als ganze einlassen, dürfen uns also nicht auf eine Auswahl beschränken, die das Gespräch mit Stimmen, die uns fremd erscheinen oder auch wirklich befremden, von vornherein abbrechen lässt. Außerdem müssen wir uns *Zeit lassen*, damit wir jedem Text in seinem inneren Aufbau folgen können, weil „der Sinngehalt eines Textes in einem Lernprozess der Wahrnehmung zutage tritt"[4]. Dadurch wird unserem Lesen die Willkür verwehrt, die den Text als Material für unsere Rekonstruktion oder auch Konstruktion von Sinngehalten missbraucht. Auch für die *Verlaufsform des Lesens*, das den Text gleichsam wieder fließend entstehen lässt, ohne ihm ins Wort zu fallen, bedarf es des unaufhörlichen Lesens in größerem Zusammenhang, es bedarf der *lectio continua*. Und schließlich tritt Williams für ein „*dramatisches Lesen*" ein: „Wir sind eingeladen, uns selbst in der Geschichte, die wir gerade bedenken, wiederzufinden, uns erneut anzueignen, wer wir jetzt sind und wer wir sein werden oder sein können in der Form der Geschichte."[5] Dieses Lesen muss sich zugleich in die *Konflikte* hineinziehen lassen, welche die biblischen Geschichten prägen[6]: Gerade wenn sie in ihrem kanonischen Zusammenhang gesehen werden, widersprechen einzelne Schriften einander häufig, oder sie ergänzen sich kritisch, sie lassen entscheidende Lücken oder hinterlassen Brüche. Konflikte entstehen vor allem durch Widerstände, die biblische Texte der Welt entgegenbringen, in der sie entstehen: Widerstände, die ein fixiertes Weltbild zerstören können, auch eine verfestigte Vorstellung von der Gemeinschaft Gottes mit seinem Volk.

Diesen letzten Gesichtspunkt überstrapaziert Williams. Wenn Schemata zerbrechen, kann dies ja auch die überwältigende Entdeckung einer Wirklichkeit anzeigen, die sich jenen Schemata nicht mehr fügt. Oder es kann der spontane Ausdruck von Sprachbemühungen um eine überraschend neue Wirklichkeit sein, die nicht mehr in die alten Wörter zu fassen ist, obwohl noch keine neue Sprache zur Verfügung steht. Dies trifft, wenn ich recht sehe, für weite Strecken des Neuen Testamentes zu. Konflikte sind Nebenwirkungen solcher „Einfälle" von Wirklichkeit, nicht aber die treibende Kraft für Wahrnehmungen – gar für sämtliche Wahrnehmungen, wie Williams anzunehmen scheint. Das Lesen der Bibel kann ja mitunter auch die eigene Lebensgeschichte und die Geschichte der Kirche unterbrechen, pausenloses kirchliches Gerede wird abgebrochen, Schulderkenntnis bricht auf, eine selbstbewusste Berufung auf die Bibel bricht zusammen. Die Bibel spricht

---

4 Williams, ebd., 58.
5 Williams, ebd., 61.
6 Williams bezieht sich hier auf W.G. Jeanrond, Text und Interpretation als Kategorien theologischen Denkens (HUTh 23), Tübingen 1986.

zeitweise überhaupt nicht mehr zu uns, in keiner ihrer Passagen, oder sie widerspricht der Kirche, oder aber sie fällt mir, dem Leser oder der Leserin, so
ins Wort, dass ich nicht weiterlesen kann oder wenigstens für einige Zeit
nicht mehr.

Im Vergleich dazu erscheint Käsemanns Darstellungsweise – sie schlägt
sich ebenso eindrucksvoll wie erdrückend in seinem Römerbriefkommentar
nieder – ungleich geschlossener, aber auch monochrom und sogar monoton,
wenn auch stilistisch farbenreich und gelegentlich rhetorisch aufwühlend.
Doch theologisch wirkt sie einförmig, und ich frage mich, ob sich hier nicht
auch ein vehement kirchenkritischer Zug bemerkbar macht. Die Einheit der
Kirche scheint für Käsemann wohl nur dann erreicht, wenn alle ihre Glieder
gleichsam auf Vordermann gebracht worden sind, mit ein und derselben
Blickrichtung, so dass der Marschbefehl erfolgen kann. Für Käsemann war
die Mobilisierung der Kirche mehr als ein Wunschbild, und sein Verständnis
der Theologie als kritischer Dienst an der Kirche richtete sich gegen eine
Volkskirche, die unterschiedliche geistliche Lebensformen und divergierende
ethische Einstellungen nur „zusammenhüten" kann und nicht über ein
Schiedlich/Friedlich hinauszukommen vermag.

2. Verbindlichkeit als Offenheit

Käsemanns Präparation der Rechtfertigungslehre als eines „Kanons im Kanon" steht m.E. in diesem ekklesiologischen Zusammenhang. Für ihn waren
nicht nur die vielfältigen theologischen Positionen der Urchristenheit „wenigstens teilweise" miteinander unvereinbar. Pluralität scheint nach Käsemanns Überzeugung leicht zur Kirchenspaltung zu führen. Dahinter steht ein
rigoroses, wenn nicht sogar ein puristisches Verständnis von „Einheit". Die
Sorge um die Herstellung dieser Einheit deckt sich durchaus nicht mit der
Frage, wie zwischen Positionen entschieden werden kann, die tatsächlich
einander widerstreiten. Eine solche Entscheidung wird nötig, wenn einem
pluralistischen „Alles ist erlaubt" gewehrt werden muss.

Käsemanns Maßregelung, die diese Frage mit jener Sorge verknüpft, will
eine jede theologisch verbindliche Schriftauslegung durch ein Kriterium
normieren, das *innerhalb* der Bibel namhaft gemacht werden kann[7], und zwar

---

7 Welche Aporien in dieser Debatte zutage getreten sind, zeigt W. Schrage, Die Frage
   nach der Mitte und dem Kanon im Kanon des Neuen Testamentes in der neueren
   Diskussion, in: Rechtfertigung. FS Ernst Käsemann, Tübingen/Göttingen 1976, 415–
   442.

so: Bestimmte biblische Aussagen sollen erlauben, das theologisch Ursprüngliche festzustellen und es sachkritisch von allem abzuheben, was sich vom Ursprung mehr und mehr entfernt hat. Eine historische Betrachtungsweise, die so verfährt, verfällt dabei leicht dem Fehlschluss, das geschichtlich Ursprüngliche – womöglich eine Art Urgestein – bilde auch den theologischen Ursprung am reinsten ab.

Etwas strukturell Anderes wäre eine interne Abstufung innerhalb des Schriftganzen. In dieser Hinsicht sollte dem Interesse am „Kanon im Kanon" m.E. die vorsichtigere Frage nach der „Mitte der Schrift" vorgezogen werden. Sie sucht den Abstand einzelner Texte zu dieser „Mitte" zu ermessen und grenzt Texte nur dann aus, wenn sie von dieser Mitte nicht nur allzu weit entfernt sind, sondern auf diese Mitte gar nicht mehr bezogen werden können. Die Frage nach der Mitte der Schrift ist dann berechtigt, wenn eine relative Ferne oder Nähe einzelner Texte zu jenem theologischen Zentrum ermessen werden soll, um das sich die Kirche in ihrem Vernehmen der Direktive der „Schrift" schart.

Es dürfte nicht zufällig sein, dass diese Frage intensiver für die Alttestamentliche Theologie als für die Neutestamentliche verfolgt worden ist. Denn zum einen lässt der (im Verhältnis zum Neuen Testament) großräumige Entstehungsprozess der heiligen Schriften Israels danach fragen, was diese Texte zuinnerst zusammenhält und sie nicht bloß geschichtlich zusammenbindet. Zum anderen werden kraft der „Mitte des Alten Testaments" dessen Schriften für die christliche Kirche verbindlich: die Mitte ist – Gott, der sich mit dem Namen „Jahwe" ebenso kundgetan wie sich darin verborgen hat, „die göttliche Person", „die unter diesem Namen gehandelt hat und die mit diesem Namen angerufen wird", „Jahwe der Gott Israels" und „Israel als Volk Jahwes"[8], zusammengefasst in der Zusage: „Ich will euer Gott sein, ihr sollt mein Volk sein."[9] Mit dieser Verheißung und dem ihr korrespondierenden Ersten Gebot tritt das Alte Testament der Kirche gegenüber, und zwar als Ganzes, nicht bloß mit einer für Christen ansprechenden Auswahl. Diese Mitte ist von der Identität des jüdischen Gottesvolkes zwar keineswegs getrennt, aber doch unterschieden. Andernfalls würde das „Judentum" nur zu den geschichtlichen Voraussetzungen des „Christentums" gehören, und wie fatal diese Sicht ist, hat sich im Verhältnis von Kirche und Israel immer wieder gezeigt. Die Verheißung des Gottes Abrahams, Isaaks und Jakobs: Er wolle der Gott seines Volkes sein und bleiben, kommt vielmehr in der Person Jesu

---

8 R. Smend, Die Mitte des Alten Testaments (1970), in: ders., Die Mitte des Alten Testaments. Gesammelte Studien I (BEvTh 99), München 1986, 40–84, S. 74f.

9 H.-J. Hermisson, Alttestamentliche Theologie *und* Religionsgeschichte Israels (ThLZ.F 3), Leipzig 2000, 31.74.

Christi von neuem und auf neue Weise zu Gehör. Darin besteht die Mitte des biblischen Kanons, die Mitte der „Schrift". Jesus Christus also die „externe Mitte" des Alten Testaments?[10] Eher: „Gott in Christus" (2.Kor 5,19): Gott an Jesus Christus und in eins mit ihm handelnd. Gott handelt hier so unerhört neu, dass das gesamte Neue Testament ein unaufhörliches Ringen darum ist, Gottes Handeln überhaupt zur Sprache zu bringen, seine Beziehungen zum früheren Gotteshandeln zu entdecken und seine Verheißung zu ermessen. Was bedeutet dies für Gottes Einheit und für die Einheitlichkeit seines Handelns? Der Gott der Väter: der Vater Jesu Christi; der Gott der Lebendigen: der Gott, der Jesus Christus von den Toten auferweckt hat! Wer Gott ist, erfahren wir mit Jesus von Nazareth aus dem Alten Testament[11] – dieser Gott hat ein für allemal, endgültig in Jesus Christus geredet. Welch ungeheure Spannung!

Das Neue Testament ist als Ganzes Christuserkenntnis in *statu nascendi*. Sollten wir etwa wünschen, jemals darüber hinauszukommen? Die Verfasser der im Neuen Testament als kohärent versammelten Schriften waren nicht dadurch ausgezeichnet, dass sie Tuchfühlung mit Jesus gehabt hätten, sondern sie waren aufgestört durch die Erscheinung Jesu Christi, und sie versuchten, dies in immer neuen erwartungsvollen Ansätzen zu formulieren, erzählend, lehrend, auslegend. Dies macht die Vielfalt des Neuen Testament aus, und so geben seine Schriften uns Anstöße, von denen wir uns immer wieder aufs neue stören und weiterführen lassen: Anstöße in diesem Sinne, nicht einen Anstoß, der einem Steinwurf gleicht, der weitere Kreise zieht, die jedoch immer schwächer werden.

Etwas anderes als diese Mitte wäre, wie gesagt, eine quasi räumlich-hierarchische Anordnung biblischer Texte. Für eine solche Ästhetik verschwimmen bei zunehmender Ferne die Kanongrenzen, und der Übergang von Schriften innerhalb des Kanons zu außerkanonischen lässt sich kaum mehr erkennen. Er dürfte dann auch exegetisch kaum mehr eine Rolle spielen.

Eine solche Sicht mag den Historiker befriedigen, solange er von den inneren Gründen der Kanonbildung absieht. Zur theologischen Geltung des Kanon kann er auch dann nicht vordringen, wenn er seine Entstehung lückenlos zu rekonstruieren vermag. Denn diese Archäologie operiert mit Einheitsvorstellungen, die sich mit dem Neben-, Gegen- und Miteinander von Texten, wie sie der biblische Kanon uns vor Augen stellt, schwerlich vertragen. An die Stelle der Ganzheit als einer innerlich reich gegliederten und dabei spannungsvollen Einheit sind Theorien getreten, die das biblische Textmaterial entwicklungsgeschichtlich anordnen. In der Regel deklarieren sie einen ge-

---

10 So Hermisson, ebd., 29f.98–101.
11 S. dazu den Beitrag von Horst Seebass in diesem Band (S. 27–43).

schichtlichen Ausgangspunkt als maßgebend, von dem her alles Frühere und
Spätere gemessen und dann auch gewichtet wird. Verschiedene Konstruktionen haben sich eingebürgert, mit deren Hilfe aus einer Entwicklung Normen
abgeleitet werden sollen.

Ein Paradebeispiel ist das Bild einer Verfallsgeschichte der Theologie im
Neuen Testament, die nach genialen Aufbrüchen bei Paulus und Johannes in
Kompromissen einer anpassungswilligen Kirche verflacht und schließlich im
„Frühkatholizismus" versandet.[12] Für Käsemann war die Mitte der Schrift
zwischen Rabbinismus und Frühkatholizismus zu suchen, aber diese Grenzlinien dürften inzwischen hinfällig geworden sein. In der alttestamentlichen
Wissenschaft treibt gegenwärtig die Tendenz einer exzessiven Spätdatierung
die seltsamsten Blüten: die meisten Texte werden in der exilischen und na-
chexilischen Zeit lokalisiert. Damit wird der Eindruck einer einheitlichen
Problemstellung erweckt, die in der Bewältigungsstrategie für Erfahrungen
des nationalen Zusammenbruches und Wiederaufbaus gipfelt. Diese gewalt-
same Rekonstruktion ebnet das geschichtliche Gefälle der Texte ein und lässt
sie nur als Antworten auf eine grundstürzende Herausforderung zur Wort
kommen. Hätten sie allein dies zu sagen, dann könnten sie uns nur beibrin-
gen, aktuelle Probleme in Fiktionen von Geschichte hinein zu projizieren und
sie artifiziell zu „lösen".

3. Die „Schrift" als dynamische Ganzheit

Durch solche Entwicklungstheorien wird aber das Gespür für die eigentümliche Einheit des Kanons auf die Dauer zerstört. Diese Einheit ist nicht schon
mit der Endgestalt der Textgeschichte gegeben, und darum hilft es schwerlich
weiter, wenn diese Endgestalt als „kanonisch" in Anspruch genommen werden soll, statt dass nach Kriterien im Laufe der Textgeschichte gesucht wird.
Die Einheit des Kanons wird plastisch erst dank der Tiefenschärfe der einzelnen Texte, und auf sie ist jede hermeneutische Bemühung um den geschichtlichen Eigen-Sinn der Texte angewiesen.[13] Entscheidend ist daher, *wie die
gegliederte Einheit der Bibel als „Schrift" konstituiert ist und wie sich diese
Einheit zur Einheit der Kirche verhält. Können wir hier eine Wechselwirkung*

---

12 Verführerisch eindrucksvoll gezeichnet von R. Bultmann, Theologie des Neuen
   Testaments, Tübingen [9]1984.
13 Siehe dazu die treffende Kritik an Brevard S. Childs von J. Barr, Holy Scripture: Canon,
   Authority, Criticism, Oxford 1983, bes. 130–171.

oder zumindest eine Korrelation erkennen?[14] Um uns diesen Fragen anzunähern, brauchen wir sozusagen die gleiche Augenhöhe wie die Alte Kirche bei ihrer Wahrnehmung der überlieferten Texte als „Schrift".

Die Wahrnehmung kirchlicher Einheit spiegelt sich darin, wie die „Fülle" der im Kanon nicht bloß gesammelten, sondern versammelten Schriften aufgefasst wird: als eine Pluralität, die nach einem Kriterium verlangt, mit dessen Hilfe eine Ordnung im Vielerlei aufgewiesen oder notfalls Ordnung geschaffen werden kann – oder vielmehr als eine *Einheit sui generis*, die bereits einen Raum bildet, in dem sich die Hörer- und Leserschaft ungezwungen und erwartungsvoll bewegen kann. Diese Einheit muss also nicht erst gebildet werden. In ihr gibt es immer wieder Anderes und Neues zu entdecken: dank der Treue Gottes, die eine Vielfalt von Erwartungsperspektiven gewährt – Erwartungsperspektiven, die derart ineinandergreifen, dass unsere Wahrnehmung nie abgeschlossen ist und auch nicht auf eine Reihe gebracht werden kann. Diese Perspektiven lassen sich weder aufeinander zurückführen noch wechselseitig abbilden. Ihre Vielfalt ist auch kein Gebilde, die kraft unserer deutenden oder assoziierenden Findigkeit geschaffen werden könnte. Die Textebene enthält mehrere Fluchtpunkte, die die Aufmerksamkeit so auf sich ziehen, dass der Blick sich immer wieder neu auf anderes richtet, ohne dass die Einheit des Ganzen verloren geht. Konsistenz und Offenheit schließen sich hier nicht aus; die Wahrnehmung ist weder beliebig noch vollständig abgeschlossen. Um mit der Konsistenz und Offenheit, die die biblischen Texte in ihrem Zusammenhang bei näherem Zusehen auszeichnet, vertraut zu werden, bedürfen wir verlässlicher Hilfestellungen, welche die „Schrift" selber gewährt: Regeln, verbunden mit Grundunterscheidungen wie „Geist und Buchstabe", „Gesetz und Evangelium", „Verheißung und Erfüllung", die uns ermöglichen, jeden Bibeltext so wahrzunehmen, wie er selbst vernommen werden will.[15]

Die Suche nach einem „Kanon im Kanon" oder nach ähnlich hierarchischen Normen hindert diese Wahrnehmung, statt sie zu fördern. Soll er in irgendeiner biblischen „Zentralaussage" oder ähnlichem fixiert werden, wird erschwert, dass die Kirche in irgendeiner Weise für die Einheit der Schrift tätig werden kann. Dergleichen wäre ja (dieser Verdacht stellt sich alsbald ein) ein erster Schritt hin zum schlüpfrigen Boden eines kirchlichen Lehramtes, das jeweils deklariert, was in der Fülle biblischer Belege verbindlich ist, von der Überfülle von Auslegungen ganz zu schweigen! Dagegen soll der

---

14 „Soviel die Bibel gilt, soviel wirkt sie. Soviel sie wirkt, soviel gilt sie": M. Kähler, Geschichte der Bibel in ihrer Wirkung auf die Kirche (1902), in: ders., Aufsätze zur Bibelfrage, hg.v. E. Kähler (TB 37), München 1967, 131–288, S. 245.
15 Näheres dazu: G. Sauter, Zugänge zur Dogmatik. Elemente theologischer Urteilsbildung (UTB 2064), Göttingen 1998, 291–296.

Kanon im Kanon – also eine interne Norm für die Zusammenstellung von Schriften (insofern zwei verschiedene Bedeutung von „Kanon") – als normative Selbststeuerung wirken und dann auch der Steuerung durch eine vermeintlich eindeutige Theologie dienen. Damit aber wird die Kanonbildung faktisch suspendiert. Oder (was auf dasselbe hinauslaufen dürfte) der Kanon soll immer wieder von neuem geschaffen werden, nämlich durch Ausgrenzung von Texten oder von einzelnen Aussagen, die nicht der Norm entsprechen. Wenn heute – etwa bei einer Ordination – mit drohendem Unterton vom Kanon als „Richtschnur" gesprochen wird (in Anlehnung an die Konkordienformel[16]), dann lässt das eher an eine Hinrichtung denken: die Richtschnur als Galgenstrick, der die Luft abschnürt. Gemeint ist mit dieser Metapher jedoch, dass die Dinge zwanglos ins Lot gebracht werden. Erst dadurch wird geistliches Leben ermöglicht.

Hängt mit einer Überbetonung der Schrift als Norm nicht *auch* zusammen, dass die Freude an einer *lectio continua* und an den Einsichten, die sie erbringen kann, heutzutage so sehr geschwunden ist? Ein andauerndes, ausdauerndes und intensives „Leben mit der Bibel", eine Freude an der Entdeckung innerbiblisch tragender und dabei spannungsvoller Zusammenhänge, erschlossen mit der Frage nach Gottes Handeln und seiner Wahrnehmung, ein darauf ausgerichteter Lernprozess und eine davon gespeiste theologische Urteilsbildung: dies alles hat bei heutigen Studierenden höchsten Seltenheitswert, ganz zu schweigen von einem „ins Große gehenden Schriftgebrauch", wie er Friedrich Schleiermacher für die Glaubenslehre vorschwebte[17]. Statt dessen hat sich ein theologischer Reduktionismus durchgesetzt, der mit einer rigorosen Handhabung eines „Kanons im Kanon" sehr wohl Hand in Hand gehen kann.[18] Inwiefern tragen auch unsere Lehrveranstaltungen mit Schuld daran?

Die „Mitte der Schrift" in den Blick zu bekommen: dazu kann die Anweisung Martin Kählers helfen, die er vor über einem Jahrhundert formulierte

---

16 Epitome, Von dem summarischen Begriff der streitigen Artikel; BSLK 769,23.
17 F.D.E. Schleiermacher, Der Christliche Glaube. Auf Grund der 2. Auflage und kritischer Prüfung des Textes neu hg.v. M. Redeker I, Berlin [7]1960, § 27.3 (S. 152).
18 Dies ist einer der Ansatzpunkte für die kritische Bestandsaufnahme von N. Appel, Kanon und Kirche. Die Kanonkrise im heutigen Protestantismus als kontroverstheologisches Problem (KKTS 9), Paderborn 1962, bes. 337–344. – Vgl. auch K. Reinhardt, Der dogmatische Schriftgebrauch in der katholischen und protestantischen Christologie von der Aufklärung bis zur Gegenwart, München/Paderborn/Wien 1970. – Beide Bücher sind charakteristisch für die Konstellation vor dem II. Vatikanischen Konzil. Was sich seither auf römisch-katholischer Seite zum Besseren hin verändert hat, zeigt das „Dokument der Päpstlichen Bibelkommission: Die Interpretation der Bibel in der Kirche" (Verlautbarung des Apostolischen Stuhls 115, Bonn 1993 [2]1996). Leider steht dieser Studie m.W. kein entsprechendes evangelisches Dokument zur Seite.

und die im wesentlichen nicht veraltet ist. Er rät, das Interesse auf die
„Hauptsache" zu konzentrieren und den „Nebensachen" nicht mehr Aufmerksamkeit zu schenken, als es erforderlich ist.[19] Dafür bedarf es allerdings
des Einverständnisses über die „Hauptsache", das wiederum von der Wahrnehmung des „Ganzen" der Schrift abhängt: Die Bibel als Ganzheit aufzufassen, heißt für Kähler durchaus nicht, sie als gleichartiges Ganzes zu verstehen, in dem jedes Stück und jeder Teil denselben Wert hat. Vielmehr erfordert ein ganzheitliches Verstehen der Bibel eine geschärfte Wahrnehmung,
deren Umgrenzung – das sind die Nebensachen, die sich um die Hauptsache
gruppieren – eine gewisse Unschärfe behalten kann, ohne dass dadurch die
Hauptsache unbestimmt wird. Kähler wendet sich mit dieser These gegen
eine seinerzeit ausgeprägte Lehre von der Verbalinspiration, die von einer
gegenläufigen Sichtweise ausgeht. „Dort heißt es: 'Weil auch die Nebensachen in Ordnung sind, kann ich mich auf die Hauptsache verlassen, *und andernfalls nicht*'."[20] Eine solche Sicht der Bibel verfällt allzu leicht der Gefahr,
die Schrift hauptsächlich über Abgrenzungen zu verstehen, denn zunächst
müssen die Nebensachen völlig bestimmt werden. Doch dadurch verstrickt
sich diese Bibeltheorie in der Problematik, die sie gern an der historisch-
kritischen Forschung anprangert, nämlich in einer Auflösung ganzheitlichen
Verstehens in unzusammenhängende Detailfragen. Hauptsächlich wird dann
über Nebensachen gestritten – etwa über Datierung, Verfasserschaft, historisch ermittelbare Abhängigkeiten – und dadurch geht der Blick für die
Hauptsache verloren. Wenn aber „die Hauptsache in Ordnung ist, wird es
auch mit den Nebensachen so sein, *aber jenes hängt hiervon nicht ab*"[21]. So
vertritt Kähler eine gleichsam an ihren Rändern offene Inspirationslehre, weil
er von der Rechtfertigung allein durch den Glauben als der Hauptsache der
Schrift ausgeht – dies freilich (anders als etwa bei E. Käsemann) dogmatisch
breit aufgefächert: in der Versöhnungslehre als „Soterologie", als Reden von
Jesus als dem Christus. Die Glaubensgerechtigkeit entlastet den Bibelleser als
Urteilenden von der Nötigung, sein Verhältnis zur Bibel durch ein alles um-
greifendes Verstehen selbsttätig aufzubauen und zu regeln, also jede Neben-
sache bestimmt zu haben und dadurch endgültige Grenzen zu ziehen.[22]

---

19 M. Kähler, Unser Streit um die Bibel (1895), in: ders., Aufsätze zu Bibelfrage (s. Anm.
    14), 17–83, S. 47: „... es ist erklärlich genug, wenn man meint, wo die Hauptsache sich
    findet, werde es auch mit den Nebensachen, soweit das erforderlich ist, in Ordnung
    sein." – Den Hinweis auf dieses Zitat verdanke ich Rainer Fischer; dessen Auslegung
    übernehme ich teilweise wörtlich aus seinem Beitrag: Offenbarung als bestimmte
    Gestalt, in: Offenbarung und Geschichten, hg. v. J. Barton/G. Sauter (Beiträge zur
    theologischen Urteilsbildung 10), Frankfurt a. M. u.a. 2000, 115–136, S. 121f.
20 Fischer, ebd.
21 Fischer, ebd.
22 Vgl. Fischer, ebd, 73.79.

Kähler richtet die Aufmerksamkeit also auf die *externe Konstitution der Ganzheit der Schrift. Sie ist – so möchte ich hinzufügen – in gleicher Weise begründet wie die Einheit der Kirche.* Was „Kirche" und was „Kanon" ist, kann nicht durch ihre Wechselbeziehung zueinander, etwa wirkungsgeschichtlich, bestimmt werden. Vielmehr sind sie gemeinsam angewiesen auf das, was sie begründet. Sie haben gleichsam eine offene Flanke: Der Anspruch, den sowohl der Kanon als auch die Kirche stellen, lässt sich nicht anders als durch ihr Verwiesensein auf Gottes richtendes und rettendes Handeln einlösen. Beispielsweise entschied sich im Donatistenstreit der Alten Kirche dass Christen kraft ihrer sakramentalen Teilhabe zur Kirche gehören, nicht aber dank der Würdigkeit derer, die das Sakrament austeilen. Dementsprechend sind die Texte, die im Kanon zusammengestellt wurden, verbindlich wegen ihrer Nähe zum Christusgeschehen, nicht dank der apostolischen Autorität ihrer Verfasser.

Diese offene Flanke entsteht gerade dadurch, dass die biblischen Texte das Christuszeugnis und das Bekenntnis zu ihm *verschriftlichen* und dass diese Notation durch die Kanonbildung anerkannt wird. Das Kanon repräsentiert von nun an das „Gegebensein" der Schrift für die Kirche, ein Gegebensein, das durch keine Aneignung im Hören oder Lesen gleichsam verschluckt werden kann.[23] Die Schriftlichkeit setzt aber auch viel mehr Auslegungen frei, als es eine mündliche Tradition könnte, die möglichst wortgetreu bewahrt werden muss und durch rituelle Wiederholung ihre Wirkung entfalten kann, durch eine Wiederholung, die das rechte Reden verbürgt. Der Kanon wird verbindlicher, weil umgreifender, als es eine mündliche Tradition erreichen kann, auch wenn ihr ein hoher Überlieferungswert zukommen mag. Der Kanon behielt allerdings die Mündlichkeit auf seine Weise bei, die nur anderes strukturiert war. Das Hören wurde nicht zugunsten des Lesens aufgegeben: bis hin zu Luthers Zeiten wurden die biblischen Texte laut gelesen. Dem Hören kommt theologisch Priorität vor dem Lesen zu.[24]

4. Die Kanonbildung als Zumutung für die Einheit der Kirche

Mit der Frage nach der lebendigen Mitte des Kanons lässt sich das Verhältnis von Kanon und Kirche nicht bestimmen, aber auch nicht umgehen. Doch so-

---

23 R.W. Jenson, Systematic Theology. II. The Works of God, New York/Oxford 1999, 275.
24 Siehe dazu I. Dalferth, Von der Vieldeutbarkeit der Schrift und der Eindeutigkeit des Wortes Gottes, in: Richard Ziegert (Hg.), Die Zukunft des Schriftprinzips (Bibel im Gespräch 2), Stuttgart 1994, 155–173, S. 158f.

bald eine – wie auch immer beschaffene – Beteiligung der Kirche nicht nur an der historischen Kanonbildung, sondern am theologischen Profil des Kanons ins Gespräch gebracht wird, fährt sich die Debatte fest.[25] Denn dann wird sie beherrscht durch den kontroverstheologischen Gegensatz: römisch-„katholische Kirche, die Schriftautorität setzt, die sich dadurch ihre Identität schafft und sichert" *versus* evangelische „Kirche, die sich zum Kanon als einer ihr externen Autorität bekennt" und sich damit unter das *verbum externum* der Schrift stellt, statt sich mittels des Kanons selber Geltung zu verschaffen.[26] So sieht beispielsweise Karl Barth die Kanonbildung als Akt des Gehorsams gegenüber der Offenbarung, als einen Akt, den die Kirche immer wieder von neuem zu vollziehen hat, um wirklich „Kirche" zu bleiben.[27] Diese Alternative ist so gewichtig geworden, dass gar nicht mehr in den Blick kommt, ob es auch eine Art selbstvergessener Anerkenntnis geben könnte, in der eine unwillkürliche Selbstverpflichtung das Maß der eigenen Beteiligung und zugleich der Verantwortung dafür zum Vorschein bringt. Die Anerkenntnis des Kanons – die ihn nicht bloß positivistisch als historisches Faktum respektiert – zeigt sich daran, dass und wie die Bibel als Ganzes im Leben der Kirche lebendig ist. Jede Reduktion der Textmenge im Gebrauch der Bibel[28] – in der Liturgie, in der Predigt[29], im Unterricht, in der Seelsorge, in der Diakonie, in der Kirchenleitung, in der Mission, im gemeinsamen und persönlichen Bibelstudium – : dies alles wäre eine heimlich-unheimliche Bestreitung der Geltung des Kanons.

Wie gelangen wir über den ökumenischen Minimalkonsens hinaus, dass die Kirche „mit der Annahme eines neutestamentlichen Kanons einen die

---

25 Dies zeigt wider die Absicht des Verfassers die äußerst gründliche und materialreiche Untersuchung von I. Lønning, „Kanon im Kanon". Zum dogmatischen Grundlagenproblem des neutestamentlichen Kanons (FGLP X/43), München 1972, bes. Kap. IV: „Kanon und Kirche – der neutestamentliche Kanon im Spannungsfeld der Kontroverse um Schrift und Tradition."

26 John Webster schlug in seinem *response* zur ersten Fassung meines Beitrages vor, die Schriftautorität, die der Kirche „gegeben" wird, d.h. ihr anvertraut und aufgetragen ist, und die zugleich dadurch gebildet wird, dass die Kirche diesen Auftrag ausführt, als eine Polarität aufzufassen. Sie sei pneumatologisch zu verstehen: Kirche und Kanon seien gleicherweise Felder des durch den Geist vermittelten göttlichen Handelns. Dem stimme ich gerne zu, muss jedoch hinzufügen, dass hier konfessionell unterschiedliche Akzentsetzungen für das Verhältnis von Geist und Kirche zu beachten sind. Vgl. als Versuch zur ökumenischen Verständigung: W. Kasper/G. Sauter, Kirche – Ort des Geistes (ÖF. Kleine ökumenische Schriften 8), Freiburg/Basel/Wien 1976.

27 K. Barth, Die Kirchliche Dogmatik I/1, München 1932, 103f.

28 Max Horkheimer bemerkte in den 60er Jahren, für viele evangelische Theologen reduziere sich die Bibel auf die Geschichte von Jesu Tempelaustreibung, aber ohne Tempel – im Klartext: auf eine Generalreinigung der Kirche von allem, was missliebig erscheint, und zwar mit dem prophetischen Gestus „im Namen Jesu".

29 Eine latente Gefahr der Perikopenordnung!

ganze Zukunft der Kirche verpflichtenden Entscheid getroffen"[30] hat? Es kommt doch wohl auf den Charakter dieses Entscheides, auf seine innere Konstitution an – im Unterschied zu den historischen Randbedingungen, aber gewiss nicht losgelöst von ihnen! Und hier reicht die Umschreibung von R. Williams nicht mehr aus: „Wenn die Gemeinschaft ihren Mittelpunkt in dieser oder jener Sammlung von Erzählungen oder Praktiken findet, wenn sie findet, dass genau *diese* ausdrücken, wem die Gemeinschaft sich selbst für verantwortlich hält."[31] „Wem die Gemeinschaft sich selbst für verantwortlich hält": in dieser unbestimmten Formulierung dürfte der Schnittpunkt zwischen soziologischer Betrachtung – die feststellt, dass und wie Gemeinschaften sich einen Richtwert wählen und sich an ihn halten – und theologischer Verantwortung zu suchen und hoffentlich auch zu finden sein: der Verantwortung Christus gegenüber, aus dessen Sterben und Leben seine Gemeinde existiert. Dieser Mittelpunkt ist nicht ohne den Kanon, aber auch nicht mit ihm allein „gegeben". Vielmehr *entdeckt die Kirche die Begründung ihrer Einheit in ihrem Leben mit der Bibel, indem sie sich dem Ganzen der Schrift aussetzt.*[32]

Dadurch wird ausgeschlossen, dass die Kirche durch ihr Lesen der Schrift diese mit konstituiert, und sei dieses Lesen noch so dramatisch und selbstkritisch! Die Schrift weigert sich – und zwar im Vollzug des Bibellesens, vor allem des gemeinschaftlichen –, zum Reflex dessen zu werden, was wir ihr entgegenbringen mögen. Sie steht der Kirche immer auch gegenüber, sie wehrt sich dagegen, zum kollektiven Ausdruck von Frömmigkeit zu werden. Ohne ein erratischer Block zu sein oder als ein erstarrtes Traditionsstück zu erscheinen, das interpretierend und kommentierend wieder lebendig gemacht werden müsste, macht sie die Kirche und jedem, jeder einzelnen in ihr auf die Externität aufmerksam, aus der sie existieren. Der Kanon ist ein Zeichen dafür, dass es keinen anderen Grund für Kirche, für Glaube, Hoffnung und Liebe gibt als den, der gelegt ist: Jesus Christus (1.Kor 3,11). Unbeschadet allen geschichtlichen Wechsels und bei aller Vielfalt des Bibellesens wahrt der Kanon ein Maß an gewährter Festigkeit, ohne die die Kirche nicht lebendig bleiben könnte.

---

30 Lønning, „Kanon im Kanon" (s. Anm. 25), 253.
31 Williams, Literalsinn (s. Anm. 3), 68.
32 Mir ist bewusst, dass „Ganzheit" für postmoderne Ohren befremdlich klingen muss und den Verdacht auf eine Totalität nähren mag, die allzu leicht totalitär werden könnte. Die Ganzheit der „Schrift" hat aber – recht verstanden – nichts gemein mit einer allumfassenden Totaldeutung, die alles schon im Vorhinein zu wissen meint. Allerdings unterscheidet sich das Folgende auch von rezeptionsästhetischen Theorien, die der Aktivität des reader-response eine schöpferische Rolle für die Textbildung zumessen; einer solchen Auffassung scheint auch Rowan Williams nicht ganz fern zu stehen.

Was wissen wir eigentlich genauer davon, wie die Alte Kirche ihre Rolle im Prozess der Kanonbildung verstanden hat? Wenn ich recht sehe, besteht eine Wechselbeziehung von Kanonbildung und Selbstklärung der Kirche hinsichtlich ihrer Konstitution als Volk Gottes und Leib Christi, eine Konstitution, die nicht gleichbedeutend ist mit einer institutionellen Selbstkonsolidierung, die sich damals auch herausbildete. Die Kirche – war sie damals eigentlich schon eine klar abgegrenzte Gemeinschaft, über Ortsgemeinden und regionale Zusammenschlüsse hinaus? – hat sich mit der Kanonbildung selber überrascht und sich zugemutet, was sie schwerlich überblicken konnte. Sie hat weder eine schon vorhandene Einheit nur noch als solche deklariert, noch hat sie eine Einheit allererst geschaffen. Vielmehr lernte sie, sich selber als Einheit wahrzunehmen, indem sie der Einheit der Texte, die sie als Kanon auflistete, auf die Spur zu kommen suchte.[33] Von der Innenspannung des Kanons ließ sie sich immer wieder von neuem zu Erkenntnissen führen, sie revidierte frühere Einsichten oder versuchte sie zumindest sprachlich zu klären. Zum Ausdruck brachte sie dies in der Lehre von der ökonomischen Trinität: Gottes Heilshandeln in der Geschichte ist der innere Grund auch der Schrift, in der Gott sich kundtut und bezeugt wird.[34] Gottes Geist ist bei der Entstehung der „Schrift"[35] ebenso wie bei ihrem Lesen am Werke. Später hat das Thema „Inspiration" die Aufmerksamkeit mehr auf die „übernatürliche" Qualität der einzelnen Texte gelenkt als auf die geistgewirkte Erkenntnis der Bibel als Einheit: als das eine Wort Gottes in, mit und unter den vielen unterschiedlichen menschlichen Stimmen der Bezeugung mannigfacher Anrede in Verheißungen und Weisungen Gottes.[36] Wie bei so vielen Konsensbildungen

---

33 So bereits Irenäus, Adv. Haer. I,10; II,28,3; III,24.1; IV,33,7. Für Irenäus sind Kanon und Kirche gleicherweise auf das Evangelium angewiesen, dessen volle und endgültige Wahrheit für sie *extern* bleibt. Und doch kann diese Wahrheit, soweit sie sich Menschen zugänglich macht, zugleich nirgendwo anders als *in* Kanon und Kirche gefunden werden, so wenig sie sich auf sie beschränken lässt.

34 Hier beziehe ich mich auf den Beitrag von John Webster in diesem Band (s.o. S. 95–126). Auch das Vertrauen auf die Allgegenwart Gottes in der „Schrift", wie es z.B. die Leseweise des Origenes leitete (M. Ludlow, Theology and Allegory: Origen and Gregory of Nyssa on the Unity and Diversity of Scripture, International Journal of Systematic Theology 4 [2002] 45–66), dürfte trinitätstheologisch begründet sein.

35 Origenes denkt u.a. an die Zusammenstellung der Evangelien: Sie sei eine geistgeleitete Entscheidung der Kirche, die mit der Vielfalt der Perspektiven der Evangelisten mehr Menschen ansprechen könne (vgl. dazu Comm. in Ioh I,2,12; I,3,20 – 4,21). Bei der Auslegung der Paulusbriefe bemerkt Origenes, dass z.B. der 1. Korintherbrief für Gläubige in einem frühen geistlichen Entwicklungsstadium bestimmt sei, im Unterschied zum Epheserbrief, den Paulus für reifere Christen geschrieben habe. Diese Vielfalt gefährde keinesfalls die Einheit des Evangeliums, das in der gesamten Schrift zu Worte komme (vgl. Comm. in Ioh I,15,85–89). Jesus, der des Guten die Fülle in sich vereinige (I,9,52–59), erlaube selber, ihn in verschiedener Hinsicht wahrzunehmen (X,2–5; bes. 5,21).

36 E. Käsemann schreibt zum Schluss seines oben genannten Aufsatzes (s. Anm. 1): „Der

in der Geschichte der Kirche ist erst später das ganze Ausmaß dieser theologischen Grundentscheidung und deren Tragweite deutlich geworden.

5. Grenzen des Verstehens
Variationen wahrgenommener Christusgemeinschaft

Können wir im einzelnen feststellen, wie diese Einheit so deutlich wie möglich wahrgenommen wurde und in welchen „Themen" sie sich äußerte, so dass im nachhinein verständlich werden kann, warum bestimmte Texte nicht in den Kanon aufgenommen wurden – weil sie tatsächlich eine andere Richtung einschlugen? Ich vermute, dass die theologischen Grenzlinien beim *Christusbild*, beim *Ethos* und bei der *Eschatologie* sichtbar werden.[37] Sie verlaufen oft haarscharf und zeigen sich nicht immer in markanten Sätzen, sondern im weiteren Textzusammenhang als zunächst fast unmerkliche, jedoch allmählich immer stärker spürbare Abweichung und Abkehr: bei der Wahrnehmung der Gestalt Jesu Christi, mit der Frage nach dem christlichen Leben und in der Rechenschaft über die Hoffnung. Diese drei Themen finden sich auch in der frühen christlichen Kunst, in der Katakomben-Malerei.

Zum ersten: *Wer ist Jesus Christus?* Ist er Lehrer und Gesetzgeber, Vorbild für die rechte Lebensführung? In solcher Gestalt kann er äußerst attraktiv sein; dies bestätigt die Missionsgeschichte bis heute. Dann erscheint die christliche Botschaft zunächst als Angebot und Aufforderung, anders zu leben als bisher – vor allem dort, wo Religion sich in erster Linie als lebenspraktische Unterweisung und Erziehung zur Verantwortung für das Gemeinwesen empfiehlt, beispielsweise im konfuzianisch geprägten China und Korea. Das Bemühen, Jesu Verhalten nachzuahmen[38], kann jedoch allzu leicht

---

Geist widerstreitet nicht dem ‚Es steht geschrieben', sondern manifestiert sich in der Schrift. Aber die Schrift kann jederzeit zum Buchstaben werden und wird es, wenn sie nicht mehr vom Geist autorisiert wird, sondern in ihrer Vorfindlichkeit Autorität sein und den Geist ersetzen soll. ... Das heißt, daß der Kanon nicht einfach mit dem Evangelium identisch und Gottes Wort nur insofern ist, als er Evangelium ist und wird. Insofern begründet dann auch er Einheit der Kirche" (223). Damit wird die Verbalinspiration durch die „aktuelle" Inspiration der Predigt des Evangeliums (warum nicht auch des „Gesetzes"?) ersetzt.

37 Diese Vermutung hat Morwenna Ludlow im ganzen bestätigt und mir eine Reihe von Belegen genannt, von denen sie einige in ihrem Beitrag auswertet (s.o. S. 69–94).

38 *Imitatio Christi* bedeutet eben nicht „Nachahmung", sondern „Nachfolge"! Irenäus macht gegen Celsus geltend, dass Jesus die Handlungsweise von Menschen nur deshalb verändern konnte, weil er Gott war (C. Cels. II,51). Erst bei den Kappadoziern bekommt das Befolgen bestimmter Gebote eine größere Bedeutung; es markierte eine Lebensführung im Sinne des „Lebens Jesu".

die geistliche Erkenntnis Jesu Christi verstellen, die uns in die Christusgemeinschaft hineinzieht: An und mit ihm hat Gott gehandelt (vgl. 2.Kor 5,19),
in ihm ist er gegenwärtig als der, dessen Todes wir gedenken, bis dass er
kommt (1.Kor 11,26). Dies allein ist der Grund, Jesus Christus zu verkündi-
gen – und darum auch Mission anders zu verstehen und zu treiben denn als
Ausbreitung des Christentums.

Die Kanonbildung traf eine für das Reden von Jesus Christus maßgeben-
de Entscheidung, indem sie vier Evangelien aufnahm, und zwar zwei grund-
verschiedene Gruppen von Evangelien: die Synoptiker und Johannes.[39] Auch
die „Christologie" des Paulus ist nicht auf einen Nenner zu bringen. Und das
Hören auf das Christuszeugnis des Alten Testaments beschränkt sich keineswegs auf einen sog. Weissagungsbeweis, sondern lernt, nach dem Verhältnis
von „Verheißung" und „Erfüllung" zu fragen. Immer wieder betonen Kirchenväter wie Irenäus und Origenes, wie entscheidend das Lesen des Alten
Testaments für das Leben und die Einheit der Kirche seien und dass die Kirche aufs Schwerste geschädigt werden würde, wollte sie das Alte Testament
auslassen. Dies alles bringt freilich auch erhebliche Spannungen mit sich, die
zu neuen Leseweisen führen, nicht zu einem uferlosen Vielerlei, vielmehr zu
einer einheitlichen Christuserkenntnis. Die altkirchliche Dogmenbildung hat
im Grunde nichts anderes versucht, als diese Einheitlichkeit in ihrer notwendigen Spannweite begrifflich zum Ausdruck zu bringen.[40]

„Was Christum treibet": was besagt diese berühmt-berüchtigte Wendung
Luthers, mit der er präzisieren wollte, was kanonisch ist?[41] Wer von uns kann
darüber befinden, was wirklich „von Christus handelt" und was nicht? Luther
meinte offensichtlich die Klarheit der Schrift und ihre „Einfalt", d.h. ihre Einheit hinsichtlich dessen, was für das Heil notwendig ist. „Was Christum treibet", treibt uns zur Fülle des Gotteshandelns hin, zu Jesus Christus gestern,
heute und in Ewigkeit. Im Hintergrund der Wendung Luthers stehen eine
weitgespannte Christologie und Trinitätslehre, die beide freilich erst aus der
Kunst des Lesens der „Schrift" immer wieder von neuem in ihrem Ausmaß
und in ihrer Tragweite verstanden werden können. Zugleich leiten sie zum
intensiven und extensiven Lesen der Schrift an, zur Entdeckung von Zusammenhängen, die einer bloß historischen Kenntnisnahme verschlossen bleiben.

---

39 Ihre Unterschiedlichkeit kann als einer der Reichtümer der Bibel gesehen werden; vgl.
    den Beitrag von John Barton in diesem Band (S. 11–26). Vgl. auch oben Anm. 35.
40 Zu Recht versteht Robert Morgan (s.o. S. 151–193) daher die Inkarnation als Grundfigur
    auch für den Kanon. Sie wurde vor allem in der Auseinandersetzung mit der gnostischen
    Verachtung der Menschlichkeit Jesu Christi bedeutsam, und gerade dafür war die
    Berufung auf den Kanon ausschlaggebend.
41 „Auch ist das der rechte Prüfstein alle Bücher zu tadeln, wenn man siehet, ob sie
    Christum treiben oder nicht, sintemal alle Schrift Christum zeiget, Rom 3[,21]. Und S.
    Paulus nichts denn Christum wissen will, 1.Kor 2[,2]" (WA.DB 7,385,26–29).

Zum zweiten: *Was charakterisiert „christliches Leben"?* Es ist immer
wieder beobachtet worden, dass weder einzelne neutestamentliche Schriften
noch das Neue Testament als Ganzes eine „neue Moral" umreißen. (Nicht
von ungefähr ist der „Hirt des Hermas" nicht in den Kanon aufgenommen
worden, obwohl er für katechetische Zwecke benutzt wurde.) Und doch werden Unterscheidungsmerkmale deutlich, die allerdings nicht mit einem bestimmten Tun und Lassen zur Deckung kommen.[42] Christliches, „neues" Leben besteht im Sein in Christus (2.Kor 5,17), „evangeliumsgemäßes" Leben
ist Leben aus und unter dem Evangelium, in der Erwartung des richtenden
und rettenden Handelns Gottes.[43] Reicht das aus, um „christliche Identität" zu
markieren? Die Versuche, christliches Leben als eine distinkte Art der Lebensführung auszuzeichnen und es dadurch zu identifizieren, in Abgrenzung
zu dem, was andere tun und lassen, verbleiben nicht innerhalb der Grenzen
des Kanons.

War dies nicht auch Grund genug für Martin Luther, als er den Jakobus-
brief eine „stroherne Epistel" nannte?[44] Er wollte ihn ja doch nicht als ein
Dokument eines pseudochristlichen Moralismus ausgrenzen, vielmehr be-
fürchtete er gerade eine Engführung des christlichen Lebens, die sich auf diese Schrift berufen könnte, eine irreführende Zuordnung von „Glaube" und
„Werken".

Zum dritten: Zukunfts- und auch Jenseitsvorstellungen drohen die ge-
währte *Hoffnung* zu überwuchern: die Hoffnung wider Erwarten, die an *Gottes Verheißungen* Anteil gibt. In der Abwehr irreführender Vorstellungen ist
die altkirchliche Eschatologie[45] sprachärmer geworden als die Bußprediger,
die meinten, sagen zu können, welches Verhalten himmlischen Gewinn
bringt, oder diejenigen, die göttliches Leben im menschlichen Dasein zu di-
agnostizieren versprachen, oder andere, die wie etwa Lactanz (*Institutiones
Divinae* VII) die Anzeichen des Weltendes aus den Zeichen der Zeit deuten
wollten. Die Verheißungen der Gottesgerechtigkeit, des Friedens, der Gottes-
ruhe, des Lebens mit Gott und der Gotteserkenntnis als vielfältige Zusage
Gottes aufzufassen, die einen einheitlichen Erwartungshorizont bilden: dafür
bedurfte es der *lectio continua* des Alten und des Neuen Testamentes. Andererseits konnten Versuche, dem Zusammenhang zwischen Altem und Neuem

---

42 Für die Alte Kirche wurde die Aristotelische Ethik mit ihrer Kultivierung von Tugenden
    maßgebend: Was „ich bin", ist viel wichtiger als das, was „ich tue".
43 Wie dies mit der Suche nach christlicher Identität einhergeht, verfolgt Michael Wolter in
    seinem Beitrag (s.o. S. 45–68, bes. Abschn. 3 [S. 53ff.]).
44 WA.DB 6,10,33f.
45 Vgl. B. Daley, Patristische Eschatologie, in: ders. (unter Mitarbeit von J. Schreiner/H.E.
    Lona), Eschatologie. In der Schrift und Patristik, Handbuch der Dogmengeschichte
    IV/7a, Freiburg/Basel/Wien 1986, 84–248.

Testament geschichtstheologisch nachzuspüren, sich als eine Falle erweisen. Wenn Irenäus meinte, das Eschaton in vielen alttestamentlichen Details vorweg abgeschattet zu sehen, lag die Gefahr nahe, daraus die Zukunft vorherzusagen. Die Johannes-Offenbarung wurde zunächst als Prophetie gelesen, die das Geschick der Kirche beleuchtet, doch bald wurde sie mehr und mehr als Beschreibung von Endereignissen aufgefasst.

Dass Gott sich mit seinem Handeln noch zurückhält – nicht obwohl, sondern gerade weil er sich in Jesus Christus ein für allemal ausgesprochen hat: dies im einzelnen auszusagen und zu denken fiel schwer. Wenn es gelang, wurde es ein Zeichen lebendiger Hoffnung, ausgespannt zwischen Gedenken und Erwartung Jesu Christi, des Kommenden. An diesem Bekenntnis der Hoffnung festzuhalten, war nur dank des Kanons möglich: nicht nur, weil sich in seinen Texten die Kontur dieses Bekenntnisses abzeichnet. Vielmehr spiegeln die Schriften des Kanons die Schwierigkeiten wider, die Hoffnung auf Gottes Handeln nicht mit einem Leben im Wartestand oder mit einer inneren Umstimmung zu verwechseln, die sich vom Lauf der Dinge und dem Gang der Welt nicht stören lässt.

Zusammengenommen ermöglichen diese drei Grenzziehungen, gerade in ihrer Beziehung zueinander, den Kristallisationsvorgang für ein immer weiter ausgreifendes und gleichwohl trennscharfes Christuszeugnis und Bekenntnis zu Gottes Gegenwart in der Geschichte Jesu Christi. Der Kanon ist darum zuallererst die „Urkunde für den Vollzug der kirchengründenden Predigt[46], eine Kunde, die weiter geht, um gehört zu werden und zum Glauben, zur Hoffnung und zur Liebe zu rufen. Dazu *ermutigt* der Kanon.

Die Kanonbildung hat Grenzlinien markiert, an denen Christen entlanggegangen sind und an denen sie erfahren haben, dass sich hier christlicher Glaube und christliches Leben geschieden haben von anderer Frömmigkeit, die sich ebenfalls auf Jesus von Nazareth berief. Es sind Grenzlinien, die immer wieder beachtet werden müssen; der Kanon hilft dazu, aber wir „haben" den Kanon nicht derart, dass die von ihm ausgeschlossenen Möglichkeiten gar nicht mehr vorhanden wären – im Gegenteil: die Unterscheidungen, die der Kanon markiert, müssen immer wieder neu getroffen werden, sie können sich leicht zu dehnbaren Toleranzgrenzen mutieren. Und es ist in der Kirchen- und Theologiegeschichte je und dann versucht worden, die Grenzlinien überhaupt zu verlegen – der Streit der Reformatoren mit Rom um die Rechtfertigungslehre ist dafür ein Beispiel von vielen. Die Grenzlinien des Kanons lassen sich auch nicht systemtheoretisch erklären: indem das Ausgegrenzte einfach als irrelevant behandelt wird. Nein, was jenseits der Kanon-

---

46 M. Kähler, Der sogenannte historische Jesus und der geschichtliche, biblische Christus, Leipzig ²1896, 22; neu hg.v. E. Wolf (TB 2), München 1956, 7f., Anm. a.

grenzen gedacht, als überzeugend empfunden und dementsprechend als lebensbestimmend angesehen wird, kann durchaus als plausibel und relevant gelten, oftmals schaut es viel attraktiver als das Kanonische aus, weil es sich einfach, schlüssig, lebensdienlich, realistisch und trotzdem vorbildlich ausnimmt. Um solcher Verwechslung nicht zu verfallen, können wir nicht aufhören, den Grenzgang entlang des Kanons weiterzugehen.[47] Das bedeutet jedoch nicht, dass die Kanonbildung fortgesetzt würde, etwa dadurch, dass auf neu entdeckte Quellen zu spekulieren wäre, die „die Schrift" erweitern könnten, ja mehr noch: die ihren Charakter verändern könnte.

Die Rolle Marcions für die Entstehung des neutestamentlichen Kanons mag früher vielleicht oft überschätzt worden sein. Gleichwohl war die Entscheidung gegen seine so herrlich profilierte und scheinbar eindeutige Theologie, die mit der Kanonbildung verbunden war, eine Selbstverpflichtung der Kirche gegen jeden theologischen Reduktionismus. Die Alte Kirche hat mit der Kanonbildung eine staunenswerte Freiheit, einen bewunderungswürdigen Mut bewiesen, indem sie sich auf eine Vielfalt von Zeugnissen einließ, die eine erhebliche Innenspannung erzeugt. Das Staunen über diesen Mut wird auch nicht dadurch geschmälert, dass die Kanonbildung mit einer Konsilidierung großkirchlicher Strukturen einherging. Sie konnte die Selbstbewegung vieler lokaler Glaubenstraditionen nicht mehr weiter gewähren lassen, wenn sie die eben skizzierten Grenzen überschritten. Die Kanonbildung ist *auch* eine Notstandsmaßnahme angesichts bedrohter Einheit gewesen. Der Kirche blieb gar keine andere Wahl, als normative Entscheidungen zu treffen, wenn sie Andersdenkende und Andersglaubende – „Häretiker" und „Ketzer" – als solche markieren musste, weil sie nichts mit ihnen zu tun haben konnte. Doch dabei geriet der Unterschied von „Richtigem" und „Falschem" viel zu sehr in den Vordergrund, statt zu sagen, woraus Christen leben können und woraus nicht: die getrübte Quelle wird wieder klar. Jetzt scheidet sich, was von Gott her unerschöpflich ist, von dem, was sich rasch erschöpft.

Die *ermutigende Zu-mutung*, sich auf ein komplexes und spannungsvolles Textgebilde einzulassen, sich seiner Wirkung anzuvertrauen, die sich nicht im vorhinein einschätzen oder gar einschränken lässt: die Ermutigung dazu gibt die Kirche mit der „Schrift" weiter – es ist keine selbstgewählte Bereitschaft, und schon gar nicht genießt die Kirche eine Vielstimmigkeit, um der Eintönigkeit zu entgehen. Dass diese Zumutung der „Schrift" immer wieder zu schaffen macht, zeigt sich beispielsweise in der Schwierigkeit, den Jako-

---

47 Auch dies gehört m.E. zur „Fortverfolgung" des Lesens, in der sich der Kanon als „heilige Schrift" erweist: als „Lesekanon", dem sich die „Lesekunst" für das verdankt, was „nützlich" für den Glauben ist; s. auch den Beitrag von Günter Bader (S. 249–288).

busbrief und die Johannes-Apokalypse als integralen Bestandteil des Kanons anzuerkennen – nicht einfach hinzunehmen und dann theologisch zu unterdrücken, sondern sie als unverzichtbare Stimmen im Kanon zu hören. All dies gehört zum recht spannungsvollen, oft anstrengenden, aber nie ermüdenden „Leben mit der Bibel". Ihre Unteilbarkeit verlangt ungeteilte Aufmerksamkeit. Sie schenkt dafür die einfältige Eindeutigkeit des ausgesprochenen Ja Gottes zu seinen Verheißungen, seines „in Christus" gegebenen Treueversprechens, in dem unser Ja befestigt wird und seinen Halt gewinnt (2.Kor 1,20). Die Aufmerksamkeit dafür muss sich die Theologie angelegen sein lassen. Sie wird ihr durch den Kanon gewährt, doch die Theologie muss sie in glaubensnotwendigen Grenzziehungen stets neu bewähren.

Der Kanon begründet also weder die Vielfalt der Konfessionen, noch garantiert er die Einheit der Kirche – auch nicht einer Kirche, die sich als eine dynamische Einheit begreifen will, die damit den Verdacht auf Uniformität abstreifen und einer belebenden Pluralität Raum geben möchte. Vielmehr ist der Kanon ein Zeugnis dafür, dass die Kirche sich an der Ganzheit der „Schrift" ausrichtet, von der sie eine endgültige Wegweisung erwarten darf. Damit wird sie der Nähe Jesu Christi gewärtig. Es ist eine Nähe, die nicht durch Authentizität der Verfasser biblischer Schriften u.ä. theoretisch abgesichert werden kann, auch wenn dies später versucht worden ist. Sie ergibt sich daraus, dass ein Ganzes (der Kanon) als eine Einheit eigener Art akzeptiert wird, die eine unermessliche Spannweite in sich enthält. Ihr vertraut sich die Kirche an. Nicht aufgenommen, ja abgewehrt wird, was den Erwartungshorizont, den die Schrift als Ganzes mitteilt, einschränken könnte. Mag die Kanonbildung literaturgeschichtlich als eine Reduktion erscheinen, so ist dies doch keine substanzielle Einschränkung. Vielmehr bedeutet es ein Sich-Aufschließen für den Erwartungshorizont, den die Kirche mit aller Schöpfung teilt. Nur so bewährt der Kanon seine Einheitlichkeit und seinen inneren Zusammenhalt.

Die Kirche hat dieses Ganze nicht zu garantieren, sie kann es auch gar nicht ermessen und ausloten. Sie wird durch die Schrift auf die externe Konstitution ihrer Einheit verwiesen, auf die Einheit, die ihr vorgegeben ist und die sie zu bewahren hat. Dafür bedarf sie der Urteilskraft für die gegliederte Einheit des Kanons, die gleichfalls extern konstituiert ist: durch das *verbum externum*, das Worthandeln Gottes an und mit Menschen. Im Leben mit der Bibel, in einer unaufhörlich spannungsvollen Lesepraxis wird die Kirche damit vertraut, dass sie dieses Wort in der Schrift vernimmt und dass sie abseits dieses Vernehmens auch nie zu ihrer Einheit finden kann. Eine buntgescheckte Textmenge strukturiert sich mit Hilfe einer Doppelgleichung: Heilserkenntnis (Christusgemeinschaft) = Ästhetik (die Grenzen des Kanons sichern Vielfalt) = Hermeneutik (Grenzen des Verstehens). So wird die Einheit der Kirche daran wahrnehmbar, wie sie sich der Einheit der Schrift aussetzt – und umgekehrt: die Ganzheit der Schrift bewährt sich im Konsens der Kirche. Die Kirche sieht sich in den weiten Raum gestellt, den die Schrift umreißt.[48]

Die Einheit der Schrift tritt dadurch in Erscheinung, dass die vielerlei Stimmen, die im Kanon hörbar werden, diesen Raum abschreiten, ohne dass sie ihn jemals ausfüllen könnten. Die Schriftzeugen stimmen darin überein, dass sie in die Geschichte Gottes mit den Menschen hineingezogen worden sind, und zwar so, wie diese Geschichte durch Jesus Christus umfangen ist. Aufgeschlossen wird sie durch die Erwartung seines Kommens und durch das Gedenken seines Gekommenseins. In diese Geschichte stimmen die Schriftzeugen ein, nicht mit einem Unisono, sondern mit einer innerlich geordneten Vielstimmigkeit. Der Kanon gleicht der gewaltigen Partitur einer Doxologie, mit vielen Bestandteilen und Formen.

Wir, die Leserinnen und Leser, die wir hier gleichsam mitspielen, wenn wir die Partitur oder Teile von ihr aufführen, haben auf den Zusammenklang zu achten, wenn wir mit unserer Stimme einfallen und dabei auch improvisieren, wo uns Raum dafür gelassen wird. Wir brauchen ein feines Gespür dafür, inwiefern die anderen Stimmen das Ihrige dazu beitragen und wie sie mit ihrem Einsatz, aber auch in ihren Pausen, zu einem vollen, reichen Gesamtklang beitragen.

---

48 Hier schließe ich mich den Ausführungen von Paul Fiddes (s.o. S. 127–149) an.

Kanon, Kanon und Wiederholung
Zu Lesekanon, Singkanon und zur kanonischen Veränderung

von Günter Bader

Man muß so lange lesen,
bis man eine Bibel findet.
Friedrich Schlegel[1]

Als ‚Theologie des Lesens' lässt sich wohl am ehesten dasjenige Exerzitium
eines auf Erfahrung gerichteten Geistes bezeichnen, das nicht nur Theologie
lesenderweise praktiziert – was vorkommen soll – , sondern vielmehr im Verfolg konsequenten Lesens Theologie allererst aufsucht und findet. Oder findet, und darum aufsucht. Keines von beidem schließt das andere aus. Aus
dem Themenkomplex, der damit zusammenhängt, wird im Folgenden lediglich *ein* Kapitel vorgetragen, wenn auch ein elementares. An sich ist nur
höchste Formvollendung dafür gut genug. Stattdessen muss hier eine bloße
Skizze genügen. Es geht um den Versuch, den Begriff des Kanons der hl.
Schrift soweit und nur soweit zu entfalten, als er auf lesetheoretischem Wege
zu konstruieren ist.

Es sei vorausgesetzt, dass die Bestimmung des Kanons der hl. Schrift in
direktem Zugriff nicht möglich ist. Daher wird in *I. Lesekanon* im Ausgang
von einem Kanontext Martin Luthers und seiner patristischen Tradition der
Weg beschritten, den Kanon der hl. Schrift auf dem Umweg über die Literatur ins Auge zu fassen. Dies führt zwar zu einem festen Begriff von Kanon,
aber nur von Kanon der Literatur. Resultat dieses Abschnitts ist der literarische Kanon, aber nicht der Kanon der hl. Schrift. In dieser Situation wird,
unter Festhaltung des in I. erworbenen Begriffs des Literarischen, eine neue
Anstrengung erforderlich. Sie läuft in *II. Singkanon* im Ausgang von einem
Kanontext des Pseudo-Dionysius Areopagita und seiner patristischen Tradition so, dass ein Weg beschritten wird, der den Kanon der hl. Schrift auf dem
Umweg über das Phänomen des rituell-musischen Kanons zu erreichen sucht.
Resultat dieses Abschnitts ist es, dass wir am Ende zwar einen festen Begriff

---

1   F. Schlegel, Kritische Ausgabe, hg. v. E. Behler, II/18. Schriften aus dem Nachlaß. Phi-
    losophische Lehrjahre 1796-1806, München u.a. 1963, 265 [Nr. 850]; Sommer 1798.

des musikalischen Kanons besitzen, nicht aber den Kanon der hl. Schrift. In dieser Situation wird, unter Festhaltung des in II. erworbenen Begriffs der Wiederholung, eine neue Anstrengung erforderlich. *III. Kanonische Verän-derung* unternimmt den Versuch, Wiederholung als das, was den Kanon zum Kanon macht, nicht nur als musisches Phänomen anzuerkennen, das dem Text stets äußerlich bleiben müsste, sondern es im Inneren des Literarischen selbst nachzuweisen. Bei dieser Aufsuchung von hl. Schrift wird dem Psalter eine ganz herausragende Rolle zufallen.

1. Lesekanon

Text-Installation

i. *Athanasius von Alexandrien* hat bekanntlich die Dreiteilung modifiziert, die zur Beschreibung des Kanonizitätsgrads eines Textes bisher gebräuchlich war. Hatte Origenes ὁμολογούμενα (allgemein anerkannte), ἀμφιβαλλόμενα (in ihrer Echtheit umstrittene) und ψευδῆ (von Häretikern untergeschobene Schriften) unterschieden, und ihm folgend Euseb ὁμολογούμενα (allgemein anerkannte), ἀντιλεγόμενα (umstrittene) und νόθα (als unecht zu verwerfende Schriften), so reduzierte Athanasius im 39. Osterfestbrief des Jahres 367, wie Wilhelm Schneemelcher behauptet, die Dreizahl der Rubriken auf eine Zwei-zahl, nämlich auf den Gegensatz zwischen kanonischen und apokryphen Schriften.[2] Jedoch die bisherige mittlere Rubrik findet sich bei Athanasius rasch wieder. Dieser unterscheidet nämlich unter den nichtkanonischen Schriften alsbald eine Gruppe, die einerseits nicht kanonisch, andererseits nicht apokryph genannt werden kann. Sie steht in auffälliger Ambivalenz zwischen beiden. Die Terminologie ist an dieser Stelle aus Gründen, die nicht Athanasius zu verantworten hat, etwas verwirrlich. Er meint mit der in Frage stehenden Zwischenrubrik eine Textgruppe, die wir nach reformatorischem Sprachgebrauch (wenigstens was das Alte Testament anlangt) „Apokryphen" nennen. Dagegen für Athanasius selbst sind die ἀπόκρυφα identisch mit den ψευδῆ des Origenes und den νόθα des Euseb. Nach der Auflistung der kanoni-schen Schriften Alten und Neuen Testaments fährt Athanasius fort:

---

2 W. Schneemelcher, Art. Bibel. III. Die Entstehung des Kanons des Neuen Testaments und der christlichen Bibel, TRE 6 (1980) 22–48, S. 42,15ff.; 43,33ff.; 44,45ff.: „Weiter ist zu bemerken, daß die Dreiteilung des Origenes und des Euseb von Athanasius aufge-geben ist. Er kennt nur die anerkannten Schriften und die von den Häretikern erfundenen Apokryphen. Lediglich einige wenige Schriften (...) duldet er als Lektüre für die neu in die Kirche Aufgenommenen."

Ἀλλ' ἕνεκά γε πλείονος ἀκριβείας προστίθημι δὴ τοῦτο γράφων ἀναγκαίως, ὡς ὅτι ἔστι καὶ ἕτερα βιβλία τούτων ἔξωθεν, οὐ κανονιζόμενα μέν, τετυπωμένα δὲ παρὰ τῶν Πατέρων ἀναγινώσκεσθαι τοῖς ἄρτι προσερχομένοις καὶ βουλομένοις κατηχεῖσθαι τὸν τῆς εὐσεβείας λόγον· Σοφία Σαλομῶντος, καὶ Σοφία Σιράχ, καὶ Ἐσθήρ, καὶ Ἰουδίθ, καὶ Τωβίας, καὶ δι-δαχὴ καλουμένη τῶν Ἀποστόλων, καὶ ὁ Ποιμήν. Καὶ ὅμως, ἀγαπητοί, κἀκείνων κανο-νιζομένων, καὶ τούτων ἀναγινωσκομένων, οὐδαμοῦ τῶν ἀποκρύφων μνήμη· ...

Aber um der größeren Genauigkeit willen muss ich, wenn ich dieses schreibe, notwen-digerweise noch hinzufügen, dass es auch noch andere Bücher außer diesen gibt, die zwar nicht kanonisiert sind, aber von den Vätern zur Lektüre für diejenigen bestimmt wurden, die neu hinzutreten und in der Lehre der Frömmigkeit unterwiesen werden wollen: die Weisheit Salomos, die Weisheit Sirachs, Esther, Judith, Tobias, die sogenannte Lehre der Apostel und der Hirte. Und wiewohl je-ne, ihr Lieben, kanonisiert sind und diese der Lektüre dienen, so sind die Apokryphen nir-gendwo erwähnt... [3]

Athanasius – soweit ist Schneemelcher zuzustimmen – kennt für die fragliche Mittelgruppe keinen selbständigen Terminus. Er beschreibt sie, indem er ihre Ambivalenz zwischen ἀπόκρυφα und κανονιζόμενα zum Ausdruck bringt. Da-bei entstehen Sätze mit einem charakteristischen μὲν/δέ. Im übrigen muss die Zwischengruppe sich mit der Beschreibung begnügen, es handle sich um Ge-lesenes: ἀναγινωσκόμενα. Doch gelesen wird viel. Es entsteht dabei das Pa-radox: Nicht nur Gelesenes wird gelesen, auch das Kanonische, auch das A-pokryphe ist prinzipiell lesbar. Somit verflüchtigt sich der Terminus der mitt-leren Textgattung und nimmt anstelle des spezifischen den generellen Sinn an: Lesbares überhaupt.

ii. *Hieronymus* hat entweder die Wendung des Athanasius direkt aufgenom-men oder erfindet sie neu. In der Vorrede zu den Büchern Salomos, die auch als Vorrede zu den Hagiographen insgesamt gilt, schreibt er, wohl im Jahr 398:

Fertur et παναρετος Iesu filii Sirach liber, et alius ψευδεπιγραφος, qui Sapientia Salomonis inscribitur. ... Sicut ergo Iudith et Tobi et Macchabeorum libros legit quidem Ecclesia, sed inter canonicas scripturas non recipit, sic et haec duo volumina legat ad aedificationem ple-bis, non ad auctoritatem ecclesiasticorum dogmatum confirmandam. [4]

Die athanasische Formel für die ambivalente Mittelgruppe οὐ κανονιζόμενα μέν, τετυπωμένα δὲ ... ἀναγινώσκεσθαι wiederholt sich bei Hieronymus, wenngleich unter Umstellung der Glieder: *legit quidem Ecclesia, sed inter canonicas scripturas non recipit.* Es gibt Lesen überhaupt. Es gibt kanoni-sches Lesen. Was ist kanonisches Lesen? Lesen auf kirchliche Lehrsätze hin?

---

3 Athanasius von Alexandrien, Ep. 39 (PG 26,1437C–1440A); deutsch auch in: NTApo⁵. I. Evangelien, Tübingen 1987, 40.
4 Hieronymus, Prologus in libris Salomonis, in: Biblia sacra iuxta vulgatam versionem, ed. R. Weber, Stuttgart 1969, p. 957; ebenso PL 28,598–602.

iii. *Hugo von St. Viktor* hat präzise das Zwar/Aber des Athanasius und des
Hieronymus im Ohr, wenn er die Aufzählung der kanonischen Bücher zwischen Altem und Neuem Testament mit der Bemerkung unterbricht:

Sunt praeterea alii quidam libri, ut Sapientia Salomonis, liber Iesu filii Sirach, et liber Iudith,
et Tobias, et libri Machabaeorum, qui leguntur quidem, sed non scribuntur in canone.[5]

Gewiss wäre es am übersichtlichsten, wenn die Menge des Lesbaren einfach
mit der Menge des Kanonischen koinzidierte, wie es der Fall sein würde,
wenn entweder überhaupt nur Kanonisches lesbar wäre – Kirchen werden mit
repressiven Bestrebungen dieser Art leicht in Verbindung gebracht –, oder
wenn erst das Lesbare insgesamt als Grenze des Kanonischen gälte, wofür –
etwa an Universitäten – nicht nur schlechte Gründe sprechen. Aber beides
trifft nicht zu. Lesbares und Kanonisches sind Mengen unterschiedlicher
Größe, wobei das Kanonische stets als Teilmenge des Lesbaren auftritt. Ein
solches Unterscheidungsbedürfnis bringt erst die Frage nach dem Kanon hervor. Aufgabe des Kanons ist es, Lesbares von Lesbarem zu unterscheiden.
Diese Funktion nimmt Hugos von St. Viktor *Didascalicon* von 1125/27 wahr.
Es sticht aus den mittelalterlichen und frühmittelalterlichen Wissenschafts-
lehren Augustins, Cassiodors, Isidors von Sevilla oder des Hrabanus Maurus
dadurch hervor, dass es verspricht, im bloßen Verfolg des Lesens – *lectio* –
zu einem Begriff von heiliger Schrift zu gelangen und demnach auch zu einem Begriff von Theologie. Theologie beruht auf der Unterscheidbarkeit von
heiliger Schrift unter den Schriften. *Theologia* ist ‚sacra‘ *pagina*. Hugo von
St. Viktor will seinen Gegenstand lesetheoretisch gewinnen. *Theologia* entsteht durch konsequentes Lesen. Konsequentes Lesen führt zu ‚divina‘ *lectio*,
wie es mit einem alten monastischen Terminus heißt. Deshalb verfährt das
Didascalicon in Ausführung des Untertitels *De studio legendi* so, dass es sich
auf den Überschritt von der *lectio saecularium artium* (lb. I–III) zur *lectio
divinarum scripturarum* (lb. IV–VI) konzentriert. Im Ganzen des christlichen
Lebens kommt aber der *lectio* nur eine beschränkte Aufgabe zu. Lesen ist
nicht alles. Die *lectio* soll den Vervollkommnungsweg lediglich initiieren,
der über *meditatio, oratio, operatio* zum Ziel der *contemplatio* führt.[6] Das

---

5 Hugo von St. Viktor, Didascalicon. De studio legendi, IV,2 (übers. u. eingel. v. Th. Of-
   fergeld, FC 27 [1997] 274,12–15). Der Text des Hieronymus aus der Vorrede auf die
   Bücher Salomos, auf den hier Bezug genommen wird, ist wörtlich zitiert Didascalicon
   IV,8 (a.a.O., 294,3–16). Dazu: R. Berndt, Gehören die Kirchenväter zur Heiligen
   Schrift? Zur Kanontheorie des Hugo von Sankt Viktor, JBTh 3 (1988) 191–199.
6 Hugo von St. Viktor, Didascalicon V,9 (a.a.O., 348ff.): De quattuor gradibus. Dazu: K.
   Ruh, Geschichte der abendländischen Mystik. I. Die Grundlegung durch die Kirchenvä-
   ter und die Mönchstheologie des 12. Jahrhunderts, München 1990, 332.360.368.370.

Initium findet aber nur statt, wenn es bereits auf der untersten Stufe gelungen ist, göttliches Lesen zu unterscheiden von Lesen überhaupt.[7]

iv. *Martin Luther* steht nahezu wörtlich in dieser Zwar/Aber-Tradition. Seit 1534 findet sich in der Deutschen Bibel beim Übergang zu den Apokryphen folgende Notiz:

APOCRYPHA: DAS SIND BÜCHER: so der heiligen Schrifft nicht gleich gehalten / vnd doch nützlich vnd gut zu lesen sind / Als nemlich /

I	Judith.
II	Sapientia.
III	Tobias.
IIII	Syrach.
V	Baruch.
VI	Maccabeorum.
VII	Stücke in Esther.
VIII	Stücke in Daniel.[8]

Neben den Kanontafeln zu Beginn der beiden Testamente dürfte dieser Hinweis wohl das einzige Exemplar eines technischen Textinstallationstextes[9] sein, das in der Lutherbibel begegnet. War es bereits bei Athanasius auffällig, dass das Erfordernis der Genauigkeit ($\dot{\alpha}\kappa\rho\acute{\iota}\beta\epsilon\iota\alpha$), das an sich streng mit dem Kanon verbunden ist, sich auch auf die Mittelgruppe erstreckte, so erstaunt erst recht Luther, der durch Bezifferung und senkrechte Anordnung den Eindruck einer kanonischen Liste hervorruft, wiewohl am falschen Platz. Das hat zur Folge, dass jetzt nicht nur, wie bereits gesehen, der Begriff des Lesens quer hindurch geht, sondern auch der Begriff des Kanons, der Kanonisches wie Nichtkanonisches bezeichnet, was wiederum paradox ist. Der Terminus des Deuterokanonischen bringt dies zutreffend, wenn auch mit entschärfender Tendenz zum Ausdruck. Deuterokanonisch ist der nichtkanonische Kanon. Nicht nur die Lesbarkeit oszilliert, auch die Kanonizität. Insgesamt bildet sich eine Hierarchie von Textgruppen, denen in absteigender Richtung Prädikate wie „Theologisch wertvoll zu lesen", „Nützlich und gut zu lesen", „Zu lesen" zugeordnet werden können, wobei die beiden ersten Prädikate durch kanonische bzw. deuterokanonische Listen zu präzisieren sind, wäh-

7   Die Hauptstrukturen des Lesens wiederholen sich; es werden hier und da unterschieden *ordo* und *modus legendi* (säkular: III,1.8f.; theologisch: IV,2ff.; V,1ff.; VI,1ff.12). Die Differenz zwischen Lesen überhaupt und göttlichem Lesen liegt in der kleineren oder größeren Anzahl der Schriftsinne (V,2ff.; VI,1ff.).

8   Martin Luther, WA.DB 12/2,1–4: waagrechte Anordnung; hier zitiert nach: D. Martin Luther, Die gantze Heilige Schrifft Deudsch, hg. v. H. Volz, München 1972, 1674,1–11: senkrechte Anordnung. Im Folgenden beziehe ich mich auf diese Ausgabe.

9   A. Hölter unterscheidet den Textinstallationstext als „Kanontext" streng von dem dadurch definierten „kanonischen Text": Kanon als Text, in: M. Moog-Grünewald (Hg.), Kanon und Theorie, Heidelberg 1997, 21–39, S. 22.

rend das dritte auf ein Gebiet verweist, das kaum noch überblickbar sein
dürfte.

Die wahre Grenze zwischen Kanonischem und Nichtkanonischem wird
damit weiter nach außen verlagert und kommt an die Stelle, an der Lesbares
überhaupt und nützlich und gut zu Lesendes aneinander stoßen. Was nun in
einzelnen nützlich und gut zu lesen ist: dafür findet sich in Luthers Vorreden
zu den Apokryphen eine ziemlich detaillierte Kriteriologie.[10] Apokryphen
haben das Griechische als Grundlage. Dementsprechend kommen Kategorien
griechischer Poetik und Hermeneutik ins Spiel. Was die Seite der Produktion
anlangt, so wird die Aufmerksamkeit des Lesers nicht nur gerichtet auf Einheit oder Vielheit des Autors,[11] sondern insbesondere auf den Grad der Inspiriertheit durch den Hl. Geist. Je geistreicher und heiliger der Poet, desto nütz-
licher der Text.[12] Allerdings ist genau zu unterscheiden zwischen der Autorschaft des Hl. Geistes selbst und der Autorschaft von Menschen im Hl.
Geist[13]; nur Letzteres trifft auf die Apopkryphen zu. Außerdem findet sich so
etwas wie eine rudimentäre Gattungspoetik. Es begegnet etwa die aristotelische Unterscheidung von Geschichte und Gedicht; wider Erwarten gibt Luther nicht dem Historischen, sondern dem Poetischen den Zuschlag.[14] Oder
das dramatisch-liturgische Spiel der Juden: Luther mutmaßt, dieses habe
einstmals die Griechen Komödie und Tragödie gelehrt.[15] Oder Phänomene
wie *nomina loquentes* und prosopopoietische Rede *sub persona*, die unter
dem Zensus des Historikers der Kritik verfielen: hier wecken sie nicht nur
kein Misstrauen, sondern werden geradezu als Qualitätszeichen poetischer
Texte gerühmt.[16] Und was die Seite der Rezeption anlangt, so finden sich in

---

10 Nützlich und gut zu lesen 1674,3; 1675,43f.; 1732,16f.; nützlich 1751,44; 1841,8.17;
    gut 1700,32; 1751,15; 1901,18.
11 Einer oder mehrere Verfasser: 1751,32ff.; 1901,4ff.
12 Autorbezeichnungen: Dichter 1675,14; 1699,6; 1731,14; Poet 1675,46; 1731,7;
    1732,18; Prophet 1675,46; 1731,14; Meister 1699,17f.; 1731,37; 1751,13.34; 1901,5;
    Sänger 1731,14; Hl. Geist als Inspirator 1675,46f.; 1701,45; geistlich 1675,17.45;
    1943,13f.; geistreich 1674,36f.; 1731,7; 1827,6; heilig 1674,17.36; 1731,4.
13 Der 111. Psalm ausgelegt (1530), WA 31/1,393,16–19: „weil der heilige geist, der ho-
    hest und beste Poet odder tichter zuvoren bereit besser und feiner lieder (nemlich die lie-
    ben Psalmen) gemacht hat, Gott damit zu dancken und loben, hab ich meine garstige und
    schnöde Poeterey odder geticht lassen faren ...“ – In XV Psalmos graduum (1532/33
    [1540]), WA 40/3,270,2f.: Et videbitis hoc, spiritum sanctum esse optimum Poetam et
    Oratorem, qui sciat regulas artis dicendi et persuadendi.
14 Geschichte/Gedicht: 1674,35ff.; 1675,7.36; 1731,4ff.; 1900,5, 1901,2; 1943,13f.20.
15 Herkunft von Komödie und Tragödie: 1731,18ff.
16 Literarische Namen und (dramatische) Personen: 1675,19ff.; 1699,11ff.; 1701,6ff.;
    1731,34ff.

Luthers Vorreden lesetheoretische Hinweise in nicht geringer Zahl.[17] So zeigt sich: Es besteht ein Qualitätsgefälle innerhalb der Apokryphen, und noch mehr außerhalb. Je tiefer man steigt, desto größer ist die Gefahr, die Limite zu unterschreiten, die durch die griechische Literatur gesetzt ist. Äsop ist besser als die schlechtesten Apokryphen.[18] Das weist schließlich darauf hin: Apokryphen sind nur Vortrupp einer größeren Textgattung. Zwischen hl. Schrift und Texte überhaupt tritt das Gebiet des Literarischen. Literatur: das ist etwas Kanonartiges am Rande und außerhalb des Kanons. Oder umgekehrt: Deuterokanonisch ist im Grunde ein Prädikat der Literatur. Nicht alles, nur das Nützlichste hat unter der Rubrik ‚Apokryphen' Eingang in die Deutsche Bibel gefunden. Der Kanon der hl. Schrift steht nicht unvermittelt unter Texten überhaupt, sondern er hat eine Art Präludium in der Zwischengattung des Literarischen. Was hl. Schrift als Lesekanon ist, wird ohne Rücksicht darauf nicht zu bestimmen sein.

Nehmen wir den Impuls auf, der durch Luthers Textinstallationssatz ausgelöst wird, so sind mit zunehmendem Schwierigkeitsgrad folgende Fragen zu stellen: Was ist Text? Was ist Literatur? Was ist hl. Schrift?

1.1. Was ist Text?

Das erste, worauf wir stoßen, ist ein Paradox. Wir beginnen mit der Frage „Was ist Text?"[19], weil uns der Begriff des heiligen Textes schwierig scheint und entzogen, der des Texts überhaupt dagegen leicht. *A facilioribus incipientes convenientior fiat disciplina.* Unser erklärtes Ziel ist es, nach Hugos von St. Viktor Vorbild allein im Verfolg konsequenten Lesens zum Begriff des Kanons und in der Folge auch zu dem der Theologie vorzudringen. Aber historisch verlief die Reihe genau umgekehrt. Was Kanon heiliger Schrift ist, war bereits klar, bevor die Frage nach Literatur eigens gestellt wurde. Das Deuterokanonische verrät bereits durch den Klang des Wortes sein abkünftiges Wesen. Man darf behaupten: Literatur als eigenes Thema taucht just zu der Zeit auf, in der erstmals der kirchliche Kanonbegriff auf klassische Lite-

---

17 Leser 1675,16; 1901,19; lesen 1674,3; 1700,33f.; 1702,21; 1732,17; 1751,6; 1841,17; zusammenlesen 1751,22f.36ff.; 1752,22; zusammenflicken 1901,5; ausraufen 1943,7; auslegen 1827,16; 1901,11; verstehen 1675,17f.; predigen 1751,6f.; singen 1751,6.

18 Äsop: 1827,13.

19 P. Ricœur, Qu'est-ce qu'un texte? (1970), in: ders., Du texte à l'action. Essais d'herméneutique II, Paris 1986, 137–159; G. Martens, Was ist ein Text? Ansätze zur Bestimmung eines Leitbegriffs der Textphilologie, Poetica 21 (1989) 1–15; Was ist ein Text? hg. v. O. Wischmeyer/E.-M. Becker (Neutestamentliche Entwürfe zur Theologie 1), Tübingen 2001.

ratur übertragen wurde.[20] Was Literatur ist, darauf meinte man die Antwort zu kennen, noch bevor die selbständige Frage nach Text überhaupt gestellt wurde. Was Text ist, ist doch klar. Dass das Klarste und Leichteste eigens thematisiert wird, das ist nun wirklich das Jüngste und Neueste. Die Begriffsgeschichte von „Text" lehrt, dass ein selbständiges texttheoretisches Interesse erst ab Mitte des vergangenen Jahrhunderts artikuliert wird.[21] Über die Interdependenz der beiden entgegengesetzten Reihen kann man wohlfeile Mutmaßungen anstellen, wie etwa diese, dass unserer Zeit heilige Texte nur noch erschwinglich sein könnten als Texte überhaupt.

Nun gibt es wie immer zwei gegenläufige Interessen, den Textbegriff so bestimmt wie möglich zu machen.

Das erste ist das Interesse an einem möglichst engen Textbegriff. Es scheint unzweckmäßig, von Text im selben Umfang wie von Sprache zu reden. Nicht alles Gesprochene ist Text. Damit lösen wir den Textbegriff von den Voraussetzungen der Antike und des Mittelalters, die die Literalität gegenüber der Oralität in sekundären Rang versetzten. Text sei ein primäres, selbständiges Kodierungssystem, das um seiner selbst willen zu lesen ist. Aber nicht alles Lesbare ist Text. Auch Spuren sind lesbar. Sie sind nicht Schrift. Unter Text verstehen wir geschriebene sprachliche Äußerungen. Texte sind ausschließlich solche Materialisierungen von Sprache, die in der Hand zu tragen, die in zeitlicher und räumlicher Hinsicht transportabel sind. Was auf solche Weise niedergelegt ist, ist niedergeschrieben. Aber nicht alles Niedergeschriebene ist Text. Bloße Ansammlungen von Buchstaben oder Wörtern sind keine Texte. Nicht einmal der einzelne Satz ist bereits Text. Sondern als Text kann erst die Zusammenstellung von Sätzen gelten. Text ist eine „transphrastische" Größe. Dies führt zu der usuellen Definition: Text sei ein materiell umschlossenes, schriftlich niedergelegtes Sprachwerk von mehr als Satzlänge, das einen Sinnzusammenhang zu erkennen gibt.[22] Auf dieser

---

20 M. Asper, Art. Kanon, HWRh 4 (1998) 869–882, Sp. 872: Der moderne Begriff von Kanon als „Liste verbindlicher Autoren" außerhalb der hl. Schrift geht „auf D[avid] Ruhnken zurück, der diesen Sprachgebrauch erst 1768 prägte, vermutlich als Metapher auf der Basis des kirchlichen Gebrauchs" (872; cf. 873.876).

21 M. Scherner, Art. Text, HWPh 10 (1998) 1038–1044 spricht von der „Herausbildung eines spezifischen texttheoretischen Interesses in der 2. Hälfte des 20. Jh." (1039). Diesen „texttheoretischen Neubeginn" beschreibt er so: „Mit dem Aufkommen von Text-Linguistik/Text-Wissenschaft/Text-Theorie und der Weiterentwicklung der Sprachtheorie in Richtung einer ,realistischen Sprachwissenschaft' (P. Hartmann) seit ca. 1965 setzt eine Entwicklung ein, innerhalb deren die Reflexion auf den Text-Begriff in einem solchen Maße zentral wird, daß die gesamte bisherige Geschichte des Text-Begriffs lediglich als vieles im Impliziten belassendes Vorläufertum eines nun beginnenden hochdifferenzierten begrifflichen Neuansatzes erscheint" (1041).

22 C. Knobloch, Zum Status und zur Geschichte des Textbegriffs. Eine Skizze, Zeitschrift für Literaturwissenschaft und Linguistik 77 (1990) 66–87: „Der alltagssprachliche Aus-

Ebene lassen sich nun auch die Kriterien für Texte aufzählen, die Klaus Weimar als Fundamentalsätze der Texttheorie nennt: Ihre situationsunabhängige Dauer, ihre Gegenwart, Unveränderlichkeit, Vollendetheit – und „Texte sind: in Linien verwandelter Laut der Sprache."[23]

Lässt sich der Textbegriff enger fassen? Ohne Zweifel. Dazu müssen wir den Spuren folgen, die in humanistischer Hermeneutik und klassischer Philologie gelegt sind. Hier wird noch einmal unterschieden zwischen Text und Kommentar, Text und Glossen, Text und Annotationen. Die jeweiligen Antonyme sind natürlich auch Texte im Sinn der eben formulierten usuellen Definition, nicht aber im Sinn der philologischen. Texte sind Urtexte. Betrifft also der engere Textbegriff nur Texte, sofern sie der Auslegung würdig, fähig oder bedürftig sind, religiöse, juristische, politische, aber auch historische und literarische[24], so engt sich beim Rückgang von der klassischen Philologie zur *philologia* bzw. *hermeneutica sacra* der Textbegriff noch einmal drastisch ein. Jetzt hat nur noch die hl. Schrift den Rang eines Textes, oder nicht einmal die Schrift als ganze, sondern dasjenige besondere Textkorpus oder diejenige einzelne Textstelle, die als Lesung, Perikope oder *dictum probans* dem aktuellen Diskurs zugrundeliegt.[25] Man merkt leicht, dass bei dieser zweiten Engführung des Textbegriffs stillschweigend der Übergang genommen wird zu Vorgängen, die als Kanonisierungsprobleme abgehandelt werden. Kanonisierungprobleme entstehen üblicherweise, wenn keine texttheoretischen Argumente mehr aufzutreiben sind, um einem Text die Textqualität abzusprechen.

Am Ende zeigt sich: Je enger der Textbegriff, desto theologischer wird er. Aber es gibt gute Gründe, den Textbegriff auf der mittleren Ebene der genannten usuellen Definition zu belassen. Es gibt vor allem auch das entgegengesetzte Interesse an einem möglichst weiten Textbegriff. Auch hier zeigt sich: Je weiter der Textbegriff, desto theologischer wird er. Mit der Thematisierung von „Text" seit der Mitte des 20. Jahrhunderts war eine zunehmende Ausweitung des Textbegriffs verbunden. Wäre Text von vornherein der literarische Text, so hätte es der selbständigen Frage nach dem Text gar nicht bedurft. Es hätte genügt, Texte als Schrift- oder Sprachwerke zu betrachten.

---

druck ‚Text' ... bezeichnet ... ein materiell abgeschlossenes und schriftlich niedergelegtes Schriftwerk" (69). „Die heute vorherrschende Bedeutung: (Schriftlich) niedergelegte Äußerung von mehr als Satzlänge, die einen Sinnenzusammenhang bildet..." (71).

23 K. Weimar, Enzyklopädie der Literaturwissenschaft (UTB 1034), Tübingen/Basel ²1993, §§ 79–86.

24 G.F. Meier, Versuch einer allgemeinen Auslegungskunst, Halle 1757, § 105 (hg. v. A. Bühler/L. Cataldi Madonna [PhB 482], Hamburg 1996, 43): „*Der Text* (textus) ist die Rede, insofern sie als der Gegenstand der Auslegung betrachtet wird."

25 Knobloch, Status (s. Anm. 22), 67; Scherner, Art. Text (s. Anm. 21), 1040.

In dem Maß aber, in dem der Werkbegriff zurücktritt, tritt der Textbegriff hervor. Das Werk hat seinen Autor und Meister; jetzt dagegen rückt der Text in die Funktion des Meisters, er wird in neostrukturalistischer Weise selbst zum Subjekt oder Quasisubjekt, bei Tod des Autors. Der Textbegriff beginnt gleichsam zu galoppieren. Nicht nur werden die Grenzen von Literatur unscharf, Alltags- und Trivialliteratur fordern Respekt, sondern Text ist Geschriebenes überhaupt, Gelesenes überhaupt, ja, unter den Begriff Text fällt bald jedwede Spur und jedwedes Zeichen. Text wäre dann alles Rede- und Zeichenvorkommen. Und endlich findet die Überschreitung des Sprachlichen statt; soziokulturelle Gebilde werden als Text bezeichnet; Institutionen, Sozialformen, Architekturen, Städtegrundrisse usw. werden gelesen – eine Bewegung, die offenbar nicht ans Ende gelangt, bis nicht die Welt selbst als Text in Erscheinung tritt, die bisher nur als Ort und Schauplatz für Anfertigung, Aufbewahrung und Transport von Texten, im übrigen aber als Nichttext im Spiel war. Der Vorgang der Entgrenzung des Textbegriffs führt unweigerlich zu einer Theologisierung des Textes. Die hochtheologische Devise lautet: *Colligite quae superaverunt fragmenta, ne pereant* (Joh 6,12).[26] Es geht ständig darum, Texte zu retten, dem Nichttext Text abzuringen, die Textwelt so lange und so weit vorzutragen, bis die Welt Textwelt ist. Wo Welt ist, soll Text werden.

Resultat: Nicht nur die Eingrenzung, auch die Entgrenzung des Textbegriffs führt, je weiter sie getrieben wird, zur einer Theologisierung des Textbegriffs. Die Entgrenzung führt dahin, dass der Text immer mehr zur Welt wird, bis schließlich die Welt einzigmöglicher Text ist. Umgekehrt führt die Eingrenzung des Textbegriffs dahin, dass der Text immer weltloser wird, bis schließlich ein einziger Text die allein noch mögliche Welt ist.

1.2. Was ist Literatur?

Die inzwischen selbst bereits kanonisch gewordene Frage „Was ist Literatur?"[27] stellt nur dann eine von „Was ist Text?" zu unterscheidende Frage

---

26 E.R. Curtius, Europäische Literatur und lateinisches Mittelalter, Bern/München [9]1978, 323: „Thomas von Celano berichtet [Prima Vita S. Francisci Ass., c. 29], der Heilige habe jedes beschriebene Stück Pergament von der Erde aufgelesen, auch wenn es aus heidnischen Schriften stammte. Von einem Jünger deswegen befragt, antwortete Franz: Fili mi, litterae sunt ex quibus componitur gloriosissimum Dei nomen."
27 Ch. Du Bos, Qu'est-ce que la littérature?, Paris 1945; J.-P. Sartre, Qu'est-ce que la littérature – Was ist Literatur?, hg. u. übers. v. T. König, Reinbek 1981; R. Wellek, Was ist Literatur?, Zs. f. Literaturwiss. u. Linguistik 30/31 (1978) 15–19; G. Picht, Was ist Lite-

dar, wenn nicht mit der Bestimmung von Text die Literatur schon mitbestimmt ist. Mit anderen Worten: Sie ist nur dann eine selbständige Frage, wenn ein ganz bestimmter Begriff von Kanon am Werk ist. Wie gesagt: Text und Kanon sind keine koextensiven Begriffe. Es genügt daher nicht, das Erscheinen von Text überhaupt bereits als das Kanonische zu bezeichnen. Anlass dazu bestünde wohl. Denn jeder Text ist immer nur eine kontingente Verwirklichung der Potentialität der Sprache, die den Text übergreift. Der Text hätte jederzeit anders sein können. Nun ist er es nicht, und deshalb ruft er ständig Texte herbei, die anders sind, usw. usf. Aber gerade als solche zeitweilige Fixation des sprachlich Möglichen, das nicht nur wie das gesprochene Wort durchrauscht, verfliegt, verklingt, hat jeder Text rein als solcher etwas an sich, was als kanonisch bezeichnet werden darf. Und zwar bezieht sich dies sowohl auf den maximal entgrenzten wie auf den maximal eingegrenzten Textbegriff. Der maximal entgrenzte Textbegriff attrahiert Kanonizität (und deshalb auch Theologizität), weil er gar nichts außer sich hat, und dies ist sein Pathos. Der maximal eingeschränkte Textbegriff beansprucht Kanonizität (und deshalb auch Theologizität), weil er alles außer sich hat, und dies ist sein Pathos. Einerlei welches von beiden: Beide Textbegriffe kommen bei maximaler Unterschiedenheit darin überein, dass alles was Text ist auch Kanon ist, und sei der Text seiner Menge nach so maximal oder minimal wie er will. Trotz der unbestreitbaren Angemessenheit der vorgetragenen Gesichtspunkte ist es unzweckmäßig, dasjenige, was bereits durch den Begriff des Textes hinreichend gekennzeichnet wurde, auch noch durch den des Kanons zu bezeichnen. Vielmehr bleibe der Kanonbegriff schon aus Gründen der Begriffsökonomie dem Fall vorbehalten, dass zwischen Text und Text unterschieden wird. Der Kanon zieht Grenzen mitten durch das Gebiet des Textes hindurch. Ist dieses, wie gezeigt, selbst begrenzt, so sind kanonische Grenzen immer noch engere Grenzen. Kanon ist Text unter Texten, der texttheoretisch nicht zu unterscheiden gewesen wäre, lesetheoretisch dagegen sehr wohl.

Insofern ist die Frage „Was ist Literatur?" im Unterschied zu „Was ist Text?" eine kanonische Frage.[28] Oder, wenn wir je über die Literatur hinaus noch etwas zum Kanon zu sagen und zu erkennnen hätten: Es ist eine zumin-

---

ratur? (1979), in: ders, Hier und Jetzt. Philosophie nach Auschwitz und Hiroshima I, Stuttgart 1980, 273–286; Weimar, Enzyklopädie (s. Anm. 23), 81: „Was ist Literatur?".

28 Ich verkenne nicht, dass in der Theologie eine traditionelle Sprechweise anzutreffen ist, die die Hierarchie zwischen Text und Literatur genau umkehrt. Es gibt „den Text" (singulare tantum); es gibt „die Literatur" (Kollektivplural), Sekundärliteratur zum Text; es gibt schließlich und endlich die von allen erstrebte „Theologische Literaturzeitung". Wir haben es aber hier nicht mit innertheologischen Relationen, sondern mit der Relation zwischen theologischen Texten und Texten überhaupt zu tun.

dest deuterokanonische Frage. Sie fragt nach einem Textgebiet, das aus dem Gesamtgebiet der Texte ausgegrenzt werden kann, soll oder muss. Aber genau darüber, ob kann, soll oder muss, entsteht kein geringer Streit. Ein „Kann" würde kaum genügen. Das würde heißen, dass man in dem, was man faktisch tut, immer noch kann oder nicht kann. Wir können aber die Frage „Was ist Literatur?" nicht der Nonchalance und dem Zufall aussetzen, mit anderen Worten: Wir können sie nicht empirisch beantworten.[29] Wiederum ein „Soll" würde zwar genügen, aber wäre gleichzeitig ein wenig übers Ziel hinausgeschossen. Es wäre mehr als genug, was abträglich ist. Wir würden Machtsprüchen wildester Art Tür und Tor öffnen oder schleichende Moralisierung bei der Kanonbildung zulassen. Dies ist nicht zu gestatten, m.a.W.: Wir können die Frage „Was ist Literatur?" nicht dogmatistisch dekretieren.[30] So bleibt nur das „Muss", und das heißt: Es muss dasjenige Phänomen vor Augen gestellt werden, das dazu nötigt, einen besonderen Textkomplex namens Literatur anzuerkennen.

Klaus Weimar hat es unternommen, den vielfältigen Komplex „Literatur" durch eine Anzahl von Kennzeichen zu umschreiben, die sich letztlich – das ist die Spitze seiner These – als „unterschiedliche Äußerungsformen eines und desselben Grundes" zwingend machen lassen.[31] Seine Argumentationskette läuft unter Beiseitelassung sämtlicher Einzelheiten so: Niemand würde Poesie nicht als Literatur anerkennen. Daher wird der Konvention folgend alles, was durch absichtlichen Reim, Rhythmus, Zeilenbruch, Bedeutungsveränderung gekennzeichnet ist, d.h. das ganze Gebiet der Poesie samt denjenigen Teilen von Drama und Epos, die poetisch sind, leichthin als Literatur identifiziert. Ein Problem entsteht erst, wenn prosaische Texte, also prosaisches Drama und prosaisches Epos, Erzählung und Roman, als Literatur nachgewiesen werden sollen, wie es ebenfalls der Konvention entspricht. Hierzu muss eine Kriteriologie entwickelt werden, von der sich zeigt, dass sie allererst in der Lage sein wird, die Identifizierung der Prosa als Literatur von der konventionellen auf die argumentative Ebene zu heben. Literarische Prosatexte, einerlei ob dramatischer oder romanhafter Art, unterscheiden sich von unliterarischer Prosa durch einen unüblichen Widerstreit zwischen der Perspektive des Beteiligten und des Nichtbeteiligten; der Dramatiker vollzieht den Perspektivwechsel durch die Unterscheidung von Haupttext und Nebentext, zwischen *Nigrum* (Rolle) und *Rubrum* (Rolleninstallation); der Romanschreiber vollzieht ihn durch die Unterscheidung zwischen Autor und Erzähler. Dadurch wird auch – rückwirkend – deutlich, dass Texte der Poesie

---

29 Weimar, Enzyklopädie (s. Anm. 23), §§ 23.89.
30 Weimar, ebd., §§ 25. 89: „dogmatisch".
31 Weimar, ebd., § 162 Leitsatz.

nichts anderes als Rollengedichte sind, zu denen die Rolleninstallation still-schweigend hinzugedacht werden muss.[32] Die dem Epos entnommene Unter-scheidung von Autor und Erzähler trägt am Ende nicht nur das Drama, son-dern auch die Poesie. Somit kann durch Kriterien, die an der Erzählung, der poesiefernsten Gattung, gewonnen wurden, schließlich auch die Literarität von Poesie zwingend gemacht werden. Kurz: Was ist ein literarischer Text? Antwort: Literarische Texte, narrative, dramatische oder poetische, sind die-jenigen, die durch den Widerspruch von Autor und Erzähler hervorgebracht wurden, oder: „Literatur ist ein Prädikat, das man allen Texten zuspricht, von denen man aufgrund bestimmter Kennzeichen annimmt, der Autor habe sie als er selbst und als ein anderer geschrieben."[33]

An dieser Stelle angelangt, können wir die Fundamentalunterscheidung zwischen Autor und Erzähler, unbeschadet der Tatsache, dass sie in ihrer terminologischen Gestalt und begrifflichen Schärfe gewiss erst auf Entde-ckungen des 20. Jahrhunderts zurückgeht,[34] in eine Beziehung zur älteren klassischen Terminologie bringen und formulieren: Literatur erstreckt sich soweit, wie Texte von einer Person *sub persona* verfasst werden, wobei aber Person und *persona*, aller verbalen Echolalie und allem Anschein leerlaufen-der Wiederholung zum Trotz, sich gegenseitig ausschließen, weil sie sich im Widerspruch zueinander befinden. Jetzt wird erkennbar, dass der Kanon der Literatur von Weimar mit denselben Gesichtspunkten aus Texten überhaupt ausgegrenzt wird, mit denen Luther, wenngleich mit einem literaturwissen-schaftlichen Instrumentarium *avant la lettre*, den deuterokanonischen Kanon der Apokryphen beschrieben hat,[35] wobei der Mangel an kategorialer, argu-mentativer Kraft bei ihm durch moralisch-religiösen Sukkurs – „nützlich[36] und gut" – kompensiert wird.

1.3. Was ist hl. Schrift?

Die geradezu nachtwandlerische Griffsicherheit, mit der Klaus Weimar den Kanon der Literatur aus Texten überhaupt auszugrenzen verstand, weckt be-greiflicherweise Eifer und Wunsch, es ihm *in theologicis* gleichzutun. Wie wäre es, im Schwung der einmal gefassten Energie fortzufahren? Wie wäre

---

32 Weimar, ebd., § 158.
33 Weimar, ebd., § 168 Leitsatz.
34 K. Friedemann, Die Rolle des Erzählers in der Epik, Leipzig 1910 = Darmstadt 1965 = Hildesheim 1977; W. Kayser, Wer erzählt den Roman? (1957), in: ders., Die Vortrags-reise. Studien zur Literatur, Bern 1958, 82–101.
35 S. Anm. 16.
36 Nützlich/utilis/ὠφέλιμος als Prädikat der von Gott inspirierten Schrift: 2.Tim 3,16.

es, wenn es gelänge, den Kanon der hl. Schrift durch Kennzeichen (*notae*) zu bestimmen, die am Ende ebenso auf einen einzigen Grund zurückführten, nur jetzt eben den der hl. Schrift? Was ist der Grund der hl. Schrift?

Es sei vorausgesetzt, die Beantwortung der Frage „Was ist hl. Schrift?"[37] liege in der direkten Konsequenz der vorangegangenen Frage nach der Literatur. Folglich wird angenommen, hl. Schrift sei eben so Teilmenge von Literatur, wie Literatur soeben als Teilmenge von Text beschrieben worden ist. Es wird also für das Folgende zugrundegelegt, man müsse nur wie bisher fortfahren, um zur hl. Schrift zu gelangen, wie es der Parole vom konsequenten Lesen entspricht. Ein Weg wird erst durch seine Konsequenz deutlich. Natürlich ist dieses Verfahren nicht unbestritten. Diejenigen, die einerlei ob sie im Sinn des engen Textbegriffs hl. Schrift als einziges Exemplar von Text überhaupt betrachten oder umgekehrt im Sinn des weiten Textbegriffs alles was Text ist bereits als im Geruche von hl. Schrift stehend wahrnehmen, wurden schon oben kritisch referiert. In beiden Fällen werden Text und hl. Schrift direkt identifiziert. Aber Texte kennen Unterschiede. Diese lassen sich nicht dekretieren, sondern müssen lesetheoretisch nachgewiesen werden. Literatur konstituierte sich, wie zu sehen war, durch einen Textunterschied. Konstituiert sich nun hl. Schrift durch einen Literaturunterschied? So sind etwa Positionen denkbar, die die von Erich Auerbach vertretene These von der hl. Schrift als *sermo humilis*[38] zum Anlass nehmen, die Nichtliterarität der hl. Schrift als die besondere Art ihrer Literarität zu behaupten.

Andere Positionen suchen bereits auf der Ebene von Text zu bestimmen, was hl. Schrift ist, ohne dass der Begriff der Literatur dazwischen träte. Carsten Colpe verfährt so. Heilige Schriften – sagt er – sind Texte, denen die Dignität des Heiligen zukommt. „Sie heben sich damit als besondere Gruppe aus anderen Texten heraus."[39] Die Untauglichkeit dieses Verfahrens erweist

---

37 Jacob Heerbrand, Compendium theologiae (1573), Leipzig [2]1587, Loc. I. 3: Quid est sacra scriptura? Quae certis prophetarum, apostolorum et evangelistarum libris constat, qui biblici dicuntur, a volumine, in quo descripti extant, et canonici: unde et canonica scriptura; Leonhard Hutter, Compendium locorum theologicorum, Wittenberg 1610, hg. v. W. Trillhaas, Berlin 1961, Loc. I q. 1: Quid est Scriptura sacra? Est verbum Dei, impulsu Spiritus sancti a Prophetis et Apostolis literarum monumentis consignatum, de Essentia et Voluntate DEI nos instruens. † Et quidem generatim Scripturae sacrae appellatione, veniunt omnes libri Biblici: κατ' ἐξοχὴν autem hoc titulo eos libros denotamus, qui sunt Canonici: Unde et Scriptura ipsa dicitur Canonica; David Hollaz, Examen theologicum acroamaticum, Stargard 1707 = Darmstadt 1971, Prol. III q. 6: Quid est Scriptura [sacra]? Sacra Scriptura est verbum DEI à Prophetis & Apostolis ex inspiratione divina Literis consignatum, ut per illud peccator informetur ad æternam salutem.

38 E. Auerbach, Sacrae scripturae sermo humilis, Neuphilologische Mitteilungen 42 (1941) 57–67; auch in: ders., Gesammelte Aufsätze zur romanischen Philologie, Bern/München 1967, 21–26.

39 C. Colpe, Art. Heilige Schriften, RAC 14 (1988) 184–223, Sp. 184f.

sich in seiner bloßen Durchführung. Colpe führt in aufsteigender Linie folgende Ebenen zur Kennzeichnung heiliger Schriften auf: 1. die „positivistische": Eine Schrift nennt sich selbst heilig: Ebene der Selbstzuschreibung; 2. die „funktionalistische": Eine Schrift ist als heilige im Gebrauch: Ebene der Fremdzuschreibung. Beide Ebenen können einzeln oder vereint darauf hinwirken, dass von einer Schrift Heiligkeit prädiziert wird. Sie können aber – darin hat Colpe Recht – selbst mit vereinten Kräften nicht die Frage unterdrücken, ob die zugeschriebenermaßen heiligen Schriften auch wirklich heilig sind. Alles entscheidend ist daher 3. die „ontologische" Ebene: Eine Schrift ist heilig dann und nur dann, wenn sie nicht nur akzidentiell, sondern an sich selbst und also wesentlich heilig ist.[40] Nur die Bestimmung, die Colpe hierfür vorgelegt hat: heilige Schriften als „Texte ..., welche die Bedeutung des Heiligen in religiöser Sprache schriftlich festhalten"[41], missversteht die ontologische Ebene als substantialistische, als ob es Heiliges und seine Bedeutung an sich gäbe, zu dem die Texte dann hinzuträten. Im Gegenteil: Wir wüssten vom Heiligen überhaupt nichts, wenn nicht der Umgang mit Texten in einer bestimmten Konsequenz darauf führte. Aber daraus folgt, dass es nicht Heiliges gibt und dann auch noch Texte als Mittel seiner Kundgabe, bei immer formal und immer gleich bleibendem Textbegriff, sondern Texte, als Medien, nicht als Mittel, verändern sich selbst, und es ist im Zuge dieser Veränderung, dass sie Heiliges und seine Bedeutung zu erkennen geben. In diesem Sinn werden sie heilig genannt, weil sie es sind. Ist Lesetheorie eine Phänomenologie der Texterfahrung, die z.B. zu erkennen gibt, wie Literatur sich aus dem Einerlei von Text überhaupt erhebt, so wird sie so gewiss in alle Heiligkeit leiten, als es Schriften gibt, die in der Tat heilig sind.

Wenn nun Literatur dadurch gekennzeichnet ist, dass ein Autor schreibt als er selbst und als ein anderer und dementsprechend ein Leser liest als er selbst und als ein anderer, so ist damit ein in sich gespannter Widerspruch im Blick, der eines Mehr oder Minder fähig ist. Zwar gibt es, zumal unter Bedingungen neuzeitlicher Subjektivität, keinerlei Nachlass von der Pflicht eines Autors oder eines Lesers, als er selbst zu handeln. Diese gilt unmittelbar und absolut. Aber darin, dass ein Autor oder Leser als ein anderer handelt, kann ein Mehr oder Minder stattfinden. Dementsprechend die Höhe der Literatur. Ein geringes Anderssein reduziert die literarische Spannung, ein stärke-

---

40 Colpe, ebd., 186: Auch Historiker und Phänomenologen haben die „Aufgabe, sich bei der Untersuchung bestimmter Schriften nicht mit einem akzidentellen Sinn des Heiligen zu begnügen, sondern mit dem Heiligen als etwas selbständig Seienden zu rechnen. Von hier aus muß sowohl die konkludente Theologie des Heiligen als auch die Semantik eines eventuell verschriftlichten Heiligen vollzogen werden können (...)."

41 Colpe, ebd., 186.

res steigert sie. An dieser Stelle liegt die Versuchung nahe, den oszillieren-
den Verhältnissen der Literatur einen Begriff von hl. Schrift so aufzunötigen,
dass man die lebendige Bandbreite möglichen Andersseins durch den
theologischen Begriff des „ganz Anderen" auszustechen sucht, um auf diese
Weise über die Literatur hinaus zu den *sacrae litterae* zu gelangen. Damit ist
nichts anderes erreicht, als dass ein eskapistischer Stichwortanschluss
vollzogen wurde, der das Fundament zerstört, auf dem wir uns der hl. Schrift
näherten. Sobald nämlich der ganz Andere oder der absolut Andere da ist, ist
der Autor oder Leser als er selbst vergangen. Aber gerade als solcher war er
in der Definition von Literatur gesetzt.

Es wird deshalb angemessen sein, auf die Vorstellung Verzicht zu leisten,
als könne man die hl. Schrift gleichsam als engeren Kreis so in die Literatur
einzeichnen, wie die Literatur selbst als enger Kreis in Text überhaupt einge-
zeichnet worden ist. Der Kanon der Literatur lässt sich mit erstaunlicher Sicherheit beschreiben. Er beschreibt eine nachvollziehbare Grenze durch das
Gesamtgebiet von Text. Doch dieser Vorgang lässt sich ohne Willkür nicht
noch einmal wiederholen, um zur hl. Schrift zu gelangen. Der Begriff des
Kanons ist mit der Literatur bereits einmal vergeben und ausgereizt. D.h.
wenn so etwas wie hl. Schrift zuverlässig in den Blick kommen soll, muss
der Kanonbegriff noch einmal der Modifikation ausgesetzt werden. Bisher
hatten wir es zu tun mit dem Lesekanon. Er vermag es, Literatur von Texten
zu scheiden. Er diente der Installation von literarischen oder gleichviel: deuterokanonischen Texten, die nützlich und gut zu lesen sind. Um aber von einem Kanon der hl. Schrift reden zu können, muss der Kanonbegriff selbst
noch eine Dimension zulegen. Er muss von der gegenständlichen Ebene auf
die transzendentale gehoben werden. Der Kanon der hl. Schrift ist kein Quan-
tum, sondern ein Quale. Das erfordert, dass über die bloße Textinstallation
hinaus der Gesichtspunkt der Liturgie und damit der liturgische Gebrauch der
Texte ins Spiel gebracht wird. Daraus aber geht ein neuer Kanonbegriff hervor, der zu dem ersten in Konkurrenz tritt.

2. Singkanon

Liturgie-Installation

Das Werk des Ps.-*Dionysius Areopagita*, dieses biblischen, wenn auch leicht
jenseits des *Jahrbuchs für Biblische Theologie* angesiedelten Theologen, ist
im Ganzen wie in allen Teilen auf die hl. Schrift als Kanon der Wahrheit be-

zogen. Seine Variante der traditionellen Kanonformel lautet: Bewahren wir die Schrift ohne alle Vermehrung, Verringerung und Veränderung, so bewahren wir dadurch uns selbst samt denen, die sie bewahren.[42] Das *Corpus Dionysiacum*, das in den Anfang des 6. Jahrhunderts gehört, trägt die Liste der kanonischen Bücher nicht primär zum Zweck der Lehre, sondern zu dem der Liturgie vor. Maßgebend ist dabei das Verständnis von Kanon als Bestand der „für die Lesung im Gottesdienst" zugelassenen, aber auch fähigen Bücher.[43] Die beiden Hierarchienschriften verfolgen mystagogische Absicht. Der Neologismus ‚Hierarchie' weist in Richtung Liturgieinstallation. Die *Kirchliche Hierarchie* bietet Hinführung zu den liturgischen Feiern der Kirche, darunter auch zur σύναξις/κοινωνία, der Eucharistiefeier. Der Gang der Abhandlung folgt dem Gang der ‚Göttlichen Liturgie', wie sie im großen und ganzen noch heute gefeiert wird. Dabei werden die großen Einheiten Proskomidie, Katechumenen- und Gläubigenliturgie zum Zweck der Analyse in kleinere Segmente geteilt. Das Liturgiesegment „Psalmen und Lesung" aus dem Übergang von Proskomidie zur Katechumenenliturgie bietet den Anlass zur Auflistung der kanonischen Bücher. Dadurch entsteht der im patristischen Umfeld wohl einzigartige Kanontext Eccl. Hier. III,4–5, dem im Gang unserer Reflexion die Aufgabe zukommt, die in I. *Lesekanon* in eine Sackgasse geratene Suche nach dem Kanon auf eine neue Ebene zu stellen. Er bedarf allerdings eines außergewöhnlichen Maßes an Geduld.

Von der Zweiheit Psalmengesang und biblische Lesung spricht Dionysius ausschließlich in stehenden Wendungen.[44] Sie ist das liturgische Grundmodul, von dem unsere Betrachtung hier immer ausgeht. Der bisher maßgebliche, allein auf das Bedürfnis von Textinstallation ausgerichtete Kanonbegriff gab zur Zweiheit von Psalmen und Lesung keinerlei Anlass. Ihm zufolge ge-

---

42 Dionysius Areopagita, De divinis nominibus II,2 (PG 3,640A): κανών im Sinn von *regula veritatis*, nicht Liste; cf. I,8 (597B) (alles). – Der griechische Text wird zitiert nach Corpus Dionysiacum I/II, hg. v. B.R. Suchla/G. Heil/A.M. Ritter (PTS 33/36), Berlin 1990/91; der lateinische Text nach Dionysiaca, ed. par Ph. Chevallier, Brügge 1937 (Nachdruck hg. v. Martin Bauer, 4 Bde., Stuttgart-Bad Cannstatt 1989); deutsche Übersetzung: Über die himmlische Hierarchie/Über die kirchliche Hierarchie, übers. v. G. Heil (BGL 22), Stuttgart 1986; Die Namen Gottes, übers. v. B.R. Suchla (BGL 26); Stuttgart 1988; Über die mystische Theologie und Briefe, übers. v. A.M. Ritter (BGL 40), Stuttgart 1994.

43 J. Assmann, Das kulturelle Gedächtnis. Schrift, Erinnerung und politische Identität in frühen Hochkulturen, München 1992, 112.

44 Psalmen und Lesung: De ecclesiastica hierarchia III (PG 3,425BC); III,5 (432BC); IV (473A); VII (556C) (umgekehrt); Oden und Lesung: III,1 (428B); IV,3 (476D); VII,3 (556BC); VII,2 (557B). – Drei liturgische Orte für die Sequenz von Psalmen und Lesung sind denkbar: 1. Orthros-Liturgie; 2. Antiphonen-Kleiner Einzug; 3. Prokeimenon-Apostolos (Epistel). Die zweite dürfte (gegen K. Onasch, Art. Prokeimenon, in: ders., Lexikon Liturgie und Kunst der Ostkirche unter Berücksichtigung der Alten Kirche, Berlin 1993, 318) die wahrscheinlichste sein.

hören die Psalmen in Reih und Glied mit den sonstigen biblischen Büchern. Weder stehen sie separat noch apart. Sie stehen daher auch den biblischen Lesungen nicht gegenüber, sind sie doch selbst eine. Und eine biblische Lesung ist wie die andere. Bücher wechseln, der Lesebegriff bleibt. Sobald aber das dionysische Doppelmodul auftritt, Psalmen und Lesung, kommt ein Moment von Liturgieinstallation zur Wirkung. Es ist die Unterscheidung zweier Orte im liturgischen Verlauf, *ψαλμῳδία/psalmodia* und *ἀνάγνωσις/lectio*, und Unterscheidung zweier liturgischer Funktionen, *ψάλτης/psalmista* und *ἀναγνώστης/lector*, wie sie in alten Ämterordnungen vorgesehen sind.[45] Die Eindimensionalität des bloßen Lesekanons weicht; indem ihm der Singkanon gegenübertritt, entsteht der Eindruck von Mehrdimensionalität.

Der einschlägige Text handelt dementsprechend von Psalmodie (Eccl. Hier. III,4) und Lesung (Eccl. Hier. III,5). Beide Abschnitte verfahren so, dass sie beide Themen invers miteinander verschränken.

Eccl. Hier. III,4: Ἡ δὲ τῶν ψαλμῶν ἱερολογία συνουσιωμένη πᾶσι σχεδὸν τοῖς ἱεραρχικοῖς μυστηρίοις οὐκ ἤμελλεν ἀπηρτῆσθαι τοῦ πάντων ἱεραρχικωτάτου. Πᾶσα μὲν γὰρ ἱερὰ καὶ ἁγιόγραφος δέλτος ἢ τὴν ἐκ θεοῦ τῶν ὄντων γενητὴν ὕπαρξίν τε καὶ διακόσμησιν ἢ τὴν νομικὴν ἱεραρχίαν καὶ πολιτείαν ἢ τῶν τοῦ θείου λαοῦ κληροδοσιῶν διανεμήσεις καὶ κατασχέσεις ἢ κριτῶν ἱερῶν ἢ βασιλέων σοφῶν ἢ ἱερέων ἐνθέων σύνεσιν ἢ παλαιῶν ἀνδρῶν ἐν ποικιλίᾳ καὶ πλήθει τῶν ἀνιώντων ἀκατάσειστον ἐν καρτερίᾳ φιλοσοφίαν ἢ τῶν πρακτέων σοφὰς ὑποθήκας ἢ θείων ἐρώτων ᾄσματα καὶ ἐνθέους εἰκόνας ἢ τῶν ἐσομένων τὰς ὑποφητικὰς προαναρρήσεις ἢ τὰς ἀνδρικὰς Ἰησοῦ θεουργίας ἢ τὰς τῶν αὐτοῦ μαθητῶν θεοπαραδότους καὶ θεομιμήτους πολιτείας καὶ ἱερᾶς διδασκαλίας ἢ τὴν κρυφίαν καὶ μυστικὴν ἐποψίαν τοῦ τῶν μαθητῶν ἀγαπητοῦ καὶ θεσπεσίου ἢ τὴν ὑπερκόσμιον Ἰησοῦ θεολογίαν τοῖς πρὸς θέωσιν ἐπιτηδείοις ὑφηγήσατο καὶ ταῖς ἱεραῖς τῶν τελετῶν καὶ θεοειδέσιν ἀναγωγαῖς συνερρίζωσεν, ἡ δὲ τῶν θείων ᾠδῶν ἱερογραφία σκοπὸν ἔχουσα τὰς θεολογίας τε καὶ θεουργίας ἁπάσας ὑμνῆσαι καὶ τὰς τῶν θείων ἀνδρῶν ἱερολογίας τε καὶ ἱε-

Eccl. Hier. III,4 [Psalmodie]: Der Vortrag der geheiligten Worte der Psalmen, wesentlich fast allen geheimnisträchtigen Vorgängen der Hierarchie verbunden, sollte erst recht von dem wichtigsten Element der Hierarchie nicht ausgeschlossen bleiben. Zwar führte nämlich jedes geheiligte Buch heiliger Schrift die zur Gottwerdung Geeigneten ein in die von Gott erzeugte Existenz des Seienden und seine Gliederung [*Gen*], oder in die Hierarchie und Verfassung unter dem Gesetz [*Ex/Lev/Deut*] oder die Verteilung und Besitzergreifung der Losgeschenke an das Gottesvolk [*Num/Jos*], die Verständigkeit von geheiligten Richtern [*Iud*] oder weisen Königen [*Reg*] oder gotterfüllten Priestern [*Par/Esdr/ Neh*], oder in die in Selbstbeherrschung unerschütterliche Philosophie früherer Männer [*Prov/Eccl*] in der Mannigfaltigkeit und Fülle der Anfechtungen [*Iob*], die klugen Ratschläge zum praktischen Handeln [*Sap/Sir*], die Lieder und inspirierten Bilderreden von göttlichen Liebeserfahrungen [*Cant*] oder in prophetische Vorhersagen der Zukunft [*libri prophetici*] oder die göttlichen Werke Jesu

---

45 *Psalmista* und *lector:* Syn. Laod., can. 15: κανονικοὶ ψάλται ... ἀπὸ διφθέρας ψάλλοντες; can. 59: Ὅτι οὐ δεῖ ἰδιωτικοὺς ψαλμοὺς λέγεσθαι ἐν τῇ ἐκκλησίᾳ οὐδὲ ἀκανόνιστα βιβλία ἀναγινώσκεσθαι; Isidor von Sevilla, Etymologiae VI, 19,9.11: De ecclesiasticis officiis II,11: De lectoribus; II,12: De psalmistis; cf. I,5: De psalmis; I,10: De lectionibus; Hrabanus Maurus, De institutione clericorum I,11: De lectoribus ac psalmistis; cf. II,48: De psalmis; II,52: De lectionibus; Smaragdus von St. Mihiel, Diadema monachorum II: De disciplina psallendi; III: De lectione (PL 102,596–598).

ρουργίας αἰνέσαι καθολικὴν ποιεῖται τῶν
θείων ᾠδὴν καὶ ἀφήγησιν πρὸς πάσης ἱεραρχικῆς τελετῆς ὑποδοχὴν καὶ μετάδοσιν ἕξιν
οἰκείαν ἐμποιοῦσα τοῖς ἐνθέως αὐτὴν ἱερολο-
γοῦσιν.

gegebene, der Nachahmung Gottes dienende
Lebensweise seiner Schüler [*Act*] und ihre
geheiligten Lehren [*Epp*] oder die verhüllte,
mystische Schau des von seinen Schülern
Geliebten, von Gott Inspirierten [*Apc*] oder
die den Bereich unserer Welt überschreitende
Kunde von Jesus als Gott [*Ioh*]. Alle diese
Bücher [*VT/NT*] sprossen aus derselben
Wurzel wie die geheiligte und gottgemäße
Symbolsprache der Weihehandlungen. Der
geheiligte Text der göttlichen Gesänge [*Ps/
Od/PsSal*] jedoch, der die Worte [*VT*] und
Werke [*NT*] Gottes insgesamt preisen und die
geheiligten Worte [*VT*] und Werke [*NT*] der
göttlichen Männer insgesamt loben will, bil-
det einen zusammenfassenden Lobpreis und
Kommentar der Wirkungen Gottes und be-
wirkt in denen, die ihn von Gott erfüllt singen, die angemessene Einstellung zu Emp-
fang und Weitergabe jeder Weihe, die die
Hierarchie vermittelt.

Eccl. Hier. III,5: Ὅταν οὖν ἡ περιεκτικὴ τῶν
πανιέρων ὑμνολογία τὰς ψυχικὰς ἡμῶν ἕξεις
ἐναρμονίως διαθῇ πρὸς τὰ μικρὸν ὕστερον ἱε-
ρουργηθησόμενα καὶ τῇ τῶν θείων ᾠδῶν ὁμο-
φωνίᾳ τὴν πρὸς τὰ θεῖα καὶ ἑαυτοὺς καὶ ἀλλή-
λους ὁμοφροσύνην ὡς μιᾷ καὶ ὁμολόγῳ τῶν
ἱερῶν χορείᾳ νομοθετήσῃ, τὰ συντετμημένα
καὶ συνεσκιασμένα μᾶλλον ἐν τῇ νοερᾷ τῶν
ψαλμῶν ἱερολογίᾳ διὰ πλειόνων καὶ σαφεσ-
τέρων εἰκόνων καὶ ἀναρρήσεων εὐρύνεται ταῖς
ἱερωτάταις τῶν ἁγιογράφων συντάξεων ἀνα-
γνώσεσιν. Ἐν ταύταις ὁ βλέπων ἱερῶς ὄψεται
τὴν ἑνοειδῆ καὶ μίαν ἔμπνευσιν ὡς ὑφ' ἑνὸς
τοῦ θεαρχικοῦ πνεύματος κεκινημένην. Ὅθεν
εἰκότως ἐν κόσμῳ μετὰ τὴν ἀρχαιοτέραν
παράδοσιν ἡ καινὴ διαθήκη κηρύσσεται τῆς
ἐνθέου καὶ ἱεραρχικῆς τάξεως ἐκεῖνο οἶμαι
δηλούσης, ὡς ἡ μὲν ἔφη τὰς ἐσομένας Ἰησοῦ
θεουργίας ἡ δὲ ἐτέλεσε, καὶ ὡς ἐκείνη μὲν ἐν
εἰκόσι τὴν ἀλήθειαν ἔγραψεν, αὕτη δὲ παρο-
ῦσαν ὑπέδειξεν. Τῶν γὰρ ἐκείνης προα-
ναρρήσεων ἡ κατὰ ταύτην τελεσιουργία τὴν
ἀλήθειαν ἐπιστώσατο, καὶ ἔστι τῆς θεολογίας
ἡ θεουργία συγκεφαλαίωσις.

Eccl. Hier. III,5 [*Lesung*]: Wenn also der die
hochheiligen Inhalte umfassende Gesang
unsere seelische Verfassung eingestimmt hat
auf die gleich folgenden heiligen Handlun-
gen und durch das gemeinsame Singen der
göttlichen Lieder die innere Gemeinschaft
mit den Gaben Gottes und mit uns selbst und
untereinander angeordnet hat, als ob es gälte,
die heilige Botschaft in einem einzigen
Reigentanz im gleichen Rhythmus darzustellen, wird der mehr verdichtete und dunkle
Gedankengehalt der Psalmenrezitation durch
reichlichere, klarere Bilder und Bekanntma-
chungen in den über alles geheiligten Lesungen von Passagen heiliger Schrift breiter entfaltet. In ihnen wird der, der in geheiligter
Weise sehen kann, erkennen, daß die dem
Einen gemäße, eine, gemeinsame Begeiste-
rung von dem einen Geist des Gottesprinzips
ins Werk gesetzt wurde. Dazu paßt es, daß in
gebührender Ordnung nach der älteren Überlieferung das Neue Testament verkündet
wird, wobei die vor alles eingegebene und
der Hierarchie entsprechende Reihenfolge
dies klar macht, daß die eine die zukünftigen
Gottestaten Jesu verkündete [*VT*], das andere
aber die Ankündigungen erfüllte [*NT*], und
daß jene in Bildern die Wahrheit darstellte

---

46 Dionysius Areopagita, De ecclesiastica hierarchia III,4f. (PG 3,429C–432A); lateinisch:
Dionysiaca II/3,1186–1195; deutsch: BGL 22,113f. Zur Erläuterung: P. Rorem, Biblical
and Liturgical Symbols within the Pseudo-Dionysian synthesis (STPIMS 71), Toronto
1984, 11–15.19.122.

[*VT*], dieses sie aber gegenwärtig zeigte
[*NT*]. Denn die Wahrheit jener bestätigte die
in diesem geschehene Erfüllung. Die Summe
von Gottes Wort [*VT*] ist Gottes Tat [*NT*].[46]

Eccl. Hier. III,4 thematisiert mit einem einzigen Satz den Gesang der heiligen
Psalmworte (ἡ τῶν ψαλμῶν ἱερολογία).[47] Seine Pointe ist der Kontrast zwischen hl. Schrift überhaupt (πᾶσα μὲν γὰρ ἱερὰ καὶ ἁγιόγραφος δέλτος) und
der hl. Schrift der göttlichen Oden (ἡ δὲ τῶν θείων ᾠδῶν ἱερογραφία). Das
μέν-δέ rührt von alter Tradition, von Basilius und Athanasius her.[48] Πᾶσα μὲν
... beginnt dementsprechend die erste Satzhälfte im Anklang an 2.Tim 3,16
und alte Vätertradition. Der μέν-Teil bietet eine Liste der kanonischen Bücher Alten und Neuen Testaments, nur dass an die Stelle der zum Kanontext
gehörigen Akribie eine gewisse leiernde Gleichförmigkeit getreten ist, erzeugt durch 14-faches ἤ, diesem untrüglichen Kennzeichen der Wiederholung. In der Tat ist eine 10-teilige AT- und eine 4-teilige NT-Liste zu erkennen, letztere besonders unakribisch und schwer rekonstruierbar. Aber alles in
allem kein Zweifel: Der μέν-Satz beschreibt das Ganze der hl. Schrift, wenngleich mit der überraschenden Ausnahme, dass der Psalter unerwähnt bleibt.
Der Psalter tanzt aus der Reihe heraus und stellt sich im δέ-Teil der Schrift
gegenüber als eigenes Korpus dar. Einerlei wie der Name dieses Komplexes
(ἡ τῶν θείων ᾠδῶν ἱερογραφία) zu verstehen ist, als ΨΑΛΤΗΡΙΟΝ/ΨΑΛ-
ΜΟΙ, als ΩΔΑΙ, vielleicht als ΨΑΛΜΟΙ ΣΟΛΟΜΩΝΤΟΣ oder als alles zusammen: es handelt sich in jedem Fall um reguläre biblische Bücher, die im
Schriftkanon der Septuaginta enthalten sind. Damit entsteht das mengentheo-
retische Problem, dass dem Ganzen der Schrift ein Teil gegenübertritt und

---

47 ἱερολογία bezogen auf Psalmen: De ecclesiastica hierarchia III (PG 3,425B); III,4
(429CD); III,5 (432ABC); IV (473A) auf Oden IV,3 (476D).
48 Basilius von Caesarea hat seine Psalmen-Homilien so begonnen: Πᾶσα Γραφὴ θεόπνευστος καὶ ὠφέλιμος (2.Tim 3,16). Jedoch: Während (μέν) Prophetie erzieht, Ge-
schichtserzählung dieses lehrt und Gesetzgebung das, und Spruchweisheit wiederum eine Gattung der Lehre darstellt, umfasst (δέ) das Psalmbuch von diesem allem das Nützli-
che und bietet darüber hinaus noch das Vergnügen der gesungenen Melodien, καὶ τοῦτο
μετά τινος ψυχαγωγίας ἐμμελοῦς καὶ ἡδονῆς σώφρονα λογισμὸν ἐμποιούσης (Hom. in ps.
1, 1 [PG 29, 212A]). – Dieses im Ohr formuliert Athanasius von Alexandrien an den E-
pistola ad Marcellinum: Πᾶσα μὲν ... Γραφὴ παλαιά τε καὶ καινή, θεόπνευστός ἐστι καὶ
ὠφέλιμος (2.Tim 3,16), das Psalmbuch aber (δέ) hat etwas ganz Besonderes. Während
(μέν) in der Schrift jede Gattung ihr Besonderes treibt und verkündet, umfasst (δέ) das
Psalmbuch wie ein Paradiesgärtlein von allem etwas und hat außerdem noch die Besonderheit aufweist, dass es in der Weise des Gesangs vonstatten geht (Ep. ad Marc. 2 [PG
27,12BC; cf. 10 [20B–21B]; 11 [21BC.24A]; 14 [25C]). Dazu: G. Bader, Psalterium af-
fectuum palaestra. Prolegomena zu einer Theologie des Psalters (HUTh 33), Tübingen
1996; ders., Was heißt „Verstummen des Psalters"?, MuK 67 (1997) 358–366.

beansprucht, auf höherer Ebene Inbegriff des Ganzen zu sein.[49] Nicht treten die göttlichen Psalmgesänge dem Schriftkanon als Teil vom selben gegenüber, auch haben sie nicht die Absicht, irgendetwas zu dessen Interpretation beizutragen. In Hinsicht auf Lehre haben sie überhaupt nichts Neues zu bieten. Die Differenz liegt im liturgischen Gebrauch. Sie liegt im Gesang, welcher durch die Verben ὑμνῆσαι und αἰνέσαι charakterisiert wird. Als zu singende treten die psalmodischen Bücher dem Schriftkanon gegenüber. Aus dem Lesekanon ist damit der Singkanon hervorgetreten.[50] Dieser ist der Art nach etwas anderes. Zwar wird alles, was Schrift ist, gelesen, der psalmodische Teil der Schrift dagegen wird gesungen.

Eccl. Hier. III,5 thematisiert die heiligen Lesungen (αἱ ἱερώταται τῶν ἁγιογράφων συντάξεων ἀναγνώσεις) nicht voraussetzungslos, sondern der faktischen liturgischen Ordnung folgend so, dass Psalmengesang vorausgeht. Heiliges wird durch mimetischen Reigentanz (ὡς μιᾷ καὶ ὁμολόγῳ τῶν ἱερῶν χορείᾳ) dargestellt. Erst wenn durch Hymnengesang (ὑμνολογία) Seelenharmonie, durch Einstimmigkeit (ὁμοφωνία) Einmütigkeit (ὁμοφροσύνη) mit Gott, sich selbst und mit Anderen hervorgebracht ist: erst dann entsteht auch ein Bedürfnis, das Dichte und Dunkle der Psalmodie durch Lesungen des breiteren und helleren zu entfalten. Und erst dann werden Altes und Neues Testament unterscheidbar, wobei jenes das verheißende Wort Gottes (θεολογία), dieses die in Jesus vollbrachte Tat Gottes (θεουργία) enthält. Theurgie ist – nach dionysischem Sprachgebrauch – die Vollendung der Theologie.[51] Aber die Differenz der beiden Testamente wird durch die Differenz zwischen Psalmodie und Lesung noch einmal überrundet. Der Lesekanon Alten *und* Neuen Testaments setzt bereits den Spiel- und Tanzkanon der Psalmodie voraus, durch den er allererst ins Werk gesetzt wird. Testamente werden gelesen, Psalmen aufgeführt.

49　Die Bedeutung des Psalters als Extrakt der gesamten hl. Schrift findet ihren Niederschlag in folgenden Psaltermetaphern: παράδεισος/*paradisus*/Mustergarten (Athanasius von Alexandrien, Ep. ad Marc. 2 [PG 27,12C]; 30 [41C]; Martin Luther, Vorrede auf den Psalter 1528/45, WA.DB 10/1,102,10; 103,10); εἴσοπτρον/*speculum*/Spiegel (Athanasius von Alexandrien, Ep. ad Marc. 12 [PG 27, 24B]; Martin Luther, Vorrede auf den Psalter 1528/45, WA.DB 10/1,104,7; 105,7); ἐγχειρίδιον/*enchiridion*/Handmesser (Hieronymus, Exc. de psalt., prol., [CChr.SL 72,177,4f.]; Martin Luther, Vorrede auf den Psalter 1528/45, WA.DB 10/1,98,24; 99,26); „klein Biblia" (ebd., 98,22; 99,24f.); „kürtze Bibel vnd exempelbuch" (ebd., 98,26; 99,28). Dazu: G. Bader, „Psalterium". Der Beitrag eines biblisch-unbiblischen Begriffs zur poetischen Theologie, in: U.H.J. Körtner (Hg.), Poetologische Theologie. Zur ästhetischen Theorie christlicher Sprach- und Lebensformen, Ludwigsfelde 1999, 82–110.

50　Selbstverständlich geht der Gebrauch von κανών im Sinn von Singkanon nicht auf Dionysius zurück (s. Anm. 42).

51　E. Bellini, Teologia e teurgia in Dionigi Areopagita, VetChr 17 (1980) 199–216; Rorem, Biblical and Liturgical Symbols (s. Anm. 46), 14f.

Nehmen wir den Impuls auf, der von der Liturgieinstallation des Dionysius Areopagita ausgeht, so sind mit wachsendem Schwierigkeitsgrad folgende Fragen zu stellen: Was ist Lesung? Was ist Psalmodie? Was ist Kanon?

2.1. Was ist Lesung?

Lesung bezeichnet im gegenwärtigen deutschen Sprachgebrauch eine spezielle Weise des Lesens, der ein gewisser Grad an Rarität und Preziosität zukommt. Man kennt Dichterlesung, man kennt die gottesdienstliche Lesung: beides eher randständige Phänomene im größeren Feld des allgemeinen Leseverhaltens. Die Lesung gehört dem lauten Lesen zu. Genauer: Sie ist Relikt des lauten Lesens. Ihre Seltenheit erklärt sich wohl aus dem Rückzug, den lautes Lesen generell genommen hat. In *I. Lesekanon* bestand noch kein Anlass, die Differenz zwischen lautem und leisem Lesen zu berücksichtigen. Ist sie einmal da, dann darf man wohl behaupten: Der Lesekanon bezog sich auf leises Lesen. Leises Lesen genügt völlig, um die in *I. Lesekanon* ausgebreiteten Phänomene zu erklären. Außerdem wird der Grad an Differenzierung und Beobachtung, wie er zu Literatur und Literaturwissenschaft erforderlich ist, viel leichter erreicht, wenn sich erst einmal der Lärm lauten Lesens verzogen hat. Dass in *II. Singkanon* über leises Lesen hinaus lautes in Betracht gezogen wird, ist nicht von vornherein einsichtig. Im Gegenteil: Es scheint unnötig. Aber auch ohne die geläufige Hypothese vom allmählichen Verschwinden des lauten Lesens im Lauf der kulturellen Evolution lässt sich der generelle Rückzug der Lesung leicht erklären. Kaum sieht man sich einer Lesung ausgesetzt, hätte man das Pensum viel lieber schnell selber gelesen, und zwar leise. Die Ursache für den kulturellen Schwund lauten Lesens ist in erster Linie die Überflüssigkeit. Weitere Gründe schließen sich daran an: Der nicht leicht zu leugnende physische Zwang, der vom lauten Lesen ausgeht; die Besetzung des Gehörs; die damit verbundene Anmaßung, als ob ein Text eine Vielzahl Hörer zu interessieren vermöchte; die Besinnung raubende Anmaßung und Ausübung von Autorität, usw. Nicht nur überflüssig erscheint das laute Lesen, sondern in erheblichem Maße lästig. Dagegen leises Lesen trägt seine Würde in sich. Es verbreitet philologische Andacht, die durch nichts zu übertreffen ist. Es erzeugt eine Stille von der Art, dass am Ende nur noch der Text spricht. Keineswegs also ist leises Lesen die bloße Verfallsform des ehemals wahren und lauten, sondern es hat eigenen Stand und Wesen.

Hat auch lautes Lesen, abgesehen von seinem fortwährenden Verschwinden, eigenen Stand und Wesen? Ohne Zweifel im Vorlesen. Illiterate Zustände am Anfang und Ende des Lebens lassen hoffen, dass laute Leser und Lese-

rinnen nie ganz verschwinden. Allerdings wollte man weder die akademische
Vorlesung noch die literarische und gottesdienstliche Lesung auf solche im
ganzen marginale Umstände zurückführen. Vielmehr gelten alle diese Lesungen auch und gerade den Literaten. Daher ist nicht alles Vorlesen auch schon
Lesung. Das Charakteristikum von Lesung dürfte sein, dass sie auf keine besonderen Umstände oder Zustände Rücksicht nimmt, die in einzelnen ent-
schuldbaren Fällen noch einmal lautes statt leisem Lesen gestatten. Lesung
hat eigenen Stand und Wesen, wenn sie in gewisser Weise rücksichtslos
wird. Die ekphonetische Lesung (ἐκφώνως[52]) bedarf im Kern keiner Gemeinde, so sehr sie in der Gemeinde stattfindet. Oder umgekehrt: Desto eher wird
Lesung in der Gemeinde stattfinden, desto eher wird sie überhaupt die Gemeinde finden, die sich um sie schart, je weniger sie um der Gemeinde willen
stattfindet. Je weniger mit zweckgebundener Absicht gelesen wird – das
könnte jeder für sich selbst, und könnte es besser –, desto mehr entsteht der
selbständige Begriff von Lesung. Lesung findet um ihrer selbst willen statt.

Hans-Jost Frey unterscheidet deshalb beim lauten Lesen zwischen dem
zweckdienlichen, instrumentalen Vorlesen in Kindergarten und Blindenheim
und der Lesung, die an und für sich und also medial geschieht. Lesung ist erkennbar an der speziellen Anziehungskraft, die von ihr ausgeht, sobald sie
nur rücksichtslos und auf sich selbst konzentriert gehandhabt wird.[53] Ist stil-
les Lesen Denken mit fremdem Gehirn,[54] so ist die laute Lesung ein Sprechen
mit rasendem, inspiriertem Munde.[55] Man muss die übliche Neigung sistie-
ren, lautes Lesen als Vollendung des leisen, oder umgekehrt leises als
Vollendung des lauten aufzufassen. Jedes von beiden vollendet sich in sich
selbst, unabhängig vom anderen. Bei allen Überschneidungen und Übergän-
gen, die faktisch stattfinden, handelt es sich letztlich um zwei Stämme einer
Wurzel. „Das laute Lesen ist nicht von der Mitteilung her verständlich. In
ihm drückt sich eine Texterfahrung aus, die sich nicht auf das Verstehen einschränken lässt, sondern eher dessen elementare Voraussetzung zur Geltung
bringt. ... Ein solches Lesen ist zunächst nicht verstehend, sondern vollzie-

---

52 Die Göttliche Liturgie kennt in ihren Rubren die Angaben μυστικῶς, ἐκφώνως
    (ἐκφώνησις) und μεγαλοφώνως. Zur Ekphonese s. G. Engberg, Ekphonetic Notation,
    New Grove 8, London ²2001, 47–51; D. Hiley, Western Plainchaint, Oxford 1993, 367–
    369: Ekphonetic Notation; K. Onasch, Art. Ekphonese, in: ders., Lexikon Liturgie und
    Kunst der Ostkirche (s. Anm. 44), 96.
53 H.-J. Frey, Lesen und Schreiben, Basel 1998, 28f.
54 J.L. Borges/O. Ferrari, Lesen ist denken mit fremdem Gehirn, Zürich 1990.
55 Heraklit, FVS 22 B 92: Σίβυλλα ... μαινομένωι στόματι ... ἀγέλαστα καὶ ἀκαλλώπιστα
    καὶ ἀμύριστα φθεγγομένη χιλίων ἐτῶν ἐξικνεῖται τῆι φωνῆι διὰ τὸν θεόν. „Die Sibylle, die
    mit rasendem Munde Ungelachtes und Ungeschminktes und Ungesalbtes redet, reicht
    mit ihrer Stimme durch tausend Jahre. Denn der Gott treibt sie."

hend."[56] Wobei zu beachten ist: Diese beiden Arten des Lesens unterscheiden sich nicht durch die Art der Beziehung zwischen Personen oder innerhalb von Gemeinden. Das machte das Lesen völlig überflüssig. Sondern sie unterscheiden sich durch die Art der Beziehung zu Personen und Gemeinden, die die Texte selbst stiften, indem sie sie herbeiführen.[57] Während das leise Lesen als verstehendes in Richtung Interpretation und Kommentar weist,[58] ist das laute Lesen mit Vollzug und Gebrauch auf dem Weg zum Schauspiel. Schauspieler ist der ehemals laute Leser, der inzwischen das Buch aus der Hand gelegt und somit die Hände frei hat.[59]

Um noch zu erwähnen, was bereits am Tage liegt: Lautes Lesen als physisches Ereignis reduziert Textmenge und Lesegeschwindigkeit, erzwingt Portionierung, Perikopierung. Nicht nur kein unendlicher, sondern endlicher, wenn nicht gar überschaubarer Text bleibt. Sobald laut gelesen wird, tendieren Texte dazu, wenige zu werden. So haben sie Zeit, sich zu wiederholen. Sie nehmen eine Kreisförmigkeit an, die dem linearen Textgebilde nicht anzumerken war. Sie gehen gewissermaßen den von Jan Assmann einseitig vorgeschlagenen Weg „von ritueller zu textueller Kohärenz" wieder zurück.[60] Poetische und liturgische Lesungen tendieren zum Zyklus.[61] Jede *biblia in nuce* ist eine zyklisch gewordene Bibel, die durch rituelle Leseordnung in Zyklizität versetzt wurde.[62] Dann befindet sich die ganze Bibel auf dem Weg zu einer Eigentümlichkeit, die bereits am Psalter diagnostiziert wurde.

2.2. Was ist Psalmodie?

Zwar stehen Lesungen durch ihr rituelles Element immer in der Gefahr, in Gesang überzugehen. Was aber bisher geschildert wurde, hält sich noch streng in den Grenzen, die asianisierenden Rednern durch Caesars Spott gesetzt sind: *si cantas, male cantas, si legis, cantas.*[63] Doch steht die Lesung nicht nur in der Gefahr, sondern sie geht faktisch zum Gesang über. Die nach

---

56 Frey, Lesen und Schreiben (s. Anm. 53), 30f.
57 Cf. Frey, ebd., 32.
58 Frey, ebd., 33.
59 Frey, ebd., 35.
60 Assmann, Gedächtnis (s. Anm. 43), 87–103.
61 G. Kunze, Die Lesungen, in: Leit. II, Kassel 1955, 87–180; P.C. Bloth, Art. Schriftlesung. I. Christentum, TRE 30 (1999) 520–558; G. Stemberger, Art. Schriftlesung. II. Judentum, ebd., 558–563.
62 Bloth, Art. Schriftlesung (s. Anm. 61) 522.
63 Quintilian, Institutio oratoria I,8,2: „Wenn das, was du da treibst, Gesang sein soll, dann singst du weidlich schlecht; soll es aber nur gelesen sein, dann muß ich dir schon sagen, daß du singst" (Übersetzung nach G. Wille, Musica Romana. Die Bedeutung der Musik im Leben der Römer, Amsterdam 1967, 472).

Lektionstönen gesungene Lesung, wie sie in der Synagoge und in den Kirchen des Ostens und Westens geübt wird, erschwert die schnelle Unterscheidung von *lector* und *psalmista*. Beide lesen, gewiss; beide singen auch möglicherweise. Aber selbst wenn die zwischen Lesung und Psalmodie bestehende Grenze nicht der Grenze zwischen Lesen und Singen entspricht, die Quintilian setzt, selbst wenn sie innerhalb des Gesungenen nachgewiesen werden muss, so sind Unterschiede gleichwohl erkennbar. Lektionstöne sind etwas anderes als Psalmtöne. Der Lektionston tendiert dazu, ein Melodiemodell pro syntaktische Einheit zu bieten. Dagegen Psalmtöne gibt es viele. Jeder Versuch sie zu zählen wäre nachträgliche Rationalisierung. Bei den Psalmen steigert sich das musikalische Element zu einer Vielzahl von Melodie- oder Psalliermodellen. Nicht Lektionstöne, erst Psalmtöne sind der Modalitätsunterschiede fähig. So vervielfältigt sich das musikalische Element, während die Grundstruktur des Psalmverses im Unterschied zum nichtpsalmischen Lesestoff immer dieselbe bleibt: *Initium – Tenor* (ggf. *Flexa*) *– Mediatio – Tenor – Terminatio* (*Differentiae*). Sie wiederholt sich durch alle Psalmtexte und -töne hindurch. So kompliziert Psalmtöne in ihrer konkreten Vielfalt auch sind, ihre Grundform ist einfach. Gerade die Simplizität des Psalliermodells schafft freie Kapazität zur Steigerung des musikalischen Aufwandes. Somit wird deutlich, dass beim Übergang von der Lesung zur Psalmodie der Wiederholung eine hervorragende Bedeutung zukommen muss. Zwar neigen Lesungen zur Wiederholung, wie oben angedeutet; aber die Psalmodie ist undenkbar ohne Wiederholung. Und das ist dann doch noch einmal etwas anderes.

Bei Dionysius Areopagita traten sich auf unterschiedlichen Ebenen hl. Schrift und Psalmodie gegenüber, so sehr auch die Psalmodie hl. Schrift ist, also mit ihr auf dieselbe Ebene gehört. Daher finden sich durchaus gleitende Übergänge. Bisher war kein Kennzeichen zu nennen, das einer Seite allein zukäme. Immer war die Psalmodie auch Lesung – was sonst. Und immer tendierte bereits die Lesung in Richtung Zyklizität, wiewohl nicht wesentlich. Aber was wäre denn bei äußerster Zuspitzung das Eigentümliche eines jeden? Was die Lesung anlangt, so ist deutlich, dass alles, was laut gelesen werden kann, auch leise zu lesen ist, und damit ist schon die Möglichkeit zugegen, einen Text aus dem Gebrauch in Interpretation und Kommentar zu überführen. Selbst Psalmtexten geschieht dies, wie bekannt. Was umgekehrt die Psalmodie anlangt, so hat sie ihr Spezialissimum darin, dass sie sich auf Dauer gegen den Interpreten und Kommentator durchsetzen will und ihn schon noch dahin bringen wird, wo er sein Handwerk niederlegt. Wie es Klaus Seybold widerfährt, indem er beim 119. Psalm eine methodisch kontrollierte Abdankung des Kommentators vollzieht und den *psalmus psalmo-*

rum unkommentiert lässt. Eine starke, im Übrigen völlig adäquate Leistung des Exegeten![64] *Explicit lectio. Incipit psalmodia.*

Cantabiles mihi erant iustificationes tuae
in loco peregrinationis meae (ps 118, 54).[65]

Und endlich gibt der Text des Dionysius Areopagita selbst Aufschlüsse, wie der Übergang von der Lesung zur Psalmodie genauer zu bestimmen sei.[66] Hierbei bietet seine Bibel, die Septuaginta, die Psalmen *und* Oden enthält, eine besondere Hilfe. Es fällt auf, dass Dionysius zwar mit dem Thema „ἡ τῶν ψαλμῶν ἱερολογία" beginnt, aber an entscheidenden Stellen von den θεῖαι ᾠδαί spricht. Psalmen oder Oden?[67] Wenn „Psalmen"[68], dann sagt Dionysius dasselbe wie die Väter Basilius und Athanasius. Immerhin mit der nicht unbedeutenden Differenz, dass sich bei Basilius und Athanasius die kompendiarische Kraft des Psalters direkt nur auf das Alte Testament bezog, während

---

64 K. Seybold, Die Psalmen (HAT I/15), Tübingen 1996, 461–475. Der Psalm „kreist" monoton in „vielen Wiederholungen" um den Zentralbegriff חשׂרה, der sich seinerseits in den sieben Variationsbegriffen דבר, אמרה, מוי, חקי, מטשׂת, דשׂת, פדי diversifiziert (473). Ps 119 „bietet kein theologisches System und keine Doktrin. Man kann ihn vorwärts und rückwärts lesen. Er bietet vielmehr Anleitung und Stoff für Exerzitien in den Glauben und in das Leben im Raum der göttlichen Tora. Die angemessene Rezeption ist Aneignung, nicht Auslegung. ... Dem Leser sei empfohlen, die konstanten (Tora-Begriffe, Gebetssprache) und die variablen Elemente (Situation, Bildvergleich, Anliegen) zu unterscheiden und darauf zu achten, daß jeder Vers eine besondere Beziehung zwischen beiden herstellen will, um eine Konkretion der ‚Lehre' zu erreichen" (474f.).

65 „Deine Rechte sind mein Lied / Jn meinem Hause" (Ps 119, 54): Wahlspruch von Heinrich Schütz, zu seinem Begräbnis vertont durch Christoph Bernhard; Text der Leichenpredigt, gehalten von Martin Geier, Dresden 1672. Dazu W. Steude, Vorwort zu: Heinrich Schütz, Der Schwanengesang. Des Königs und Propheten Davids 119. Psalm in elf Stücken ... SWV 482ff., (Neue Ausgabe sämtlicher Werke [NSA] 39) Kassel 1984, VIII; M. Heinemann, Heinrich Schütz und seine Zeit, Laaber 1993, 264. – Im übrigen: Th. Seedorf, Art. Cantabile, Handwörterbuch der musikalischen Terminologie, Wiesbaden 1999.

66 Dionysius Areopagita bietet folgende Beschreibung des Verhältnisses von Psalmodie und Lesung: Während die Psalmodie gegenüber dem Rest der Schrift das Ziel des Lobens (ὑμνῆσαι) und Preisens (αἰνέσαι) aller ihrer Inhalte verfolgt und dies auf die Weise der Verallgemeinerung (καθολικὴν ποιεῖται) des Gesangs der göttlichen Dinge (τῶν θείων ᾠδήν) und ihrer Darstellung (καὶ ἀφήγησιν) tut, hat die Lesung die Aufgabe, das eher Abgekürzte und Verschattete (τὰ συντετμημένα καὶ συνεσκιασμένα) des Psalmengesangs durch klarere Bilder und Ansprachen auszubreiten.

67 Psalmen und Oden erscheinen bei Dionysius promiscue: Eccl. Hier. III,4 (PG 3,429CD); III,5 (432AB); VII (556C).

68 W. Völker, Kontemplation und Ekstase bei Pseudo-Dionysius Areopagita, Wiesbaden 1958, 87 Anm. 1: „Die Worte ἡ δὲ τῶν θείων ᾠδῶν ἱερογραφία beziehe ich auf die Psalmen, denn nach der Ausdrucksweise zu urteilen, muß es sich um eine hl. Schrift handeln, nicht etwa um liturgische Gesänge, und zwar um eine Schrift poetischen Inhalts. Nun sind die Bücher der Propheten sowie das Hohelied bereits zuvor erwähnt, so daß eigentlich nur die Psalmen übrigbleiben."

der Bezug zum Neuen durch den *sensus christologicus* suppliert werden musste. Dagegen setzt Dionysius – wie gesehen – die „heilige Schrift der göttlichen Gesänge" (ἡ τῶν θείων ᾠδῶν ἱερογραφία) dem Kanon Alten *und* Neuen Testaments entgegen. Wenn aber „Oden" im präzisen, von Psalmen zu unterscheidenden Sinn, dann bezieht sich Dionysius auf dasjenige Buch, das die Septuaginta und nur sie dem Buch der Psalmen in fließendem Übergang folgen lässt, die ΩΔΑΙ.[69] Weicht die Septuaginta der christlichen Gemeinde bereits durch die Kompilation alttestamentlicher Oden vom hebräischen Text ab, so setzt sie ihrer Abweichung vollends die Spitze auf, indem sie mit unverkennbarer Dreistigkeit mitten ins Alte Testament einige Texte des Neuen platziert, neutestamentliche Oden. Und damit nicht genug. Sie beschließt die Odenkompilation mit dem Engelshymnus, der zwar an die Schriftdoxologie Lk 2,14 anknüpft, im übrigen aber frei komponiert ist und trinitarische Elemente sowie eine Epiklese Jesu Christi enthält.

Was sind ΩΔΑΙ?[70] Größtenteils Bibelepitome, bestehend aus *Cantica* Alten und Neuen Testaments. Mit Recht dürfen sie beanspruchen, ein Kompendium des Kanons beider Testamente zu sein, loziert inmitten des Alten Testaments. In der Fassung des Codex Alexandrinus enthalten die ΩΔΑΙ neun Hymnen, die zum Morgenlob ("Ορθρος) der orientalischen Kirchen gehören; die freikomponierte zehnte, die Schlussdoxologie, steht unter dem *Rubrum* "Υμνος ἑωθινός.[71] Hier wird deutlich, dass die hl. Schrift vollends dabei ist, vom Lesebuch zum Gesangbuch (*Solfeggio*) zu mutieren. Beginnend mit dem Psalter, spätestens aber mit den Oden der Septuaginta ist die hl. Schrift zugleich Schrift und Ritus, *Nigrum* und *Rubrum*. Sie ist es sogar so sehr, dass sie zum einmal gegebenen Ritus neue Texte produziert und sich inkorporiert.

---

69 Es muss offen bleiben, ob die Oden der LXX als selbständiges „Buch" oder als Fortsetzung der Psalmensammlung konzipiert sind. Septuaginta, id est VT graece iuxta LXX interpretes II, ed. A. Rahlfs, Stuttgart 1935, 164: „Inscriptionem ωδαι ego addidi; non est in mss."

70 Die ΩΔΑΙ enthalten (in der Anordnung der LXX ed. A. Rahlfs): I. Novem Odae ecclesiae graecae: 1. Ὠιδὴ Μωυσέως ἐν τῇ Ἐξόδῳ (Ex 15,1–19). – 2. Ὠιδὴ Μωυσέως ἐν τῷ Δευτερονομίῳ (Dtn 32,1–43). – 3. Προσευχὴ Αννας μητρὸς Σαμουηλ (I Reg [1.Sam] 2,1–10). – 4. Προσευχὴ Αμβακουμ (Hab 3,2–19). – 5. Προσευχὴ Ησαιου (Jes 26,9–20). – 6. Προσευχὴ Ιωνα (Jon 2,3–10). – 7. Προσευχὴ Αζαριου (Dan 3,26–45). – 8. "Υμνος τῶν τριῶν παίδων (Dan 3,52–88). – 9. Προσευχὴ Μαριας τῆς θεοτόκου (Lk 1,46–55) und Προσευχὴ Ζαχαριου (Lk 1,68–79). – II. Odae aliae: 10. Ὠιδὴ Ησαιου (Jes 5,1–9). – 11. Προσευχὴ Εζεκιου (Jes 38,10–20). – 12. Προσευχὴ Μανασση (apokryph). – 13. Προσευχὴ Συμεων (Lk 2,29–32). – 14. "Υμνος ἑωθινός (Engelshymnus; Große Doxologie).

71 Euchologion, Venedig 1872, 31; Horologion, Venedig 1868, 48–63.69ff. – P. Wagner, Einführung in die gregorianischen Melodien. Ein Handbuch der Choralwissenschaft I, Leipzig ³1911, 7 nennt deshalb den Cod. Alex. des 5. Jahrhunderts „[d]as älteste auf uns gekommene liturgische Gesangbuch". Dazu K. Onasch, Art. Oden, in: ders., Lexikon Liturgie und Kunst der Ostkirche (s. Anm. 44), 289–291.

Diese Koinzidenz mag Dionysius Areopagita im Auge haben, wenn er behauptet, heiliger Text und heilige Handlung seien derselben Wurzel entsprossen (συνερρίζωσεν).[72] Was sind also ΩΔΑΙ? Sie sind das einzigartige Dokument einer dem Kanon der hl. Schrift inokulierten Schalt- und Andockstelle, an der Schrift unmittelbar in Liturgie übergeht und Liturgie unmittelbar in Schrift, oder mit Dionysius Areopagita: an der der Singkanon der Psalmodie, mit dem die Liturgie beginnt, übergeht in den Lesekanon der Schrifttexte – und umgekehrt.

Unter Text stellen wir uns etwas vor, was ins Unendliche läuft. Auch Literatur hat „kein Ende". Und selbst die hl. Schrift möchte sich als *lectio continua* Geltung verschaffen. So ist der Text überall mit der Vorstellung einer fortlaufenden Linie in elementarer Weise verbunden. An der Psalmodie bricht sich der vorwärts drängende Lesefluss. Es ist, als ob der Text begänne, sich um sich selbst und in sich selbst zu drehen. Die kanonische Linie beginnt sich zum Kreise zu biegen. Die zyklische Gewalt der Psalmodie setzt den Text unter Zwang, so dass leises Lesen zu lautem und lineares zur Lesung wird. Wiederholung tritt ein in etwas, was sich an sich nicht notwendig wiederholt. Der Zeilenbruch ist erstes Zeichen hierfür. Perikopierung wird danach verständlich als eine Art Zeilenbruch im Großen. Auf unterschiedlichen Stufen von Textmenge sind Zeilenbruch und Perikopierung äußere Anzeichen des spannungsreichen Vorgangs, wie etwas sich nie Wiederholendes sich in gewisser Weise wiederholt. Ist dies der Weg zum Kanon? Kanonisierung als Perikopierung in großem Stil?

2.3. Was ist Kanon?

Die Gedankenwelt des Dionysius Areopagita besticht durch synthetischen Schwung. Sie ermuntert dazu, Differenzierungen, die im Lauf des kulturellen Prozesses selbstverständlich geworden sind, wieder rückwärts zu denken. Im dionysischen Schwung steckt ein regressives Moment. Am Ende ist alles mit allem verwandt. In unserem Fall lädt die dionysische Synthesis dazu ein, dem Paradigma des Liturgiemoduls Lesung und Psalmodie zu folgen und den Lesekanon als Singkanon zu denken. Was daran in der Sache ansprechend ist, wurde dargestellt. Jetzt aber stellt sich die Aufgabe, das von Dionysius initiierte Spiel mit den beiden *canones* anhand unserer vergleichsweise genaueren Kenntnis der Geschichte des Kanon-Begriffes kritisch zu durchleuchten. Es löst sich in ein leeres Spiel mit Äquivokationen auf. Soll der Kanonbegriff

---

72 Dionysius Areopagita, De ecclesiastica hierarchia III,4 (PG 3,429D).

nicht zur Kanonade verkommen, so gilt es, einen Zustand terminologischer Differenziertheit wiederherzustellen. Dann wird auch der Blick auf die Sache an Differenziertheit gewinnen.

Was den Lesekanon anlangt, so beruht dieser auf einer kirchlichen Sprachbildung. Das antike Wort hatte das Schilfrohr (קָנֶה) vor Augen, das dem Handwerker als Instrument dient, und implizierte durch Abstraktion von Geradheit vier Bedeutungen: 1. Maßstab, Richtlinie, Kriterium; 2. Vorbild, Modell; 3. Regel, Norm; 4. Tabelle, Liste.[73] Der kirchliche Gebrauch hingegen führt nur die dritte und vierte Bedeutung weiter. Die dritte: Die Maßstäblichkeit von Normen und Regeln führt zum κανὼν τῆς ἀληθείας und κανὼν τῆς πίστεως. Synodal- und Konzilsbeschlüsse, wenn mit Sanktion versehen, sind Kanones und weisen in Richtung kanonisches Recht und Kanonistik. Die vierte: Während nach alexandrinischer Gewohnheit Listen von Büchern, wie Bibliotheken sie brauchten, als κατάλογοι oder πίνακες bezeichnet wurden,[74] trat im kirchlichen Sprachgebrauch an diese Stelle die Bezeichnung κανών. Damit geschah eine Umformung, die für das europäische Bewusstsein die wirksamste gewesen sein dürfte. Nicht auf dem klassischen, auf dem kirchlichen Sprachgebrauch beruhen die heutigen Verwendungsweisen. Seitdem Athanasius die genaue Liste der zur Lesung im Gottesdienst zugelassenen Bücher als τὰ κανονιζόμενα bezeichnete, ist Kanon eine Liste, die eine begrenzte Textsammlung auszeichnet. Nicht dass bisher Kanon und Buch nie in Beziehung getreten wären; von Polyklet und Demokrit sind Werke dieses Titels überliefert, Lehrschriften, die durchaus Kanonisches, Maßstäbliches schildern. Aber abgesehen davon, dass sie jeweils ein Werk sind und nicht Sammlung mehrerer, verweisen sie den Leser von sich weg auf das Maßstäbliche hin, das sie abschildern, während der kirchliche Kanon ausschließlich ins gegebene Buch hineinweist.

Was ist Lesekanon? Lesekanon ist seit Athanasius die an die Geradheit des antiken Arbeitsinstruments erinnernde lineare Bücherliste. Gelesen wird im Westen allerdings auch der *canon missae.* Hier taucht ein Kanonbegriff

---

73 Assmann, Gedächtnis (s. Anm. 43), 103–114; Asper, Art. Kanon (s. Anm. 20), 869.872f.; H. Ohme, Kanon ekklesiastikos. Die Bedeutung des altkirchlichen Kanonbegriffs (AKG 67), Berlin 1998, 406.

74 Zwar geschah in Alexandria der Übergang vom bloßen Inventar zum Verzeichnis (πίναξ): s. Kallimachos, Πίνακες τῶν ἐν πάσῃ παιδείᾳ διαλαμψάντων καὶ ὧν συνέγραψαν. Dazu U. Jochum, Kleine Bibliotheksgeschichte, Stuttgart 1993, 28–30. Aber die dabei entstandenen Listen „nannte man in der Antike *nicht* ‚Kanon'" (Assmann, Gedächtnis [s. Anm. 43], 112).

auf, der ohne das rituelle Element des Singkanons nicht erklärt werden könnte.[75]

Was den Singkanon anlangt, so nennt die Musikwissenschaft einige
Schwerpunkte des Sprachgebrauchs.[76] Am wenigsten hat die älteste pythago-
räische Gebrauchsweise mit praktiziertem Gesang zu tun. Die Pythagoräer
werden von den Akusmatikern als Kanoniker (κανονικοί) unterschieden. Ihr
κανών ist das Monochord, das den Musiktheoretikern zur Berechnung der
Tonproportionen dient. Die Grundoperation ist die κατατομὴ κανόνος/sectio
canonis.[77] Das Erklingen ist dabei unwesentlich. Nicht so beim byzantinischen Kanon. Er führt in nächste Nähe zu Dionysius Areopagita, ohne dass
sich die Beziehung präzisieren ließe. Dionysius kennt vielleicht das Phänomen, den Terminus kennt er nicht. Als κανών wird die jüngere der beiden
Hauptgattungen der byzantinischen Hymnographie bezeichnet.[78] Im 7. Jahrhundert entstanden, steht der Kanon einerseits in Konkurrenz zur monastischen Psalmodie[79], andererseits zum älteren Kontakion (κοντάκιον), der zweiten Hauptgattung, die durch ihn zunehmend verdrängt wurde. Kanon ist eine
Zusammenstellung von Gesängen nach dem Muster der neun von der Septuaginta zum Morgenlob dargebotenen Oden ('Ωιδαί), zunächst unter Verwendung des biblischen Textes, dann in freier poetischer Paraphrase, je nach Titel und Rang des Tages, dem der Gesang galt. Ein Kanon umfasst somit einen

75 H. Cancik, Kanon, Ritus, Ritual. Religionsgeschichtliche Anmerkungen zu einem litera-
    turwissenschaftlichen Diskurs, in: Kanon und Theorie (s. Anm. 9), 1–20. Canciks These
    wird von der Herausgeberin M. Moog-Grünewald korrekt zusammenfasst in dem Satz:
    „Kanon ist Ritus" (ebd., ix).
76 P. Cahn, Art. Kanon, MGG² S 4 (1996) 1677–1705; K.-J. Sachs, Art. Canon/Kanon,
    Handwörterbuch der musikalischen Terminologie, Wiesbaden 1999.
77 Das arabische Vorführinstrument für die sectio canonis, das zwar nach dem Griechi-
    schen ‚qanun' genannt wurde, sich aber vom Monochord unterschied durch Mehrsaitig-
    keit und Trapezförmigkeit, gelangte im Hochmittelalter durch spanisch-maurische Ver-
    mittlung ins Lateinische. „Canon" war die Bezeichnung einer Art von „Psalterium". Da-
    zu: E. Bubert, Art. Psaltérion ou Canon, Dictionnaire de la Musique II, ed. par M. Ho-
    negger, Paris 1976, 841–842; Sachs, Art. Canon/Kanon, a.a.O. (s. Anm. 76), 10–12.
78 W. (v.) Christ, Ueber die Bedeutung von Hirmos, Troparion und Kanon in der griechi-
    schen Poesie des Mittelalters, erläutert an der Hand einer Schrift des Zonaras (SBAW),
    München 1870, 75–108; E. Wellecz, A History of Byzantine Music and Hymnography,
    Oxford 1949, 168–215; ²1961, 198–245; M.M. Velimirovic, The Byzantine Heirmos
    and Heirmologion, in: W. Arlt (Hg.), Gattungen der Musik in Einzeldarstellungen. Ge-
    denkschrift Leo Schrade, Bern/München 1973, 192–244; H. Schmidt, Zum formelhaften
    Aufbau byzantinischer Kanones, Wiesbaden 1979; Ch. Hannick, Art. Byzantinische
    Musik, MGG² S (1995) 288–310, Sp. 289ff.
79 Das Gerontikon des Abtes Pambo berichtet von dem ägyptischen Mönch, der aus Ale-
    xandrien in die Wüste zurückkehrt und fragt: Ἀπελθόντος γάρ μου ἐν Ἀλεξανδρείᾳ εἶδον
    τὰ τάγματα τῆς ἐκκλησίας, πῶς ψάλλουσι, καὶ ἐν λύπῃ γέγονα πολλῇ, διατὶ καὶ ἡμεῖς οὐ
    ψάλλομεν κανόνας καὶ τροπάρια; Scriptores ecclesiastici de musica sacra, ed. M. Gerbert
    I, St. Blasien 1784, 2–4. Zur Datierung: O. Wessely, Die Musikanschauung des Abtes
    Pambo, AÖAW.PH 89 (1952) 46–62.

Satz von neun Oden, wobei jede einzelne davon wieder durchsetzt sein kann von drei nichtbiblischen Troparien, deren jeweils erstes dem ganzen Stück als Leitstrophe (εἱρμός) dient.[80] Man kann sich fragen, ob der byzantinische Kanonbegriff überhaupt ein musikalischer Begriff ist oder nicht vielmehr ein textorientierter. Erst seit dem 14. Jahrhundert bezeichnet *Canon* den mehrstimmigen Satz, der aus einem Melodiemodell gebildet wird. Trotz des fugierten Einsatzes liegt kein *Contrapunctus* vor; alles was erklingt, ist immer nur die eine Melodie. Obgleich einstimmig notiert, erklingt der Kanon vielstimmig. Das Notat bedarf dazu des *CANON*, der Anweisung, in welcher Weise die Wiederholung geschehen soll. Zunächst ist *CANON* der Wortlaut der Aufführungsregel (*regula*), von der dann auch das Musikstück seinen Namen hat.

Was ist Singkanon? Das erste Resultat muss gewiss lauten: Singkanon hat mit Lesekanon weder historisch noch sachlich etwas zu tun. Zwischen beiden Termini besteht nichts als Äquivokation. Statt linearer Geradheit impliziert der Singkanon die Vorstellung von Zirkularität, die bekanntlich die Geradheit verbiegt. Die allerjüngste musikalische Verwendung befördert die Idee von Kanon als Wiederholung. Kanon ist ein musikalisches Gebilde, das sich nur noch um sich selbst dreht. Aber gerade so verleiht es dem uralten Phänomen ritueller Repetition einen hochrationalen musikalischen Ausdruck. Der musikalische Kanon vollzieht, was der Ritus schon immer vollzogen hat. Und vollzieht es weit besser, als Texte es in ihrer Linearität je vermöchten. Ritus und Texte nehmen einen verschiedenen Weg.[81] Mit Leerlauf hat dies übrigens nichts zu tun. Reine Repetition löste die Polyphonie in Monotonie auf; sie wäre bereits musikalisch eine Nullstufe. Vielmehr gehören zum Kanon kanonische Schemata wie etwa einfache Wiederholung, Spiegelung, Umkehrung (Krebs); *per augmentationem* oder *per diminutionem*; *alla prima, alla secunda* ... usw. Ein Kanon ist nicht leer. Von Anfang an ist er über reine Repetition hinaus. Kanonische Wiederholung geschieht durch Veränderung. Das ist der Begriff der kanonischen Veränderung,[82] die maximale Gebundenheit und maximale Freiheit vereint.

---

80 S. Anm. 78. K. Onasch, Art. Kanon, in: ders., Lexikon Liturgie und Kunst der Ostkirche (s. Anm. 44), 184–186; Art. Oden, in: ebd., 289–291.

81 Assmann, Gedächtnis (s. Anm. 43), 87ff. Die These: „Repetition und Interpretation sind funktionell äquivalente Verfahren in der Herstellung kultureller Kohärenz" (89), verkennt m.E. die die Gleichwertigkeit überwiegende Ungleichwertigkeit.

82 Johann Sebastian Bach, Einige canonische Veraenderungen, / über das / Weynacht-Lied: / Vom Himmel hoch da / komm ich her, BWV 769 (Nürnberg 1747), in: Die Orgelchoräle aus der Leipziger Originalhandschrift, hg. v. H. Klotz (Neue Ausgabe sämtlicher Werke [NBA], Serie IV/2), Kassel 1958, 197–211.

3. Kanonische Veränderung

Wiederholungs-Installation

An dieser Stelle will sich eine Kindheitserinnerung nicht abweisen lassen. Sie betrifft Gebärde, Ton und Wort von Frau S., der Nachbarin in der Nachkriegszeit. Sie sprach einen hessischen Dialekt, der, in Relation zur ortsüblichen schwäbischen Weltoffenheit, fremdländisch ans Ohr drang. Ihre Reden fanden nicht nur Kommentare zuhause, sondern Imitation. Zur Aufspießung eignete sich insbesondere die Wendung:

Schönes Wedda isses heit,
hab gsacht: *Schönes Wedda isses heit.*

Dieser Satz, an sich schon Vollzug einer Veränderung, ist weiterer Veränderung fähig. Mit Blick auf den ferneren Lebenslauf von Frau S. könnte man fortfahren:

hab gsacht: *Schönes Wedda isses ...*
hab gsacht: *Schönes Wedda ...*
hab gsacht: *Schön ...*
hab gsacht: *S ...*
hab gsacht: ...

... solange nur die Wendung selbst vollziehbar bleibt! Ich muss bei Frau S. Abbitte leisten: Ich habe sie damals nachgemacht. Aber das Schlimme ist die Unaufrichtigkeit der späten Abbitte, die sich selbst verrät. Trotz stattgehabter Belehrung gleicht der Erwachsene immer noch dem Kind in seiner damaligen Unbelehrtheit. Ich werde sogleich gezwungen sein, Frau S. noch einmal zu imitieren. Frau S. macht ihre Aussage in einem Satz zweimal. Dieser Vorgang – so die These – ist in mustergültiger Weise kanonisch und ist kanonischer Veränderungen fähig. Die Aussage beginnt sich um sich selbst zu drehen.

Folgender Weg wird eingeschlagen: Ausgang zu nehmen ist bei der schrillen Äquivokation der beiden Kanonbegriffe, die das eindeutige, unwiderrufliche Resultat der beiden bisherigen Gänge war. Diese hat ihren Sitz in der Unterscheidung von Interpretation und Gebrauch, wenn diese nur richtig vollzogen wird. An dieser Stelle spielt noch einmal und jetzt erst recht der Psalter eine erkenntnisleitende Rolle. Der Parallelismus, immer schon prototypisch an den Psalmen erkannt, lehrt die Zyklizität des an sich linearen Textes. So wird endlich der rare Ausblick auf einen Text getan, der sich nur noch um sich selber dreht. Das ist der Kanon der hl. Schrift.

3.1. Interpretation und Gebrauch

Der Ausgangspunkt der nun anzustrengenden Überlegung lässt sich durch das Begriffspaar Interpretation und Gebrauch bezeichnen. In den beiden zurückliegenden Kapiteln wurden zwei Formen des Umgangs mit Texten unterschieden: Texte als Gegenstand von Interpretation (I.) von Texten, sofern sie sich im Gebrauch befinden (II.). Die Opposition der Termini Interpretation und Gebrauch dürfte dem Leser Umberto Ecos wohlvertraut sein, der hier in Anspruch genommene Sinn dagegen weniger.

Umberto Eco handelt mehrfach von der Entgegensetzung Interpretation und Gebrauch,[83] wobei der Sinn allerdings einfach bleibt, und zwar dieser: Der Umgang mit „offenen" Texten droht sich ins Unendliche zu verlieren. Dagegen ist ein Umgang mit Texten, der Interpretation genannt zu werden verdient, ein diszipliniertes, regelhaftes Geschehen. Je disziplinierter die Interpretation, desto deutlicher ihre Grenzen. *I limiti dell'interpretazione*: ein Thema, das um der Deutlichkeit des Interpretationsbegriffs willen gestellt werden muss. Beim „geschlossenen" Text dürften Grenzen selbstverständlich sein. Aber auch und gerade der offene Text fordert Grenzen der Interpretation: „Ein Text ist nichts anderes als die Strategie, die den Bereich seiner – wenn nicht ‚legitimen', so doch legitimierbaren – Interpretationen konstituiert." Was jenseits dieser Limite ist, nennt Eco freien Gebrauch. Während die Interpretation abhängig bleibt vom ständigen Vollzug eines Wechselspiels „zwischen der Strategie des Autors und der Antwort des Modell-Lesers", löst sich die einseitig leserbezogene Strategie daraus und wird zur Praxis eines „freien, abweichenden, begehrlichen, hinterlistigen, boshaften Gebrauchs der Texte", die durch den Text nicht mehr gedeckt ist. An dieser Grenze muss man sich „entscheiden", „ob man die Semiose in Bewegung halten oder einen Text interpretieren will."[84] Was ist Gebrauch? Gebrauch ist wilde, illegitime Interpretation. Er ist Missgestalt von Interpretation, z.B. Überinterpretation. Folglich gilt es, die Interpretation gegen den Gebrauch stark zu machen. Gebrauch klingt daher so *abusive*, als ob es sich um bloße Benutzung von Texten handele. Im Sinne von Eco ist Gebrauch geradezu Missbrauch der Texte.

---

83 U. Eco, Lector in fabula. Die Mitarbeit der Interpretation in erzählenden Texten, München 1990, 72ff.: „Gebrauch und Interpretation". – Die Grenzen der Interpretation, München 1995, 47ff.: „Interpretation und Benutzen der Texte". – Zwischen Autor und Text. Interpretation und Überinterpretation, München 1996, 76: „Interpretieren und Gebrauchen"; „benutzen" – „interpretieren"; 79: „Interpretation und Gebrauch".
84 Eco, ebd., 73f.

Jedoch: *Abusus non tollit usum.* Gegen Eco wird hier der unzweideutige
Sinn von „Gebrauch" wiederhergestellt. Anders als in der Nachfolge Augustins bezeichnet *usus* im Humanismus oder bei Luther eine unübertreffliche
Weise angemessenen Seins bei den Dingen, fern von *abusus.* In unserem
Kontext macht der Gebrauch keinen Anspruch, etwas zur Interpretation beizutragen. Wenn kein Anspruch, dann auch keine Konkurrenz. Zwischen Interpretation und Gebrauch besteht eine Differenz wie zwischen leisem literarischen und lautem liturgischen Lesen, wie zwischen Lesekanon und Singkanon, oder wie zwischen Text allein und Text in Darbietung, Aufführung, Aktion. Kurz: Gebrauch ist ein ritueller, sich wiederholender Vorgang. Er ist
weit entfernt davon, als Terminus für ungezügelte Interpretation herhalten zu
sollen. Ein Psalmtonmodell etwa interpretiert keinen Text, sondern installiert,
portiert ihn. Auch strebt der Gebrauch nicht dahin, den Text in irgendeiner
Weise zu verändern. Im Gegenteil: Er bewahrt ihn in seinem Bestand. Was
die Textualität des Textes anlangt, so fügt der Gebrauch nichts hinzu und
nimmt nichts hinweg. Was allerdings die Materialität des Textes anlangt, so
fügt der Gebrauch immer nur hinzu, der Missbrauch dagegen nimmt immer
nur fort. Durch Gebrauch soll ein Text bewahrt werden über die Verfasstheit
in Tinte und Papier hinaus. Der Gebrauch lenkt die Aufmerksamkeit vom
Signifikat zurück zum Signifikant, und zu diesem, nicht zuletzt aus mnemotechnischen Gründen, in möglichst satter Materialisierung. So impliziert etwa
der klassische Text Dtn 6,5–9 insgesamt acht Mnemotechniken, Weisen von
Textgebrauch. Währenddessen bleibt der Text selbst, das *Š^ema Jisrael* Dtn
6,4, gänzlich unverändert und zur Interpretation bereit.[85] Was ist Gebrauch?
Gebrauch ist Textinstallation, erweitert um den Mehraufwand von Liturgieinstallation. Der liturgische Mehraufwand zielt letztlich immer auf die
Darbringung von Leibern (Röm 12,1). Der Gebrauch steigert somit ohne
Zweifel die Festlichkeit eines Textes. Wenn dann die Interpretation beginnt,
endet das Fest.[86]

   Nachdem nun der Gebrauch in einem Sinn fixiert ist, aus dem vollends
das letzte Echo auf Eco getilgt wurde, sind endlich die Voraussetzungen gegeben, um eine *erste* tentative Formel für hl. Schrift zu bilden. Was die Seite
der Interpretation und des Lesekanons anlangt, so konnten wir bisher sagen,
was ein literarischer Kanon ist. Was die Seite des Gebrauchs und des Singka-

---

85 J. Assmann, Die Katastrophe des Vergessens. Das Deuteronomium als Paradigma kultu-
     reller Mnemotechnik, in: A. Assmann/D. Harth (Hg.), Mnemosyne. Formen und Funkti-
     onen der kulturellen Erinnerung, Frankfurt/M. 1991, 337–352, S. 339ff.; ders., Gedächt-
     nis (s. Anm. 43), 218–221.
86 Frey, Lesen und Schreiben (s. Anm. 53), 33: „Das Verständnis verschüttet das Fest der
     Sprachentfaltung. Mit dem leisen Lesen beginnt das Zeitalter der Interpretation und der
     Sekundärliteratur in jedem Sinn des Worts."

nons anlangt, so konnten wir bisher sagen, was ein ritueller oder musischer Kanon ist. Beide *canones* bleiben sich in unwiderruflicher Weise äußerlich. Ihre Begriffe sind äquivok. Wenn nun aber, wie gezeigt, das Ineinanderspiel von Psalmodie und Schriftlesung das Grundmodell für die Kanonizität der hl. Schrift bietet, so lässt sich behaupten: Hl. Schrift heiße unter Texten und literarischen Texten ausschließlich derjenige Text, bei dem Interpretation und Gebrauch in eine innere Beziehung treten, m.a.W.: Hl. Schrift heiße ausschließlich ein Text, der die unauflösliche Äquivokation der beiden Kanonbegriffe als Zusammenspiel präsentiert.

3.2. Parallelismus

Deutlich genug verrät sich der soeben zum besten gegebene erste Satz durch sein Übermaß des Wünschens. Als bloßes *pium desiderium* kann er nicht bestehen; es bedarf eines zweiten Satzes zur Stütze. Der zu lösende Antagonismus wird bereits durch die bildliche Vorstellung deutlich, die mit Kanon von Anfang an verbunden ist: Wie soll der Inbegriff von Geradheit Biegung, Krümmung, Inkurvation annehmen, wie Zirkularität, die dem musikalischen Kanon eigen ist? Wie soll er, ohne auf der Stelle aufzuhören Kanon zu sein? Ein gekrümmter Kanon hat ausgedient. Schon im Bilde ist die Äquivokation der beiden Kanonbegriffe unüberwindlich. Noch deutlicher wird der Antagonismus durch die Sache selbst. Wie soll ein Text, der ohne Linearität nicht zu denken ist und also, sich selbst überlassen, dazu neigt, stetig und endlos geradeaus zu gehen, plötzlich die Richtung ändern, sich einwärts bewegen oder gar beginnen, sich um sich selber zu drehen? Wie soll er, ohne auf der Stelle aufzuhören Text zu sein? Jeder Aufgeklärte fürchtet sich vor der Gebetsmühle; sie ist zwar Text, aber der Leerlauf der liturgischen Aktion hat dem Lesen ein Ende bereitet. Kanonische Linearität und kanonische Zirkularität verharren in ungemilderter Äquivozität.

Nur eine Möglichkeit gibt es. Wenn Zirkularität dem Text nicht mit mechanischer Gewalt von außen aufgenötigt werden soll, dann muss sie in ihm selbst nachgewiesen werden. Sie muss sich als inneres Textphänomen aufspüren lassen. Nun gibt es zwei Textsorten, Prosa und Poesie, und nach einer ansprechenden Etymologie ist Prosa als *oratio prosa-prorsa-proversa* das, was sich stets vorwärts richtet, während die Poesie mit ihren *versus* genau die umgekehrte Richtung einschlägt,[87] wiewohl auch sie immer unter Bedingungen von Textualität. Psalterien sind keine Gebetsmühlen, gewiss

---

87 R. Jakobson, Poetik. Ausgewählte Aufsätze 1921–1971 (stw 262), Frankfurt/M. 1979, 265.

nicht; aber erhaben über jeden Vergleich mit Gebetsmühlen sind sie nun wieder auch nicht. Denn das Kreisen um sich selbst, das Klaus Seybold als Ausnahme des 119. Psalms beobachtete, nicht das mechanische, das von außen kommt, sondern das klangfigürliche, das vom Text selbst und von nichts anderem ausgeht, ist den Psalmen insgesamt eigen. Nicht nur Psalm 119, alle Psalmen bilden sich durch die Form des poetischen Parallelismus. Damit setzen sie eine Figur in die Welt, die die Zirkularität mit texteigenen Mitteln produziert.

Roman Jakobson hat in zahlreichen späten Studien den Parallelismus aus seiner Zerstreutheit in Nationalliteraturen gesammelt und zu einem einzigen strahlenden Fokus komprimiert.[88] Jakobson nimmt dabei geradezu die Gestalt eines *Lowth*[89] oder *Herder redivivus*[90] an. Er entdeckt im Parallelismus zunehmend das Grundprinzip alles Poetischen.[91] Gerade diesen Parallelismus,

---

88 Roman Jakobson hat sich zum Parallelismus u.a. in folgenden Arbeiten geäußert: Zwei Seiten der Sprache und zwei Typen aphatischer Störungen (1956), in: ders., Aufsätze zur Linguistik und Poetik, München 1974, 117–141, S. 135.138; Linguistik und Poetik (1960), in: ders., Poetik (s. Anm. 87), 83–121; Poesie der Grammatik und Grammatik der Poesie (Fassung 1961), in: ders., Poetik (s. Anm. 87), 233–263; Poesie der Grammatik und Grammatik der Poesie (Fassung 1968), in: ders., Aufsätze zur Linguistik und Poetik (s.o.) 247–260; Der grammatische Parallelismus und seine russische Spielart (1966), in: ders., Poetik (s. Anm. 87), 264–310; Ein Blick auf die Entwicklung der Semiotik (1975), in: ders., Semiotik. Ausgewählte Texte 1919–1982, Frankfurt/M. 1988, 108–135, S. 128f.

89 Robert Lowth, De sacra poesi Hebræorum prælectiones academicæ Oxonii habitæ, Oxford 1753, ²1763; ed. with a new introduction by D.A. Reibel, Oxford 1995; hg. mit Annotationen v. J.D. Michaelis, Göttingen 1758, ²1770. Der Parallelismus wird dreifach (*parallela synonyma, antitheta, synthetica*) in der 19. Vorlesung entwickelt; ders., Isaiah. A new translation, with a preliminary dissertation, and notes critical, philological, and explanatory, London 1778; ed. with an new introduction by D.A. Reibel, Oxford 1995. Die Termini „Parallelismus", „parallele Zeilen" und „parallele Ausdrücke" werden in The Preliminary Dissertation eingeführt (p. X-XI); Jakobson, Poetik (s. Anm. 87), 267: „Lowths kühne, aber vorzeitige Leistung muß auf einer neuen Ebene wiederaufgenommen werden."

90 Johann Gottfried Herder, Vom Geist der ebräischen Poesie. Eine Anleitung für die Liebhaber derselben und der ältesten Geschichte des menschlichen Geistes, Dessau 1782/83; Werke 5, hg. v. R. Smend, Frankfurt/M. 1993, 661–1308. Im ersten Gespräch entwickelt Herder – „Großer Verteidiger des Parallelismus!" (686,16) – den „Ebräischen Parallelismus" als poetisches Prinzip von Rhythmus, Tanz, Antiphonie und Reim (684–688).

91 Gerald Manley Hopkins, Poetic Diction (1865), in: The Journals and Papers of Gerard Manley Hopkins, ed. by H. House, London 1959, 84f.: The artificial part of poetry, perhaps we shall be right to say all artifice, reduces itself to the principle of parallelism. The structure of poetry is that of continuous parallelism, ranging from the technical so-called Parallelisms of Hebrew poetry and the antiphons of Church music up to the intricacy of Greek or Italian or English verse. But parallelism is of two kinds necessarily – where the opposition is clearly marked, and where it is transitional rather or chromatic. Only the first kind, that of marked parallelism, is concerned with the structure of verse – in rhythm, the recurrence of a certain sequence of syllables, in metre, the recurrence of a

den er mit einer so universalen Erwartung befrachtet, nennt Jakobson zu unserem hellen Vergnügen den „kanonischen Parallelismus".[92] Ihm gegenüber sind, wie zu Lowths, wie zu Herders Zeit, zunächst Vorurteile abzulegen. Der härteste Vorwurf ist gewiss der der Tautologie.[93] Konzilianter klingt es, wenn man ihn entschuldigt etwa als Relikt eines archaischen Wiederholungszwangs, als Überbleibsel chorischer Antiphonie, als Notbehelf unter Bedingungen vorliterarer Oralität, oder als Hilfsmittel, das zu mnemotechnischen Zwecken erfunden worden sei.[94] Fehldeutungen dieser Art entstehen, sobald gemutmaßt wird, der Parallelismus stehe für irgend etwas, sei es als Ausdruck von ... oder als Mittel zu ... Er steht überhaupt nicht für etwas; er steht in erster Linie für sich selbst. Als transzendentalpoetisches Prinzip invariant, äußert er sich in einer freien Vielzahl von Variationen, die „alle ... einen autonomen poetischen Wert" besitzen.[95] „Poetisch" heißt nach dem Satz des frühen Jakobson, „daß das Wort als Wort, und nicht als bloßer Repräsentant des benannten Objekts oder als Gefühlsausbruch empfunden wird."[96] Hier

---

certain sequence of rhythm, in alliteration, in assonance and in rhyme. Now the force of this recurrence is to beget a recurrence or parallelism answering to it in the words or thought and, speaking roughly and rather for the tendency than the invariable result, the more marked parallelism in structure whether of elaboration or of emphasis begets more marked parallelism in the words and sense. And moreover parallelism in expression tends to beget or passes into parallelism in thought. This point reached we shall be able to see and account for the pecularities of poetic diction. To the marked or abrupt kind of parallelism belong metaphor, simile, parable, and so on, where the effect is sought in likeness of things, and antithesis, contrast, and so on, where it is sought in unlikeness. – Deutsch bei Jakobson, Poetik (s. Anm. 87), 107f. 264.

92 Jakobson, Poetik (s. Anm. 87), passim.
93 Zu Luthers Äußerungen über Tautologie und Alternation in der Psalterexegese: G. Hammer, Historisch-theologische Einleitung zu D. Martin Luther, Operationes in psalmos (AWA 1), Köln/Wien 1991, 392f.; Johannes David Michaelis hat in der ‚Praefatio editoris' zu Robert Lowth vor der Imitation des Parallelismus in europäischen Sprachen gewarnt (I, ²1770, XIX): Molestius autem peccatur, si ea imitamur, quae poësi Hebraicae priva ac propria sunt, ut, parallelismum duorum hemistichiorum, de quo noster in praelectione XIX. pulcherrime egit: qui vel in carmine vernaculo intolerabilis foret, ac tautologiae molestissimae nomine notaretur. Et tamen video, multos tunc demum sibi pulcros videri, si preces publicas ad hunc modum mere Orientalem conforment, auresque perpetuis repetitionibus, Orienti jucundis, Europae invisis, laedant, prudentioribus stomachaturis, dormitaturis reliquis. Nec tamen antiphonias nostras aut litanias hic carpere videri velim, sed prosas preces, ab uno fusas oratore sacro. Illae, si vel metro careant, sunt tamen quodammodo ob musicam modulationem poëticae: nec quidquam est peregrini auribusve molesti, in duorum chororum antiphonia, sed in unius precantis tautologia. Zur Tautologie auch ebd., I,392. Dazu: J.G. Hamann, Kreuzzüge des Philologen – Kleeblatt Hellenistischer Briefe, in: Schriften 1758–1763, hg. v. J. Nadler (Sämtliche Werke 2), Wien 1950, Erster Brief: 170,37ff.; Zweyter Brief: 175,17ff.; Herder, Vom Geist der ebräischen Poesie (s. Anm. 90), 674,35ff.
94 Jakobson, Poetik (s. Anm. 87), 296f.
95 Jakobson, ebd., 297.
96 Jakobson, ebd., 79.

hat der Parallelismus seinen notwendigen Sitz. Einerseits „aktiviert" er als
„durchgehender Parallelismus ... alle Ebenen der Sprache"[97], diversifiziert
sich in phonematischen, grammatischen und semantischen Formen und er-
öffnet Freiheit zu abwechslungsreichsten Variationen. Aber andererseits auch
umgekehrt: „Sobald der Parallelismus zum Kanon erhoben wird,"[98] hört die
Freiheit der Prosa zu endlos fortlaufender Textlinearität auf, und in der Linearität geschieht anderes als Linearität, nämlich Inversion von Linearität.

Jakobsons Studie über die Polarität der Aphasien beschrieb die Sprachfä-
higkeit des Menschen als Oszillation zwischen der senkrechten Achse der
Similiarität und Metapher und der waagrechten der Metonymie und
Kontiguität, die es zu vermeiden gelte wie Scylla und Charybdis oder wie
Broca und Wernicke.[99] In Variation dieses Schemas gelangte Jakobson dazu,
die Poesie als „Projektion" der Ähnlichkeit von der Similiaritätsachse auf die
Achse der Kontiguität zu definieren.[100] Um es für unseren Zweck kurz und
bündig zu sagen: So entsteht Parallelismus. Parallelismus ist ein auf die me-
tonymische Fläche der Textlinearität projizierter Wirbel der Metapher, einerlei ob hoch oder tief. Er ist die unsichtbare Senkrechte in dem vor Augen lie-
genden Anschein des Waagrechten, der stets dominiert. Er ist die unerhörte
Plötzlichkeit im zeitlichen Kontinuum des Hörbaren, bis zur Unauffälligkeit
und Langeweile darin versteckt. M.a.W.: Parallelismus ist Wiederholung.
Und plötzlich wird die *usque ad nauseam* bekannte Wiederholung durchsichtig. Sie lichtet sich zur Wiederholung.[101] Im Schnitt der beiden Achsen erhält
das eine Wort Wiederholung „entgegengesetzte Bedeutung".[102] Das ist der
fruchtbare Augenblick. Mitten in die Linearität des Textes ist Zirkularität
eingetreten. Oder – Synthese von *I. Lesekanon* und *II. Singkanon* trotz fort-
bestehender Äquivokation – Kanon ist Kanon. Was ein wenig klingt wie:

---

97 Jakobson, ebd., 297; s. auch 118: „Ein Missionar warf seiner afrikanischen Herde vor,
   ohne Kleider zu gehen. ,Und wie steht es mit dir?' Man zeigte auf sein Gesicht, ,Bist
   nicht auch du irgendwo nackt?' ,Ja, aber das ist mein Gesicht.' ,Bei uns', gaben die
   Eingeborenen zurück, ,ist überall Gesicht.' So wird in der Dichtung jedes sprachliche
   Element in eine Figur dichterischen Sprechens verwandelt."
98 Jakobson, ebd., 108.
99 Jakobson, Aufsätze zur Linguistik und Poetik (s. Anm. 88), 117–141.
100 Jakobson, Poetik (s. Anm. 87), 94.242; ders., Aufsätze zur Linguistik und Poetik (s.
   Anm. 88) 253.
101 Deutsches Wörterbuch von Jacob Grimm und Wilhelm Grimm XIV, Leipzig 1960,
   1046: „*in trennbarer komposition* wiederholen *i.s.v.* zurückholen (*unter* A), *in fester
   komposition* wiederhólen *mit der bedeutung ,noch einmal sagen oder tun'* (*unter* B)." –
   P. Handke, Aber ich lebe nur von den Zwischenräumen. Ein Gespräch, geführt von Her-
   bert Gamper (st 1717), Frankfurt/M. 1990, 190: „Ich weiß nie, wie ich das betonen soll:
   Soll ich sagen, die Wieder*holung*, oder die *Wieder*holung."
102 S. Kierkegaard, Die Wiederholung, übers. v. H. Rochol (PhB 515), Hamburg 2000,
   23,19; cf. 3,20.

Wiederholung ist Wiederholung. So ist es, so soll es sein. Nun lässt sich ein *zweiter* Satz zur hl. Schrift formulieren, der dem ersten spürbar zu Hilfe eilt: Hl. Schrift heiße derjenige Text, der zwischen den aphasischen Bedrohungen „mitten hindurch geht", in dem die Linearität der prosaischen Wiederholung durchsichtig, durchhörig wird auf die Vertikalität der poetischen Wiederholung hin, die sich in ihr darstellt und bricht.

3.3. Text, der sich um sich selber dreht

Um nun auch gleich den *dritten* und letzten Satz vollends an den Tag zu geben: Hl. Schrift heiße der und nur der Text, der sich ausschließlich um sich selber dreht. Dieser Satz, der natürlich sobald er laut wird an der Grenze zur Abgeschmacktheit liegt, beschreibt die Kanonizität des Kanons als Resultat von Wiederholung. Kanon als etwas, das an sich sich nur um sich selber dreht, wird auf Linearität projiziert und produziert *da*durch allererst die üblicherweise mit Kanon verbundene Geradheit. Was zunächst das schon phonetisch ärgerliche „Sich-selbst" anlangt, von dem wir hier viel zu viel sprechen, so kann dies im Grunde nicht befremden. Es darf an die reiche Überlieferungsgeschichte des mit der hl. Schrift verknüpften Sich-selbst erinnert werden, die allerdings kaum je im Zusammenhang betrachtet wurde. Wenn nach Luthers bekanntem Satz die hl. Schrift dadurch von anderen Schriften unterschieden ist, dass sie sich selbst interpretiert (*sui ipsius interpres*)[103], dann öffnet sich hinter diesem oft für spezifisch reformatorisch gehaltenen Satz eine lange Tradition, beginnend mit dem zuerst neuplatonischen[104], dann patristischen[105] Satz von der sich selbst auslegenden Potenz der für kanonisch gehaltenen Schriften, und gipfelnd in zeitgenössischen Wendungen, die so etwas wie ein Sich-selbst sei es der Sprache,[106] sei es des Textes[107] suggerieren, bis an die Grenze der Quasisubjektivität von Sprache und Text hin. Wäh-

---

103 Martin Luther, Assertio omnium articulorum (1520), WA 7,97,23; cf. 98,18; 99,1; Ein Sermon von S. Jakob (1522), WA 10/3,238,11: „sich die schrifft selbs auslegt"; Deuteronomium Mosi cum annotationibus (1525), WA 14,556,27: „[scriptura] velit seipsam interpretari".

104 H. Chadwick, Antike Schriftauslegung, Berlin 1998, 11f.

105 M. Tetz, Η ΑΓΙΑ ΓΡΑΦΗ ΕΑΥΤΗΝ ΕΡΜΗΝΕΥΟΥΣΑ. Zur altkirchlichen Frage nach der Klarheit der Heiligen Schrift, in: Theologie in Geschichte und Kunst. FS Walther Elliger, Witten 1968, 206–213; J. Pépin, Art. Hermeneutik, RAC 14 (1988) 722–771, Sp. 757ff.

106 G. Bader, Art. Sprache/Sprachwissenschaft/Sprachphilosophie. VI. Systematisch-theologisch, TRE 31 (2000) 765–781, S. 775: „Die Sprache selbst/Die Sprache spricht/Die Sprache spricht sich selbst."

rend somit das Sich-selbst gerade in seiner abstrakten Höhe ziemlich vertraut klingt, verwundert es nun doch ein wenig, warum dies ausgerechnet mit dem sinnlichen Moment der Drehung verbunden sein soll, das die Assoziation von Leerlauf fast zwingend herbeiführt. Aber in dem Maß wie der Psalter, der hier alles inneviert, mit Parallelismus, und der Parallelismus mit Chor und Choreia zu tun hat, kann auf Drehung (*twist*) kein Verzicht geleistet werden. Und selbst der Leerlauf soll, wie zu sehen sein wird, seinen angemessenen Sinn erhalten. Dass ein Text sich dreht, hat allemnach zwei Bedeutungen, eine auf der Ebene der Interpretation, und eine auf der des Gebrauchs.

Im ersten Fall geschieht die Drehung *im* Text; ein Element des Textes, etwa ein Wort, wiederholt sich. Und folglich ist die Drehung im Text genau das, was wir soeben als lineare Wiederholung geschildert haben. Das Wort, das zweimal statt einmal vorkommt, verändert bei der Wiederkehr seinen Status. Nach allem, was man von Heraklit weiß, heißt Drehung nicht, dass das Wort noch einmal an der Stelle vorbeikommt, an der es beim ersten Mal stand. Im Gegenteil! Das Wort, das beim ersten Auftritt seine Bedeutung darin hatte, dass es bedeutend, d.h. referentiell war, lockert, wenn es sich dreht, diesen Bezug. Das wiederholte Wort steht nicht mehr der Welt gegenüber, in der es sich gebildet hat, und ohne die es sich nicht gebildet hätte. Es hat sich weitergedreht. Jetzt steht es sich selbst gegenüber. Die Selbstbezüglichkeit des Wortes formiert sich auf dem Hintergrund verblassender Weltbezüglichkeit. Jetzt tritt die Situation der Anfechtung ein, in der „das Wort als Wort" die gesammelte Aufmerksamkeit auf sich zieht.[108] In dem Maß, in dem es auf sich zieht, zieht es von allem sonstigen ab. Sobald einmal die weltbezogene Bedeutung in den unausbleiblichen Sog der Evakuation geraten ist, beginnt das wiederholte Wort, um seine alte Bedeutung erleichtert, den verheißungsvollen Reigen und Tanz, dessen wesentliche Bedeutungsleere auf neue Erfüllung wartet:

Vacate et videte ... (*ps* 45, 11).[109]

---

107 M. Scherner, „Text". Untersuchungen zur Begriffsgeschichte, ABG 39 (1996) 103–160, S. 152: Roland Barthes und Jacques Derrida.

108 Frey, Lesen und Schreiben (s. Anm. 53), 70–72. – Jakobson, Poetik (s. Anm. 87), 79: „das Wort als Wort". Aber auch: „Anfechtung lehrt auf das Wort merken" (Jes 28,19 [Luther]).

109 Regula Benedicti 48,4.10.13f.17.22: vacare lectioni. Dazu: M. Van Assche OSB, ‚Divinae vacare lectioni'. De ‚ratio studiorum' van Sint Benedictus, SE 1 (1948) 13–34; A. Wathen, Monastic *lectio*. Some clues from terminology, MonS 12 (1976) 207–215; H. Hauke, Der Stellenwert des nichtliturgischen Lesens im Mönchsleben des Mittelalters, in: Viva vox und ratio scripta. Mündliche und schriftliche Kommunikationsformen im Mönchtum des Mittelalters, hg. v. C.M. Kasper/K. Schreiner (Vita regularis 5), Münster/W. 1997, 119–134. Man beachte, dass sich in der monastischen Tradition *vacare lectioni* und *vacare deo* überschneiden.

Im zweiten Fall geschieht die Drehung *mit* dem Text. Man kann sie sich am bequemsten klar machen, wenn man das isolierte Wort als Modell dafür nimmt.[110] Das isolierte einzelne Wort büßt, sobald es seines Kontexts beraubt ist, die Naivität seiner ersten Bedeutung ein. Es büßt die Naivität seines ersten Bezuges auf Welt ein und verstrickt stattdessen in sich selbst, und dies nicht nur einmal. Wieder und wieder begegnet es als dasselbe; wieder und wieder begegnet es auf andere Weise, in einer unabsehbaren Flucht neuer Bedeutungen. Es wird zum Abgrund, vielleicht aber zur Himmelsleiter, zum Aufgrund. Obgleich dem isolierten einzelnen Wort von außen, schon weil es ersichtlich eines ist und nicht zwei, keinerlei Wiederholung anzumerken ist, wiederholt es sich. Es dreht sich in sich und um sich selbst, vertikal, nicht horizontal. Es bildet eine Spirale. So auch, wenn man sich das einzelne Wort erweitert denkt zum isolierten Text oder Textkorpus. Kanon, als isolierter Text, entsteht der bekannten These zufolge durch Kontextvernichtung.[111] Der Text wird aus seinen primären Referenzen gelöst. Gerade als so destabilisierter Text, der um seine erste, auf die vorfindliche Welt gerichtete Bedeutung erleichtert wurde, beginnt der Kanon sich zu drehen und zu tanzen. Vielleicht war Dionysius Areopagita der erste, der den Kanon in dieser zirkulären Bewegung zu schildern vermochte. Der Kanon wird an sich selbst zur Wiederholung, obgleich ersichtlich einer und nicht zwei. Er dreht sich, wie eine Textrolle (*rotulus*), inkurviert in sich selbst, sich um sich selbst dreht. So entsteht allererst, und zwar sinnenfällig vor unseren eigenen Augen, ein Sichselbst der hl. Schrift, das wir von ferne und *in abstracto* bereits zugestanden hatten. Das Dümmste wäre offenbar, den Kanon wieder an den alten Ort zurückstellen zu wollen. Dann wäre man ihn als Kanon, d.h. als psalterförmig in Drehung und Tanz versetztes zyklisches Buch,[112] los. Und den neuen Ort könnte er nicht weisen, auf den er in seinem verheißungsvollen Leerlauf allerdings ausgestreckt ist. Aber was ein rechter Kanon ist, kann warten.

Paul Ricœur, den wir bereits aus Anlass von „Was ist Text?" kurz annotierten,[113] schlägt mit erstaunlichen Worten einen Bogen vom Beginn bis zu der Frage, die hier am Ende auf Spitz und Knopf zu stellen ist: „Was ist Text, der sich um sich selber dreht?" Das ist in der Tat die Frage, bei der unsere Suche nach dem Kanon der hl. Schrift inzwischen angelangt ist. Text, der

---

110 Frey, Lesen und Schreiben (s. Anm. 53), 72f.

111 A. Goldberg, Die Zerstörung von Kontext als Voraussetzung für die Kanonisierung religiöser Texte im rabbinischen Judentum, in: A. Assmann/J. Assmann (Hg.), Kanon und Zensur (Archäologie der literarischen Kommunikation 2), München 1987, 201–211.

112 J.L. Borges, Die Bibliothek von Babel, Stuttgart 1974, 48: „(Die Mystiker behaupten, daß die Ekstase ihnen ein kreisförmiges Gemach offenbart, mit einem kreisförmigen Buch, dessen Rücken rund um die Wand läuft; ... dieses zyklische Buch ist Gott.)"

113 S. Anm. 19.

sich um sich selber dreht, so Ricœur, ist in Wahrheit das implizite Telos von Text überhaupt, sofern dieser sich davon emanzipiert hat, nur ein sekundäres schriftliches zum primären mündlichen Zeichensystem zu sein. Gegenüber der mündlichen Situation des Dialogs und ihrem kurzatmigen Eingebundensein in die sinnliche Präsenz der wirklichen Welt hat der Text die Tendenz, sich vom sinnlichen Moment zu lösen. Eine Wahrheit kann bekanntlich dadurch, dass man sie aufschreibt, nicht verlieren. Der Text überdauert das Hier und Jetzt.[114] Er suspendiert die unmittelbare Beziehung auf die Welt, auf die sich zeigen lässt. Mit innerster Konsequenz läuft ein Text darauf hinaus, nicht von dieser Welt zu sprechen. „Car, si on ne parlait pas du monde, de quoi parlerait-on?"[115] Allerdings muss man bei einem Text, der sich in dieser Weise nur noch um sich selbst dreht, peinlichst darauf achten, jede Hypostasierung oder Ideologisierung zum absoluten Text zu vermeiden. Die Drehung um sich selbst ist keine Versponnenheit. Die Referenz auf Welt ist ja nicht aufgehoben, sie ist unterbrochen. An die Stelle der Referenz erster Ordnung tritt die Referenz zweiter Ordnung. Immerhin: „dans ce suspens où la référence est différée, le texte est en quelque sorte ‚en l'air', hors monde ou sans monde".[116] Das ist Text im originalen Zustand von Kanonizität. Aber die wesentliche Weltlosigkeit des Textes, der sich von der Welt abkehrt, um sich fortan nur noch um sich selbst zu drehen, hindert nicht, dass eben dieser Text seine eigene Welt herbeiruft, der er sich „stracks" und „mit ganzer Wendung" zukehrt. Der Text hat dann eine kanonische Veränderung oder eine Wiederholung vollzogen. Nicht mehr zeigend auf diese Welt, weist er auf jene.

---

114 G.W.F. Hegel, Phänomenologie des Geistes (Werke 3), Frankfurt/M. 1970, 84: „eine Wahrheit kann durch Aufschreiben nicht verlieren". Man beachte, dass Hegel die Loslösung aus der sinnlichen Gewissheit des Jetzt und Hier mit einer komplementären Figur durchführt. Vom Jetzt löst er sich durch Vertextung: „Wir schreiben diese Wahrheit auf" (84), vom Hier durch Wendung: „Ich wende mich um" (85). Beide Figuren – so lautet der Anspruch des Kanons – sind im zirkulären Text eins.

115 Ricœur, Qu'est-ce qu'un texte? (s. Anm. 19), 140.

116 Ricœur, ebd., 141.

Register

Bibelstellen

Personen

Mitarbeiter

Dr. Günter Bader, Professor für Systematische Theologie an der Evangelisch-Theologischen Fakultät der Universität Bonn

Revd. Dr. Dr. h.c. John Barton, Oriel and Laing Professor of the Interpretation of Holy Scripture an der Theologischen Fakultät der Universität Oxford

Revd. Dr. Paul S. Fiddes, M.A., D.Phil., Professor of Systematic Theology an der Theologischen Fakultät der Universität Oxford und Principal of Regent's Park College

Dr. Morwenna T. Ludlow, S.A. Cook Bye-Fellow at Gonville and Caius College, Cambridge

Revd. Robert C. Morgan, Lecturer in Theology (New Testament Studies) an der Theologischen Fakultät der Universität Oxford

Dr. Dr. h.c. mult. Gerhard Sauter, Professor für Systematische Theologie an der Evangelisch-Theologischen Fakultät der Universität Bonn

Dr. Caroline Schröder-Field, Wissenschaftliche Assistentin für Systematische Theologie an der Evangelisch-Theologischen Fakultät der Universität Bonn

Dr. Horst Seebass, Professor für Altes Testament an der Evangelisch-Theologischen Fakultät der Universität Bonn

Revd. Dr. John Webster, Lady Margaret Professor of Divinity an der Theologischen Fakultät der Universität Oxford

Dr. Michael Wolter, Professor für Neues Testament an der Evangelisch-Theologischen Fakultät der Universität Bonn